# CHARTING THE SOUL

Psycho-Spiritual Astrology

# CHARTING THE SOUL

## Astrology, Characterology and the Human Energy Field

**Rebekah J S Hirsch**

# CHARTING THE SOUL:

## Astrology, Characterology and the Human Energy Field







Available from Amazon.com and Amazon.co.uk

ISBN-13:978-1532918643
ISBN-10:153291864X

www.chartingthesoul.com

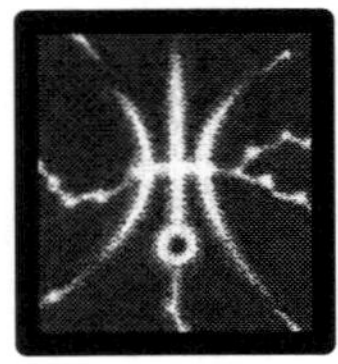

For Mum and Dad

# ACKNOWLEDGEMENTS

I come from a large wild family, all of whom are terribly important to me and who created around me a field of laughter and openness of mind for which I am eternally grateful. My Mum was a writer with a great love of the Arts and she gave me her unlimited faith in the importance of my creative expression. My Dad was a mathematician and the artistic path was not his way. But he also had total faith in my endeavours and, when the chips were down he gave me the financial support that I needed to complete this project. My brother Robin also helped, never questioning my need for support and without Dad and Robin I might not have made it through. I also have to thank the Urania Trust for the generous grant they gave me to see me through the final stages of writing.

Top of the list I need to thank my beloved friend Fern, who is a wise woman and a truly great astrologer. Fern patiently read through the chapters as I churned them out and was a good enough friend to come back to me and show me the places where I'd lost it. When I made sweeping, inaccurate Sagittarian/Aquarian generalisations she brought exquisite Virgoan precision to find just the right word and without Fern this book would have been much diminished. I also want to thank my dear sister Rachel who enthusiastically read the chapters as they arrived and whose job it was, whenever I lost heart, to keep on reminding me how important it was for me to write this book.

My younger son Mikey was still at home in those years and I need to thank him for keeping me sane, his unfaltering faith in me and his understanding when coming home to a Mum who yelled, "Don't speak to me" when he walked in the door, wouldn't say another word until she had finished the next chapter and then came down and burned the sausages. Which was not a bad thing because that's when Mikey started taking over some of the cooking. My elder son Matthew avoided most of the burned sausages but was equally supportive; another reader giving me vital feedback with Virgoan precision and wisdom.

And I want to go back to the 1980's and thank my women friends who were there with me when I first stumbled out on to the path of an astrologer and a healer. I owe so much to Alison who taught me to meditate and to Tricia, Yvonne, Leticia, Nancy and Di who brought me up short when I was coming from my head and ignoring my heart..

I cannot sufficiently express my gratitude to my two lifelong friends Hilly and Barbara who I met long ago at Art College. Hilly who has been so incredibly patient and helpful in sorting out the design of this book and Barbara who sat up through the night with me designing my web-site. Thanks also to my editor Jane Struthers and to David Price who helped me to make Word do what I wanted it to.

Beyond the warmth and support of my family and friends I have had the privilege of studying with some of the most amazing teachers of our time. Back when Uranus was transiting my Sagittarius Midheaven it was Liz Greene and Howard Sasportas, two of the great astrologers of the twentieth century who launched me into the stratosphere of astrology. At the same time I was learning about the creative process from Robert Fritz and having eureka moments learning Rogerian communication skills from Ivan Sokholov at the Parent Network in London. Glorious years culminating in a life-changing decision to go and study in the USA at the Barbara Brennan School of Healing. I am eternally grateful to Barbara and to all my teachers at BBSH and the fantastic friendships that I formed there. I want to mention Mike Mervosh who stands out as the person who really helped me to understand Characterology backed up by my friends on the Advanced level training who lined up for me to look at their charts and test out my theories about the astrology of Characterology. And I want to thank my dear friend Christine who gave me the healing in which I first experienced the palpable light of my own Core Star and who always, unfailingly, reminds me of who I really am.

More recently, my thanks go to Pete Dellensen and Trilby Fairfax who believed in me enough to bring me on to the staff at their Voice Dialogue training in Dorset.

And beyond this dimension, thanks to all my ancestors who have sometimes felt like a tangible presence with me on this amazing path.

# CONTENTS

## PRELUDE



## PART I

## THE CONCEPTUAL FRAMEWORK



## PART II

## THE FIVE CHARACTER TYPES

**Characterology: in the Psyche, the Human Energy Field and the Horoscope**

## THE GERMINATION OR SCHIZOID STAGE

# PRELUDE
# How I Got Here

In the long hot summer of 1976 I was having a whale of a time! I had moved into a squat in Finsbury Park in London. Utopianism was rife and the squatters in the next row of houses had created a commune, knocked down all the fences between the gardens and kept goats and chickens. I had just seen Peter Schaffer's psychological play *Equus* and I was excited to discover that a lot of the people in my squat were in therapy with the radical psychotherapist RD Laing. Some of them were pretty wild. By being part of such a group I really knew that I had arrived!

The very first morning after I moved into the squat I was woken up by a commotion, with loud banging and shouting coming from the kitchen. I rushed in to see two men involved in a peculiar struggle. The younger one was making all the noise. He had picked up a chair and was using it like a lion tamer to try and trap the other man, who was crouching on the floor in a corner while intermittently yelling and taking rapid puffs from the cigarette dangling from his lips. I stood there bewildered, trying to take in the scene. I noticed that someone had spilled sugar on the floor and decided the trapped man, who was holding a dustpan and brush, had been trying to sweep it up. Other people appeared who quickly calmed things down and gently removed the chair from the young man's hands.

This was my introduction to Willie. Half-French, half-Vietnamese, and abandoned by both parents, Willie was diagnosed as schizophrenic and had severe mental health problems. I imagined that Willie, dismayed by the spilling of the sugar, had sensed anger radiating from the man on the floor and had used the chair to protect himself. Willie lived in a world in which he saw aliens in the garden. He talked to them regularly and sometimes he got very scared.

After a while I discovered that Willie liked me. If Willie came and sat with me while I was drawing or listening to music he would calm right down and only occasionally talk quietly to the aliens in the garden.

I was very pleased to know that he could find peace around me. This wasn't so good for my husband, who had to put up with Willie jealously muttering hostile things whenever he came in and repeatedly stabbing his cigarette butt in my husband's direction. After I left the squat I heard that Willie was admitted to a psychiatric hospital but when I went to visit him he had had electroconvulsive therapy and couldn't remember me at all.

Before I came to the squat I had led quite a sheltered existence in which madness was only something that happened to people in books. Willie opened my eyes to a different reality. I could see that the human mind was much bigger than I had previously considered: oceanic, with unfathomable depths well beyond the control of the rational, optimistic thinking I was brought up on. Whereas I had lived my life in a pool of fairly shallow sunlit waters, Willie had been swept a long way out and was trapped in a fierce current that he didn't know how to escape.

In those irresponsible anarchistic days, recreational drugs were everywhere and when I was twenty-five I took a trip on LSD. My husband, my brother and I managed, with difficulty, to chop an extremely small black tablet into three. Then we stood for some time, in the bright airy front room of the squat, holding our tiny portions on the palms of our hands, gazing at each other with unconcealed anxiety. However, there was no going back so, as one, we gulped them down. Fifteen minutes later we were laughing uncontrollably as we were hit by 'the rush'.

An older man, another of RD Laing's patients, had dropped in for a visit and kindly talked us through the first stage of the trip. He brought out a book from his pocket and showed us an excerpt of writing by Jean-Paul Sartre. I remember as he read some description of sunlight on the snow I gasped aloud because I could so intensely see the snow lit up with violet shadows and glittering diamond sparkles. We were astonished, transported and ecstatic over the poetry of the words and beauty of the imagery. When our older friend saw that we were well on our way he smiled, picked up his book and left us to it.

Soon, as we all calmed down, my experience deepened and I shifted into an exalted state of perception in which I discovered that every single thing in the world was exquisitely, luminously beautiful. The most everyday things became fascinating: flowers on a poster began sprouting from the wall; food on the plate started, rather uncomfortably, to move and tasted extraordinary, though not necessarily nice.

When we went outside the grey path through Finsbury Park became a river of liquid rose-pink in the dusk while streams of violet light ran up tree trunks and out through the branches into the darkening sky. We squealed like children as magical, glowing underground trains hurtled past and when we went home we danced for hours with giant shadows thrown up on the wall by candlelight.

Over the next two years I took six more trips, experimented with magic mushrooms and once with some form of dried fungus that came from America. Every one of my trips was a journey of spiritual revelation as I watched the limitations of the 'real' world dissolve into rivers and vortices of light and meaning. I felt sure, and still do, that the luminous, intensely beautiful and poetically meaningful world that opened up for me did not go away when I was not tripping; it was still there, still real, only I was no longer able to see it.

The American mushrooms were special. On a soft summer afternoon we sat in dappled shade under the trees on Hampstead Heath and chewed our way, with comical disgust, through the bag of dried mushrooms like a group of overgrown children, innocent of both the dangers and the possibilities of what we were doing. That trip took me to a transcendental place of connection with Spirit that changed my life. I can remember very little of it but I know that at one point I was talking to the sky, a flowing mandala of opalescent light. My Little Mind was at one with the Universe. I was completely at peace and I understood absolutely everything there was to be understood, all my questions answered. As the effects of the mushrooms wore off and I started to 'come down' I realized that this blissful state would not stay with me and I made a huge effort to retain something to take back with me into my everyday life. The only scrap of information that I was able to bring back was simply this:

## How I Got Here

Nothing bad can possibly ever happen.

As soon as we left Hampstead Heath I had to deal with something 'bad' as one of my friends who was tripping started to get seriously frightened. And since that time many things that felt extremely bad have happened to me, and wars and catastrophes have happened in the world. But always I have sustained the awareness that there is a parallel reality in which there is no such thing as 'bad'. Many years later in the introduction to *A Course in Miracles* I found these words:

*Nothing real can be threatened.*
*Nothing unreal exists.*
*Herein lies the peace of God.*

I took the last of my trips indoors on a dark winter's night. In the dim glow of the lamplight the walls of my room dissolved into darkness and the pinewood floor became an ocean of honey-gold particles of shimmering light, flowing out to infinity. Two waves rose up out of the golden sea forming into the shapes of two human figures, the outer layers of light particles turning into more opaque cells, covering and containing the two bodies. Features started to appear and I realized these two figures were those of my husband and myself. I saw that we remained eternally connected to the sea of light and to each other even though we also appeared to be separate inside our dense skin boundaries.

When I looked upwards away from the sea of light I saw that the two figures were fantastically complex organic structures, galaxies of living light moving majestically across the velvety black void of space. I was breathless with awe at this miracle of Creation and almost beside myself with wonder when I realized that these vast constructions of light had a central consciousness capable of unified thought and communication. Time slowed down, almost to a standstill, as I witnessed the miracle of sound emanating from one of the beings – huge invisible waves rolling slowly through the darkness to reach the other where amazing patterns of light burst forth as the receiving consciousness registered comprehension of the meaning of the sounds.

I believe that in this vision I was privileged to witness a profound truth about human existence. We are each a walking universe of stars, summoned out of Creation and formed by the intention of our personal, individual consciousness. Every human being is made of vast complex networks of light and energy. That these energies know how to combine to make up the cells and organs of our bodies is, in itself, a miracle. When we see at the heart of that amazing functioning network of life a Consciousness that is capable of communication and creating sound and movement, the beauty and wonder of it is almost unbearable.

It has been more than thirty years since I had that vision. I did not realize it at the time but my trips were an initiation. They inspired in me a longing so deep that it became the central quest of my life to seek out and understand the unseen world of Spirit and energy that in my expanded state I could perceive. And I discovered that I wanted to explore this other reality with my full consciousness, through meditation and healing practices, not through mind-altering drugs. I realized, rather wistfully, that I would not take LSD again.

I never have returned to drugs but my quest for understanding, for confirmation and for pathways that lead me to a transcendent awareness of life has never left me and only grows stronger with the passage of time. Over the years I have found teachers and schools where I have studied meditation, astrology, communication, creation, perception and energy healing, always looking for patterns and meaning. I am undoubtedly a mystic but I am also rational – the explanations I seek have to have logic and consistency, i.e. they have to make sense. What I have found is a continual affirmation of my original vision.

This book is for my fellow travellers on this path; for the mystics and healers and all those who journey into the non-physical realms. In our quest for understanding it is useful to remember the fable of the six blind men and the elephant; each one is touching a different part of the elephant but each one thinks he has got the whole picture. I think we are all partially blind as we feel our way into that other reality. I am, like you, an explorer of the unseen world and this book is a map of the little bit of the elephant that I know.

> *What is it we are questing for? It is the fulfilment of that which is potential in each of us. Questing for it is not an ego trip; it is an adventure to bring into fulfilment your gift to the world, which is yourself. There is nothing you can do that's more important than being fulfilled. You become a sign, you become a signal, transparent to transcendence; in this way you will find, live, become a realization of your own personal myth.*
>
> Joseph Campbell *Pathways to Bliss*

# PART I

# THE CONCEPTUAL FRAMEWORK

Charting the Soul brings together three approaches to understanding a human being – psychology, energy healing and astrology. These are three distinct methodologies but to my mind they are naturally intertwined as they are all ways of reading and relating to a person's Human Energy Field. It is important to read through this section, which provides an overview of each approach, sometimes summing up the traditional understanding sometimes coming from a very new perspective. The concepts outlined here are the foundation for understanding the psychological, energetic and astrological descriptions of the five character types in the main sections of the book.

1

# Awareness

> *Each person's life – each life-form, in fact – represents a world, a unique way in which the universe experiences itself.*
> Eckhart Tolle *A New Earth*

## The Human Energy Field

This book is founded on a spiritual viewpoint. The fundamental premise is that every living being is a unique facet of consciousness arising from the eternal source of Universal Consciousness. Each one of us is born as an exquisite star emerging from the infinite void. Each spark of consciousness radiates its own field of energy and the essential qualities of that individual consciousness appear as vibrational patterns in their energy field. Every person has a Human Energy Field (HEF); in fact, every person *is* a Human Energy Field.

So, people are bigger on the inside than they appear from the outside! A human being is a powerful, immortal soul temporarily taking form in the world of matter by building and inhabiting a physical, biological, mortal body. The consciousness of a human soul creates a Human Energy Field and it is the HEF that supports the life of the body. And the way that a person's life on earth develops is a manifestation of the qualities of consciousness and the vibrational patterns running through their HEF.

Well, this is all very grand but it is clear that coming to experience life in the physical plane is a complex and confusing business! The first thing we do is forget who we really are; that seems to be a major part of the story. So we humans stumble around creating tangles and log-jams in the flow of our energy field and having dismayingly unwelcome life experiences. One way of thinking about this is to accept that even though human life can get very messy, that doesn't mean it's a mistake. The value of the human experience lies in the journey, in the struggle to manifest our uniqueness, in learning how to embody Essence through Awareness.

> *Get this in your head! You must have negative experiences in order to grow. Those experiences are not meant to defeat you; they serve a purpose and that purpose is to enlighten you. You needed to find out what door is closed, so that you can start searching for a door that is open. You needed to find out what hurts, so that you can discover what heals. You needed to realize what must come to an end so that you can have a new beginning.*
> James Weeks *Across The King's River*

So, from the labyrinthine density of our human confusion, what we want is a map, a pointer to direct us towards the door that will open. We need a way of becoming conscious of the vibrational energy patterns that underpin our personal dilemmas and we want techniques for disentangling blockages that impede the flow of energy in the HEF. And, most of all, we need to start remembering who we really are. A lot of the time we cannot see the wood for the trees – our view of the road is impeded by our identification with old wounded ways of being, old pain, old defences, powerful beliefs about 'the way it is': images that cloud and obscure our perception and our ability to allow our lives to flower.

## Awakening

In this book I use the word Awakening to describe a process of bringing these old wounded tangled places into consciousness. The more we can release the grip of old fear-based ways of thinking, the more we are freed up to make different choices and the more we can create spaciousness in the psyche to allow our true Essence to shine through.

## Awareness

One of the things that I teach is an approach to Awakening called Voice Dialogue (the creation of Doctors Hal and Siddra Stone). In the Voice Dialogue model we refer to something that exists outside the distortions of our habitual thinking. This is the place of Awareness.

Awareness exists outside our personal, emotional reactions; when we are in Awareness we simply observe everything without judgement and this experience is imbued with profound stillness and peace. When we are able to bring our human entanglements into consciousness and to witness them from Awareness then transformation occurs and we are released from the grip of the old ways. In Voice Dialogue, we describe the process of building an Aware Ego – bringing old patterns into consciousness, disidentifying with the old distortions and beliefs and developing more and more spaciousness and freedom to express our true Essence and spontaneous creativity.

I will go one step further and say that developing our ability to move into Awareness is developing our ability to experience our own divinity. The more we develop the Aware Ego the more access we have to inner guidance, to Presence, to Stillness, to remembering who we really are. Living from the Aware Ego we are able to open to allow life to move through us. Instead of rolling helplessly down a road dictated by unconscious conditioning, our access to Awareness increasingly allows us to become energy dancers moving in and out of the currents in the river of life. And this view gives us strength to embrace the difficulties we encounter as human beings; the struggle is the road and Divine Consciousness itself is expanding through our human Awakening.

> *One day Confucius and his pupils were walking by a turbulent river, which swept over rapids, rocks and waterfalls. They saw an old man swimming in the river far upstream. He was playing in the raging water and went under. Confucius sent his pupils running downstream to try and save him. However, the old man beached safely on the bank and stood up unharmed, the water streaming from his hair. The pupils brought him to Confucius, who asked him how on earth he managed to survive in the torrent among the rocks.*

*He answered, 'Oh, I know how to go in with a descending vortex, and come out with an ascending one.'*
*He was, of course, a man of the Tao.*
Philip Rawson and László Legeza *Tao*

2

# Three Roads On The Map

In this book I bring together the three approaches of psychology, energy healing and astrology; three roads on the map leading towards the unknown territory of consciousness. All three approaches are doorways that open into the mystery that we are; each of them brings us a greater understanding of 'how we work' and all three are about the process of Awakening, of becoming increasingly conscious, of developing Awareness.

To be more specific, in this book the three roads on the map that I am looking at are:

- **Characterology** – an aspect of Body-Mind Psychology, originally the work of the psychologist Wilhelm Reich who described five different character types emerging from five stages of child development.
- **Energy Healing** – using extrasensory perception to observe the Human Energy Field (HEF) and discern patterns of energy including the five character types as they appear in the HEF. The model I follow is based on the work of the healer and physicist Barbara Brennan.
- Jungian based **Psychological Astrology** focusing on the archetypes associated with each of the planets in relation to the five character types.

## Characterology

There is a universally held understanding that a person's character is powerfully shaped by their life history. All branches of psychology recognize the long-lasting impact of our experiences in childhood and the damaging effects of unresolved trauma. To my mind, Wilhelm Reich's theory of Characterology is one of the clearest and most valuable ways of understanding what happens during the early years of childhood and the significant effect of trauma on the subsequent development of the personality. Today, this concept of five stages of child development and the emergence of five character types is accepted and included in a variety of psychological approaches (e.g. Neo-Reichian Bodywork, Bioenergetics, Core Energetics, Hakomi and Brennan Healing Science).

Obviously we know that there are more than five types of people in the world, just as with astrology we know that there are more than twelve kinds of people in the world. However, understanding how the emphasis on one particular stage of child development leads to the emergence of a distinct and recognizable aspect of character can be extremely helpful when dealing with the complexity of human behaviour. And so I have used the exploration of the five stages of development and the five character types as the basic framework for this book.

The energy healer, using a psycho-spiritual approach, can expand on the psychological view. For example, a healer sees that in addition to the psychological impact of events in this life a person will have unresolved issues and talents and gifts that have been passed down the ancestral line or that arise from past life experiences.

A psychological astrologer will see both experiences in childhood and the ancestral inheritance as they show up in the horoscope.

There is already a vast range of books available for study on the subjects of Characterology, energy healing and psychological astrology and I am deeply grateful to all those who have contributed to this pool of wisdom. In this book my aim is to take the next step, go beyond the established knowledge and show how integrating the three approaches expands the understanding in each area and increases our access to Awareness. So what I am doing is weaving the three strands together, more closely than has been done before.

Twentieth-century psychology tended to come from a dualistic, judgemental viewpoint and my intention is to present a more compassionate and affirming approach to Characterology. In the main section of the book where I describe each of the five character types I start with the Reichian model of the impact of trauma and wounding experienced in childhood and the development of Characterological defence mechanisms. However, I then move on to the spiritual viewpoint where my emphasis is on the realization that tremendous gifts of soul and Essence are associated with each of the five character types. In the heart of even the darkest places is the light of the soul waiting to come through. Finally, and most importantly, it is by making the links between psychology, energy healing and the astrological archetypes of the planets that everything starts to open up and it becomes clear what it is that is struggling to break through. So this book should be of interest to anyone working in the fields of psychology, energy healing and astrology, as well as anyone on a path of personal growth.

**The psychologist:**

- can develop their understanding of the spiritual dimension of psychotherapy. They can discover how psychological issues are rooted in energy patterns in the Human Energy Field and they can develop their ability to perceive, sense and support the flow of energy as part of the therapeutic process (many psychotherapists already do this intuitively or they will have had some training in this approach). A counsellor or therapist who includes the spiritual dimension understands that it is in opening to Awareness and entering into Presence that transformation takes place.
- can recognize astrology as a brilliant diagnostic tool! A person's horoscope reveals so much that might otherwise remain unconscious and it also affirms a person's sense of their authentic nature. Astrology both shines light into the shadowy corners of the psyche and illuminates the pathway to healing.

**The energy healer:**

- can recognize the powerful impact that a person's psychological history, emotions and beliefs have on their HEF.

Learning to recognize a person's Characterological make-up is an invaluable tool in understanding what is happening in the HEF, above all in getting to know the appropriate healing response that will help the energy in the field to move from the armouring of defence into the flowering of the gifts.

- can learn to recognize a person's astrological chemistry as a core vibrational pattern in the HEF and recognize the archetypal gifts and drives that want to be expressed.

**The astrologer:**

- can expand their understanding of astrology by learning about the psychology of the five character types and seeing how they are represented by the planets and the houses in the horoscope. Relating the archetypes of the planets to the different character types also deepens our understanding of the planets.
- can learn to recognize each planet's own distinct vibrational signature and expand their knowledge of the planets by seeing how they appear as a distinct pattern running through the HEF.

For all my readers, this book presents an opportunity to explore the balance of your own Characterological make-up, gradually deepening your understanding through the book. You may begin by recognizing a pattern of childhood experiences that left you with some kind of issue and my hope is that by the end of the book you will be able to see the inner butterfly of soul that might be ready to struggle out of this particular cocoon or recognize the phoenix of Essence that might rise from that heap of glowing ashes!

**Astrology**

Most psychotherapists and process facilitators are intuitively aware of what is happening in the HEF. Most energy healers are effortlessly aware of the importance of understanding a person's psychological process. However, not enough people working in the helping professions have a real understanding of the value of astrology. For so many people, the perception of astrology is warped by the prevalence of 'magazine astrology' and the number of astrologers who speak from a shallow place of judgement and dualistic thinking. A real, fully trained and experienced astrologer can see in the horoscope so much that otherwise remains in shadow and can open up the way that Essence is seeking to find. So, above all, this book aims to demonstrate the value of astrology on the path of Awakening.

## How to Use this Book

There is a lot of information in this book and some readers may already feel they have expertise in one of the three areas I am bringing together. So in places it will be fine to skim through things that you already understand and look for the bits that bring a new perspective, the sections that seem most inspiring and most relevant to your own approach to Awakening. For example, several friends have helped me by offering to read the book. My friend who is a professional astrologer already has a profound understanding of the archetypes of the planets. But she was delighted to learn about the five character types and to explore the ways in which they appear in the horoscope. Another friend is a Brennan Energy Healer and already has an excellent understanding of the five character types and how they appear in the HEF. She was able to enjoy reading quickly through the sections about energy healing, expanding and affirming knowledge she already had, but she experienced excitement and wonder when she started to see how the planets relate to the character types and how they illuminate and make sense of the patterns in the energy field.

It is important to read Chapters 2–6 in which I outline the fundamental concepts that underpin this book:

- Reich's idea of the five stages of childhood giving rise to the five character types
- A description of the Human Energy Field
- A lay person's outline of some of the key features of the horoscope

One of the most important sections is on pp 32 – 33 when I talk about the Creative Process; hoping to introduce a fundamental shift in our way of thinking about the Character types. Instead of focusing on pathology and trauma occurring in five stages of childhood I introduce the idea of the Character types as representatives of five intrinsic stages of the Creative Process: five stages of the soul's journey moving from a state of pure energy to take form in the world of matter.

The main part of the book is divided into five chapters exploring each of the five character types in depth, starting with the psychological model, proceeding with the spiritual view and finishing with a description of the archetypes of the planets associated with each stage. This is the core of the book for psychologists, energy healers and astrologers learning to understand and recognize the five types.

The first two parts of the book are written with the intention of being easily comprehensible to non-astrologers as my focus is on the archetypes of the planets rather than the complexities of chart interpretation. However, I refer quite often to the system of the 'houses' of the horoscope. If you have ever had your chart done, it might be helpful have a copy of your chart to hand and ask an astrologer to help you note which planets are in which signs and which houses they occupy.

The third and final part of the book is written for astrologers and for people with enough understanding of the language of astrology. This section is made up of five case studies of the horoscopes of famous individuals whose life stories and achievements are a good illustration of each of the five character types.

A last word about my intention in writing this book: many people, possibly all people, live with a deep-rooted belief which is some version of 'There is something wrong with me'. But on the level of Essence, there is no doubt that you are fundamentally, profoundly good! This is the paradox of spiritual awareness; for the rational mind alone this is incomprehensible because, obviously, many people in this world commit truly atrocious acts of cruelty, etc., and we all say and do things that we regret. But in the place of Spirit, inside even the darkest shadows is the light of Essence waiting to come forth and unravel the knot. Every living being who comes to this earth is running their own, totally unique, pattern of Universal energy with tremendous power to heal and transform the old patterns of wounding. So how can we learn to live from Essence? In this astro-psycho-spiritual quest of a book, what I can offer you are ways to have MORE of yourself – how to know yourself better, how to awaken to the parts of you that you didn't know were there, how to get out of your own way and deepen and expand and transform your expression of your unique individuality – above all, to know your Divinity. No matter how good or bad you think your life is, at the centre of your being you are a star: a little piece of God who has come to this planet so that the Divine can experience life on earth through you!

> *'Purity means that our true nature is already perfect and complete,' he continued. 'None of our confusion and fear can change this inner purity. It doesn't get worse when we suffer or improve when we become enlightened like the Buddha. We don't need to add anything to it or take anything away, nor do we have to do something to get it. It's here with us each and every moment, like a diamond in the palm of one's hand.'*
>
> Yongey Mingyur Rinpoche

3

# An Introduction to the Human Energy Field

*Everything that is created in the physical world must first exist in the world of life energy.*
Barbara Brennan *Light Emerging*

Using clairvoyant perception, a human being appears as part of an extensive sphere of light – a magnificent network of beautiful, shifting, changing, rippling light. The physical body itself is at the centre of this field of light, built around energy structures at the core of the field.

The field is born from a central point of light, that also exists in another dimension. Energy from this source flows into the material world and radiates out to form a luminous field that extends far beyond the body. It is this dynamic living light energy that sustains and underpins all life forms in the material world. This halo of light is known in most spiritual traditions as the 'aura'; energy healers refer to it as the 'Human Energy Field' (HEF).

Descriptions of the aura appear in most systems of spiritual beliefs, from tribal shamanic traditions to all the major religions. There is a huge amount of literature already available on this subject and considerable variation in the detail of the descriptions of the aura. It seems likely to me that, at this stage of human evolution, we are not yet capable of creating a precisely accurate map of the non-physical realms, just as early man could not have created an accurate geographical map of the world. So, what I shall be doing here is describing the HEF as it appears to me and in ways that are relevant to the subject of this book.

My understanding of the Human Energy Field was derived, in the first place, from my years of study at the Barbara Brennan School of Healing. (Barbara Brennan is the author of *Hands of Light* and *Light Emerging* and the founder of the Barbara Brennan School of Healing.) We are greatly indebted to Brennan, who expanded on the traditional concept of the aura and provided us with a structured and much more extensive description of the Human Energy Field. Here, I also refer to concepts from the ancient Chinese Taoist practice of Qigong.

### The HEF as an Expression of Soul and Psyche

One of the main themes that appear in descriptions of the aura is that a person's energy field changes according to their state of consciousness. So, the light of the individual's unique essential nature, their changing emotions as well as any issues that block their expression of self, will appear as some kind of recognizable pattern or formation in their energy field.

### The Chakras

Another widely accepted idea, rooted in Hindu beliefs, is that the aura contains a system of chakras – energy centres that appear as vortices drawing universal energy into the HEF to sustain the life of the individual. In this book I will be referring to the seven major chakras, each of which has specific psychological and physiological functions.

### The Hara

I will also be referring to a deeper level of the HEF known as the level of the Hara. The Chinese practice of Qigong and many martial arts traditions describe a vertical column of energy deep in the core of the HEF. This central Hara line has three major centres which are the seat of individual personal power and are the driving energy sources for this life. In the Brennan model of the HEF, the activity of the chakras occurs on an outer level of the field and this level is supported and sustained by the powerful structures held on the deep inner level of the Hara.

So, on the outer level of the field are the chakras, which are very fluid and liquid, opening and closing, reacting and responding to the individual's experience of life. And deeper into the core of the field we have the level of the Hara – powerful lines and centres of energy which are much less affected by everyday events and hold a profound sense of the life purpose that brings this unique soul into incarnation.

## Overview of the Structure of the Human Energy Field

In what follows I shall give a more detailed description of the HEF. As always, there are difficulties in talking about the non-physical world in language designed for describing the physical world.

## Core Star

In the Brennan model of the HEF we see that a living being is born from a star that arises in another dimension beyond the limitations of the physical world. This star is a drop in the infinite ocean of Universal Consciousness, one tiny spark of light which is divine, eternal and cannot be harmed. This unique facet of Universal Consciousness contains the essential qualities of the soul and the divine purpose of an individual life. When we connect to this level of being we experience bliss and wonder at the beauty of creation.

## Hara

The living light of the Core Star flows into the manifest world onto the level of the Hara. Energy on the level of the Hara forms powerful lines of light which are the structures that support the HEF. Running through the centre of the field is the central line of Hara which is rooted deep into the centre of the earth and which rises up to connect to the non-physical realms of Spirit. So when our focus is on the level of the Hara we experience ourselves as a bridge between heaven and earth, between our divine nature and our biological form.

On the level of the Hara we hold our soul intention to live a life in the manifest world. One of the signal qualities of experience on the level of the Hara is stillness. Here we are not rocked by the emotional turmoil of human life. Instead we feel the sense of our own divinity and the sacred and solemn purpose of our life here on earth.

There are three main centres of energy situated along the central Hara line, which are known in Qigong as the Tan T'ien or Dantian. Situated deep within the belly is the Lower Tan T'ien. This centre, strongly rooted into the earth, is the source of the raw instinctual biological power that sustains physical life. When it is energized it may feel hot, almost like a core of molten lava, and it radiates a red-gold light. In western society we are very inclined to focus our energy upwards into the head. Anyone who has had the experience of allowing their focus to sink away from the head down into the area of the Lower Tan T'ien in the pelvic cradle will appreciate the immense sense of personal power and Presence that is available when we are connected to this centre.

The second centre is situated in the area of the heart. It is traditionally known as the Middle Tan T'ien. Barbara Brennan refers to it as the Soul Seat and sees it situated a little above the heart. Whereas the Lower Tan T'ien holds concentrated raw power, the energy of the Soul Seat, or the Middle Tan T'ien is much more diffuse and tender and it vibrates with the energy of the heart. This is the meeting place of heaven and earth. Here we feel the passion of our love for the Divine, including our love for all beings, and it is where we experience our longing to fulfil our life purpose and allow our celestial light to shine through into the manifest world.

In traditional Qigong the third centre, the Upper Tan T'ien, is situated in the middle of the head or a little above the head. Barbara Brennan refers to a point over three feet above the head, which she calls the ID point or individuation point. Whereas the Lower Tan T'ien connects us to the earth, to gravity and the concentrated energy of our biological existence, the Upper Tan T'ien, or the ID point connects us to the non-physical realm, to the world of Spirit, to Divine Consciousness. The Upper Tan T'ien has a white light which can be brilliant and very powerful, and at other times still and soft like snow. The Upper Tan T'ien is as powerful as the Lower Tan T'ien but it is our connection to infinity and so it has the quality of spaciousness and expansion.

### The Chakras

Most spiritual traditions recognize seven major chakras (and there are also minor chakras) connecting into the vertical column of energy that runs through the centre of the body, parallel to the spine. The chakras are often described as radiating the seven colours of the spectrum, from red at the base chakra to violet or white light at the crown chakra.

1. The 1st chakra or the base chakra is situated at the bottom of the torso, aligned with the central column of energy pointing downwards to the earth. It has a low rate of vibration, close to the heavy vibration of matter, and its primary function is to support the health of the biological body and deal with all the issues of survival in the physical world. The light of the base chakra is often seen as red and its sound is deep and earthy like the sound of drumming or of a didgeridoo.
2. The 2nd chakra, also known as the sacral chakra, is situated a little way below the navel. This is the centre of sexual and procreative energy and it supports the reproductive system as well as sexual and sensual pleasure and the joy of being in a physical body. This chakra also the place of self-love and self-nurturing. The 2nd chakra has a faster, more fluid vibration than the base chakra and its colour is orange. On the deeper level, the 1st and 2nd chakras are supported by the primal power of the Lower Tan T'ien.
3. The 3rd chakra, also referred to as the solar plexus, is situated just below the sternum. The 3rd chakra is concerned with mental activity: the way we think about things, the beliefs and judgements we make about life and ourselves. It is also the seat of our sense of personal power. The vibration of the 3rd chakra is finer than that of the lower chakras and its light is yellow.
4. The 4th chakra is the heart chakra, which has everything to do with our emotions, our relationships and our ability to open to love. On a deeper level, the heart chakra connects to the Middle Tan T'ien and our connection to universal love. The colour of the heart chakra can be seen as a peaceful green like the light of Nature and the heart also gives off the beautiful rose light of love.
5. The 5th chakra is situated in the area of the throat. The throat chakra has to do with speech and communication. It also has to do with our ability to take in nourishment and with our

trust and faith in life. The 5th chakra has some of the energy of the Upper Tan T'ien and it has a crystalline light that connects to the stillness and harmony of Universal Consciousness. It has a fine, high vibration and gives off a clear blue light that is the colour of the sky.

6. The 6th chakra, also known as the third eye, is situated in the forehead. The 6th chakra is the major centre for imagination, understanding and perception, including all kinds of higher sense perception, intuition and vision. It is through this chakra that we are able to perceive the non-physical realms and experience the celestial love of the angels. It has a fast, fine high vibration, far removed from the slow, dense vibration of the physical realm. The light of the 6th chakra is the deep indigo blue of the night and it also has a silvery radiance like starlight.
7. The 7th chakra, also known as the crown chakra, is situated at the top of the head, aligned with the central column of light pointing upwards to the sky. The crown chakra has to do with all higher mental activity and our connection to the Mind of God. It has a very high vibration and is closely related to the non-physical world of Spirit. It has a brilliant, white-gold light. On the level of the Hara, the 6th and 7th chakras are closely connected to the Upper Tan T'ien and to the clear light of the Mind of God.

When the seven chakras are functioning well, they appear as glowing centres of light drawing in energy to sustain and nourish the HEF. When a person has issues of unresolved pain and difficulty, these will show up in the relevant chakra. That chakra may be small and weak or even completely shut down, it may be overcharged and splayed open, or it may appear to be torn or damaged in some other way. Its colour may be dim and washed out, darkened by shadows or weighed down with clouds like mucus which appear around energy blocks in the HEF. The chakras may also contain 'objects' associated with old wounds, as well as signs and symbols related to ancestral issues. A chakra can be restored to full health in a number of ways but, in particular, when a shift of consciousness occurs with the release of old beliefs and emotions. A healer can assist this process by working with the energy field, making repairs, clearing away mucus and running in energy, light, colour, sound and love to rebalance the chakras.

The HEF extends both outwardly, a long way out beyond the physical body, and inwardly to vast depth at the core of the field. Moving towards the upper chakras and towards the outer levels of the field, the energy takes on an increasingly fine and high vibration, ultimately dissolving into the vast emptiness of space and the unshadowed light of the stars. Closer to the physical body and nearer to the Earth, the vibration of the field becomes increasingly contracted and more dense, connecting to the raw power of the Lower Tan T'ien and inwardly into the deep vibration at the core of the manifest world.

Thinking in terms of the Daoist idea of yin (feminine) and yang (masculine) energy, we can sense that the chakras and the outer levels of the field have the tendency towards expansion and the energy of light and Spirit, which is the yang energy, while the lower chakras and the inner levels of the HEF have the tendency towards contraction and the soft energy of darkness and Matter, which is the yin energy.

## The Physical Dimension

We start with one individual spark of consciousness sending light flowing out into the manifest universe, firstly at the level of the Hara, then moving on to engage more closely with the physical world on the level of the chakras and, last of all, the life force coalesces into Matter, taking form as the cells and tissues of the physical body. All the biological systems of the body are constructed around the energy structures held in the HEF. When the field is clear then the physical body is energized and healthy, and where the HEF is weak or damaged the health of the physical body deteriorates.

The HEF is not obviously detectable to people whose everyday perception is attuned only to the physical world. In order to perceive the dimensions of the non-physical worlds we have to use clairvoyant, clairaudient, intuitive senses also known as Higher Sense Perception

(HSP). All beings have HSP, nobody is born without it, but in our materially oriented cultures children lose faith in their HSP and learn to limit themselves to the accepted materialistic interpretation of the world. But for many of us, from childhood onwards, the perceptions of the non-physical dimensions keep seeping through as Spirit calls to reawaken us to remember who we really are.

4

# A Psycho-Spiritual Approach to Healing the Human Energy Field

> *From the holistic perspective, the physical cannot remain healthy unless the emotional does too.*
> Barbara Brennan *Hands of Light*

## The Effect of Psychological Trauma on the HEF

Whatever a person is experiencing in life has a direct impact on their energy field. Experiences of love and joy make the field light up or feel full, or exquisitely sensitive or electric! Intense mental activity can make the field buzz and spin, while in states of meditation and deep peace the field becomes still like a millpond. When a person has a painful experience an area of their HEF will react, perhaps by going into a state of tightly held contraction, or it might be disturbed by bursts of discordant energy, like electric shocks.

Often people cannot cope with the emotions that accompany a painful experience and they repress their feelings. If these uncomfortable feelings are never allowed into consciousness the blocked emotions accumulate into a zone of stuck energy in the HEF. The trapped emotional energy forms a blockage in the flow of the life force that supplies energy to the physical cells of the body and, over time, this begins to cause a breakdown in physical health. Energy blockages are the original cause of all disease and difficulty in human life but their root is often buried in the mists of time. They may also be directly inherited as an issue for the whole ancestral line and they may also result from past life experiences. Every human being has these areas of stagnation in their HEF – shadows wrapped around the pain of an old wound – and they are not easy to bring into consciousness.

When a healer looks at a person's HEF they perceive that while much of the field is radiant, luminous and vibrant they can also sense the areas where the flow of energy is blocked. These blockages may look dark and cloudy, feel heavy, sticky, cold or hard or there may be places that are overcharged and burning, or something else that feels difficult. The patterns of flow or disturbance in the HEF are directly related to a person's physical health and their psychological state of mind, and the discordant areas signify some kind of tangle of physical and/or emotional dis-ease. Psycho-spiritual healing is a two-pronged approach that combines energy healing with psychotherapy. In this approach, working directly in the energy field to clear blockages can initiate psychological release as well as physical healing; simultaneously, psychological breakthroughs arising from 'process work' bring about shifts and clear blocks in the energy field.

### Body-Mind Psychotherapy

The depth psychologists of the twentieth century brought tremendous advances in human understanding by opening the door to the vast inner world of the unconscious. One of the early psychologists was Wilhelm Reich, originally a student and colleague of Sigmund Freud. Reich proposed the idea that repressed emotions become locked in the physical body. He developed the technique of working with the body, asking his clients to take up strenuous physical postures so that the tension in the muscles would release, bringing a major discharge of emotion. Reich saw that a person's physical and psychological well-being are directly linked, not separate but two expressions of the same root. This is the fundamental theory of Body-Mind Psychotherapy, and the principle that a person's state of mind has an effect on their physical body is the basis of all holistic approaches to healing.

### Core Energetics

The discoveries of Reich were taken up by his students, Alexander Lowen and John Pierrakos, who developed the Body-Mind approach of Bioenergetics. John Pierrakos's wife Eva was a gifted psychic who channelled a body of material of profound spiritual and psychological insight known as The Pathwork. John Pierrakos took Reich's work to the next level and developed Core Energetics, an approach born from the synthesis of his understanding of Body-Mind process work and Eva's material on psycho-spiritual development:

> *Energy and consciousness are in a continual state of interaction: energy is shaped and directed by consciousness which is itself driven by energy.*
> John Pierrakos *Eros, Love & Sexuality: The Forces That Unify Man and Woman*

In the late 1970s Barbara Brennan trained with John and Eva Pierrakos and became a facilitator of both The Pathwork and Core Energetics. By the end of the twentieth century Brennan became recognised as one of the great contributors to the development of the psycho-spiritual approach. She continued to expand on the work and developed Brennan Healing Science in which the energy healer is constantly moving focus between the worlds of the psyche, the body and the Human Energy Field.

A psycho-spiritual healer works both in the physical world and with the 'unseen world' of Spirit, so they are able to see beyond a person's immediate situation, whatever appears to be the presenting physical and psychological issue. From a healer's view a person is born from their Divine Core Star and is much, much more than a victim of circumstances. A healer has an expanded understanding of what is going on for their clients because, in addition to a person's psychological and medical history, a healer receives information directly from the HEF, including issues related to reincarnation and the inheritance of ancestral patterns.

From the spiritual perspective our birth into human existence is a choice, an act of consciousness. Children do not arrive as a blank slate: the child is new but the soul is not and both the unresolved problems and the creative talents developed in past lives can be perceived in the HEF. Healing is what occurs when we are able to bring our wounds into consciousness, hold them in the light of the Core Star and allow the old shadows to dissolve and transform. Every individual has an immortal soul which is infinitely greater than their psychological issues. Time and again, we see the human spirit rise like a phoenix from the fires of adversity, and locked inside a person's shadows are great human gifts in which the light of the soul is waiting to be released. So a healer constantly moves between the Body-Mind awareness of the presenting issues of a person's current life and psychic awareness of the bigger picture of what is happening in the non-physical dimensions and the unfolding journey of the eternal soul.

## Characterology

An important aspect of Body-Mind Psychotherapy is the theory of Characterology. In his work with his clients Wilhelm Reich observed that the psychological effect of trauma experienced in early infancy differed from the effect of trauma experienced in an older child. He noticed that if a person's history emphasized one particular stage of childhood this led to the development of specific psychological and physical characteristics. Based on these observations Reich mapped out the psychological development of the personality through five stages of infancy associated with the emergence of five basic types of Character. Each of the five Characters has a distinct physical and psychological profile, including specific patterns of neurosis and defence which block the healthy expression of the Self.

Everybody has been through the five stages of child development so everybody has some signs of all five of these Character types. However, some people have a dominant emphasis on one of the types, while most people have an emphasis on a mixture of two or three. Character Structure, or Characterology, is the term used to describe the balance of these five personality types in a person's make-up. A psycho-spiritual healer can learn to quickly recognize a person's Character Structure in their physical appearance, their psychological nature and the energy patterns in their HEF. I have found this understanding so valuable that I have made it the central structure of this book.

However, again, as a healer I go a step further by remembering that within the cocoon of the personality lies the butterfly of the soul. So in this book we look beyond the limitations of traditional Characterology to recognize that though each of the five Character types suffers from negative patterns of defence, they also bring through wonderful gifts of the soul such as vision, compassion, creativity, courage and wisdom.

In Part II of this book I use the five Character types as a framework from which to make an exploration of the Human Energy Field. So Part II is organized into five sections. Each section is divided into three parts:

- An outline of Reich's description of psychological wounding and defence in the Character types as they emerge from each of the developmental stages.
- A description of the five Character types as patterns appearing in the HEF – including
  specific gifts that emanate from the Essence of the soul.
- A description of how both the psychological wounds and the gifts of the soul are represented by specific planets in a person's horoscope.

This method integrates the ancient art of astrology with the psycho-spiritual approach to energy healing and the Body-Mind approach of Characterology. It expands our understanding of all three disciplines and creates a new approach to working with the HEF. What follows in the next section is an introduction to characterology.

# 5

# The Psychological View: Characterology and Five Stages of Child Development

> *Defence – 'The purpose of ego defence mechanisms is to protect the mind/ self/ ego from anxiety and to provide a refuge from a situation with which one cannot currently cope.'*
> www.britannica.com

In the twentieth century the early psychologists began to understand the long-term effects of childhood trauma. A view emerged that when a child has a painful experience they repress their feelings and develop psychological defence mechanisms which help them to maintain control in order to avoid being overwhelmed by suffering. One of the most common defences is the defence of detachment – when the child 'freezes' their feelings, goes numb and represses all emotion. Sometimes a child who feels threatened will develop the defence of aggression or they may become hypersensitive, clingy and over-anxious to please and appease. Everyone develops defence mechanisms; it is part of being human and without their defences the psyche of the child might not survive. But if the defences become ingrained they distort the natural flow of the Life Force. Therefore, childhood trauma causes blockages to develop at the foundations of the new life, and the younger the child the more damaging the effects of trauma.

Wilhelm Reich observed that when a person is in defence their repressed feelings have an effect on the physical body. Certain areas of the body contract or collapse in reaction to the pressure of control and eventually this will develop into a blockage of chronic muscular tension or 'armouring'. Reich observed that the physical appearance of a person's body has a distinct correlation with their pattern of psychological defence so that certain features, such as long, stringy, gangling bodies as opposed to short, compact, stocky bodies, are associated with particular psychological characteristics. In addition, he realized that these distinct body and personality types are linked to specific patterns of experience in childhood. Reich concluded that not only a person's psychological development but also the actual physical stages in childhood.

- **The Schizoid Type** The Schizoid type is associated with the developmental stage that extends from conception through the gestation period and on into the critical time of labour, birth and the earliest days of life. Wounding and defence in this stage arise from the experience of terror – the primal fear of physical death and annihilation. The Schizoid defence is associated with extreme mental detachment and fragmentation.
- **The Oral Type** The Oral type is associated with the period that extends from birth through the first year of life while the baby's survival remains totally dependent on receiving care and nourishment from others. Wounding and defence arising from this stage centre on the experience of deprivation – the fear of abandonment and hunger. The Oral defence is associated with extreme emotional dependency and collapse.
- **The Masochist Type** The third type is the Masochist type, associated with the second and third year of life when the child develops mobility and speech and begins to assert their autonomy. Wounding and defence in this stage arise from experiences of being dominated and humiliated – the fear of powerlessness and shame. The Masochist defence is associated with stubborn resistance and experiences of defeat.
- **The Psychopathic Type** The fourth type, the Psychopathic type, is associated with the older child, aged three to five, who is ready to focus on the area of relationship and begins to explore their sexual identity in relationship to the parent of the opposite sex. Wounding in this stage arises from the experience of the breakdown of trust in relationship – the fear of betrayal. The

Psychopathic defence is associated with aggression and the experiences of betrayal.

- **The Rigid Type:** The fifth type, the Rigid type, is associated with the child between five and seven years old, who is learning the social rules of how to fit in with their family, their tribe and their community. Wounding and defence arising from this stage centre on the experience being criticized or rejected – the fear of failure. The Rigid defence is associated with issues of extreme control and judgement.

The analysis of an individual's personality based on the five Character types is known as Characterology. Clearly there are more than five types of people in the world so Characterology is a simplification of something which is highly complex.

I will go through the Reichian view of all five Character types in Part II of this book. We shall see that Reichian Characterology was very much focused on the damaging effects of the defence mechanisms of the five types. Learning about the different Character types is fascinating but it is easy to have a negative reaction to the uncomfortable descriptions of childhood trauma, wounding, distortion and defence. Reich named the five Character types using terms from classical analytical psychology – Schizoid, Oral, Masochist, Psychopathic and Rigid – so the names themselves have painful associations with mental health problems.

People reading the descriptions quickly find themselves identifying with one or more of the Characterological types. Almost without exception readers go into a state of judgement: against themselves for being flawed, against their own parents who 'wounded' them and/or into a state of guilt about their own failings as a parent! Yet Characterology only describes the results of a child's struggle to deal with their circumstances as they grow through the developmental stages. We build a defence as a way of coping when difficult things happen and it is a simple fact that, in life, difficult things do happen. While it is clear that some people suffer appalling neglect and abuse in childhood and become profoundly damaged, even children from stable and loving homes have their issues. The development of individually distinct patterns of Characterology is as intrinsic to human psychological development as the growth of ten fingers with unique fingerprints is to physical development.

6

# The Spiritual View: Essence and Five Stages of the Creative Process

> *You are the light of Presence, the awareness that is prior to and deeper than any thoughts and emotions.*
> Eckhart Tolle *A New Earth*

For a psycho-spiritual healer, whatever is happening in a person's HEF is directly related to their psychological make-up, including their Characterology. In the energy field we can see the impact of life events – areas of contraction where pain is held and areas of light where the soul has been able to flower.

From the psychological view alone it is easy to fall into a judgement that regards a person's defence patterns – their Characterology – as a symptom of something that has gone 'wrong' that needs to be 'fixed'. Living life from a place of fear, walled in by our defences, is undoubtedly painful, sometimes intolerably painful. However, from the spiritual view it is possible to look at even very grim scenarios in a different way. For the healer, a person's wounds and defences can be seen as the tip of an iceberg, a sign of something much deeper and potentially valuable that has not yet emerged, and this point is critical to understanding this book and the nature of healing. The psychological defences and blocks in the HEF are congested tangles of consciousness that have not yet found expression in our world of form – of Essence that has not yet come to fulfilment. Like the caterpillar wriggling in its cocoon or the bald fledgling squawking from the nest, our defences represent our struggle with incarnation at a stage when we have not yet learned how to fly.

So, when we encounter patterns of defence, the question is not 'What is wrong or sick or diseased about this person?' but 'What energy is trapped in this knot – how can we free the Life Force that is wanting to be liberated here?' From this perspective we see the unfolding psychological development of a child not as a series of unfortunate mistakes but as the soul's struggle for expression. And when we regard all human life forms as individual waves arising from the universal source then we can see that beyond our personal dilemmas we embody a power far greater than the fear and pain that confront and absorb our attention.

Seen this way, the experiences we have in childhood with our families are the outcome of a meeting between the energy patterns already emanating from our own consciousness and the energy patterns in the environment we meet.

From my twenty-five years' experience as an astrologer I know that a person's horoscope accurately reflects all of their life, including the nine months of the gestation period *before* birth. It is clear to me that we do not enter this world as empty vessels. From the moment of conception a person is already running patterns of energy arising from qualities of consciousness distilled from past lives and from their ancestral and genetic inheritance. Many mothers will recognize a certain quality or resonance that they experienced during pregnancy as a powerful aspect of the personality of the child they later get to know. From conception and through gestation the incoming soul is already radiating the qualities of their Essence. Each human soul, parent and child alike, has deliberately incarnated in order to create a life in the material world and all experiences are reflections of their intentions as creators.

This does not deny us our legitimate feelings of grief or rage when people treat us unkindly or when life does not go our way – far from it. Denial and repression of our emotional experience is exactly that which blocks and tangles the flow of our energy. The more that we learn how to feel our emotions and to experience authentic responses to our life predicaments while holding everything in the light of Consciousness, then the more we will be able to allow the life force to flow and to engage fully in the creative process of living.

The ultimate power in a person's being is the eternal light of their Core Star. Somehow, in the intensity of our human struggles we forget that everyone who incarnates on this planet is a God-like creator of life with an energy field capable of running an immeasurably complex biological body, a life purpose of embodying a unique aspect of Divine Consciousness and a sacred task of bringing forth their Creative Essence into the manifest world!

## The Creative Process

The Creative Process is a term I use to describe the way in which all of life begins as an initial spark that has to follow the laws of time and structure before it becomes manifest in the physical world and this is one of the most important themes running through this book. Creation is the act of bringing something into being – to start with nothing and end up with something. When I talk about the Creative Process I am referring not only to artistic endeavours but to creativity as a fundamental aspect of being alive. The Jesuit philosopher Teilhard de Chardin spoke of human creativity as a vital aspect of the evolution of human consciousness. To live is to create, as together all living beings co-create the evolving story of 'life on earth'.

So the Creative Process is the business of life. We are doing it all the time, from invisible creative processes in the cells of the body to everyday acts like cooking breakfast, to the creation of magnificent events and ideas that change the world. We recognize and admire creativity in great works of art, music and literature but creativity can also be a piece of graffiti on a railway carriage or a child's first attempts at handwriting. It is the construction of any kind of object, from fantastically expensive cars and architect-designed buildings to the putting up of a garden shed. It means life-sustaining activities like running a home or the cultivation of crops. It can be scientific discoveries and inventions from the building of a magnificent sandcastle to the design of a rocket that will fly to the Moon. All human enterprise is creative, from starting up a small business to writing the constitution for a nation. One of the most profound acts of creation is giving birth to a child and the capacity to reproduce is one of the fundamental signatures of life. And the single most important creation of any human being is the making up of their own life story.

Two of my teachers, Barbara Brennan and Robert Fritz, both speak on the subject of the Creative Process. Robert Fritz, with the Sun in Taurus, focuses more on the stages of the Creative Process in the physical world. Barbara Brennan, with the Sun in Pisces, focuses on the Creative Process moving through the non-physical realms.

In his book *The Path of Least Resistance*, Robert Fritz describes how the Creative Process goes through distinct stages:

- the first stage is the initial surge of energy that accompanies the birth of an idea – the Germination phase
- the second is the stage of active growth and development – the Assimilation phase
- the third stage is the conclusion of the process with a finished manifest result – Completion.

This idea of a sequence of progressive stages in the Creative Process can also be applied to Reich's theory of five stages of child development. In both, there is a moment of conception, then a period when everything is fluid and still changing and eventually there is a conclusion i.e. when the child's life reaches a plateau and a foundation of character has been established or when a creative idea has become manifest in the physical world.

In developing this connection I have added two more stages to Robert Fritz's idea of the Assimilation phase – so we end up with five stages of the Creative Process to match Reich's five stages of psychological development. And this idea of five fundamental stages of creation also applies if we take the spiritual view of a soul travelling from the non-physical realms to incarnate in the world of Matter moving through five progressive stages from conception through to successfully building a life in the material world.

One of the key concepts of this book is the idea that these stages of the Creative Process will be found in all aspects of human development and human activity. And when we are able to look at Reich's five Character types in this way it enables us to move away from the judgemental thinking that interprets Characterology in the light of defence mechanisms and as a problem to be overcome. Instead, we can appreciate the value of each of the Character types as a vital stage in the Creative Process.

So, the connection is as follows:

- Five stages of the Creative Process – moving from initiation through to completion
- Five stages of the soul's journey to incarnate and live a human life in the manifest world
- Five stages of child development going from conception and birth through the first seven years of childhood

In order to help us think differently about Reich's five Character types I decided to link this sequence with the steps of the Creative Process by naming the developmental stages after five stages in the growth of a plant.

**Five Stages of the Creative Process**

- **Germination** The life of a plant begins with a seed. Every tiny seed holds the blueprint for the growth of the entire plant through to maturity. The creative process starts when the seed initiates the process of cell division and multiplication and develops the first microscopic signs of a shoot. This stage is known as Germination.
- **Rooting** In order for the seed to survive and grow it must get nutrients from the soil. So the seed develops a root system, anchoring it in the earth and giving it access to the water and minerals it requires. This stage is the Rooting stage. In temperate climates both the Germination and the Rooting stages occur underground, out of sight during the dark days of winter.
- **Budding** With a network of roots established, the first green shoots push their way above the ground seeking out the light of the sun. With light from the sun and nourishment from the roots the shoots develop young leaves and buds, and the seed

is now well on the way to fulfilling its potential. We can call this the Budding phase. In temperate climates this stage occurs during the beautiful days of spring.

- **Flowering** When the plant is sufficiently mature and the conditions are right, there comes the time of flowering. This is the time of sexual activity when the plant blossoms and does whatever is necessary to attract insects or to make use of the elements in order to pollinate, cross-pollinate and ensure the fertilization of the seeds its flowers have brought forth. This stage is called the Flowering phase. In temperate climates this stage begins in the spring and carries on during the sultry days of summer.
- **Harvest** In the final stage the blossoms fade, the petals fall and the plant goes on to ripen its harvest of fruits, nuts, berries and pods, which carry the treasure of further seeds and the perpetuation of the creative cycle. This stage is called the Harvest phase and this is the completion of the creative cycle. In temperate climates this stage occurs during the time of autumn when the trees put on their most beautiful displays of colour before the fading of the light. After the fulfilment of the harvest, the energy of the plant retreats underground for the cold days of winter and the secret underground germination of new life.

Every human life goes through all five stages of development, from the initial spark of Germination, which is conception and birth, through to the Harvest stage which represents everything that we achieve and bring to completion in the course of of life. And in our creative human endeavours we repeatedly go through this cycle from the initial concept through the stages of growth and (hopefully) on to fruition and completion.

Similarly, this sequence of steps gives us a framework for thinking about the soul's journey descending from the world of Spirit into the world of Matter. The pure light of a soul arises in the non-physical realms and flows out towards the physical dimension where it is channelled into powerful lines and centres of energy at the deep level of the Hara. Further on into the physical realm the energy radiates out into the luminous sphere of light which is the aura and the chakras and lastly takes form in the biological cells and tissues of the physical body. The five stages of the Creative Process can be applied to this journey into physical form and throughout this book, I use the terms Germination, Rooting, Budding, Flowering and Harvest interchangeably with the Reichian names for the five stages – Schizoid, Oral, Masochist, Psychopathic and Rigid. Each stage has a very different vibration, which appears as specific, recognisable pattern of energy in the HEF.

## The Creative Process in the Human Energy Field

In the Brennan model of the HEF, Brennan refers to seven levels of the field, associated with the seven chakras. Thus the 7th level of the HEF extends far out from the body towards the realm of Spirit and has a very fine high vibration, whereas the first level is very close to the physical body and has a slow dense vibration near to the vibration of Matter. One way of looking at the Creative Process is as if the wave of creation first emerges on the 7th level of the HEF, cascades down through all the levels of the field until it emerges into manifest form in the physical world.

The Creative Process appears on the grand scale as a giant wave moving through every life from birth to death. Barbara Brennan also describes how the Creative Process moves through the levels of the HEF in an unfolding sequence of steps, which occur on a daily basis from the most simple activities to major human achievements.

To illustrate the Creative Process as it appears in the Human Energy Field this is a description of what happens in the HEF in the humble, everyday process of creating a garden.

## The 7th Chakra or Crown Chakra

In the creative process, the moment of conception, when an idea is born occurs in the 7th chakra and in the 7th level of the field. It appears as a burst of brilliant light in or around the 7th chakra. The 7th chakra shines with a crystalline white light and the 7th level of the field appears as a fine shimmering network of white-gold light, which holds pure mental awareness close to the perfection of the Divine Mind. The 7th chakra is remote from the nitty-gritty of everyday human life and so the patterns that appear here represent spiritual ideals. In the example we are looking at in the 7th chakra the soul's higher purpose in creating a garden might be to celebrate the relationship between humanity and Nature.

## The 6th Chakra or the Third Eye

Like the 7th chakra, the 6th chakra also has to do with inspired vision and ideals and it runs at a very high vibration. The 6th chakra is softer and more emotional than the 7th and it has to do with our experience of Divine love and spiritual ecstasy. This is the place where we feel our connection with the angelic realms and everything here is illuminated with the silver starlight of celestial love. The ideal concept of the garden held on the 7th level evokes an emotional response on the 6th level, which becomes illuminated with the gardener's delight and soul love for Nature.

The 6th chakra is also the place where we become aware of non-physical beings, such as the support of angels. In this chakra the gardener may perceive the overlighting presence of Nature spirits and they may have a connection to an individual angel particularly attuned to the creation of this specific garden.

## The 5th Chakra or Throat Chakra

The 5th level of the HEF radiates very clear light; it is spacious and still, reflecting the harmony of the Universal Energy Field. When the 5th chakra is fully open it is filled with peace born from trust in the Divine and willingness to surrender to Spirit.

The 5th chakra is more closely related to the physical world than the abstract ideals of the 7$^{th}$, as if it were an octave down from the high vibration of the 7th chakra. This is the chakra which links the vibration of sound to the vibration of matter and it holds a perfect template for forms that exist on the physical level.

On the 5th level the creative idea develops into a coherent structure – a clear energy blueprint for the garden through which the gardener can express the ideal concept of the 7th and the soul love of the 6th chakra.

## The 4th Chakra or Heart Chakra

The 4th chakra is sometimes said to be the most important of all the chakras. It is here in the heart, through love and longing for communion, that a human life becomes the bridge between the worlds of Spirit and Matter.

The 4th chakra is sometimes radiant with a beautiful peaceful green light like the light of Nature. It can also be full of feeling – intense, moving, sometimes turbulent – like a fountain of light and emotion illuminated with the passionate, rose light of love.

The 4th level of the field is fluid and full of movement and colour. This is the theatre of the human imagination and it is the place we go to when we dream, also known as the Astral Plane. It is a level of extremes, angels and demons, Heaven and Hell, and here we find both our dreams of happiness as well as old wounds, the grief of loss, the lingering issues of past lives and some of our deepest fears. So it is here in the 4th chakra, and those below it, that as we move closer to the struggles of human incarnation we may encounter increasing difficulty and resistance to the Creative Process.

In the 4th level the creative idea of the garden shifts from the quiet, perfect structures held in the 5th chakra. Here it fills out into recognizable images from the physical world. The gardener's vision becomes much more personal, filled with all kinds of recognizable objects. There will be a jumble of emotional images: not only the hope for an ideal outcome but also any fears and doubts associated with this plan. There may be emotionally charged memories of previous gardens and there may be people here, such as the memory, happy or sad, of the parent who first introduced the gardener to gardening or there might be something like a vision of the future with children or grandchildren playing in the garden.

If, for some reason, the gardener's creative impulse gets entangled with painful memories and associations full of grief or failure they may, at this point, abandon the idea of the garden altogether. If they have more positive associations and remain hopeful then the vision will proceed, now coloured with the qualities of the memories and associations that the prospect of the garden has evoked.

## The 3rd Chakra or Solar Plexus Chakra

The 3rd chakra is associated with linear, rational thinking and all forms of mental activity. It radiates a fine, fast-flowing network of clear, shimmering yellow light out into the 3rd level of the HEF. Here the fluid emotional energy of the 4th level can begin to crystallize, taking on structure including practical items such as a garden plan with specific plants and dates for planting. This is one of the most critical stages of manifestation as the individual uses their personal will to transform free-flowing energy of the mind into a list of practical, manageable, real world events.

The 3rd chakra is also associated with our sense of personal power, self-worth, competence and worldly effectiveness. It is here in the 3rd chakra that the creative idea departs from the perfect vision of the higher levels and takes on the limitations of human capability.

For example, if the gardener has experienced a lot of criticism in their life they will be habitually worried about failure and the whole project can become besieged with the tension of their anxiety. Then all the vibrational structures around the idea may be weakened and sabotaged by the fear of failure, and the 3rd chakra is the place in which many good ideas founder. A gardener blessed with more self-confidence will have more trust (linked with the 5th chakra), giving them access to inspiration (connecting up to the 7th chakra), generating positive energy for good mental planning (3rd chakra) which supports the functioning of the lower chakras in the journey towards manifestation.

## The 2nd Chakra or Sacral Chakra

The 2nd chakra is the place where we experience our emotional response to human life on earth. Here we find self-love and our tangible, sensual, sexual pleasure and delight in living in a biological body in a physical world. The vibration of the 2nd level of the field is more liquid, heavier and more dense than that of the upper levels. When the 2nd chakra is open it radiates a brilliant orange light, like a bright flower or the juicy flesh of a fruit. It has the feeling of satisfaction associated with the gratification of our desires and the 2nd level may be lit up with a warm sunset glow.

However, the 2nd chakra is also where we may hold fears that we are not lovable and negative beliefs that we are not entitled to fulfilment. The 2nd chakra can be the Garden of Eden but it can also be the expulsion from the Garden: abundance or starvation, the longing for paradise or the experience of exile. Often the transition of the creative idea through the 2nd chakra leaves the vision diminished and distorted by negative beliefs of scarcity and deprivation or drained by feelings of unworthiness.

Here, our gardener may be filled with self-doubt and the dread of disappointment, or they could fill with pleasure imagining the sensual delight of the garden and feeling the appreciation of other people. Whichever way they proceed with the plan their creation will be imbued with the emotions of their 2nd chakra: anything from severe anxiety creating a self-filling prophecy of failure to their delight in the sensual pleasure of gardening and finding joy in the process no matter what the outcome!

## The 1st Chakra or Base Chakra

The 1st chakra is the closest to the physical world and it is in the 1st level of the field that we hold the energy structures around which our biological cells cluster and organize to form the biological body. The Base chakra is the support for all our worldly physical functions and the 1st level of the field holds the matrix upon which matter collects to form material objects and real world events. And so it is the heaviest, the most dense of all the chakras, more fixed and much slower to change than the upper levels.

Here on the 1st level of the field the vision of the garden takes on its final shape prior to manifestation in the world. Any mistrust of the physical world will show up here and this can weigh down, dilute and sometimes drastically distort or sabotage the final outcome. When the base chakra is strong, the outcome will reflect that confidence and if the base chakra is weak a lot of things may not work out well. Whichever way the energy flows, the final garden plans are put into action and so the original concept comes into some kind of physical manifestation

In this example I have tried to give a clear description of the Creative process by starting from the 7th chakra and working down. However, this is only one possibility – on another occasion inspiration might rise up from the base chakra, directly from our connection to the earth or some impulse of the body. Wherever it arises we see how the creative impulse turns into emotionally charged energy in action, welling up and cascading through the energy field and out to take form in the physical world. A person's state of consciousness, their thoughts and feelings, beliefs and self-confidence create unique personal patterns in their HEF. These patterns shape and direct the flow of energy so that every manifest outcome is imbued with the qualities of the individual whose will and passion have brought this creation into being.

*On the Auric level energy and consciousness cannot be separated.*
Barbara Brennan *Light Emerging*

The Creative Process of vision, commitment, action and result occurs a thousand times a day; it is the substance of our lives. It occurs every time we bring anything into manifestation in the physical world, even in the split second it takes us to decide whether or not to make a cup of coffee. We spend our whole lives in this creative continuum, stopping, starting, getting stuck, giving up, renewing our vision, tripping up or gliding through in an endless variety of ways as we struggle on a daily, weekly, yearly basis to create our human stories.

Human life is not easy. Suffering is an intrinsic part of life and every human being carries distortions in their HEF. Always the eternal light of the Core Star shines from within, for no matter how extreme the human experience it cannot damage the Core Star. As the light of the Core Star flows forth it encounters places where movement gets choked by tangled knots of energy, occluded by clouds of mucus or walled in by armour like steel plates. With the HEF distorted by this kind of constriction, built up over many lifetimes, it is not surprising that our human lives do not always go the way we want them to! What is amazing is how successful the experiences of human beings are, how the light of love finds its way into the darkest night, how the phoenix of the soul always rises from the ashes of catastrophe, how kindness is always there even alongside cruelty.

The psychologists of the twentieth century brought tremendous new insight with their exploration of the unconscious. The awareness that aspects of the psyche are hidden from everyday consciousness allows the possibility of profound healing by bringing the hidden root of trauma into consciousness.

> *Every part of the human person, from the structure of the body to the clarity of the perception, is moulded by internal energy. Genetic inheritance, family background, societal conditions, and many other influences affect us. But we create our lives ourselves through what we do with our energy: where we decide to go with it and how we direct it.*
> John Pierrakos *Core Energetics*

7

# The Astrological View: An Introduction to Astrology

> *The soul of the newly born baby is marked for life by the pattern of the stars at the moment it comes into the world, it unconsciously remembers it, and remains sensitive to the return of configurations of a similar kind.*
> Johannes Kepler *Harmonics Mundi*

A psychotherapist builds a picture of an individual's character structure through listening to them and observing their body language. A healer uses Higher Sense Perception to perceive the Human Energy Field in the non-physical dimensions. An astrologer looks at a person's horoscope as a kind of chemical read-out for this life – body, mind and spirit.

At one time, astrology and astronomy were the same subject. So, in the first place, a natal chart is an astronomical map of the heavens for a given moment of time, showing the positions of all the planets of the solar system as seen from the Earth. However, an astronomer's role is only to observe and plot the movements of planets but an astrologer sees each of the planets as having a distinct nature and significance, and so the changing pattern of their movement across the heavens has profound meaning. Astrology is the meeting place of rational and intuitive thinking – whereas the astronomical position of the planets is exact, their astrological interpretation is not. Astronomy speaks the precise language of mathematical calculations but astrology is a language of the soul, written in metaphors made from the mysterious combination of archetypes and arithmetic.

So the horoscope is a psycho-spiritual blueprint of potential for the life of a person. With my energy healer's voice I would say that astrology is a way of reading a person's Human Energy Field. It is vastly more complex than the foolish whimsy of predictions in the daily papers and to begin to comprehend the significance of a horoscope requires in-depth study. But when the basic language of the planets is understood there comes a moment in which the arcane glyphs and angles weave into a cohesive whole and light up with meaning.

It is a delight for me to speak the language of astrology to my fellow astrologers. Astrology is the language of psyche and soul, and my hope is that this book will help non-astrologers to begin to understand this magical language. What follows is a simplified overview of some of the basic principles of chart interpretation starting with three separate areas of the chart – the twelve signs of the zodiac, the eleven heavenly bodies (the eight planets of the solar system, the Sun, the Moon and the planetoid Chiron) and the twelve houses of the horoscope.

## The Ecliptic – the Wheel of the Zodiac

The great circle of the zodiac is a representation of the ecliptic, which is the apparent path that the Sun takes through the sky, mapped against the background of the constellations. Astrologers divide the ecliptic into twelve equal sections, which we know as the twelve signs of the zodiac. The signs of the zodiac each have a specific quality or vibration. Each sign of the zodiac has a planetary 'ruler' and it is the archetypal energy of the ruling planet that gives meaning to the signs. A zodiac sign is like the energy field radiating from the Essence of its ruling planet.

## The Planets

> *Astrology consists of symbolic configurations: the 'planets' are the gods, symbols of the powers of the unconscious.*
> CG Jung, *Letters 1951-1961*

The basis of astrology lies in understanding the nature of eleven planets used in the interpretation of a chart: the Sun, Moon, Mercury, Venus, Mars, Jupiter, Saturn, Uranus, Neptune, Pluto and Chiron. Four of these are not actually planets – two are the Sun and the Moon and the others are Chiron and Pluto which are known as trans-Neptunian objects. Nevertheless, astrologers are in the habit of referring to all of them as 'the planets'.

The eleven planets represent basic elements of human life and each one corresponds to a distinct archetypal aspect of the psyche. Jung used the term 'archetype' to describe universal aspects of the mind common to all human beings. Archetypes arise from the human collective – a deep, unconscious source from which the intrinsic themes of human life emerge – and the planets are symbols of these elemental aspects of the soul. Thus, everyone has a primary experience of having a mother (represented by the Moon) and a father (the Sun); everyone has the urge to relate (Venus), everyone feels the urge to assert their individuality (Mars), everyone has the urge to communicate (Mercury).

The sign of the zodiac in which a planet falls gives it a resonance, like a type of mask or costume that the archetype is wearing in this person's life drama. The Psychosynthesis therapist Pierro Ferucci once said,

*Each one of us is a crowd!*

We each have many, many different aspects of our personality, different voices in our minds, different actors on our stage. We can never consistently be only one way – it depends which 'voice' is uppermost at the time. Transpersonal Psychology calls these different expressions of the mind 'sub-personalities' and in astrology we see the sub-personalities represented by the configurations formed by the planets in the chart. People tend to identify with the qualities of their personality that seem most acceptable – areas where they feel happy and successful – and they try to repress those parts of their personality which are more shameful, fearful or painful. But in astrology nothing is hidden. We can see all the planets, all the sub-personalities, all the actors in the play – Iago sabotaging everything from the shadows as well as noble Othello and innocent Desdemona dancing unconsciously to his tune.

## Aspects

In astrology, we find that the angles formed between the planets in the horoscope (or important points such as the Ascendant), have a meaning. At certain specific junctures (e.g. when two planets are at right angles to each other), the planets involved have a powerful influence on each other. We refer to these dynamic relationships between the planets as aspects. The aspects formed between planets and other important points in the horoscope is one of the main features of chart interpretation. e.g. if a planet or the Ascendant is in aspect to Mars (God of War) it will express in a very different way to the same planet in aspect to Venus (Goddess of Love).

In the astrological sections of the book I continually refer to the aspects between planets. By this I mean that the archetypal expression of the planets in aspect to each other will be significantly changed according to the nature of the planets involved. This is particularly important when a planet is in aspect to the Sun, the Moon or the Ascendant (the three cornerstones of the horoscope).

For more advanced astrologers, in the earlier sections of this book I use the term 'aspect' very broadly – referring to any of the major aspects: conjunction, square, opposition, trine, sextile, inconjunct, quintile. My intention is to focus on the archetypal nature of the planets and the way that any contact between planets will affect and change their expression. In the case studies in Section III I go into much more detail about the different effects caused by 'hard' and 'soft' aspects.

## The Houses

The twelve houses of the horoscope represent another dimension separate from the zodiac signs and the planets. The houses are about timing. They represent the entire passage of life from birth to death proceeding around the chart in chronological order like twelve slices of a pie. At the beginning, on the left side of the chart, is the Ascendant or Rising Sign which signifies the moment of birth. Following on from this the six houses in the bottom hemisphere of the chart represent the individual's experiences in childhood: from infancy through to becoming an adult. The next six houses, moving into the top hemisphere of the chart, describe the way the individual steps out into the world and enters into relationship – from significant partnerships with another, to relationship with society at large and lastly in relationship to the world of Spirit.

So the houses set the scene – they tell us when and where in the person's life the drama of the planets is being acted out. The great astrologer Dane Rudhyar describes the houses as 'fields of experience'. For example, if we find a gathering of planets in the 3rd house we know that the energy of those planets comes through in that area of the chart which has to do with communication, speech, words and all kinds of networks. If we find planets gathered in the 7th house of the chart we know their activity is focused on the area of significant relationships and partnerships.

Even in this small overview we can already see the weaving of many threads that come together in a natal chart, and how could it be anything less than complex when we are looking into a symbolic map of a person's energy field? Just to glance at a horoscope we see the energy patterns formed by the planets scattered around the great wheel of the zodiac. All the different aspects of the chart are linked; nothing stands in isolation in this glorious kaleidoscope of dynamic energies.

Some unusual charts are dominated by one planet, one sign or the activity in one house. In other charts there is a more even distribution of emphasis or sometimes, in a more conflicted personality, rival groups of planets compete for attention.

### The Ascendant, the Moon and the Sun

However complex the chart, the three cornerstones of any chart are the Sun, the Moon and the Ascendant.

### The Ascendant

The Ascendant is the sign of the zodiac that was rising over the Eastern horizon at the moment of a person's birth. The sign on the Ascendant and any planets sitting close to the Ascendant give us direct information about what was happening at the time of this person's birth. The Ascendant, signifying birth itself, becomes a template for the way a person goes out into life and it lays down a pattern for the way they begin or initiate anything. When you meet a person for the first time, what you meet is their Ascendant, their 'persona' – the face they present to the world. Even more than that, the Ascendant and any planets in aspect to the Ascendant describe something fundamental about a person's sense of identity and speak of the Essence of a person's fundamental way of being alive. We can imagine the entire horoscope, the complete domain of the psyche, as a jewelled cavern, full of treasures and talents, the full spectrum of the energies of the soul. The Ascendant is the lens through which we radiate the light of the planetary energies from within and through which we receive our subjective perception of the world. If the entrance to this container of consciousness is blocked and distorted then the beautiful spectrum of the soul's energies cannot emerge into the light of the manifest world. So a major part of our life's journey centres around developing the qualities of the Ascendant.

Astrologers give the utmost importance to the Ascendant. The planets and the signs of the zodiac are celestial, they turn our eyes heavenward, but the Ascendant has to do with a unique human life lived down here in the world of matter. The expression of the Ascendant is not a static thing. Liz Greene describes the Ascendant as 'a developmental pattern'. The Ascendant represents qualities that we learn to embody, with ever greater depth, over the course of a lifetime.

### The Moon

The archetype of the Moon has a vast domain ruling all areas of life to do with the feminine principle, the yin energy and the power of the Goddess. The Moon represents our experience of the Divine Feminine.

In the first place, the Moon symbolizes pregnancy and the womb; the gentle dark into which the seed of life is sown and the ground in which the incarnating soul roots; the emotional and biological container that nurtures the light of the incoming soul.

The Moon symbolizes the beloved archetype of mother and child and describes the nature of our relationship with our own mother. It is in the safety (or otherwise) of our primary relationship with our personal mother that we develop a pattern in relation to our physical and emotional feelings and lay a foundation of trust (or otherwise) that our needs will be met. So the continuum of the Moon describes all our images of the Feminine from the womb to the Maiden to the Mother to the Crone. It includes fertility, menstruation, conception, gestation, pregnancy and birth on to infancy, childhood, our experience of 'home' and family, our roots, our ancestors and our genetic and spiritual inheritance, all threaded through with the overlighting presence of the Goddess.

The Moon also represents the realm of the unconscious: the non-rational, instinctive, intuitive wisdom of our inner world. The glimmering light of the Moon softly illuminates the dark, fecund world of feelings and emotions, the dream world and the vast internal domain of the body with its cellular networks, functions and instinctual drives, all of which remain, at least partially, unconscious.

The Lunar energy can be equally strong and is equally relevant to the charts of both men and women. It is the basis of the adult woman's sense of identity as a woman and it also represents a man's anima, his inner 'female' nature, which is the basis for his perceptions and expectations of women, family and relationship.

The Moon is central to the study of child development and Characterology because it is the primary indicator of a person's infant experience, childhood and the family home. When the Moon is prominent in a chart (i.e. involved in aspects with many planets), then the feminine issues of physical and emotional nourishment, relationship, feelings, sensuality and touch are central to this person's life. When the Moon is not very involved with other planets this shows that this feminine energy of feeling is not emphasized; if the Moon is very lonely in the chart this can indicate an awkward disconnection from the feelings.

## The Sun

Most people are at least dimly aware of their Sun sign – that is the sign that the Sun was in on the day they were born. The Sun is the symbol of the bright, yang, masculine principle. Whereas the Moon represents the inner stillness of 'being', the Sun represents the extroverted fire of 'action'. The path of the Sun is the path of the hero, questing through the adventure of life, meeting challenges, taking the initiative, bringing change, transformation and growth.

Just as the Sun in the solar system is the source and the centre of all light and life, the Sun in the horoscope represents the bright light of rational consciousness and creative self-expression. The Solar energy gives us our unique sense of individuality and healthy self-importance. It warms us with self-confidence and self-belief and is the raw energy from which we generate direction and purpose. In those moments when we are required to rise to a challenge and cross over the threshold into the unknown it is the Sun in the chart that lights the way and warms us with faith, courage and vision.

When looking at the archetypal meaning of the Sun it is important to remember that the Sun in a chart is not the same as the ultimate Essence of the self. What the chart reveals is a pattern of energies – like the colours on the artist's palette or a range of chemical elements. Each one of the planets in the chart contributes to this spectrum of colour through which the light of Essence shines to create a unique personality and an individuated life. So the Sun does not represent the totality of the self but it is the warm light of consciousness, illuminated by the qualities of our Essence, which we have come to develop and express in this life.

As the Moon speaks to us of infancy and our relationship with the mother, the Sun in the chart describes the life of the older child – active, curious, playful, creative, innocent and free – and the Sun is the symbol of relationship with the father. In the arms of the Lunar Goddess we trust and rest in the peace and stillness of 'being'.

Following in the footsteps of the Solar God we learn to use the creative power of the Will and come alive in the joy of 'doing'. In the face of the Mother we seek acceptance, but reflected in the eyes of the Father we find a challenge to arise and show ourselves, the urge to individuate. The active, masculine yang energy requires us to reveal ourselves through creativity, self-expression and in our willingness to be true to ourselves and take action in the world. The energy of the Sun in the horoscope is a mirror of our self-belief and our faith and trust in life.

## The Nodes of the Moon

In the astrological sections of this book I sometimes refer to the North Node of the Moon. I think the Nodes of the Moon are important enough for anyone with an interest in astrology to get a grasp of their meaning.

The North Node and South Node are exactly opposite each other, in opposing signs at either end of an axis crossing the wheel of the horoscope. Because I have a basic belief in reincarnation I think of this axis in relation to the ongoing development of the soul over many lifetimes. Roughly speaking, the sign, house and any planets aspecting the South Node indicate qualities that are well established in a person's character, i.e. qualities that have been developed in a previous life and do not need to be refined any further in this life. The sign, house and aspects to the North Node indicate an area of life that this person needs to develop, to work to bring into Awareness in this life.

So, the axis of the Nodes represents a vast continuum extending over a lifetime. In youth a person may rely heavily on the qualities of the South Node, which come easily to them. As the years go by there is an increasing pull to develop the qualities of the North Node and the affairs of the South Node feel increasingly stale and unrewarding.

Over a lifetime, all the activities of the archetypes of the planets contribute to a continuous cycle of increasing consciousness and, in the end, it is the qualities of the placement of the North Node where this developed consciousness can really shine.

## The Horoscope and the Human Energy Field

The Ascendant, Sun and Moon give an astrologer direct information about a person's early life: the quality of their childhood experience, the relationships within the family and patterns of psychological development. Beyond that, astrology gets more complicated as the placement of the planets in the wheel of the zodiac forms into a kaleidoscope of patterns and networks of connection which I shall refer to as the 'aspects'. For a healer, this kaleidoscope of planets and aspects shows up as recognizable patterns in a person's Human Energy Field.

The energy pattern of the Ascendant comes across with the vibration of distinct qualities that speak of the person's unique individual nature. It shows up in the way they present themselves and relate to others, but the qualities of the Ascendant are also strong when the person is alone – the Ascendant sounds a distinctive individual note that is always there, whatever the person is doing. In the HEF the vibrational pattern of the Ascendant is easily apparent, like the first layer of energy that you meet. In the HEF the energies of the Sun and the Moon both appear close to the centre of the field where the light of the Core Star emerges. In some people the energy of the Sun appears more prominent and other people appear more identified with the energy pattern of the Moon. However, the energy signature of both the Sun and the Moon are always a powerful presence radiating out from the centre of the aura. The golden light of the Sun will expand upwards, warming the 3rd and 4th chakras and lighting up the face and the head, the seat of the rational mind. The soft, silvery light of the Moon will contract inwards and downwards to rest in the pelvic cradle and connect with the dark inner world of the body, the non-rational feelings and the dream world.

Each of the planets in the horoscope focuses the Core Star light in a different way. Looking at the HEF from the view of the astrologer, the light of a person's Core Star shines through the energy pattern of the planets like light shining through a prism and breaking up into the spectrum of the rainbow.

*If I have manna in my constitution, I can attract manna from heaven. Saturn is not only in the sky, but also deep in the ocean and Earth. What is Venus but the Artemisia that grows in your garden, and what is iron but the planet Mars? That is to say, Venus and Artemisia are both products of the same essence, while Mars and iron are manifestations of the same cause. What is the human body but a constellation of the same powers that formed the stars in the sky?*
Paracelsus, *Paragranum*

**Conclusion**
The mind of a human being is built on layers of experience and we run our consciousness through a maze of hard-held beliefs about ourselves and our world. Many of these beliefs are largely unconscious and many are negative, e.g. 'This world is very dangerous', 'I am not lovable', 'There's something wrong with me'. Unfortunately, unconscious beliefs like these help to shape our reality. Instead of following our spontaneous impulse towards life we hesitate, go about things in a convoluted way or decide not to move at all and our Life Force gets trapped, confirming our worst suspicions about the way things are. You can see this as a repeating cycle in which layers of negative experiences come to obscure the light of the Core Star. When we are able bring these powerful limiting beliefs into consciousness, the new awareness magically untangles the old web and the Life Force is liberated. Sometimes awareness is just the beginning of a long process of restoration of the flow of the Life Force. Hal Stone, the founder of Voice Dialogue, talks about learning to become an 'energy dancer'. When all aspects of self, all the sub-personalities, are welcomed into consciousness they no longer obscure our awareness and instead we become free to dance from one to another, making a moment-to-moment choice about which energy to express. When there is no

longer a need to censor any of our inner voices then this is the moment when the light of the Core Star can truly shine.

Over time many people lose the joy of physical existence. The openness of childhood and the raw intensity of adolescence fade into memory as we become increasingly weighed down with burdens that seem to trap us in habitual struggles that shut out the Light. When we are confronted by difficult challenges we recoil into a state of defence but the defence cuts us off from the Life Force. Staggering through our dark labyrinths of defence we seem to become punch-drunk and semi-conscious. Somehow, in the intensity of our human drama we forget that everyone who incarnates on this planet is actually a god-like creator of life with an energy field capable of running an immeasurably complex biological body, a life purpose of embodying a unique aspect of Divine Consciousness and a sacred task of bringing forth their Creative Essence into the manifest world!

So, when we understand that our defences are the very things that block the flow of our Essence, then we might ask this question: how is it that we became so defended in the first place? The next section of this book attempts to answer that question. It is an exploration of what happens to us in our early years, looking at five basic Character structures that emerge over five stages of early child development. Each section opens with a brief overview of the traditional psychological view of each Character type, including the defence mechanisms associated with each one. The second section explores the creative impulse and the gift of each of the Character types seen from the spiritual view. Lastly there is an outline of the astrological patterns associated with each Character type with a description of the appearance of the planetary energies in the Human Energy Field.

# PART II

# THE FIVE CHARACTER TYPES

## Characterology: in the Psyche, the Human Energy Field and the Horoscope

This section of the book is an exploration of the five basic Character structures emerging over five stages of child development. Each section opens with a brief overview of the traditional psychological view then moves on to explore the creative impulse, the Essence and the gift of the Character types as seen from the spiritual view. Lastly there is an outline of the astrological patterns associated with each Character type, with a description of the archetypes of the planets most relevant to each stage.

8

# THE GERMINATION OR SCHIZOID STAGE

Reich named the first of the stages as the Schizoid stage – extending from conception through the gestation period and on into labour, birth and the earliest days of life. This period is filled with the raw experience of coming into physical incarnation with bodily sensations ranging from ecstasy and bliss to extremes of unbearable discomfort or physical pain. It is likely that many souls react with utter terror to the experience of inhabiting the vulnerable and limiting container of the biological body, constantly overhung by the threat of physical death and annihilation. In traditional Characterology the Schizoid defence is associated with extreme mental detachment and fragmentation as the infant disassociates from the unbearable terror of being alive in the world of matter.

# 9

# The Germination or Schizoid Stage

# The Psychological View: Wounding and Defence in the Schizoid Stage

> *Therapeutic experience with clients who share this type of history suggests that, sooner or later, they make two core feeling decisions: (1) 'There is something wrong with me' and (2) 'I have no right to exist'.*
>
> Stephen M Johnson, *Character Styles*

**Developmental Stage**

The first developmental stage extends from conception through the gestation period to labour, childbirth and early infancy. The incoming soul makes the incredible journey from the unbounded vistas of the non-physical realm through the gateway into physical incarnation and the limitations of the biological body. At the moment of birth the infant makes the awesome discovery of what it is to inhabit a biological body and cope with the demands of physical existence: heat, gravity, breath, hunger and thirst, with all the vital functions of the body overhung by the ultimate threat of death. The challenge here is the terror of living and dying, the dread of physical annihilation, the extreme vulnerability of living in a physical body.

By the time we reach adulthood most of us have learned to live as though we have become oblivious to the fundamental issue of our mortality. And yet in any instant the people and things that we hold dear or our own physical health or our entire existence can be swept away. So we can imagine that the awareness of a newborn baby may be flooded by the issues of biological vulnerability. In the process of adjusting to this new reality the baby is, of course, dependent on the good will and loving support of the family into which they are born.

From conception through to birth and infancy, the child is dependent on others for its survival and at no other time in life do we experience such a complete state of helplessness. Adults instinctively respond to the defencelessness of the newborn baby with great gentleness and care and are moved to protect and nurture the young. Notwithstanding the tenderness of mothers, fathers and carers, a baby's first days of life are fraught with the hitherto unknown challenges of breathing, feeding, touching, feeling, digesting, excreting, sleeping, waking, changes of temperature, being picked up and put down, and so on. The whole system, which includes the baby's health, the mother's health and the state of the entire family, is brand new and difficulties can arise at any time!

Even during pregnancy the foetus may be affected by a variety of issues. The mother's physical health and diet will affect the unborn child and the mother's emotional state will also have an impact. Whatever the mother's overall state of being, her emotional history and her biological inheritance, hers is the world into which the embryonic cells of the new life are born. Hopefully, in the vast majority of cases we can imagine that much of the baby's time in utero is a harmonious period of safety and soulful communion between mother and child.

Following this, the impact of labour and childbirth is huge as the baby makes the extreme transition from complete protection and unity into utter vulnerability and separation. Many babies enter this world in a state of distress, though this is not always the case. Whatever the circumstances, the child's entry into human incarnation is a kaleidoscope of the energies of everyone involved, fraught with moments of difficulty, confusion, alarm and relief while, hopefully, the whole journey is illuminated with the light of love and joy that a baby brings.

Clearly what is needed is a time for the newborn infant to receive loving reassurance that this physical body, physical family and physical world are actually safe. Very often this is a wonderful time when the child begins to bond with the parents and a beautiful period of calming contact and communion follows, with a joyous welcome from the extended family. Soothing experiences of gentle touch, comfort, continuity, being held and supported enable the infant to stabilize and begin to trust in this new embodied life.

## Wounding

When serious difficulties are experienced during these early days the impact is huge. Any trauma can have the effect of an earthquake, sending out a shockwave of terror and shattering the protective boundary of trust and containment that the child needs. Obviously, we can never get a direct description of what a pre-verbal child experiences. But we can understand that a newborn baby has no understanding of time, no concept of 'the future' and their moment-to-moment experience fills their awareness with undiluted intensity; they are awash in an ocean of feeling and sensation. In the baby's state of extreme openness, experiences of even unintended neglect may feel life-threatening and a sense of hostility coming from either of the parents or primary carers is overwhelmingly terrifying.

Yet anyone who is a parent knows that the whole business of pregnancy, childbirth and the early days following a birth can be extraordinarily difficult for the parents, and for the mother in particular. All kinds of issues arise and, even without going into nightmare scenarios like death or severe health problems for parent or child, the normal experience of new parents is extremely challenging. Even though the early days with a newborn baby can be some of the most wonderful days in a parent's life, they are likely to be an emotional roller-coaster as everyone tries to adjust to the new reality. And it's important to remember that between 10 and 15 per cent of both mothers and fathers experience a significant period of post-natal depression.

So, life with a new baby is just not the same as before and a certain amount of turmoil and disturbance is normal and unavoidable. However, in some families the parents simply cannot cope with the pressure of the responsibility of a baby. For whatever reason, the atmosphere in the family is riven with some kind of conflict. When a child is born into a family where there is a persistently hostile environment, where the baby's crying is not soothed, then fear becomes internalized.

> *The Schizoid often feels possessed by an alien demon who hates him and feels he has no right to exist.*
> Stephen M Johnson, *Character Styles*

A state of chronic anxiety or even dread starts to become the norm. Into the foundations of the new life the belief is built that living in a biological body is extremely dangerous – the paradoxical belief that 'Being alive threatens my life'. Regression exercises in psychotherapy can help people to uncover memories of intense emotion from these earliest stages of infancy. For many newborn babies the experience of taking up residence in a biological body is terrifying. Living with this level of fear is intolerable and in a primitive, emotional way the infant starts to build a defence.

> *The infant's natural response to a cold hostile and threatening environment is terror and rage … but this is an untenable position from which to lead a life … so the infant turns against herself.*
> Stephen M Johnson, *Character Styles*

In my own therapy I have had the experience of regressing to a pre-verbal, infantile state. In my regression I felt myself alone in darkness, paralysed with fear. I had the image that above me shone a brilliant white star that was infused with rage, a terrifying white heat of fury. It was as if the beams of light shooting from the star were razor-sharp and slicing through me, dividing everything in the world between the acceptable and the unacceptable. The star seemed to be an expression of helpless rage transmuted into an attack on life, and on myself.

That session made me reflect on the Christian story of Adam and Eve tasting the fruit of the tree of the knowledge of good and evil. Perhaps in the fragmentation of the Schizoid wound we find humanity's original sin? In the earliest moments of life, when our experience becomes intolerable, we split into duality, dividing the whole of existence into good and evil.

The Schizoid stage is about the impact of being born into the physical world and the splitting and fragmentation that can occur when the infant does not receive the containment and support that it needs to anchor successfully into their new body.

## Defence

When the child in the Schizoid stage experiences terror, the infant goes into something like a state of shock, withdrawing consciousness from the tangible experiences of the physical world. The infant learns to freeze out the emotions and sensations that are so distressing and retreats into a detached state of mind which blocks out much of their physical and emotional experience. The more often the experience of terror is repeated the more entrenched the numbing defence pattern becomes and this primary coping mechanism develops into a chronic pattern of freezing – rejection of feelings, splitting experience into acceptable and unacceptable components. Instead of learning to tolerate the wholeness of their experience, the young being clings to the safety of a frozen, dream-like withdrawal from physical reality, while their repressed emotions – including their furious rejection of life itself – are pushed away and buried deep in the unconscious.

This is the Schizoid wound and defence – the terror that shatters the child's sense of wholeness and leads to splitting and fragmentation in the development of the personality. As they mature into adulthood the Schizoid type develops an automatic, almost involuntary habit of living only in the mental world of thinking and imagination while their physical and emotional feelings remain numb.

> *The key to understanding the Schizoid structure is the disconnection of the individual from life processes – from the body, from feelings, from intimate others, from community.*
> Stephen M Johnson, *Characterological Transformation*

## Recognizing the Schizoid Defence

In adulthood, the person we recognize as the Schizoid type is someone who is often mentally brilliant, imaginative and intuitive but clumsy, awkward and uncomfortable with living in a physical body. In company with someone with the Schizoid defence we get the feeling that they are not fully with us – sometimes their attention can seem to switch in and out of focus like an electrical fuse shorting out! In conversation they may be perfectly friendly but they feel remote, unreachable and they seem to blank out on us from time to time. The Schizoid type is detached, emotionally unavailable and they react to emotional issues with mental analysis! If someone tries to force an emotional exchange or conflict onto them their underlying fear and sensitivity will start to show through and they will 'space out'.

People with a lot of Schizoid wounding find it hard to cope with everyday material reality. They overlook things, bump into things, break things, spill things, lose their keys and forget to put the milk in the fridge. They accumulate information and think about things, analyse and explain things but they do not FEEL! The person with Schizoid wounding is missing a huge chunk of reality, which is their own authentic emotional and physical response to life and relationship. They can invest with intensity in a fantasy computer game or a political campaign but they are unconsciously afraid of heartfelt intimate communication with another person. The Schizoid types feel safe drifting through a world of ideas and fantasy because nothing there is truly real. All spaced-out individuals, from computer geeks speaking Klingon to Pollyanna mystics living in rainbow-land, are attached to this form of denial. One of the core beliefs of the Schizoid type is 'I'm not really real and neither are you.'

The Schizoid type stumbles along through life, caring about 'the masses' but not able to cope with intimacy. They make wonderful inventions but they can't remember to post a letter! They can see auras and channel guidance from the higher realms but they can't heal the pain of their own fragmentation. They are fantastic at taking an intelligent, detached overview of things but their inability to access their frozen emotions means that they never fully enter into relationship.

## The Puer and Puella Aeternus

The Germination/Schizoid type has some similarities with the Jungian archetype of the *puer aeternus*. *Puer aeternus* means 'eternal youth' and in mythology it denoted a child-god (often Cupid/Eros, the son of Venus/Aphrodite) who remained forever young. The feminine term is the *puella*. In Jungian psychology this archetype represents an adult person whose emotional life has got stuck at an adolescent level. The *puer/puella* is unable to fully engage with adult life due to the fear of being trapped in a situation from which it might not be possible to escape. They have a pathologically unrealistic attachment to the ideal of freedom, they cannot cope with boundaries and limits or tolerate anything they perceive as a restriction. The *puer* brings the gifts of romantic youthful vision, imagination and creativity but they have great difficulty coping with adult responsibilities and the demands of intimate relationships. Clearly this pattern relates to the Germination/Schizoid type and I will refer frequently to the archetype of the *puer* and the *puella*.

The Schizoid type is immensely creative, full of ideas, but often their inability to sustain their inspiration through the challenges of physical manifestation leaves their creative endeavours unfulfilled and in their chaotic passage through life they can leave a trail of uncompleted projects. A typical example of the Schizoid type is the absent-minded professor bumbling through the day with his mind continually focused on 'higher' things. At the negative end of the spectrum an example would be a completely detached serial killer, disassociated from human warmth and empathy, living in distorted fantasy, exploring the fragility of biological existence in the most negative way.

## Physical Appearance

We recognize the Schizoid type in specific characteristics of their physical appearance. The face and physical body of the classic Schizoid type reflects their primary experience of fragmentation so that they look disjointed and uneven, as if the parts of the body have not been assembled quite correctly! The body is awkward and gangling, with an imbalance between the left and right sides of the body, reflecting a kind of inner motion of twisting away from something. In the HEF, when a person with Schizoid wounding gets frightened they energetically 'leave' the body as their energy surges up to the top of the head and twists away as they retreat to the 'safety' of the higher chakras and the upper levels of the HEF. The Schizoid type often has the distinguishing feature of wide-open, slightly staring eyes with a lot of the whites of the eyes showing, like an animal that is afraid, even though they may be reckless, fearless individuals, numbly overriding the instinctive fears of the body.

**Myths**

In the development of twentieth-century transpersonal psychotherapy it was understood that the myths and legends of a culture are representations of core psycho-spiritual issues working through the collective unconscious. The whole of western culture has its roots in the ancient Mediterranean cultures of Greece and Rome and so I refer often to the mythology of those times, as well as to fairy tales and other stories that speak to themes arising in the collective. This early Greek/Roman Creation myth helps to illuminate the Schizoid condition.

(I apologize to classical scholars as I am not consistent in my use of the Greek and Roman names for the Olympian gods and goddesses. For example, I will more often refer to the Roman goddess Minerva by her Greek name, Pallas Athena. However, I will usually refer to the Greek god Ares by his Roman name, Mars. In astrology we use the Roman names for the gods and so Ouranos is called Uranus, Cronus is called Saturn and Aphrodite is Venus.)

**Ouranos the Sky God**

In the very beginning there was Gaia, the goddess of the Earth, who gave birth to Ouranos (Uranus), the god of the sky. Every night,

Ouranos came down and lay with Gaia and from time to time she presented him with their offspring. Unfortunately, Ouranos was not satisfied with his progeny, who he considered to be incredibly ugly, and he hurled them back into the Earth where they lay groaning in Gaia's womb. Gaia became enraged by Ouranos' behaviour and when she gave birth to her next child she hid him away from his father. The child, who she named Cronus (Saturn), grew secretly to manhood, hidden in a cave and suckled by a mountain goat until, when the time was right, Gaia brought him out of hiding. Then Cronus crept up on Ouranos, took a sickle and castrated him, then flung the severed genitals down into the ocean. At the place where the genitals sank from sight there was a stirring and commotion in the water and up from the bottom of the sea rose Aphrodite, the goddess of love and beauty, born from the foam of the seed of Ouranos.

Like the Schizoid type, Uranus rejects the flawed, imperfect reality of physical existence. His son and adversary is Saturn, the law-keeper of biological existence: the god whose domain is exactly that which Uranus rejects – the structures and limitations of the physical world. Uranus embodies the principle of creativity but he prefers to live in the world of ideas; visions that are beautiful in their perfection but two-dimensional without the flesh of manifest form.

Saturn will not tolerate this situation and removes from Uranus the possibility of spawning any more fruitless rejected creations. The miracle is that from this bloody conflict is born Venus, the goddess of love and beauty.

10

## The Germination or Schizoid Stage

# The Healing Response to the Schizoid Defence

From the healer's viewpoint, a person with Germination/Schizoid energy is likely to have unresolved past life issues around bodily suffering – a lifetime when they endured great physical pain – so that coming into physical incarnation evokes fear even before birth. Whatever the cause, for the Schizoid type the experience of being in a physical body is terrifying. Any premature attempt to force them to fully engage with their physical and emotional experience will only send them spinning further off into fear and fantasy. So, in the first place, the healing response to the Schizoid type is to meet them in their comfort zone, which is the world of thoughts and ideas: the high vibration of the 6th and, particularly, the 7th chakra. When contact and a feeling of sufficient safety is established at this level, it then becomes possible for a healer to begin to induct the denser vibration of the lower chakras and to open the possibility of a deeper engagement with the life of the body.

At the heart of the Schizoid wound is an extremely vulnerable newborn infant. So the healing response to the Schizoid needs to be as sensitive and gentle as if we were approaching a baby. There can be no hurry, no force, no loud noises, no sudden movements. Even gentle, well-meaning physical touch can feel threatening to someone in the grip of the Schizoid defence, and right from the start the healer needs to establish just how close they can approach before the Schizoid person starts spacing out and energetically 'leaving' their body. 'Safety' is the keyword for healing the Schizoid type. Beneath their rational, logical exterior the Schizoid type holds an irrational terror of entering into embodied physical contact and emotional experience.

## The Healing Response to the Schizoid Defence

The healer needs to work vibrationally to bring their own energy down into the vibration of the lower levels of the field, anchoring into the body and grounding deep into the heart of the Earth. Holding this state, they can gently induct this vibration into the HEF of the Schizoid who begins to experience their own energy sinking safely down to connect with the physical body and the possibility that life on Earth could be safe. This is a vital experience for the Schizoid type, helping them to begin the journey down from their castle in the clouds to discover what it is to live in a human body and love with a human heart.

There is not a person on the planet who does not have Schizoid wounding. It is a universal experience and we all have to find ways to deal with the dread of our own mortality. However, for some people the Schizoid splitting dominates their way of living. It is a major journey for a person with profound Schizoid wounding to recover from their primary terror, relinquish their demand for a perfect world and surrender to the wholeness of human experience. They must learn how to contain their primal terror and risk again the vulnerability and flaws of emotional contact and love. In other words, they must develop ways that make it possible for them to engage with the messiness that is an unavoidable part of being a member of the human race. Until they do, they will experience much frustration in their inability to connect with the physical world and much loneliness in their denial of their repressed human longing for relationship.

The Schizoid mind is a beautiful mind, luminous with vision and imagination. And the struggle of the Schizoid life is to incorporate their expanded awareness into the embodied forms of the physical world – the unalterable limitations of the physical body and the one-way passage of time.

# 11

# The Germination or Schizoid Stage

## The Spiritual View: the Gifts of the Germination Stage

The Schizoid phase extends from conception to birth and clearly this period corresponds to the first stage of the creative process: the Germination phase when the first spark of life comes into being and initiates the cycle of life. In the Germination stage there is very little manifest form, only a seed. However, inside this tiny handful of cells is a huge concept, the entire idea, the whole potential of the life to come!

Out of emptiness, out of the velvety black void, out of nothing comes something. Germination/Schizoid souls are those, like Uranus, who love this first moment of creation – the unlimited world of potential – creative conception. Inside the clumsy, awkward, Schizoid types are Germination souls who bring gifts of inspiration, innovation, completely radical original thinking and intuitive leaps of genius into biological incarnation. The Germination soul is the magician who conjures into being the first idea, the embryonic possibilities of life.

### The Nature of the Incoming Soul

In their mind, the Germination type has a memory of the non-physical realm where the soul glides freely through an effortlessly responsive vista of vision and possibility. There, a shift of imagination immediately initiates change – sounds, colours and shapes spontaneously reflecting shifting thoughts and feelings. Accustomed to ranging the vast expanses of the Universal Energy Field, the Germination soul finds such limitations as gravity and time claustrophobic. From the very moment of birth, the Germination soul struggles with the ponderous laws of the physical world; the difficulty for the Germination soul is in coming down to Earth! The Germination soul has a memory of a state of consciousness that extends beyond the boundaries of the Earth and even of the solar system. In their minds they can still receive knowledge filtering down from the distant reaches of the non-physical realms and, like Uranus in the myth, these are souls who are at home in the perfect world of ideas, vision and imagination and this is their gift.

With the mind attuned to the outer edges of the HEF, the Germination soul has access to all kinds of information that transcends the boundaries of earthly logic. Unlike more practical and earthbound individuals they do not struggle with slow, methodical analysis but are able to make intuitive leaps of understanding. Without being particularly conscious of a detailed thought process, a Germination soul will suddenly understand something without fully knowing where the information is coming from.

And so the Germination souls bring innovation and genius to our world. They are pioneers of knowledge and understanding, bringing radical shifts and original thinking to science, art, politics and culture. These are the dreamy, imaginative children, living in magical worlds and talking to invisible friends. This is also the world of the autistic child, retreating from the experience of relationship but capable of extraordinary mental focus. These are the artists and visionaries, seeing pictures, hearing music and poetry and retrieving fragments of the Divine Mind which they struggle to bring into manifest form on the Earth plane. These are the scientists pushing at the frontiers of physical knowledge, mentally journeying to the edge of the universe, working through the night puzzling over abstract patterns of meaning that the everyday mind can barely grasp. And these are the mystics and healers, automatically aware of the energy fields that surround them, feeling the presence of the dead and the living, sensitive, telepathic, clairvoyant, clairaudient, using Higher Sense Perception to see beyond the physical world, struggling to decipher a wealth of information to pinpoint the relevant truth of the present moment. And the challenge for the Germination soul is to learn how to bring their beautiful, ethereal, fluid and shifting ideas into the acute focus demanded by the limitations of time and matter.

## The Appearance of the Germination or Schizoid Stage in the Human Energy Field

> *The Schizoid typically does not live in his body but lives in his head.*
> Stephen M Johnson, *Characterological Transformation*

From the view of an energy healer, the Germination/Schizoid soul appears as a recognizable pattern of energy in a person's energy field. One of the key hallmarks of wounding in this stage is a sense of coldness in the HEF, sometimes extreme freezing with unyielding icy energy around the core. As we feel into the aura we get the sense of disconnected fragments of energy, which can appear like shattered glass, giving off the cold prickly sensation of fear, sometimes with bursts of energy leaking out of the fractures like electric shocks. A key indication of Schizoid wounding is weakness at the joints of the skeletal structure where we find energy leaking away.

When a person is in the Schizoid defence this causes distortions in the HEF that feel like numbing, splintering and shock. However, when a person is expressing the gifts of Germination the energy pattern manifests in a very positive way. The gifts of the Germination/Schizoid soul relate to the function of the higher chakras, particularly the 7th chakra, the place where we are connected to the Divine Mind. Here the HEF of the Germination/Schizoid soul has a brilliant, exciting, electric quality that lights up the energy field around the 6th and 7th chakras, extending far out above and around the head. The upper energy field is big and highly energized, with a feeling of freedom and expansion directed upwards and outwards towards the stars; flickering and changing with every thought, moments of inspiration appearing like lightning arcing across the sky in an electric storm.

However, very often from the shoulders down the energy quickly loses its brilliance and becomes cold and pale. Much of the lower part of the HEF is contracted away from the ground and the entire field has a sense of withdrawal from the Earth, and twisting away upwards as if to escape from the constraints of the body.

When working with a person with Schizoid wounding I often start by spending a long time at the person's feet. Feeling as though I am connecting with a very young child, I wait for the moment when the child opens to trust in me and to the presence of the Divine, and at that moment the whole field comes alive and energy flows down into the feet, connects to the Earth and starts to circulate around the whole HEF.

# 12

## The Germination or Schizoid Stage

## The Astrological View: the Astrology of the Germination/Schizoid Type

> *Let me think that there is one among those stars*
> *that guides my life though the dark unknown.*
> Rabindranath Tagore, *Stray Birds*

The planets in a horoscope represent universal, archetypal drives of the human psyche. The two planets that carry the energy of the Germination/Schizoid stage are Uranus, ruler of the sign of Aquarius, and Mercury, ruler of the signs of Gemini and Virgo. By exploring the archetypal nature of Uranus and Mercury we find new insights into Essence of the Germination/Schizoid soul. The principles of Uranus and Mercury both belong to the element of Air, representing the realm of the mind: logical, rational, reasoning, talking, words, numbers, analysis, ideas, ideals, imagination, invention, concepts and abstractions.

# 13

# The Germination or Schizoid Stage
## Uranus, Ruler of Aquarius

The planet Uranus was discovered in 1781, during a turbulent period of history, the time of the French and American Revolutions. In keeping with the innovative nature of Uranus, this was the first time in the history of astronomy that a planet was discovered that took human knowledge of the solar system beyond the orbit of Saturn and it was also the first planet to be discovered using a telescope. As the god of the sky, Uranus is ruler of the vast emptiness of space and symbolizes the spirit of freedom, breakthrough, innovation, revolutionary upheaval and change.

### Planetary Archetype – Essence

Uranus rules electricity and comes as a cosmic lightning bolt of brilliance, genius and inspiration, which is the Essence of the gift of the Germination/Schizoid phase. Uranus's association with electricity includes electrical activity in the nervous system, computer science and all kinds of networks, and the Uranian soul lives in a world of ideas, ideals, concepts, theories and formulas – abstract geometries and logical perfect visions.

As the bringer of change, Uranus is also associated with sudden shocks, lightning strikes, earthquakes and all kinds of accidents and disruptive experiences that demolish the status quo. Into human life, Uranus brings radical leaps of the mind, the birth of previously unimaginable ideas, shocking originality, creativity, freedom, change, rebellion, revolution, innovation, invention, the ideal, the complex, the abstract and scientific nature of things, intuition, telepathy and channelling.

Uranus takes the human capacity of thinking to the highest, most exalted state of the mind. Through the inexplicable process of direct knowing, like quantum particles connecting across the universe, Uranus is our link to the Universal Mind.

Uranus represents the mind at its best and its worst. Uranus is completely detached from the heat of human passion and desire, aloof from emotional turmoil, perceiving the struggles of human relationships in almost mathematical terms and offering fair, unbiased analysis, like balancing a quadratic equation. In psychological process work, Uranus plays a vital role in bringing the clear perception of the Witness. As the Witness, Uranus has the detachment needed to be able to name the issues without becoming identified with any one side of things.

### Wound

Uranus's function is to understand things and to conceptualize, imagine and create. But the energy of Uranus is always detached and it is not the function of Uranus to feel or empathize or identify with emotion. So Uranus will respond to an emotional crisis with mental analysis. A Uranian individual is uneasy when dealing with feelings, and when they are engulfed by too much emotion they start to feel as though they are drowning, gasping for the air of mental clarity. To the Uranian individual, the world of logic, explanations and rationalization gives a sense of a cosmic symmetry and order, whereas the emotions and physical needs of the body seem irrational, messy and threatening. So a Uranian soul, with their highly developed mental focus, is very likely to stumble and fall when it comes to the challenges of human relationships.

The Uranian individual can be callous, aloof, emotionally awkward and unfeeling. When Uranus is dominant in a chart, or in a difficult combination of planets (e.g. with Mars in its warrior aspect or Saturn in its role as judge), this can indicate a person capable of pathological detachment, casting a shadow of cold-blooded heartlessness onto the psyche.

In his role as the sky god – the original creator – Uranus was obsessed with perfection. A person with Uranus strong in the chart is likely to suffer from the effects of the Perfectionist Inner Critic who judges everything they do with a merciless eye. Uranian perfectionism can be crippling, making it impossible for a person to have a realistic sense of the value of their efforts. This can mean that the Uranian person never manifests any of their brilliant ideas: the fear of failure drains the life force out of the creative impulse before they get started. Uranus and/or the sign of Aquarius in combination with other perfectionist signs such as Virgo or Libra can be an indication of a 'killer critic' – a relentless perfectionist who can drive a person to despair and suicide. Here we see Uranus at the heart of the Schizoid wound, unable to live with the imperfections of being human.

As the bringer of change, Uranus is associated with sudden unexpected crises, including major catastrophes and disasters. Above all, Uranus seeks freedom. Like the *puer aeternus* Uranus has no tolerance for restriction but, unlike the *puer*, Uranus has no concerns for the challenges of being human. Like a bolt from the blue, Uranus demolishes, smashes and shatters old habits and structures, indifferent to human shock and terror, intent only on liberation and the opportunity for new growth. When this brilliant but unpredictable, shocking, detached, unfeeling planet appears around the Ascendant or in aspect to the Moon we are clearly looking at the potential for Schizoid wounding.

### Story – Prometheus

We have already met Uranus in the form of the creator god. The myth of Prometheus the Titan relates to Uranus as the ruler of Aquarius.

Prometheus was a Titan, one of the ancient gods who supported Jupiter, the king of the gods, in his battle for the throne of Olympus. Jupiter did not particularly care for human beings but Prometheus was kind and wise and he loved mankind; he had a special relationship with members of the human race and raised them up from ignorance, teaching them agriculture, astronomy, mathematics, medicine and healing. Jupiter was not impressed with human progress and when Prometheus asked if he could give mankind the gift of fire Jupiter angrily refused. Prometheus was blessed, and cursed, with the gift of foresight. Even though he foresaw the terrible fate that awaited him he defied Jupiter, stole the sacred flame from Olympus and taught mankind the use of fire.

Jupiter was enraged. He cursed mankind by sending down Pandora's Box which, when she opened it, released a plague of spites on to the human race – old age, labour, sickness, insanity, vice and passion – though Prometheus had managed to ensure that among them was also the spirit of hope. Jupiter punished Prometheus by having him chained naked to a pillar in the mountains where, every day, an eagle flew down and tore out his liver. Prometheus was immortal so every night his liver grew back ready to suffer the same fate the following day. Jupiter intended this punishment to be eternal but eventually Chiron, the king of the centaurs, exchanged his life for Prometheus' who was, at last, set free.

Prometheus was an altruistic visionary; he wanted to give the human race a chance to evolve, he wanted to make things better. This is a kind of pride known as 'hubris': thinking he could improve on Jupiter's plans for mankind, defying the gods in order to bring through a vision of a better world. Like a typical, revolutionary Aquarian, he defied authority, broke the law and sacrificed himself in order to give mankind the gift of fire, symbolizing the light of consciousness which would transform human destiny.

This story illuminates the gift of the Uranian soul. The suffering imposed on humanity by the Spites and the agony inflicted on Prometheus speak of the Schizoid difficulty with being human. But Prometheus has overlighting awareness and his vision was that mankind should have the chance to evolve and bring the light of consciousness into the dark of matter.

### In the Human Energy Field

In the HEF the energy of Uranus creates a brilliant, fast-flowing surge of light. It focuses energy up towards the head and through the brain into the nervous system. Uranus is particularly connected to the 7th chakra, our link to the Mind of God, and it focuses the light of consciousness far out to the perceivable limits of the field and beyond. When Uranus is active it moves through the HEF as a wave of neon silver/white light and moments of Uranian inspiration come as bursts of dazzling electrical flashes or even explosions of sparks and ripples of brilliant light radiating out from the head. When the energy of Uranus is momentarily stilled in deep reflection it darkens into the velvety black void of space until the flashing, radiant light surges again. When there is a lack of grounding in the HEF then the energy of Uranus becomes overcharged and destructive – overloading the chakras in the head and creating shockwaves and fractures in the HEF.

## Uranus in Aspect to the Ascendant, the Moon and the Sun

The Sun, the Moon and the Ascendant are the elements of the chart that speak of both our most fundamental aspects of character and also give us clear information about experiences in childhood from birth (Ascendant) and our relationships with our parents (father – Sun, mother – Moon). Electric Uranus has the Essence of brilliant mental activity but its effect also works through shock and shattering. So, when Uranus is in aspect to the Ascendant, Sun or Moon we see the possibility of Schizoid wounding in childhood as well as the gifts of the Germination stage coming through one of the parents or as a notable presence in the family dynamics. (For astrologers, the hard aspects – squares, conjunctions, oppositions and inconjuncts – are more likely to indicate wounding and the softer aspects – trines, sextiles and quintiles – are more likely to indicate the gift of the Germination soul.)

## Uranus in Aspect to the Ascendant

In its wounded expression when Uranus is close to the Ascendant this indicates that there was some kind of shock or terror around this person's birth. Often there were medical complications or surgical interventions. For example, this aspect would be commonly found in the charts of babies who had to spend their first days or weeks of life in an incubator, but it could also be some other kind of unpredictable drama around the birth. The positive expression of this placement means that some kind of brilliant, electric or revolutionary energy or some energy of breakthrough was associated with this person's birth.

A person with Uranus aspecting the Ascendant may have been confronted by the terror of the vulnerability of the body at birth but, even if this was not the case, this person will have experienced at least a certain amount of Schizoid wounding so they are not at ease in the body and are likely to appear awkward in some way. They are also likely to be rebellious, unpredictable and eccentric. Uranus connects us to the Divine Mind through intuitive knowing so the Uranian individual will suddenly know, with very little warning, that they must change everything and take a different and completely unexpected course. People with this aspect may be extremely accident-prone as Uranus decides to turn some corner with complete lack of concern for the human, physical or emotional consequences!

Though the Uranian individual may often be disruptive, their Essence and their longing is for freedom and their core qualities are brilliance and originality. However much Schizoid wounding is present, it is the mental qualities of intense creativity, imagination and genius that want to shine through when Uranus is in aspect to the Ascendant.

### Uranus in Aspect to the Moon

The Moon is the symbol that represents the archetype of mother and child. The unpredictable electric energy of Uranus does not sit well with the extreme sensitivity and tenderness of this, the most fundamental of relationships. Uranus in aspect to the Moon is likely to indicate some experience of shock or threat or lack of safety in relationship with the mother. Some of the most extreme negative examples could be if the mother had severe mental health problems, was a terrified mother living in an abusive relationship or a displaced homeless mother living in a time of famine or a war zone, but even when these kinds of dramas are not applicable there is some way in which a lack of emotional or physical contact undermined the bonding between mother and child. Contact between Uranus and the Moon is likely to bring difficulties but it also indicates a mother with creative, mental gifts and a longing for freedom. There may have been an unusual childhood, very likely chaotic and unstable but with a lot of space for freedom of self-expression and radical original thinking, and these gifts are built into the soul of the individual with Uranus aspecting the Moon. A Moon-Uranus aspect can be a great gift in the work of psychotherapy and healing as it gives the capacity for far-seeing Awareness, the quality of the Witness who can perceive all the ramifications of an issue without judging or becoming emotionally involved.

## Uranus in Aspect to the Sun

A Uranus aspect to the Sun is less likely to be an indication of wounding because the archetypal energy of the Sun is warm and powerful, much more resilient than the Moon, and at ease with the rational world. The Sun is associated with the energy of the father, so negative Sun-Uranus contacts can indicate wounding from coldness, cruelty or ideals of inhuman perfectionism coming from the father. When the relationship with the father is less destructive this is a very positive indication of a free-thinking father bringing the mental gifts of Uranus.

Like Prometheus, Uranus wants to make things better. So the Uranian individual is interested in all kinds of social and political theory and can always see how society could be improved with radical ideals about freedom, justice and social change. Uranus is associated with revolution and it is the Uranian souls who are found manning the barricades, devoting their lives to improving the human condition. The individual with a Sun-Uranus aspect may have great concern for the fate of the human race but they can be aloof and hard to reach in personal relationships. For some Uranian souls it is not their destiny to get involved in the imperfect world of human relations. Instead they will be found tucked away in computer rooms, academic institutions, artists' studios or scientific research centres, working away at imponderable theories that are beyond the comprehension of most of the people for whom their inventions and breakthroughs are designed to serve.

The principle of Uranus is transpersonal – it is about freedom, innovation and change. Uranus can bring clarity, objectivity and understanding to the arena of human relationships but Uranus is the least emotional of all the planets, not concerned with the warm, illogical needs of the human heart, and the Uranian energy can form a serious barrier to personal human contact, constantly slipping away into analysis and explanations rather than simply feeling the feelings. There needs to be a strong emphasis on some of the other planets in the chart if the Uranian soul is also to know the happiness of warm, human relationships.

# 14

# The Germination or Schizoid Stage

## Mercury, Ruler of Gemini and Virgo

In the solar system, Mercury is a very small planet, fast-moving and the closest to the Sun. One side of Mercury always faces the Sun; thus one side is in eternal light and the other in eternal darkness, and in psychological terms Mercury symbolizes the duality of the conscious and the unconscious mind. In mythology, Mercury was the son of Jupiter, the king of the gods, and Lady Maia, an aspect of the goddess of Night – thus again he embodies the most fundamental duality of the light of Spirit and the darkness of the void.

In astrology Mercury is the ruler of both the signs of Gemini and Virgo. I shall give a special mention to Virgo later and for now speak more about Mercury as the ruler of Gemini.

Mercury was the messenger of the gods and wore a pair of winged sandals that enabled him to fly swiftly through the skies. He was the only god who had access to both the Solar realm of Olympus and Pluto's dark realm of the Underworld, so he represents the ability of the human psyche to make connections, to retrieve material from the dream world and bring it into the light of consciousness.

### Planetary Archetype – Essence

Mercury rules the mind. The cerebral processes of analysis, comprehension, deduction, understanding and imagination bring us to the mental gifts of Germination as well as the fragmentation of Schizoid wounding.

In traditional astrology Mercury rules the nervous system, including the pathways of the brain. In the brain and nervous system we store a massive library of knowledge, information and memories. Mercury represents the process by which we manage this giant archive using a kind of supersonic filing system, a vast network of connections that enables us to make sense of things. One of the primary functions of Mercury is discernment: the ability to differentiate one thing from another, which enables us to make a coherent picture from the sea of information that we receive from our senses and other perceptions. Mercury is the symbol of the astonishing human ability to think about things – to synthesize and integrate both objective experience (current perceptions) and subjective awareness (reactions, responses and memories) so that, in an instant, we can extrapolate a meaning from our experience and make a choice. Mercury also brings us the amazing human faculty of imagination, the ability to envision different futures and the joy of storytelling and all forms of artistic expression.

Above all, silver-tongued Mercury represents our ability to communicate. Mercury gives us words and images, spoken and written – the use of symbols, and all forms of language, from the highest spiritual texts and poetry to the lowest forms of gossip and deceit. Mercury brings us mockery, irony, wit and humour; without Mercury there would be no laughter! In mythology Mercury is said to have invented the lyre and the Mercurial soul is associated with music and all the arts. It is common to find Mercury prominent in the charts of writers, artists and performers where their imagination, verbal dexterity and wit shine through in poetry, song, dance, theatre and art. Mercury also rules the hands, those marvellous instruments, executives of the creative impulse, which are such a distinguishing feature of human beings. and Mercury is associated with all kinds of skills and crafts. Mercury is just plain clever! A strong Mercury will always be a factor in the charts of scientists and teachers and anyone who works with numbers, from the purest abstract algebraist to a shopkeeper counting his cash. With swift insight the Mercurial soul brings their perception, intelligence and communication skills into any area of life that requires analysis, study or research. The Mercurial type is eternally curious, drawn to the acquisition of any kind of knowledge from the profound to the profane.

In mythology Mercury had the office of psychopomp, the guide of souls on their journey to the Underworld, so he has a special function as the bridge between the conscious and the unconscious mind. He represents the psychological process by which messages and meaning emerge from the unconscious through dreams, omens, images and symbols that bring insight, transformation and healing. As the psychopomp, the guide of souls, Mercury is likely to be prominent in the charts of psychologists and psychotherapists, bringing tremendous communication skills, helping them to retrieve the lost treasures of the unconscious and bring them into the light of day. He carries the caduceus, the symbol of healing, a magic wand with two snakes entwined around it, said to represent the polarities of good and evil, masculine and feminine, day and night.

The archetype of Mercury appears in the mythology of cultures from around the world, often as a trickster god, such as Loki or Coyote, a cunning magician with many faces and the disguises of a chameleon. He is known as many things: the prince of thieves and liars, the ruler of magic and divination, the bringer of dreams and the god of the crossroads. Mercury is the Essence of curiosity, a quicksilver soul with a brilliant mind, flitting like a butterfly from one thing to another, gathering information like pollen from a flower and casually passing it on to the next person they meet. A Mercurial soul's purpose is communication and whatever their inquisitive minds discover they are immediately urged to pass on, networking, distributing and bridging wherever they go. In his capacity as a disseminator of information Mercury is associated with all forms of literature from newspaper gossip columns to works of genius in science or literature. Into even the darkest places, Mercury brings the sound of laughter and with Peter Pan playfulness the Mercurial soul brings stories, connection and communication into human life.

## Wound

Like Uranus, but both more fluid and more fragile, Mercury represents the activity of the mind, possibly the greatest gift of being human. But our wonderful mental abilities can cause serious problems when our objective ability to think and analyse gets out of balance with our subjective ability to feel. When a person allows themselves to feel what they hold in their hearts and emotions, they find their tenderness and vulnerability. All too often people attempt to avoid the pain or fear of vulnerability by focusing on rational mental activity, in which they feel much more in control. So a person with a strong Mercury will often try to live from the detached, objective analytical mind where things seem light, rational and logical and they can use their intelligence to gain some sense of mastery. In their attempt to avoid feeling vulnerable they repress their subjective inner world which is emotional, irrational and very difficult to control. This focus on the rational mind becomes pathological: a person becomes so detached that they disassociate from their emotions, reject their feelings of tenderness, empathy and compassion and become capable of acts of cruelty and destruction. Once again we have arrived at the splitting of the Schizoid wound.

With the archetype of Mercury we see that the human process of acquiring knowledge entails dividing and separating, breaking information down and sorting it into a kind of mental filing system – creating polarities, dualities and making judgements. In itself duality is not a problem; it is a fundamental part of human life. Taoist philosophy describes the primal duality – Yang, the masculine, principle of light and Yin the feminine, principle of darkness – and everything that there is emerges from the union of this original duality. The problem occurs when one thing is judged as welcome, superior and good, while the other is rejected as inferior and bad – then the sense of the sacred, holistic oneness of all life is lost. It is part of the function of Mercury to seek to understand things by dissecting, analysing and categorizing the world but in its negative expression Mercury often takes on the role of the Critic or the Judge. When discernment turns to criticism, Mercury can be merciless, mocking and scornful, and whatever is on the dissecting table is likely to wither and die under the knife of Mercury's heartless scrutiny.

In its wounded expression people with a strong Mercury are likely to suffer from difficult mood swings, when the aspects of self that are repressed struggle to gain entry into consciousness. This is particularly so when there is an emphasis on Gemini, the sign of the Twins, with its imagery of the polarity between the light and the dark, the good and the bad. The negative face of Mercury and Gemini can be linked to the classical psychological descriptions of mental health problems of splitting – schizophrenia, multiple personality syndrome and particularly bipolar disorder with pathological shifts from manic euphoria to black depression. So a negative Mercury is often restless, moody and fickle, easily bored and ready for flight at any moment. This unpredictable energy does not sit well with the steady gentleness, patience and perseverance required when caring for the newborn.

## Story – Castor and Pollux

Mercury appears in numerous myths but the story that is most relevant to the understanding of the splitting of the Schizoid wound is Gemini's story of the twins, Castor and Pollux.

Castor and Pollux were the sons of Leda, wife of Tyndareos, King of Sparta. Jupiter, king of the gods, decided to pursue Leda, mated with her in the form of a swan and she then gave birth to two eggs. From one egg emerged Castor and his sister Clytemnestra who were both mortal, the children of Tyndareos, and from the other egg came Pollux and his sister Helen, who were divine, the immortal children of Zeus.

The twin brothers, Castor and Pollux, known as the Dioscuri, were inseparable and grew up to become great warriors. The Dioscuri were pugnacious and quarrelsome and their sisters were also involved in conflict and strife: Helen became Helen of Troy and both she and Clytemnestra played key roles in the Trojan War.

One day, in battle with another pair of twins (Idas and Lynceus), Castor, the mortal twin, was killed. Pollux was grief-stricken at the loss of his brother and refused to accept his immortal status unless Castor could share it with him. Jupiter compromised by decreeing that together they should alternate their days, spending one day in the divine realm of Olympus and the following day in the Underworld with the souls of the dead.

The story of Castor and Pollux illustrates the wound of polarization and duality associated with Gemini. Mercury is the astrological ruler of Gemini, the sign of the Twins, one twin being human and the other divine, and the myth illustrates our human struggle to bridge the polarities of life – Spirit and Matter, mind and emotion, male and female, light and dark.

In the process known as Voice Dialogue, hearing from the many inner voices of the psyche, we find that different sub-personalities go in pairs, into polarities. One of the sub-personalities may be dominant – e.g. a driving pusher determined to achieve – while the other is rarely heard – e.g. the voice of an oppressed and Vulnerable Child who desperately needs some time to play. People tend to identify with one voice and disown the other but, actually, both of these aspects of the psyche have something to offer and both need to be heard. One of the highest expressions of Mercury, the messenger of the gods, is the capacity to move between two polarities; to bring what is disowned and unconscious into Awareness. The more of our inner Voices or sub-personalities that we can bring into Awareness, the more freedom we have to express all of our life force. Hal Stone, one of the creators of Voice Dialogue, speaks of becoming an 'energy dancer' moving effortlessly between the different Voices of the Selves and this quicksilver dance is the gift of Mercury.

### In the Human Energy Field

In the HEF the light of Mercury appears as a network of shimmering streams of clear yellow-gold light, usually arising in the head and radiating out through the field. Like a current of electricity the energy of mental activity runs in rivulets of pulsating golden light. Specific areas of the field and body will become charged and brilliant with this pulsing golden light wherever there is a focus of attention or intense mental activity. For example, the hands of a craftsperson or a musician will be lit up with the intensity of focused skill when they are working and often someone undertaking intense mental activity will feel the force of the speeding pulsing golden light surging around their head.

In the wounded state, when there is a lack of grounding and an overemphasis on Mercury, the mind becomes overcharged and the delicate threads of Mercury's network become thick with a hot yellow energy. When Mercury is very overactive, there is frantic whirling, spinning and loud buzzing in and around the head and the whole field starts to break up into disparate, disconnected and incoherent streams.

Mercury is the principle of communication and is strongly associated with artistic creativity. With all communicators, and particularly with actors and singers, we can see Mercury's delicate golden matrix focused through the 5th chakra, which is the speech centre. Mercury also has to do with skills and likes to reach up to the vision and imagination of the 6th chakra and direct it outwards either through the verbal expression of the 5th chakra or through artistic or mechanical skills of the hands. When Mercury is functioning harmoniously its energy creates beautiful quicksilver patterns of words, music, laughter, movement and vision that dance and sparkle though the HEF.

**Mercury in Aspect to the Ascendant, the Moon and the Sun**

Mercury rules everything to do with the mind and communication, including the electric impulses in the nervous system. When it aspects the Sun, Moon or Ascendant, Mercury's qualities of quicksilver movement and flow will be a strong presence in the HEF. Like Uranus, Mercury is associated with tremendous mental gifts but it is also associated with duality and splitting. When Mercury is in aspect to the Ascendant, Sun or Moon, we see the possibility of Schizoid fragmentation in childhood as well as the gifts of the Germination stage coming through one of the parents or as a notable presence in the family dynamics. (For astrologers, the hard aspects – squares, conjunctions, oppositions and inconjuncts – are more likely to indicate wounding and the softer aspects – trines, sextiles and quintiles – are more likely to indicate the gift of the Germination soul.)

**Mercury in Aspect to the Ascendant or the Ascendant in Gemini**

In its wounded expression, when Mercury is in aspect to the Ascendant or when the Ascendant is in Gemini, this can indicate a tense or unstable energy at the time of birth. Mercury does not bring the sudden catastrophic shocks associated with Uranus but is more associated with worry and anxiety. This is a fracturing of the sense of containment as the insecure child finds that their world lacks consistency: things are constantly shifting, polarizing into light and dark. Family members may suffer from Mercurial mood swings and they can be brittle, tricky and unreliable. The destabilizing atmosphere of tension and anxiety is the negative expression of Mercury when energy is focused on mental control and disconnected from the slow, unknowing wisdom of the body.

The positive expression of Mercury in aspect to the Ascendant is a person who radiates the gifts of Mercury – wit, humour, intelligence and perception. People with Mercury in aspect to the Ascendant, or the Ascendant in Gemini, have the ability to take their verbal skills and intelligence into any kind of network and they are among the great communicators of the world. These Mercurial souls radiate a Peter Pan youthfulness and charm with the ability to shift mood and subject with deftness, speed and grace. Mercury brings a light touch to even difficult moments of communication, with easy access to laughter and to the true meaning of what is arising – able to express the humour or the poetry in any situation. With astonishing swiftness the Mercurial soul will perceive the Essence of what is being communicated and immediately give it voice with the detachment of the Witness and the wisdom of the archetypal Mercury who has access to both the seen and the unseen worlds.

### Mercury in Aspect to the Moon

In its wounded expression, when Mercury is in aspect to the Moon or the Moon is in Gemini, this can indicate a mother with the unstable, moody, fickle energy of Mercury. This aspect can be a sign of mental health problems in the mother such as bipolar disorder or schizophrenia; less dramatically, it can indicate a mother who is brittle, fragile, unfeeling, anxious, restlessness or unstable. Mercury has the quality of youthfulness and a Moon-Mercury aspect can be the sign of a mother who finds it very hard to be tied down to the adult responsibilities of parenthood: a *puella* – a mother who is more identified with her own inner child than the adult role of a parent. Negative Mercury in aspect to the Moon can mean that inconsistency, instability and unpredictable mood swings undermine the infant's trust that the emotional centre of the family is strong enough to contain the new life.

On a positive note, Moon-Mercury aspects can indicate a mother who is youthful, charming, delightful, witty, playful and a great communicator. This aspect is very often found in the charts of writers and artists as the Moon-Mercury combination gives access to the realms of the dream world and the imagination. This aspect, with Mercury as the bridge between the conscious and the unconscious, will also be found in the charts of psychotherapists and healers.

**Mercury in Aspect to the Sun**

Mercury never strays further than 28° from the Sun, so the only major aspect that Mercury can make to the Sun is a conjunction, which is a very common aspect. When Mercury is closely aligned with the Sun this aspect is known as 'combust': the cool objectivity of Mercury is overwhelmed by the heat of the subjective grandiosity of the Sun. This aspect is not associated with the Germination/Schizoid type but with the fiery nature of the Flowering/Psychopathic type.

The Sun is the representative of the father and this aspect can be an indication of mental health problems, mood swings, fickleness and irresponsibility associated with the father – again, the father as the *puer aeternus*. However, this aspect does not indicate the same level of Schizoid wounding as Mercury aspects to the Moon or the Ascendant. When Mercury is conjunct the Sun this indicates that mental gifts, artistic talents and the skills of communication are part of the unique 'gift' that this person brings to the world.

# 15

## The Germination or Schizoid Stage
## Virgo: the Wisdom of the Body

The signs of Virgo and Gemini are both ruled by Mercury. Gemini is happy in our technologically advanced cultures; in fact Gemini's gift of mental brilliance is one of the most highly valued qualities in our world today. Virgo also excels at mental activity but I am giving it extra space here because Virgo has a deeper level of meaning that is only just beginning to regain its true value in human collective consciousness.

Virgo is one of those signs that often gets a bad press in magazine astrology. While Virgo can express the positive qualities of Mercury – intelligent, articulate and skilful – they also express the negative end of the spectrum – nervous, fussy and critical. One of the functions of Virgo is to create order, but when out of balance Virgo can get lost in obsessive attention to detail, hyperactive list-making and, eventually, serious anxiety disorders.

One of the main issues for Virgo is the physical health of the body. People with Virgo strong in their charts often suffer from health problems. When the focus is on the challenges of living in a physical body this is an indication of the challenges of the Germination/Schizoid type. Virgo deals with the Germination/Schizoid difficulty of living in a vulnerable, biological, mortal body but they are coping with it in a very different way from Gemini and Aquarius. Virgo is an Earth sign and so a Virgo is not drawn to escape the confinements of the body through some cosmic out-of-body experience!

Virgo speaks, more than any other sign, of the wisdom of the body. By that I mean a form of direct knowing – non-analytical, non-rational, intuitive understanding that arises from being attuned to impulses and instincts arising within the body. So the Virgo path asks a person to learn how to become fully present in the body, i.e. able to respond, moment to moment, day to day, to the intuited needs and a form of guidance that comes directly from the body. **In its Essence Virgo describes the healing response to the Schizoid wound – learning, through daily, minute-to-minute attention to trust again in the wisdom of the body.**

In our societies we have long departed from the harmonious connection with the cycles of the Earth that is known to tribal peoples. In times past it was a matter of life and death for people to follow the cycles of the seasons, the time for planting seeds, the time for hunting, the time when the rain would come, and so on. People with an emphasis on Virgo love and honour all the fauna and flora of the earth, and they have an innate sense of the need to live in harmony with Nature. Their path is to seek out ways to live their lives attuned to the rhythms of the body, the order of the seasons and cycles of Nature and to honour the spirit of the earth. And it seems that in our time this aspect of Virgo is coming into its own. Increasingly today we see a worldwide surge of interest in sustainable living, the emergence of shamanic wisdom onto the world stage, a growing awakening to new forms of healing, respect for the wisdom of the body and a longing to live in good relationship with Nature.

Virgo is related to a particular aspect of energy healing. In meditation, walking in nature and in practices like yoga and T'ai Chi, we can learn to quiet the overactive mind, and this is a prerequisite for energy healing. When the mind surrenders into silence then it becomes possible to sink deep down inside the body and witness the heart beating, the blood rushing, the expansion of the lungs or the electrical pulsing of the nervous system. This deep focus of attention is known as 'cellular awareness' and it is the basis of energy healing. Mercury, the ruler of Virgo, carries the caduceus, a symbol associated with medicine and healing. The caduceus is a rod entwined by two serpents forming a double helix pattern that resembles cellular DNA patterns. The healer's ability to connect with the consciousness of the cells at this level requires a precision of sensitivity and focus and this is the gift of the way that Mercury expresses through Virgo. This Virgoan ability to focus consciousness right down into the heart of the material body is very much like the Uranian ability to take consciousness out to the edge of the universe, only travelling in the opposite direction!

## Story – The White Snake

This is an old European fairy tale called The White Snake. Once there was a king who was renowned for his wisdom. His servant was a kind young man called Peter. One day Peter discovered that every day the wise king ate a piece of the flesh of a magical white snake. Peter decided to try a piece of the white snake for himself, and when he swallowed the mouthful he was astonished to find that he could now understand the speech of animals.

Peter set out to find his fortune. On his travels, overhearing the voices of animals, he frequently came to the aid of creatures in distress. He rescued some fish that had become trapped out of water, he avoided trampling through the pathway of a column of ants and he helped three fledgling crows to return to their nest.

When Peter arrived at a strange town he decided to try for the hand of a haughty princess who was seeking a husband. To test him, the princess set him three tasks, which she thought to be impossible but each time the animals came to Peter's aid.

First the princess flung a ring far out to sea and told Peter to retrieve it, but it was brought back to him by the grateful fish whose lives he had saved. Then the princess scattered a sack of millet seed over the palace lawns and told Peter that every seed must be back in the sack by morning. When the dawn came Peter discovered that the ants he helped had come in the night and returned all the grain to the sacks. Lastly, the princess told Peter that she could only marry a man who brought her a golden apple from the Tree of Life. This magical task was accomplished for Peter by the crows he had saved. So Peter married the princess and became the wisest king in the land.

Peter's magical connection to the animal kingdom symbolizes our human capacity to listen to the wisdom of the body and the instincts. By humbly listening, Peter makes relationships with the animals and is rewarded with their help through even the most impossible tasks. For a person with Schizoid wounding this story shows the potential for healing held by connecting to the magical, instinctual wisdom of the body. When we quiet the mind and tune in to a deeper level of Awareness, then we gain access to consciousness of the cells where physical healing and transformation can occur.

One of the qualities of Virgo is kindness and respect for that which appears humble and small. Peter's respect for this world of the little, seemingly unimportant animals is the gift of Virgo to see value in small things, in that which is easily overlooked. Sitting quietly, listening for the still small voice, unknowing but trusting that guidance will come, is the quality of the Virgo Essence that is the antidote to the cold mental judgements of the Schizoid wound.

16

# The Germination or Schizoid Stage
# Chiron: the Wounded Healer

In 1977, a small but significant object was discovered in the solar system that followed a path between the orbits of Saturn and Uranus. It was classified as a planetoid because it was neither a planet nor an asteroid but had its origins in the space debris of the Kuiper Belt at the outermost edge of the solar system, beyond the orbit of Pluto. It was given the name of Chiron after the mythological king of the centaurs. When we see that Chiron has an irregular orbit between Saturn and Uranus we can begin to suspect that Chiron might have something to say about the Schizoid wound. In fact, Chiron speaks to the issue of all kinds of wounding and healing, for he represents the archetype of the wounded healer.

**Planetary Archetype – Essence**

The discovery of Chiron was synchronous with the emergence of the new paradigm of 'holistic' healing that emerged in the collective consciousness of the western world during the 1960s and 1970s. With the dawning of the Age of Aquarius in the late 1960s the people of the west developed a surge of interest in the philosophies, religions and medical and healing systems of the Orient. For a decade, young adults set off along the 'hippy trail' to India while American soldiers returned to the US with their eyes opened to the culture of the people of Vietnam. It was the beginning of what we call 'the New Age' and Chiron's discovery was a sign of the collective consciousness of the west opening to a more holistic, mystical and 'body-mind' orientation.

Astrologers watched the advent of this new heavenly body with interest, waiting to observe Chiron's area of influence in the horoscope. By the mid 1980s it was clear that Chiron in the chart did, indeed, represent the archetype of the wounded healer. The emphasis was on alternative, integrated, holistic healing as much as on the study of medicine, and Chiron's discovery signalled the first wave of interest in the personal growth movement.

**Wound**

It was soon realized that when Chiron was active in a person's chart it brought experiences of profound, often agonizing wounding. The wounding of Chiron has a bewildering quality of senselessness – we cannot discover a cause or reason why such a calamity has befallen a person and we are thrust into a place of extreme helplessness. In these situations we have no choice but to find some way to accept and come to terms with our fate. These are our darkest days when we have no choice but to surrender to the greater forces of life and death.

Human beings like to seek happiness and security and we do not voluntarily set out to journey into dark and difficult places. But when Chiron becomes active and we are struck down by some terrible blow or unbearable loss then we have no choice but to look beyond our everyday thinking and embark on a quest for healing. Often we find that the loss cannot be reversed. However, Chiron brings both wounding and healing and we discover that painful experiences open us to a much deeper level of understanding and acceptance of ourselves and what it is to be human. Healing is not what we thought it would be but comes in unexpected forms, and emerging from a journey with Chiron we find that we now see the world in a completely different way and often develop a new set of priorities in life.

One of the hardest things for materially oriented thinkers to understand is that, on the soul level, healing does not necessarily mean the eradication of a disease or a safe return to 'normal' life. Sometimes a miracle occurs and a problem disappears but at other times, despite faith and diligence, the problem persists and takes us somewhere we would not willingly go. And I do not know anyone who knows how, why and where that choice is made; the answer lies beyond the scope of human comprehension. When the sick child does not recover, when the cancer returns, when divorce is the only option, then Chiron symbolizes healing that comes as compassionate acceptance of self and others and the willingness to retain our capacity for love and faith even in our darkest hour.

**Story – Chiron the Centaur**

Chiron was the king of the centaurs, half-horse and half-human, so again we find a duality: human and animal, the mind and the body. Chiron was an immortal, a half-brother of the gods of Olympus and a son of Saturn. Chiron was learned and wise and he was the first physician, the first to understand the medicinal properties of herbs. He was tutor to many of the young Greek heroes such as Achilles and Hercules to whom he taught the martial arts, archery, navigation and astronomy as well as healing. One day, when Chiron and Hercules were out hunting, Hercules accidentally dropped an arrow which pierced the flank of Chiron's horse body. Tragically, Hercules' arrow was tipped with the deadly poison of the monster the Hydra and so, despite all his knowledge of herbalism, Chiron's wound was incurable, leaving him in constant pain. Chiron wandered the earth looking for a remedy for his wound. He taught and studied healing wherever he went and gained in wisdom until he became the greatest of healers. But there was no antidote to the poison of the Hydra. Chiron could not heal himself but because he was immortal he could not die and was condemned to a life of suffering. Eventually, Chiron persuaded Jupiter to allow him to die by offering his immortality in exchange for Prometheus' freedom, and Chiron was allowed to descend to the Underworld and live in peace in the happy Elysian Fields.

Chiron has the upper body of a man and the lower body of an animal. And it is in his horse's flank – his instinctive, animal nature – that he is wounded. This symbolism speaks of a split in consciousness formed from the division of mind from body and separation from the instincts. The other centaurs, Chiron's subjects, were a wild and unruly bunch and we can see the benefits of Chiron's serene wisdom in gaining control of the more violent and destructive urges of the instincts. But in asserting mental dominance we lose access to the mysterious and numinous wisdom of Nature and the body.

## In the Human Energy Field

In his books *The Power of Now* and *A New Earth*, Eckhart Tolle talks about the 'pain-body', an accumulation of old negative emotion that human beings carry in their Energy Fields.

> *The remnants of pain left behind by every strong negative emotion that is not fully faced, accepted, and then let go of, join together to form an energy field that lives in the very cells of your body ... This energy field of old but still very-much-alive emotion that lives in almost every human being is the pain-body.*
> Eckhart Tolle, *A New Earth*

Chiron, more than any other planet, even Saturn or Pluto, carries the energy of the pain-body. In the HEF Chiron appears like a tangle of dark veins carrying energy that feels toxic – hard to approach because of the pain that surrounds it. When a negative Chiron is connected to the Moon in the horoscope then it appears in the HEF as a mass of toxic energy attached to the Moon's silvery light radiating from the core, seated in the pelvic cradle.

When Chiron is in aspect to the Sun its dark thorny energy will appear higher up in the HEF above the 3rd chakra. When there is an aspect from Chiron to Mercury the dark knot may be lodged in the throat chakra or it may extend through much of the nervous system. Chiron in aspect to Venus extends its tentacles into the area of the heart or shrouds the Middle Tan T'ien in a thorny mass, and when Chiron is in aspect to Mars the dark tangle appears in the base or the 2nd chakra.

One way of looking at this is to see that the toxic energy of Chiron is like the seed in the oyster that creates the pearl and this is how the healing energy of Chiron works in the HEF. Because it is painful we cannot ignore it. As we become more able to bring consciousness, awareness and understanding into the wounded place of Chiron, we open a channel to the Core Star and celestial love. Acceptance is the key to healing Chiron's wounds. When we are able to let go of our attachment to what might have been, acceptance allows the light of Divine Peace to flow into the wound. Then the pain of

Chiron can be transformed, and the wounded area of the HEF becomes transparent, giving off ripples of a pearly light similar to the angelic light of the 6th chakra and closely connected to the Essence of the soul. This transformational journey is the heart of the path of healing.

We humans seem to learn through suffering, so the place where we are wounded becomes our teacher. Our pain propels us on a journey in which we are forced to abandon superficial thinking and break through old patterns of denial, and thus our attention leads us to a doorway we would not otherwise have known existed. Eckhart Tolle talks about creating 'spaciousness' by focusing our total attention and awareness in the present moment and Barbara Brennan talks of sinking down through the 'deep soft pain' into a revelation of a new Awareness. The shift comes with our ability to remain present in our total experience including our pain, not from taking evasive action! Chiron in the chart brings the experience of intense human suffering, but out of our darkest hour a silver light dawns – a totally new way of being and a renewed and deeper connection with life.

### Chiron in Aspect to the Ascendant, the Moon and the Sun

Chiron is pertinent to all five of the developmental stages but Chiron in aspect to the Ascendant or the Moon is another indication of Schizoid wounding.

### Chiron in Aspect to the Ascendant

Chiron in aspect to the Ascendant often indicates some life-threatening difficulty during pregnancy or childbirth, an immediate confrontation with the biological frailty of the human body. Even when the delivery of the baby is without complications, Chiron in aspect to the Ascendant indicates that some form of wounding has been a major factor in the development of this person's sense of identity. They may have had to deal with some persistent difficulty that will not go away, leading to the Schizoid belief that there is something deeply, fundamentally wrong with them – as if, in their very Essence they are flawed and unlovable.

## Chiron in Aspect to the Moon

The Moon is a complex symbol that represents both the archetype of the mother and the experience of the child within the family. When Chiron aspects the Moon this is an indication of something painful, specifically associated with the mother. Chiron often has to do with the body so it may be that the mother suffers from a physical illness or she herself is wounded in some way that makes her unable to fully meet the needs of her baby, no matter how much she may wish to.

In early years, the relationship with the mother makes a foundation for our experience of being in a body. Chiron in aspect to the Moon is a sign of Schizoid wounding when something occurs that undermines or even shatters the infant's sense of safety so that the natural instinctual experience of living in a body comes to feel toxic. The Moon also represents the need for relationship and so Chiron in aspect to the Moon indicates something intrinsically painful coming through the experience of relationship.

## Chiron in Aspect to the Sun

Aspects between Chiron and the Sun are not an indication of Schizoid wounding but of a later stage of child development, the Masochist stage.

17

# The Germination or Schizoid Stage

## The Houses: Where to Look for the Germination/Schizoid Stage in the Chart

In a natal chart:

- The gestation period is represented by the 12th house
- The moment of birth is represented by the Ascendant
- The 1st house represents early life

The signs and the planets found in the 12th house, around the Ascendant or in the 1st house paint a picture of what was happening during pregnancy, at the time of this person's birth and in the early weeks of life. When there are several planets grouped here that in itself indicates an emphasis on the Schizoid/Germination phase.

**The 12th House**

The signs and planets found in the 12th house tell us several things. Firstly, they give us information about what was happening during pregnancy. For example, when Venus, the planet that symbolizes love and harmony, appears in the 12th house this can indicate that pregnancy was a time of happiness in the mother's life and the unborn child enjoyed a blissful gestation period. When Pluto, the planet associated with death, appears in the 12th house this can indicate some serious threat to the life of the unborn child, such as when there has been a question of terminating the pregnancy.

The 12th house is associated with the unconscious, the dream world and our connection to the non-physical world of Spirit. The 12th house also speaks of the collective of human consciousness and it is one of the places where we see the nature of our ancestral inheritance coming down the genetic line. Planets in the 12th are not easy to bring into consciousness and they do not find ordinary expression in the physical world. Nevertheless, planets in the 12th house have a very powerful influence on a person's life. They come through either as a gift, an inherited talent or as a sign of unresolved ancestral issues, an energy that the family has disowned and that becomes a major but unconscious drive, in urgent need of attention.

When Uranus, Mercury and/or Chiron is found in the 12th house the negative expression appears as experiences of shock, fragmentation and wounding during the baby's gestation period. At the positive end of the spectrum, Uranus and Mercury in the 12th house are signs of mental gifts coming down the ancestral line, with the possibility that the person will express the gift in a way that affects the human collective. The presence of Chiron here indicates that an issue of wounding and healing is an important part of the ancestral inheritance and, again, something that this person may offer to the collective.

### The Ascendant

The Ascendant is one of the most important places in the chart because it is the moment of birth, the doorway into incarnation, the bridge between the manifest and unmanifest worlds. When Uranus, Mercury or Chiron are found close to the Ascendant (or in aspect to the Ascendant), or when the Ascendant is in the sign of Aquarius, Gemini or Virgo, this is an indication of experiences of shock or fragmentation associated with birth and a prime indication of a soul with Germination/Schizoid energy.

### The 1st House

The 1st house is the extension of the energy of the Ascendant as the baby establishes a life in the physical world. When Uranus, Mercury or Chiron are found in the 1st house this shows the likeliness of Schizoid wounding in the child's early days and the Germination/Schizoid energy built into the foundation of their sense of identity.

### The 2nd and 6th Houses

The Schizoid stage is about the very earliest experiences in life and so is primarily associated with the Ascendant and the 12th and 1st houses.

However, the Germination/Schizoid type is one who has difficulty with the experience of living in a biological body and both the 2nd and 6th houses relate to the experience of material bodily existence.

The 2nd house is associated with the nurturing stage in infancy and an emphasis on this house is an indication of either the Rooting/Oral energy or the Harvest/Rigid energy. However, when Mercury, Uranus or any of the more challenging planets – Saturn, Pluto or Chiron – fall in the 2nd house they indicate an underlying foundation of Schizoid terror in bodily existence which compounds the deprivation anxiety of Oral wounding and underpins the Rigid defence.

The 6th house is complex in that it relates to a range of issues. On one level it is the house associated with our daily routines, including our everyday work in the world. It is the house of service and those who take a practical behind-the-scenes role in organizing and supporting creative projects. In this respect this house might seem to be more associated with the work of the Harvest/Rigid soul. However, the 6th house falls below the horizon of the chart; the focus is still internal – on personal development rather than on social or collective work. As with the sign of Virgo, there is a fragility and sensitivity to 6th house affairs – there is often a struggle with the challenges of the material world which is more typical of the Germination/Schizoid soul.

The 6th house also has to do with issues of physical health, and planets here indicate the kind of health problems a person might have as well as the ways in which they maintain their health. As we saw with the sign of Virgo, health problems have the effect of focusing a person's attention within on the needs of the body. When there is an emphasis on the 6th house, particularly if the Sun, the Moon or the North Node are found here, the health of the physical body will be a major concern in this life and an important area of personal development and awareness. With this focus on the body the 6th house represents the Germination/Schizoid soul a little further on from the raw terror of birth trauma – now learning how to care for their physical health and the possibility of developing a sense of peace and well-being in the experience of being in a body.

## The Houses:
## Where to Look for the Germination/Schizoid Stage in the Chart

### The Parental Axis – the 4th and 10th Houses

The 4th and 10th houses represent a child's perception of their mother and father so these two houses are extremely important in the study of Characterology. Astrologers have a tendency to assign the 10th house to the mother and the 4th house to the father (but this is variable). Perhaps this is because the mother is frequently the dominant figure in childhood so it is her values that set a stamp on the aspirations (10th house) of the developing child.

The 4th house appears at the base of the chart and represents life at home in the family – the ground into which this life is rooted. Planets in the 4th house tell us about the person's childhood experience in the bosom of the family. Planets here show the influence of the ancestors in a more direct and personal way than planets in the 12th house.

The 10th house – at the top of the chart – is associated with career and life out in the world but a person's direction in life is unconsciously steered by the influence of one or both parents. So planets in the 10th house also give us information about the person's relationship with their parents. When Uranus, Mercury or Chiron are found in the 4th or 10th houses they indicate that the Germination/Schizoid energy is a major factor in the family

### Summary

Indications of emphasis on the issues of the Schizoid/Germination stage:

- Uranus or Mercury in aspect to the Ascendant or the Moon (the Sun to a lesser extent)
- Uranus, Mercury or Chiron in the 1st, 2nd, 4th, 6th, 10th or 12th house
- The Ascendant, the Moon or the Sun in the sign of Gemini, Virgo or Aquarius
- Challenging planets – Chiron, Saturn or Pluto – in aspect to the Ascendant
- The North Node in the 6th house

18

# THE ROOTING OR ORAL STAGE

The second stage is associated with the period that extends from birth through the first eighteen months of life. While the baby still cannot walk or feed itself the infant remains totally dependent on receiving care and nourishment from the parents or other carers. Trauma in this stage arises from experiences of neglect, hunger, any kind of deprivation and the fear of abandonment. Wounding in this stage can lead to a permanent anxiety around getting needs met and the Oral defence is associated with extreme emotional dependency and collapse.

19

# The Rooting or Oral Stage
## The Psychological View: Wounding and Defence in the Oral Stage

*If I need too much I will be despised and abandoned.*
Stephen M Johnson, *Character Styles*

The Oral stage follows the Schizoid as the infant moves into the nurturing phase, lasting from birth through the first eighteen months of life. The incoming soul is anchoring into the physical body: discovering the biological necessity of nourishment; the cycle of hunger, feeding, digestion, absorption and satisfaction.

At this stage the infant is totally dependent on their parents for survival. The energy field of a baby is not yet fully formed and they get protection from the HEF of the parents. The baby has only just learned what it is to be separate and they need to continue to feel merged, at one with the mother or carer, for quite some time. They build trust in the secure bond with their primary carers through the feeling of being securely contained and it is not healthy for them to be too quickly precipitated into feelings of separation and aloneness. The experience at the heart of the nurturing phase is the relationship between the mother/carer and child – ultimately, the experience of loving and being loved.

From the spiritual view, love is not an ephemeral feeling that comes and goes, it is a fundamental state of being. Love is the essential state of the universe, it is indestructible and it is eternally available to us in all our little stories and creations. There is a profound link between love and nurturing. The giving and receiving of nurturing is a direct expression of loving and being loved, of entitlement, of belonging, of having a place in the universe. The question, in the Oral stage, is whether the experience of the incoming soul is one that reassures them or undermines them in their confidence that they are loved.

With the extreme dependency of an infant in this stage, the care of the baby requires an upwelling of unconditional love in the mother or primary carer who has to meet continuous demands on their time, physical strength and health. In doing so, mothers and carers become empathically sensitive to their baby's needs, as they tenderly and patiently work to ensure that the child is comfortable and content. When the bonding with the mother/carer goes well then the child builds a healthy feeling of containment – a deep confidence that they are loved and lovable, that the world is safe and that the physical body is a good place to be.

In her book *The Continuum Concept*, anthropologist Jean Liedloff describes living in the jungles of Venezuela with the Tauripan Indians who, she said, were the happiest people she had ever met. Liedloff came to the conclusion that their child-rearing practices were the basis for the Tauripan's happiness. She observed that young babies were never left alone, were constantly held in contact with another human being until the time came when the baby initiated a moment of separation. She watched the babies experiment with crawling away from the mother, then returning, building confidence in their independence at exactly their own pace. It is not possible to emulate the security of a tribal upbringing for a child in western society but we often make matters worse for our children by thrusting them too soon, sometimes at a very early age, into separation. And at the extreme negative end of the spectrum we see the tragic experience of the Romanian orphans left alone in their cots while only their most basic survival needs were met. Utterly deprived of human warmth and interaction the orphans were later found to have suffered severe damage to both their psychological and physical development. Without emotional bonding and loving contact an infant's development is retarded on every level.

## Wounding

All sorts of things can cause problems during the nurturing stage, from global tragedies like war and famine to post-natal depression, illness or other personal problems in the life of the mother/carer. There may be normal, everyday issues around the care of the baby who is learning to cope with minor disturbances, e.g. hurry or impatience in a harassed, working mother who does not have time to let the child finish feeding satisfactorily. At the other end of the spectrum there may be major instances of neglect, brutality and abuse in a family that cannot cope with their own needs let alone those of the baby.

The infant in the Rooting/Oral stage is exquisitely sensitive, with an open, unshielded energy field, and this means that they receive the emotional state of the family as a direct transmission. Learning to ride the ups and downs of emotional waves is part of being human but when there is a chronic painful situation running in the family the infant is in trouble. The baby gets overwhelmed by the pain and conflict of those around them while the family have reduced capacity to give soothing attention to the baby. It is as though the infant can hear everyone but nobody can hear them.

Experience is raw and immediate at this young age. When nobody responds to the baby's distress, when the child is too often left cold, hungry, frightened or alone, then a pattern of anxiety develops which grows into a chronic fear of abandonment and a deep-seated belief in deprivation. So the child with Oral wounding grows up with the sense that they have a bottomless pit of need inside them. This develops into a belief that, in themselves, they are simply 'not enough'. This belief sets the framework for a lifetime of waiting for someone else to fulfil them, eternally waiting for Mummy to finally show up and take care of them.

As always, it is fear that causes a breakdown in the Oral soul's connection to their Core Star. Instead of being sustained by the calm strength of their inner light, the lost Oral soul turns in the opposite direction, foraging outside their own energy field, searching for any contact that will assuage their hunger and loneliness. Their unsatisfied need for merging means that they never develop a healthy sense of personal boundaries and they put up with being invaded and violated by others who overwhelm their space – because negative contact is better than no contact at all. Fear of abandonment becomes the driving factor behind all their relationships as they spend their lives searching, looking through hopelessly rose-tinted spectacles, for 'the one' who will not leave them; the relationship in which they will, at last, find the love and nurturing they never received. As long as they are still awaiting the arrival of the fantasy 'beloved' on whom they can depend, the Oral type remains unable to take authentic adult responsibility for their own life and relationships.

### Defence

In adulthood the sensitive, anxious Oral type is hyper-vigilant to the state of another person's energy field. Like the infant in the Oral stage they automatically attune to the other person's vibration and feel what the other person is feeling. They have difficulty with self-assertion and use their empathic sensitivity to pre-empt conflict, falling into a pattern of pleasing and appeasing others which takes them ever further from their own centre. Their innate authentic wish to give becomes distorted into self-sacrifice and martyrdom. The true loving instinct of the Rooting soul has been appropriated by their belief in deprivation and so they try to ensure that they can get sustenance from others by being 'good'; constantly putting their desperate need for approval above their own self-realization.

Some Oral types are overtly clinging and demanding, repeatedly collapsing into a state of neediness and dependency on others. They specialize in finding someone else to shoulder responsibility for them and to this end they are adept at summoning compassion from others with their hard luck stories and childlike appeal. Until recently, this was the widely held romantic ideal for a young woman: vulnerable, childlike, helpless and in need of rescuing – catch any Puccini opera and see how they end up! Inevitably their appeal becomes wearing and irritating over time as the 'rescuer' starts to feel horribly drained by the constant neediness of this permanent victim.

Another, equally common, version of the Oral defence is when the child copes with their fear of abandonment and shame of inadequacy by going into a state of denial. To feel the anguish of their need is too painful and they compensate by constructing a mask of self-sufficiency designed to say 'I'm fine, I don't need anyone, I can do it all by myself.' In childhood this type, known as the 'compensated Oral', developed a pattern of 'caretaking' when the child started caring for the parent's well-being instead of the other way round. They use their hyper-vigilant perception to be supersensitive to the needs of others, learning to anticipate the needs of the parents and to completely repress their own vulnerability and neediness. In Voice Dialogue we recognize this as a very common Primary Self – the Voice of the 'Pleaser' – a dominant, automatic urge to please others no matter how detrimental to the person's own well-being. I once heard a Voice Dialogue student refer to his 'Pleaser' as a 'Killer-Pleaser' because his polite urge to please would override even his most basic instinct for survival.

Underneath all the Oral disguises is the belief that their needs are so great that they will overwhelm others, and this often becomes a self-fulfilling prophecy when some 'rescuer' finally gives up the impossible task of saving them. Whether they present as a die-away heroine or a self-reliant 'caretaker' it is extraordinarily difficult for the Oral type to move beyond their fundamental belief that they cannot make it on their own. Consciously or unconsciously they pursue the desperate hope that if they are 'good' enough someone will, eventually, take care of them.

## Recognizing the Oral Defence

When they are in their defence the helpless Oral type appears as a weak, clinging, unassertive individual, easily victimized, a target for bullying and always on the verge of collapse. The compensated Oral type will appear to be much stronger, often efficient and competent, the 'brave little soldier' sorting out everyone else's problems and denying their own. Many nurses and schoolteachers operate from the position of the compensated Oral. Underneath the persona of giving and pleasing is the infantile belief system that has never yet resolved the dilemma of dependency and merging versus autonomy and self-sufficiency.

**Physical Appearance**

The physical appearance of the classic Oral type reflects the feeling of undernourishment so their bodies have a childlike quality, weak and thin with a frail, drooping, low-energy, willowy look. They have a caved-in chest area, curved shoulders and their spine is bent protectively around their tender hearts with feeble arms and legs reflecting their feeling of imminent collapse. Like the Schizoid, the Oral type often has large eyes but where the Schizoid's eyes are wild and focused on something far away, the eyes of the Oral type are childlike, watery, soft and appealing, but sometimes extremely demanding in their yearning for contact. Another distinguishing feature of the Oral type is that they often have what is referred to as a 'verbal defence' – running a constant patter of conversation, often a continuous stream of meaningless, inconsequential chatter like the prattle of a child, overwhelming the other person with a 'wall of words'. This kind of communication is very different from the brevity, clarity and precision of communication from the Germination/Schizoid type. The Oral type use their 'verbal defence' to hold the attention of another person while attempting to hide their underlying feelings of vulnerability. So the Oral type babbles on, hardly pausing for breath as they use their energy field to put out energy 'tentacles' to hold the other in a 'mental grasp' while sucking energy from their energy field. They often accompany this by fixing the person with the gaze of their soft appealing eyes, feeding off the ensnared attention until the other manages to break away, feeling quite exhausted by the exchange!

Individuals with severe Oral wounding go through life in a continual cycle of impoverishment. Their underlying belief in deprivation extends to difficulties with money, security or any other sign of containment, nourishment or abundance. However gifted they may be, they continually fail to find financial stability or emotional security in the world. All forms of addiction stem from Oral wounding as the individual desperately seeks for something to fill the inner void, whether it be drugs, alcohol, sex, food, money or co-dependent relationships. But no matter what comes their way in terms of romance or money or possessions, it will always disappear into the inner emptiness; there will be a repeating pattern of abandonment and a constant feeling of 'not enough': not enough money, not enough support, not enough time, not enough love.

On a more positive note, the sensitivity of the tender-hearted Oral gives them real emotional intelligence, even a kind of telepathy that allows them to reach out and commune with all kinds of human beings. People with the Oral/Rooting energy are gentle souls with the sensitivity of a child. They empathize with anyone or anything that is in a vulnerable or victimized state and as well as feeling great concern for any kind of underdog they tend to be very fond of animals and children who give them the unconditional love they can never get from adults.

Aspects of the Characterology of the Oral type will be found in the make-up of the best among those in the caring professions, including doctors, nurses, healers, counsellors and therapists, teachers and social workers whose sensitivity enables them to identify and empathize with those in need.

### Story – The Little Match Girl

The Little Match Girl lived with her father on the streets of Amsterdam. Her father tried to make a living by putting together boxes of matches, which she sold on the streets, but they were not very successful in their endeavours and their days went from bad to worse.

One evening, in the bitter cold of winter's twilight, the Little Match Girl sat on the street corner waiting for her father as the sun went down. To take her mind off the intense cold she recalled happier times when her grandmother was alive and told her magical stories about angels. The light faded and the cold deepened and still the Little Match Girl waited patiently. The sky turned to inky black and the stars shone bright but her father never came.

At last she stood up and wandered off through the dark, frosty streets. Shivering with cold, she paused by the window of a big house that was glowing with light. Inside she saw a roaring fire, a table heaped with food and a Christmas tree, lit with candles and piled at the foot with wrapped presents. It was the most beautiful sight she had ever seen and, spellbound, the Little Match Girl pressed up against the window to drink it all in.

Suddenly, as she watched, a door burst open and a group of excited, happy children tumbled into the room. It was Christmas Eve and time for them to open their presents. The Little Match Girl gazed through the window as the gifts were opened, marvelling at the sight of such abundance. But after a while, the children departed, the happy scene was over and the Little Match Girl drifted aimlessly along the street. Looking up at the glittering stars she saw a shooting star fly across the indigo sky.

'Oh!' she exclaimed to herself, 'I remember Grandmother told me that when you see a shooting star it means that somebody has died, and their soul is on the way to Heaven. I wonder who has died?'

At that very moment she suddenly saw her own dear grandmother walking towards her down the dark street. Overjoyed, she ran into her grandmother's open arms.

'Oh, Grandmother, how happy I am to see you,' she said, glorying in her grandmother's warm embrace.

'Do you know, Grandmother, just before you came I saw a shooting star. That means that somebody has died, doesn't it?'

'Yes, indeed, my dear,' replied her grandmother. 'It is you who have died and I have come to take you to Heaven.'

Happier than she had ever been in her short life, the Little Match Girl floated up into the sky, safe in her grandmother's arms, and that is the end of the tale of the Little Match Girl.

I don't think this story needs much explanation. I imagine a large number of readers will easily identify with the image of the Little Match Girl pressed longingly up against the window, outside looking in. We all, at some time, suffer from a sense of being cut off from joy and abundance as if by some invisible screen or membrane, the feeling of being excluded from life itself. The Little Match Girl is totally impoverished and abandoned and yet she does not question her situation. There is not even any mention of envy when she is watching the children opening their Christmas presents. She does not question her fate but she also does absolutely nothing to help herself. She could, for example, have knocked on the door of the wealthy house and asked for shelter but it does not even occur to her to act on her own behalf, so deep is her belief that she is entitled to nothing at all except the love of the angels.

# 20

## The Rooting or Oral Stage

## The Healing Response to the Oral Defence

When working with the Oral wound, the therapist or healer needs to be aware of the urge to buy into the Oral's neediness and try to 'rescue' them. Unfortunately, the time when the Oral type could be saved by having someone else do it for them is long past. For example, when a child is very little they need someone else to tie their shoelaces for them, because they simply can't do it. But the day comes when it is no longer helpful for the adult to do it for them – the child needs to learn how to do it for themselves. So the healing response to the Oral type is, with patience and compassion, to support them to get off the floor and stand on their own two feet. The healer needs to hold the awareness that this person is actually a mighty soul with a Core Star of unlimited power and the innate capacity to grow strong and stand alone. Working in the Oral's energy field, the healer can hold the vibration of the Oral's Core Star and Hara so as to support them in reconnecting with the strength of that vibration in their own HEF.

For the Oral type, the journey towards rediscovering their true strength and power is a hard one. They need to undergo disillusionment, letting go of the magical hope that someone will finally come and look after them – Mum, Dad, God, Father Christmas! As they move away from enmeshment they reach what psychologist Melanie Klein called the 'depressive position': an acceptance of the realities of being human – separate and self-responsible. This is the final part of relinquishing the 'merging' of the Oral stage. The Oral type will find that at the heart of their depression lies their infantile fury at being so neglected. This buried rage is made of raw, suppressed life force and fuels the drive to build a new, adult sense of self, new boundaries and a new life.

The healer supports the Oral type in learning to take full responsibility for themselves. This includes learning to be persistent, not giving up in the face of difficulty but sticking to their intention through whatever challenges may come. Part of healthy self-reliance means learning to reach out and ask for appropriate help. Asking for help does not mean collapsing into the arms of a rescuer. It means overcoming the shame and dread of our human vulnerability and learning that part of being self-responsible is to acknowledge the need for relationships of equals with other human beings.

When they have mourned the passing of childhood and acknowledged their resistance to self-responsibility, the Oral type is liberated into a new self-respect and self-confidence so that, at last, they can begin to bring through the beautiful gifts of the Oral/Rooting type.

The Schizoid and Oral stages lay the foundations of experience for the life of the individual. Every human being on the planet has to deal with the experience of living in a fragile physical body and every one of us has to deal with the issues of nourishment and dependency. We all have Schizoid and Oral wounding to a greater or lesser degree and the beliefs (positive or negative) that we hold about the primary issues of surviving in a physical body and receiving nourishment are at the core of all our stories.

# 21

## The Rooting or Oral Stage

## The Spiritual View: the Gifts of the Rooting Stage

> *And if I have prophetic powers, and understand all mysteries and all knowledge, and if I have all faith, so as to remove mountains, but have not love, I am nothing.*
> *1 Corinthians 13:2*

In the creative process, the Oral phase corresponds to the Rooting stage when, underground and out of sight, the sprouting seed establishes a root system, anchoring it into the earth and absorbing moisture and nutrition. This stage of the creative process is about taking in nourishment, sustaining life by receiving the physical abundance of the earth. In human development it also includes creating emotional stability within a network of belonging. Just as important as receiving food, the baby gains emotional nourishment from the love and security it receives from the parents, carers and family. Our experiences in our families during this stage lay the foundations for our expectation around physical and emotional security, containment and well-being.

Recent research into the biochemistry of the body supports Wilhelm Reich's original theory that our emotions and our physical bodies function as different aspects of one intelligent and unified system. When we experience a particular emotion this appears to trigger the activity of specific peptides and enzymes. It is these enzymes which give instructions to our biological cells, i.e. our emotions speak directly to our bodies through the chemical activity of the enzymes. In *Molecules of Emotion*, Candace Pert says:

> *Emotions live in the body as informational chemicals.*

At the level of the cells, our emotions are the guidance system for the functioning of our bodies, so our feelings exist in both the non-physical world of the mind and in the physical world of the body.

> *The emotions move back and forth, flowing between both places, and in that sense they connect the physical and nonphysical.*
> Candace Pert, *Molecules of Emotion*

Pert goes on to describe a 'field of information' that extends from the Divine Consciousness of the soul through to the human mind and on into the cellular networks of the physical body. Seen this way, our emotions represent a chain of communication from the non-physical Awareness of the soul through to the actions of the physical body in the physical world. Thus a vital aspect of the Rooting stage involves establishing a healthy flow of emotional communication within this 'field of information'. Whereas concepts and ideas are the expression of the Germination phase, emotional responses and choices are the expression of the Rooting phase.

The Rooting stage is based in communion and nurturing in relationship. The Essence of the Rooting soul lies in the tender archetype of the mother and child, earth and seed, the bliss that comes from love and nourishment. The Rooting soul comes from the heart; they live life through their feelings and bring the greatest of all the gifts of humanity – love.

## The Nature of the Incoming Soul

The Rooting/Oral soul has an unconscious memory of life in the realm of Spirit; of divine communion, oneness and unbounded love. It is natural for them to attune their energy field to the vibration of those around them and to merge with other beings by setting up flowing, liquid exchanges of energy. The Rooting soul longs to be a vehicle for the expression of Universal Love on earth. Ultimately, the Rooting soul has come here to transmit Divine Love, the Essence of the message of Jesus Christ.

The difficulty for the newly incarnated Rooting/Oral soul is the earthly experience of separation. The limitations of biological incarnation create problems for a consciousness that is attuned to non-physical existence. In the physical world the incoming soul must learn to communicate without merging and to centre their awareness in an individuated self. Here in the dense, beautiful world of matter, time teaches humanity to focus into the present moment, learning to bring our precise attention to each particular instant. In this highly focused school of awareness, we need a clear sense of our distinct separate individuality in order for us to express our unique Essence and purpose.

But in the confusion of Oral wounding, the human process of individuation feels like a contradiction of the urge to merge! It is difficult for these individuals to grasp the paradox that in order to realize their soul's purpose of communion and oneness they must first establish a firm and contained sense of self. They cannot fulfil their purpose and bring through their gifts of love until they are fully anchored and grounded in their own inner Source.

In childhood the Rooting/Oral soul's uncertainty around boundaries was reflected in their family's difficulty in giving healthy nurturing and support. Some families will have had extremely rigid boundaries, leaving the child feeling terrifyingly alone. Often the Rooting/Oral soul is born into a family with chaotic and weak boundaries, so the child feels constantly invaded and overwhelmed.

The Rooting/Oral type needs to repair the broken continuum of their development towards autonomy, differentiate themselves from others and learn to establish healthy boundaries. With a better sense of containment they can discern the place where they end and another person begins, and then it is clear when their giving is giving and their receiving is receiving. On the physical level the most obvious boundary is simply our skin, which sets an inarguable limit on our physical form. We also have other less tangible boundaries – mental, emotional and spiritual – which all require conscious attention and maintenance.

With their focus on relationship, the Rooting/Oral souls are among the great communicators of the world, with expression ranging from the most profound and heavenly poetry to the soothing lullabies of a mother. All members of the caring professions, doctors, nurses, practitioners of complementary medicine, vets, teachers, social workers, counsellors and therapists are motivated by the Rooting soul's urge to heal and care for their fellow human beings and other living creatures. With their intuitive vibrational awareness of the energy field of others, many healers, channels and people with 'psychic' awareness have the focus of the Rooting soul. In their Essence the Rooting soul knows the oneness of all living beings and their life purpose is to create relationships of love, care and communion in the world. They are not interested in conquest and they do not exclude, despise or make war on any group of people. They are the peace-makers, always able to find common ground in relationships.

The Rooting soul walks a difficult path but from their own suffering they learn to empathize with others in need. The despised Rooting/Oral type may experience much pain in this life but it is through their gentle childlike heart that we gain the priceless human gifts of love, empathy and compassion.

## The Appearance of the Rooting/Oral Stage in the Human Energy Field

Like the Germination type, the Rooting soul has access to the outer edges of the field where super-sensory, telepathic communication takes place. Whereas the Germination type seeks the clear expression of the mind, the Rooting soul longs for the flowing communion of the heart. The Germination type loves the certainty and precision of abstract concepts but the Rooting soul loves the ever-changing tides and currents of feelings. The Germination type radiates electric brilliance while the Rooting soul has a soft shimmering glow like moonlight in the mist or sunlight shining through water. Rooting souls are extremely sensitive and their energy fields react and respond instantaneously to the environment, flowing out towards tenderness and beauty and contracting away from discord and aggression.

When the Rooting type becomes afraid and goes into the Oral defence their energy field starts to feel sticky and clammy as they contract like a sea anemone or send out suckers to feed from another person's energy field. When the individual turns away from their inner Core, the HEF has a sense of something caving in and collapsing inside. They focus their energy upwards to access the Higher Sense Perception in the 6th chakra which they use as a form of protection. This overloads the 6th chakra and weakens the lower chakras. In this state any sexual connection (2nd chakra) becomes entangled in co-dependency and the desperation of unmet infantile needs. The structures around the base chakra are similarly weak, overstretched and collapsing.

When they express themselves in a positive way, the Rooting soul is happiest in the fluid, unstructured and emotional chakras – the 6th, 4th and 2nd chakras. They are particularly at home in the 6th chakra and at that level the energy field is big and beautiful, luminescent with the pearly light of Celestial love and lit up by connection to the angels. The Rooting soul also has a strong focus in the heart chakra, which is full of their longing for love and their empathy and compassion for others as well as the pain they experience about any form of cruelty. In the 2nd chakra the sensual ecstasy of sexual contact, the wild joy of music and dance, the sheer loveliness of the human body or the breath-taking beauty of the Earth can light up the 2nd chakra with a rainbow of intense colour.

22

# The Rooting or Oral Stage

# The Astrological View: the Astrology of the Rooting/Oral Type

### The Planets

In the horoscope the planets that symbolize the watery, feeling nature of the Rooting/Oral type are Neptune and the Moon. Whenever these planets are strong in the chart we can recognize the signature of the Oral or Rooting stage.

# 23

# The Rooting or Oral Stage
## Neptune, Ruler of Pisces

In mythology Neptune was the god of the sea, and both the Moon and Neptune belong to the element of Water – the waves, tides and currents of the non-rational realm of feeling.

### Planetary Archetype – Essence

Just as Uranus resonates with the core of the Schizoid/Germination phase, Neptune is the Essence of the Rooting/Oral phase. Like Uranus, Neptune takes us to the non-physical realms, opening our awareness to the love of the Divine and to the unbounded ocean of life where limitations dissolve and there is only oneness, union and communion. Neptune evokes in us a memory of perfect unity, a longing to return to the Cosmic Womb and the infinite Light from whence we came.

Neptune has the most sensitive and ethereal vibration of all the planets and it brings us to the Light of Christ as the personification of Divine Love for life on earth. Neptune is strongly linked to the story of Jesus Christ, representing the undying connection to the Divine that lives in each of us and to Jesus' qualities of unconditional love, compassion and His dedication to a life of service and healing. The themes of suffering, redemption and resurrection are at the heart of the nature of Neptune; faith in the immortal life of soul that transcends whatever cruel fate arises in human life.

Arising in the universal ocean of life, where all is one, Neptune represents the Essence of union – the blissful moment when two beings, who appear to be separate, become united. In this respect Neptune and the sign of Pisces are associated with transcendent sexual union and all kinds of sublime, magical experiences that surpass physical world limitations and light up everyday living with exquisite beauty. In Sacred Geometry, when two separate spheres join together, the area where they are united, where the two spheres overlap, is known as the 'Vesica Piscis', so-named because it resembles the shape of a fish. (The zodiac sign of Pisces, the sign of the Fishes, is, of course, ruled by Neptune.) The Vesica Piscis is the place where boundaries dissolve, where two separate entities merge and from the flow of their exchange something new is created. This is the realm of Neptune.

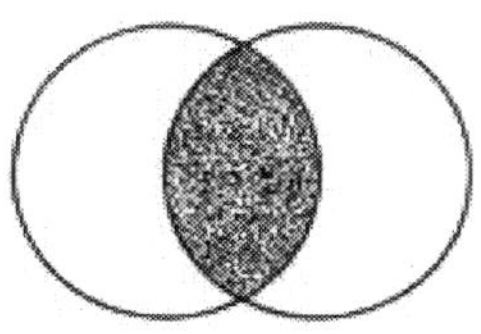

VesicaPiscis

Refined Neptune does not particularly like the nitty-gritty physicality of biological existence but it does have an extremely mystical function in the functioning of the human body. Neptune represents the mysterious means by which communication happens between our Soul Consciousness and our biological body.

To refer again to her book *Molecules of Emotion*, neuroscientist Candace Pert talks about a level of consciousness which she refers to as the 'field of information', the means by which the mind, which is formless, is able to give instructions to the biological cells of the body in the world of form. The mind sends out an impulse through the 'field of information' and this activates chemical hormones and enzymes in the body. It is the changes and movements of these enzymes which convey biological instructions for activity to the physical cells.

> *Emotions travel between the two realms of mind and body as the peptides and their receptors in the physical realm and as the feelings we experience in the non-material realm.*
>
> Candace Pert, *Molecules of Emotion*

Traditionally, Neptune rules chemical processes. Whether it is the exchange of enzymes at the cellular level or union between two people,

Neptune is the symbol of that moment of merging when boundaries are dissolved and some form of mutual exchange occurs.

Neptune sometimes figures strongly in the charts of scientists. In the area of scientific research Neptune, like Uranus, gives direct access to the higher mind and the ability to intuitively make connections and see possibilities that are not visible to those with a more earth-bound focus.

Neptune also loves the arts, and many seek the lost world of perfect unity that they long for by escaping into the magical world of the imagination. Neptune will be strong in the chart of any artist but it is particularly associated with music, dance and the glamorous, fantasy world of cinema and photography.

It is the planet most associated with spirituality, mysticism and healing, psychic abilities, empathy, telepathy and all forms of Higher Sense Perception. Neptune loves the silence of contemplation when it becomes possible to hear the quiet voice from within, and the shaman in the forest, the guru on the mountain, the novice in the chapel or the businessman on retreat all seek to find Divine communion in silence and stillness. But away from the peace of Nature or the tranquillity of a monastery, the Neptunian soul is swept along and buffeted by the prevailing currents in whatever part of the human ocean they surface.

### Wound

An individual born with a strong Neptune has great difficulty in coming down to earth! The Essence of Neptune is formless and it comes as a shock to discover that perfect, flowing, loving communion is hard to sustain in the turbulence of physical incarnation. Ethereal Neptune feels claustrophobic within the dense confines of the biological body and is inclined to seek out-of-body experiences in a variety of ways, ranging from advanced studies of the cosmos and meditation through to promiscuity, alcoholism and drug addiction. While a Uranian soul may reject the life of the body they remain great seekers of 'Truth', but when reality becomes too ugly for Neptune the longing for beauty leads them down the road to fantasy, illusion, delusion and deceit.

## Neptune, Ruler of Pisces

With the eyes of the soul turned anxiously to the skies searching for the lost celestial home, ears straining to hear the song of the angels, Neptunian individuals have great difficulty coping with such practical, worldly limitations as time, money and the needs of the body. Attuned with the sensitivity of a baby to the energy fields of those around them, they feel great pain when rudeness, crudeness, aggression or brutality shatters their vision of harmony.

Failing to cope, a Neptunian life often descends into a chaotic struggle which is most often carried out in the arena of relationships. Desperately grasping at any straw, they try to escape the pain of life through romantic, sexual encounters. But the Neptunian individual has difficulty in holding boundaries, in making clear distinctions and facing up to tough realities. The urge to merge overrides the urge to protect the self (which is the province of Mars) and they easily fall prey to all kinds of confused and inappropriate relationships and frequently end up in the role of victim or martyr. It is as though the tender infant from the Oral stage lives on in the psyche, exerting a powerful influence over adult choices, and the disowned Martian energy of individuation and separation keeps coming at_them in the form of brutality and disempowerment. But all too often Neptunian sensitivity and confusion make it very hard for them to deal with unwelcome aspects of the reality of their relationships. With Oral wounding in infancy the Neptunian individual became accustomed to neglect and never developed a healthy sense of entitlement to love and protection. So when the perfect partner starts to show feet of clay, even to the point of serious abuse, the Neptunian soul remains deluded, clinging beyond reason to their fantasies, hopes and illusions while their desperate urge to please continually undermines the chance of finding their own, authentic inner strength. Neptunian souls need to discover that self-love and truthful assertion of their legitimate needs are major milestones on the road to love.

Like Uranus, Neptune can bring the icy touch of idealism and perfectionism. A truly Neptunian soul is only a breath away from the memory of the perfection of the non-physical realm and they struggle to find a way to accept human flaws and failings. So a Neptunian individual can suffer greatly from attacks from the Voice of their 'Inner Critic, for whom nothing is ever good enough. The intense, unprotected vulnerability that we experience in infancy, in the Oral stage, is the very spot, the wound, from which we grow the voice of our Inner Critic. In Voice Dialogue we say that the louder and more insistent the domination of the Inner Critic, the younger the age of the infant who first tried to make sense of it all by deciding 'There is something wrong with me'.

So, at one end of the spectrum Neptune is associated with the Christ energy: universal love, mysticism, compassion, union, empathy and telepathy and the highest expressions of science, beauty and art. At the other end we find the lost souls of our society whose fragility leads them into breakdown and madness; all those who escape from suffering into any form of addiction and co-dependency or those who simply collapse and end up in the gutter.

**Story – The Little Mermaid**

The Little Mermaid falls in love with a human prince. Obsessed with her love she goes to see a witch who turns her fishy tail into human legs. But the price she pays for her entry into human life is that she has her tongue cut out and every step she takes causes her pain. She finds the prince but she is unable to speak to tell him of her love and he falls in love with another woman whom he marries. The heartbroken Little Mermaid is told that if she kills the prince and his bride and sprinkles their blood on her legs she will be able to return to her life as a mermaid. But the Little Mermaid chooses instead to sacrifice herself and throws herself into the ocean where she is turned into sea spray.

Sacrifice and martyrdom are one of the themes of Neptune and there is intense pain in the Little Mermaid's longing for love and the relentless emotional and physical cruelty of her fate. One way of looking at this is to say, in Voice Dialogue terms, that when someone is so identified with gentleness and sweetness that they deny their capacity for self-assertion then the disowned energy comes at them in the form of hardness and cruelty. Neptune rules the feet, the place where we touch the earth, but every time the Little Mermaid's magical feet touch the ground it is as if she is walking on knives, illustrating Neptune's difficulty in grounding and engaging with earthly life. The imagery that she is walking on knives symbolizes the phallic, warrior energy which she lacks but which she cannot embrace.

The other part of her magical contract is that she has paid with her tongue for the spell that makes her human. She cannot talk and in this we can see how Neptune's intuitive, telepathic sensitivity does not easily find expression in the left-brain, logical, analytical nature of human languages. In the end, the Little Mermaid chooses love over everything; she sacrifices her own life and joins her Essence with the spray of the ocean rather than hurt the one she loves.

The tale of the Little Mermaid illustrates the wounds but does not say enough about the gifts of Neptune. So the story I am going to tell now is an old Russian fairy tale.

### Story – The Snow Child or Snegurochka

Once upon a time, there lived a couple named Ivan and Maria. They were good, honest people and would have been very happy, except that they had no children. The years passed, yet however much they longed for a child, the cradle remained empty.

On the first day of winter, the couple went out to play with the village children who were building snowmen. However, instead of making a jolly snowman, Ivan and Maria sculpted the snow into the form of beautiful, tiny child. An old man passing through the village paused to examine their work. Ivan and Maria spoke courteously to the stranger and offered him food and drink. But after the mysterious old man went on his way a miracle occurred. The couple were amazed and overjoyed to discover that their little snow-baby had come to life! At last they had a child of their own and they named her Snowflake.

Snowflake grew quickly, far more quickly than a human child. By the time the winter drew to a close she was as big as a ten-year-old. Everyone loved this wonderful child who was never anything but kind and gentle and brought happiness wherever she went.

When spring came, the villagers rejoiced in the returning warmth of the sun. But as the days grew longer, Snowflake became ever more pale and subdued. At midsummer the villagers lit a bonfire to celebrate the summer but at the sight of the flickering flames Snowflake crept away. She knew she could not stay near the heat and so she slipped away into the forest and set off towards the snow-capped mountains of the north. Back in the village, when Snowflake's absence was discovered the villagers searched high and low for the beloved child. In deep distress, Maria went to visit an old wise woman to tell of her trouble. The old woman listened and then said, 'The old man who gave life to your child was King Winter. He gave you this gift so that you should know the joy of parenthood. But the child is not of this world, she comes from another place and now she must return.'

Meanwhile, Snowflake travelled on and when she spied a great eagle circling overhead she called to him, begging him to carry her up into the mountains. The eagle lifted her onto his back and flew her up to his eyrie, high in the mountain peaks. Then, as night fell, Snowflake saw the grand figure of King Winter coming to her across a bridge of moonbeams.

'Oh, dear, kind King Winter,' cried Snowflake, 'please tell me who I am. I feel I am near to my home. Can you help me?'

King Winter replied, 'You are a snow child. Your true home is a palace of ice, far beyond the Moon. I myself gave you to Maria and Ivan to fulfil their dearest wish and bring them joy but your task is over now and it is time for you to come home. Go once more to your earthly parents and bid them farewell.'

Then Snowflake returned to the earth in a wisp of cloud. Ivan and Maria were beside themselves with joy when Snowflake appeared before them and she told them everything King Winter had said.

'I am grateful for your love,' said Snowflake, 'and I will always think of you when I am up there in the sky. I was sent to you from Heaven and now I must say farewell.'

Ivan and Maria were sorrowful but filled with gratitude. Then, as the sun rose the Snow Child dissolved into a tiny shimmering cloud and floated up into the sky. She was carried to her home beyond the Moon where her brothers and sisters awaited her. They never tired of hearing Snowflake tell the story of Ivan and Maria and the miracle that came to them through her.

This story is about moments of grace. The state of grace that Snowflake embodies cannot be a permanent fixture in our lives, and to cling on to it will only destroy it. The spiritual Essence of Neptune is perfect love and when the gift of grace comes into our lives we may find ourselves in a magical state of blissful union with the Divine, we may create a work of art, we may fall in love like a teenager or find ecstasy and oneness in the arms of a lover. And when the wave passes, we need only to feel grateful, like Maria and Ivan, and trust that the Divine never really leaves us but will come again in another different, unexpected form.

### In the Human Energy Field

In the HEF Neptune tends to lift the energy upwards to the higher levels of the field. In the 7th chakra Neptune merges with the perfection of the Divine Mind to receive direct knowledge, understanding and spiritual insight. The 6th chakra is where Neptune is most at home, basking in a sea of Celestial love and communing with guides and angels. Neptune energizes a flow of connection between the 4th and 6th chakras, opening up the highest levels of love and compassion in the sacred human heart. Neptune is also at home in the 4th level of the field, which is the astral plane, the dream world, the imaginal realm where epic mythic stories are played out. Neptune also lights up the 2nd chakra with the ecstasy of sexual union and the sensual beauty of life on earth. One of the most powerful experiences of human bliss comes in those moments when a stream of energy flows between the celestial love of the 6th chakra through the passion of the heart to the sensual pleasure of the 2nd chakra.

People with Neptune strong in their chart radiate qualities of sensitivity, tenderness and compassion. The HEF is lit up by the beauty of Neptune, giving them radiance and charisma, and Neptune is often prominent in the charts of some of the most glamorous stars of the silver screen. Neptune is strongly associated with acting and performance, and people with a strong Neptune have a liquid energy field that easily flows into changeable masks and disguises. With a sensitivity approaching telepathy, a person with a strong Neptune will pick up on another's vibration and effortlessly shift, like a chameleon, to adjust their energy field to match the other person's.

In the HEF the positive expression of the energy of Neptune can look exquisitely beautiful and delicate, flowing in soft, shimmering waves that reach far out into space in a mist of violet and rose or like silvery stardust. The sound of Neptune is like remote, fine, high music, poetry, words of spiritual wisdom or the silence of snow falling. The felt sense is of profound gentleness, compassion and spiritual bliss.

### Neptune in Aspect to the Ascendant, the Moon or the Sun

When Neptune is in aspect to the Ascendant, Sun or Moon, the beautiful gentle magical radiance of Neptune will be a tangible presence in a person's HEF. Neptune seeks communion, oneness and merging and so brings the possibility of Oral wounding in childhood as well as the gifts of the Rooting stage coming through one of the parents or as a notable presence in the family dynamics. (For astrologers, the hard aspects – squares, conjunctions, oppositions and inconjuncts – are more likely to indicate wounding and the softer aspects – trines, sextiles and quintiles – are more likely to indicate the gifts of the Germination soul.)

### Neptune in Aspect to the Ascendant

When Neptune is found close to the Ascendant this indicates that there was some kind of Neptunian energy around at the time of the person's birth. In its wounded expression, Neptune is associated with all kinds of chemicals and drugs and also with things that are foggy and confused. So Neptune close to the Ascendant may indicate that there was some kind of confusion around the birth or possibly that the mother was offered a lot of pain relief through drugs. Neptune on the

Ascendant could also indicate a very beautiful and gentle birth, in which mother and baby are in communion with each other and with Spirit.

Neptune in aspect to the Ascendant brings tremendous sensitivity and the longing to be lovingly attuned to others. However, it can also indicate some of the negative qualities of Neptune as the prime indicator of Oral wounding. This aspect is a classic indication of the Neptunian individual who is going to have difficulty with boundaries – difficulty in asserting their own needs, difficulty in saying 'No', difficulty in allowing another person some space, difficulty in handling any kind of aggression and, very often, difficulty in telling the truth. To a more assertive individual the Neptunian soul can appear as the classic Oral victim – clingy, needy, devious and demanding.

The positive expression of Neptune means that the qualities of compassion, empathy, telepathy, imagination, romance, artistry, mysticism, spirituality and vision will be an integral part of the person's sense of identity and their way of relating to others. When Neptune is in aspect to the Ascendant, particularly when it is in the 1st house, the person is touched with the charisma and the beautiful silvery radiance of the Neptunian Essence and when the aspect is very intense it can make a person seem glamorous, larger than life.

### Neptune in Aspect to the Moon

Neptune in aspect to the Moon is an indication that the child's perception of the relationship with the mother (represented by the Moon) is strongly coloured by the qualities of Neptune. This can be a very beautiful placement where the mother is gentle, sensitive and attuned to the needs of the baby; an exquisitely empathic mother with compassionate understanding and she can also be a mother with a great imagination and the ability to enter into the magical world of the child.

The difficulty with a Moon-Neptune aspect is that the mother is very likely to lack a clear sense of personal boundaries. This loving, empathic mother will do very well while the baby is in arms and needs to remain merged. But Neptune in aspect to the Moon frequently indicates a mother who has unmet Oral needs of her own and the risk is that she will unconsciously come to depend too much on the unconditional love of the child. In more severe cases the mother may appear as some kind of victim and be seriously needy. She may have been taken advantage of, abused or abandoned in many of her relationships. She may be a great spiritual seeker but she may also be a hopeless dreamer, living in a fantasy world or escaping through alcohol or drug addiction. This aspect is a common indication of issues of co-dependency in the family, which makes it extremely difficult for the growing infant to escape from enmeshment in everybody else's needs but particularly the mother's.

Neptune can indicate the cold touch of perfectionism and a Moon-Neptune aspect can bring self-judgement – the belief that the person is in some way not good enough. The person may be defeated by their own idealism, seeking after perfection, unable to cope with harshness in the physical world or flaws in the physical body. The Moon has to do with nourishment and this aspect is often associated with eating disorders. The extreme vulnerability of the child evokes the Perfectionist Inner Critic, easily slipping into a painful sense of failure that is out of proportion to the reality of a situation. The feelings of low self-esteem and unworthiness, and the difficulty in asserting the self, lead to a lack of a sense of entitlement so that individuals with Moon-Neptune aspects are likely to have problems with money and prosperity.

Away from the difficulties with boundaries and perfectionism, Neptune in aspect to the Moon is a very beautiful placement. It brings an enormous capacity for love, more so than any other combination of planets. This is also one of the major indications of a visionary soul, often expressing through some form of artistic ability as well as through psychic gifts and natural healing abilities.

## Neptune in Aspect to the Sun

When Neptune is in aspect to the Sun the person's father may express the positive qualities of Neptune: he may be sensitive, imaginative, artistic and visionary. With the negative expression of Neptune, the father may have been weak in some way, a victim, unable to maintain proper boundaries or assert his authority. At the worst end of the spectrum, a Sun-Neptune aspect can be a sign of a father whose lack of boundaries extends to the possibility of sexual abuse within the family. A negative Neptune in aspect to the Sun can be a sign of a father who was an alcoholic, a drug addict, a fraudster or a man who has collapsed into total chaos. Often a Neptune aspect to the Sun goes with an absent father. This might be the *puer aeternus*, a Peter Pan soul who could not cope with the responsibilities of parenthood. Or it may be that the father's work takes him away from the home, such as a sailor who is at sea most of the time. For whatever reason, he is not at home with his children and supporting the mother. The lack of a strong, clear Solar energy contributes to the collapse of boundaries within the family and to the Oral cycle of chaos, loss, deprivation and abandonment.

The energy of Neptune brings sublime sensitivity, gentleness, compassion and a profound longing for communion. The soul with a strong Neptune may spend a lot of this life falling into painful states of desperation and heartache, collapsing, clutching on to others, ready to make almost any sacrifice rather than face their dread of loneliness. At some point the individual must let go of the illusion that they can get what they seek from another and, instead, turn inwards to make an authentic spiritual connection to their own Core Star. The relationship that they long for can only happen when they have first established that relationship with themselves.

# 24

# The Rooting or Oral Stage

## The Moon, Ruler of Cancer

The Moon is the ruling planet of the Water sign of Cancer. We have seen that the Moon is the symbol associated with the Feminine principle – the Yin energy. It represents birth itself, the mother, the child, the family, the ancestors, the physical body and the womb. Because the Moon is the symbol of experience in infancy, whatever is happening with the Moon in the chart speaks directly of the Rooting/Oral stage.

**Planetary Archetype – Essence**

We have seen that Neptune is very closely connected to the world of Spirit. When the soul incarnates in the physical realm the Moon is a symbol for our container in the world of matter; the body as the temple of the Spirit. A child's sense of bodily contentment and safety is anchored in their relationship with their mother/primary carer and is reinforced by the love and security they find in their family. The Moon symbolizes a continuum that runs from the child to the mother, the family, the home, the ancestors. Like the little seed putting out roots, the strength of the relationships within the family continuum gives the child a fundamental sense of security and being anchored in life. So the Moon represents all the things that hold and support us, including our physical body. In the horoscope, the sign in which the Moon is placed and any planets in aspect to the Moon give us a description of what will give this person the feeling of being contained in life, their way of taking in nourishment of body and soul. The sign and aspects of the Moon also indicate the gifts and the challenges that come down to us through our genetic inheritance and through the ancestral line.

The Moon and the Sun are a duality. The Sun represents the bright light of consciousness and the Moon represents the dimly seen image of what is emerging from the unconscious. The Solar principle is action – the Lunar principle is receptivity. The Moon is home, the place where we go to rest and find peace and stillness of being. In the Taoist text the *I Ching*, the first two hexagrams represent the primal duality of the Masculine and Feminine. The Feminine principle is known as K'un, the Receptive.

> *Perfect indeed is the sublimity of the Receptive. All beings owe their birth to it, because it receives the Heavenly with devotion.*
> Richard Wilhelm Translation, *The I Ching*

**Wound**

The Lunar principle represents home and the tender bond of mother and child. Difficulty for the Lunar principle occurs when something harsh enters the childhood scenario, threatens the vulnerability of the child and breaks up the peace of the family. Any kind of serious stress within the family, from depression to domestic violence, will shatter the foundation of physical security and trust which the Lunar principle represents.

**Story – The Annunciation**

One of the most universal symbols connected to the Lunar archetype of the Feminine is the Madonna, Mary, mother of Jesus Christ. If Neptune is associated with the light of Christ, then the Moon is the symbol of Mary, the part of our consciousness that is willing to undertake the sacred task of bringing the Christ Light into form.

> *It is the Creative that begets things but they are brought to birth by the Receptive.*
> The I Ching, K'un the Receptive, *Richard Wilhelm Translation*

In many versions of the story of the Annunciation, Mary is sitting spinning when the Archangel Gabriel appears to her. In a moment of surprise she drops her spindle and questions whether she is worthy of the holy task that is being asked of her. But her doubt is only momentary and in the time that it takes for her to pick up the spindle she steadies herself and opens to the Divine Will. We can imagine that Mary might have had the hopes of any young girl but she surrenders her notion of what she thought her life would be and willingly embraces the task that the Angel of the Annunciation has presented to her.

The Moon as the symbol of Mary represents our ability to respond to life, to allow whatever arises in the moment to be what it is, without judgement. In this context, we interpret Mary's virginity as her ability to be wholly present, completely open to the will of the Divine, unattached to the past or the future but ready to embrace whatever the moment offers, free of any preconceived agenda.

How simple, yet how difficult, it is for us to accept the moment, without judgement, and allow the current to carry us in the river of life. How many years or lifetimes do we spend standing on the bank, watching the river flow by, waiting for it to be the way we think it ought to be, or paddling hopelessly upstream? Paradoxically, this is not to advocate a passive approach to life. To be born into this world is to be a creator of life and we all have desires and dreams, a unique Essence to express and a life purpose to fulfil. So often, fear blinds us and we try to resist the Divine guidance upwelling inside. But Spirit is greater than the Little Mind and, sooner or later, life will present us with inescapable dilemmas designed to break us out of our prisons and free us to enter once more into the flow.

Mary is the Essence of the archetype of the Feminine embodying the qualities of trust, surrender, openness and willingness to be the channel through which Spirit flows into life. In this we see the Moon, the Goddess and the body represented as the Holy Grail, the container of the light of the Divine.

> *When you are open, the Divine can pour itself into you.*
> Mother Meera, *Answers*

Another aspect of the archetype of the Moon is symbolized by the Roman goddess of the Moon – Diana the Huntress. Diana was a virgin goddess who gave herself to no man but lived in the forests, wild and free. She symbolizes the most primal aspect of the Feminine principle: Nature, in the raw, the wild untameable cycles of birth and death that underpin every aspect of life. This is the other end of the spectrum from the gentleness of Mary. Diana represents the instinctual laws of Nature with a power that completely transcends the little egoic mind of civilized man.

## In the Human Energy Field

In the HEF the energy of the Moon appears as a source of soft, silvery light arising within the core of the body, close to the central vertical power current. The light of the Moon will shift and change, moment to moment, rippling and shimmering with every fluctuation of feeling.

The sign that the Moon occupies and any planets in aspect to the Moon will show up in the appearance of this source of light. So, when Neptune is in aspect to the Moon or the Moon is in Pisces, the light will be very beautiful, soft and diffuse – more inclined to shimmer upwards towards the stars than to anchor downwards into the earth.

When Saturn is in aspect to the Moon or the Moon is in Capricorn, the container of light will appear more opaque – stony and cold in its negative expression, full of strength and purpose, deeply rooted in the earth, in its positive expression, and capable of holding whatever life brings.

We have already seen that when there is Schizoid wounding, the energy of Uranus shatters the light of the Moon, bringing fracturing and fragmentation that can feel like broken glass. However, when expressing as the creative gifts of Germination, Uranus brings an exciting, electric brilliance radiating out into the cosmos.

In its wounded expression Chiron in aspect to the Moon shows up as shadowy, dark veins that are toxic and full of pain and that seem to strangle the light of the Moon. To approach this Moon energy feels like approaching a battered child who flinches away from the threat of more pain. When expressing the gifts of Chiron, the dark veins are transformed and in their place is a feeling of strength, peace and the pure and silvery light of celestial love.

### The Moon in Aspect to the Ascendant or the Sun

The Moon represents the non-rational world of feelings, bodily sensations and emotions. When it is in aspect to the Ascendant or the Sun (or when the Ascendant or Sun are in Cancer) it brings through enhanced sensitivity and the changing tides of emotions. Sometimes the feelings can be overwhelming and may create a difficulty in recognizing individual boundaries. So the Moon in aspect to the Ascendant or the Sun can be an indication of Oral wounding as well as a sign of the ability to make loving connections, which is the gift of the Rooting stage.

### The Moon in the 1st House

When the Moon is in the 1st house (particularly if it is close to the Ascendant) it has a powerful effect on the person's sense of identity. Whether they identify themselves as a child in need of nurturing or as a mother whose role is to give nurturing, the issues of nurturing, caring, relating and belonging are going to figure highly in this person's way of relating. When they are in the Oral defence they identify themselves either in the role of 'caretaker' – mothering and sometimes smothering everyone around them – or in the role of a continually needy and demanding child, often in a state of collapse. When they embody their Rooting gifts they radiate the true Essence of caring, loving and giving from a place of authentic strength.

### The Moon in the 12th House

The 12th is the most mysterious of all the houses because it has to do with our connection to Spirit and the non-physical world. This is also the house of the collective, and people often bring through 12th house planets in the form of gifts to the collective. We have seen that the 12th house is associated with the gestation period and it speaks of other pre-birth matters such as past lives and our ancestral inheritance.

The 12th house is the house of the unconscious, and planets here are difficult to access. It often takes half a lifetime before an individual is able to bring 12th house planets into consciousness, to really have them in their personal life and know them as part of who they are. So, particularly with a young person, planets in this house often represent an area of difficulty – genetic, physical or psychological – an unresolved issue passing down the ancestral line waiting to be healed. The Moon in the 12th house is one of the strongest indications of Oral wounding.

It is as if, in infancy, the person's legitimate need for nurturing, protection and care has been overlooked. Perhaps the mother or another family member was ill and their needs superseded those of the infant. This placement could be found in the chart of someone who had been orphaned or born in a time of famine. However, even in families where there has not been this kind of drama, somehow the needs of the child have not been recognized and honoured. The Moon in the 12th is always a sign of some form of deprivation or abandonment during the Oral phase.

The 12th house is the place where we connect to a world that is infinitely larger than the physical realm, the dream world, the numinous world of Spirit. A person with the Moon in the 12th may struggle to get their needs met in the physical world but they have an effortless connection to the non-physical realm. The Moon is where we go to rest, and when the Moon is in the 12th house, the sense of home and safety is found in the world of Spirit. People with the Moon in the 12th can be a great channel for Divine love. They often have a tremendous ability to give to others; the capacity for nurturing and care becomes much larger and is played out on the world stage.

## Planets in Aspect to the Moon

In the chart the planets in aspect to the Moon give a description of the nature of this person's sense of containment in life, the quality of energy that sustains them and meets their needs. In the negative expression, planets in aspect to the Moon represent something that blocks or distorts a person's sense of safety and containment. In our primary relationship with mother we lay down a template for both our experience of the physical body and our feelings of safety in relationship. Difficult planets in aspect to the Moon can be an indicator of both health issues and problems in relationship.

Aspects from any of the outer planets – Saturn, Uranus, Neptune, Pluto and Chiron – all signify a disturbance in the harmony of the Moon energy but even the personal planets (the Sun, Mercury, Venus and Mars) can have a difficult impact on the supersensitive Moon. However, the three planets that are the prime indication of Oral wounding are Saturn, Chiron and Neptune.

**Saturn**

Saturn in aspect to the Moon is one of the most difficult placements in a chart. A negative Saturn brings a cold, critical energy and often manifests in a child's life in the role of a harsh disciplinarian, a rigid authority figure who despises vulnerability, which they see as weakness. The Moon is the tender archetype of the mother and child and represents a vulnerability that is completely polarized by a patriarchal Saturn. The Moon in this situation appears like a child in the grip of a merciless tyrant and this placement is a common indication of Oral wounding. Saturn is associated with the Harvest/Rigid type so a Moon-Saturn connection is also an indication of the Harvest/Rigid soul – hard-working and disciplined, very unlike the collapsing Oral type. So this placement is a prime indication of the Compensated Oral type. This is the child who has given up on the possibility of receiving nurturing and goes into a state of denial of their own needs. They becomes expert 'caretakers', Mummy's little helper, getting approval for organizing and supporting everyone else and hopelessly ashamed and rejecting of their own vulnerability which they fear is a bottomless pit of need.

Saturn always improves with time and the positive expression of Saturn in aspect to the Moon is a person who is mature, steadfast, loyal and capable of the disciplined, steady, hard work necessary to see a project through into manifestation.

## Chiron

We have seen that when Chiron is in aspect to the Moon wounding is in some way an intrinsic part of the mother-child relationship – something painful, such as a bereavement or loss or the physical illness of a family member, undermines the nurturing phase.

In the positive expression, a Moon-Chiron aspect is often found in the charts of healers, therapists and any who bring tremendous gifts of caring, compassion and understanding of the human condition.

## Neptune

Neptune in aspect to the Moon is a very beautiful placement, signifying a gentle soul of extreme and exquisite sensitivity. This may be an indication of a very loving mother who bonded well with her baby. However, we have seen that this placement also goes with a mother or a family with weak boundaries; mother and child become enmeshed, making it extremely difficult for the child to develop healthy boundaries and an authentic sense of identity. A Moon-Neptune contact often indicates a mother who is some kind of a victim, or an alcoholic or drug addict. This can be a sign of a Little Match Girl childhood of impoverishment, or a Little Mermaid child who finds life in this harsh world agonizing.

In its positive expression, Moon-Neptune is often seen in the charts of artists, giving them effortless access to the dream world and the imaginal realms. Moon-Neptune is also common in the charts of spiritual teachers, healers and therapists, bringing effortless compassion and empathy into their work.

## The Sun in Aspect to the Moon

The meaning of aspects between the Moon and Sun varies according to the nature of the aspect. A difficult aspect indicates that there is a split or rift between the two principles of the Feminine and the Masculine. This often appears as a struggle between the two parents in the family. A harmonious aspect between the Sun and Moon is a sign of a healthy balance between the Masculine and Feminine though sometimes this harmony is superficial and comes at the expense of a deeper level of truth. When the Moon and Sun are conjunct, this can be a sign of a powerful personality, sometimes rather self-obsessed; someone who is driven by an intense combination of the creativity of the Sun and the emotionality of the Moon.

# 25

## The Rooting or Oral Stage

## The Houses: Where to Look for the Rooting/Oral Stage in the Chart

In order to see what happened during a person's nurturing phase we look at the houses associated with early life; the 1st and 2nd houses are specifically to do with the early years and the 4th house describes the overall experience of family life. Although the 10th house is not associated with childhood, we have seen that the signs and planets there can give us information about the individual's perception of their parents, particularly the mother. The 2nd house represents the experience of being in a physical body and the pleasures of the senses, and it is particularly relevant to the Oral stage because it shows us all the issues around nourishment and sustenance (including money, prosperity and abundance). Also, all the Water houses – the 4th, 8th and 12th – have something of the quality of the Oral stage because they are associated with the non-rational, inner world of feelings, sensations, instinct and intuition.

### The Moon in the 12th House

The placement of the Moon in the 12th house is one of the strongest indications of Oral wounding. Twelfth house planets do not express in the ordinary way, so the Moon here is an indication of a child who received more sustenance from contact with the world of Spirit than from contact with their biological family, perhaps because the mother was absent, ill or not available in some other way. Paradoxically, in adult life, this person radiates powerful Lunar energy. Though the individual may be dogged throughout life by the feeling that they never get their own needs met, nevertheless others perceive them as bringing through the Lunar qualities of compassion and caring on a grand scale and this is their gift to the collective.

### Neptune in the 12th House

Neptune in the 12th house also emphasizes the Rooting/Oral stage but with less emphasis on wounding and more on the Rooting soul's wonderful gifts of empathy, compassion, capacity for universal love and Neptune's effortless connection with the world of Spirit.

### The 1st House

We have seen that the 1st house gives us information about the earliest experiences of being alive. Difficult planets here (Saturn, Uranus, Chiron or Pluto) represent Germination/Schizoid energy but they can also indicate the energy of the Rooting/Oral stage.

### The 2nd House

The 2nd house is also associated with early life but whereas the 1st house shows the first raw initiation into life energy – *'I am here, I have arrived, I live!'* – the 2nd house shows the new life anchoring into physical form – *'I sense, I feel, I am real, I have a body!'*

In the 2nd house the focus is on the physical experience and the sensual pleasure of inhabiting a biological body. In the security (hopefully) of their mother's arms and in their wider experience of the nurturing phase the baby lays down a basic pattern of comfort (or otherwise) in their physical body and ease (or dis-ease) in their emotions. Signs and planets in the 2nd house tell us what happened during the 'nurturing stage' and the person's foundation in the sensual experience of being in a body. In traditional astrology, as well as being the house of the body, the 2nd house is associated with money and possessions and in this way planets here also represent the energy of the Harvest/Rigid stage. However, the Harvest/Rigid stage is always an 'overlay' of issues from an earlier stage. From the view of a healer there is a clear connection between a person's infant experience during the nurturing phase and their subsequent relationship to all kinds of sustenance, including money. Signs and planets in the 2nd house describe a person's ease or difficulty with their beliefs around abundance or deprivation (Rooting/Oral issues), and this becomes the foundation of their adult experience around money and possessions (Harvest/Rigid issues).

### The Parental Axis – the 4th and 10th Houses

The 4th house shows a person's experience of their home and family, including the direct influence of the ancestors, so planets here also speak directly of the Oral or Rooting stage. The 4th house falls at the lowest point in the chart and astrologer Dane Rudhyar refers to it as:

> *The soil in which the 'human-plant' is rooted.*
> Dane Rudhyar, *The Astrological Houses*

Signs and planets here tell us if this person's 'human-plant' has grown from the soil of a family life that was sustaining and nurturing or otherwise. Some signs and planets indicate a benign presence with healthy support for nurturing and rooting. Other signs and planets show conflict, disturbance – an unhealthy and even toxic environment for Oral development.

The 10th house is not associated with family life. However, planets in the 10th house give us additional information about the parents, most often the mother. A negative Saturn in the 10th house is a sign of Oral wounding, a mother who was cold and rigid, not able to merge well with a babe in arms. A positive expression of Saturn in the 10th house would be a mother who was strong and responsible with great loyalty to her family. Negative Neptune in the 10th could be a sign of a mother with Oral wounding of her own – very inclined to merge with others and to become enmeshed and dependent on her children. The positive expression of Neptune in the 10th would be a mother who was tender, compassionate, spiritual or artistic.

## Summary

Indications of emphasis on the issues of the Rooting/Oral stage:

- Neptune and/or the Moon in aspect to the Ascendant, Moon or Sun
- Neptune and/or the Moon in the 1st, 2nd, 4th, 10th or 12th house
- The Ascendant, Moon or Sun in the sign of Pisces or Cancer. (When there are no other difficult planets present, the Moon or Cancer on the Ascendant is an indication of the gifts of the Rooting stage rather than the wounds.)
- The North Node or any other emphasis on the 2nd, 4th or 12th house
- Saturn, Chiron or Pluto in the 2nd or 4th house

Neptune and the Moon are both Feminine planets: they represent aspects of the principle of relationship. They are receptive, emotional and sensitive. Neptune represents the highest spiritual and visionary aspect of the Feminine – our connection to the wisdom of the Divine, the breath of the Holy Spirit that illuminates life with a magical hope and longing. The Moon is much earthier for she is the primary energy of the mother, the containment that anchors us in the physical world and provides us with the miraculous home of the body.

Whenever Neptune or the Moon is strong in the chart we know we are looking at an exquisitely sensitive soul but one who is very likely to suffer from Oral wounding. The negative expression of Neptune is a deluded, escapist dreamer adrift in this harsh world, not coping but collapsing, one of life's victims. Neptune in aspect to the Moon or the Sun is often the sign of the *puer* or the *puella aeternus* – one who is stuck in an adolescent fantasy view of life. If this kind of Neptunian soul does not find a turning point they may die young.

Similarly, with the negative expression of the Moon a person gets stuck in the role of a clinging, demanding child, refusing to grow up and take adult responsibility for their life and they risk creating that which they dread, ending up impoverished and alone.

But the soul never gives up. Sooner or later, in one life or another, the turning point is found and the Rooting/Oral soul finds the strength to stand up and take the long and winding road towards self-realization. It may feel painful to begin with, like the Little Mermaid walking on knives, but eventually, through self-nurturing and developing inner strength and perseverance, the Neptunian or Lunar soul is finally able to bring through the greatest of all gifts, the love of the sacred human heart.

26

# NARCISSISTIC WOUNDING

The issue of the first eighteen months of life is survival – meeting the physical needs of the biological body and the emotional need for a sense of belonging. During this first stage of life the infant learns that moments of pain and difficulty can be endured and survived and, hopefully, they find a level of security and continuity in their family relationships. With the basic framework for physical survival established, the next three developmental stages focus on the struggles of individuation – the child's need to develop their own sense of identity and authentic self-expression.

As they move into the second year of life the infant leaves behind the total dependency of babyhood. They start to crawl, they learn to feed themselves and they begin to speak. This stage, in which the infant begins the journey of separation from the parents and carers, is known as the 'rapprochement' phase. In the rapprochement phase the infant encounters two sets of dilemmas; unity versus individuation and grandiosity versus vulnerability.

- The dilemma of unity versus individuation. From conception onwards the baby is developing in a line that leads from complete symbiosis with the mother in utero, through infancy when the baby still needs to feel merged with the mother/carer, and on into separation and independence. During the rapprochement phase the child begins to experiment with moments of separation from the mother/carer and this becomes a dance between the safe sense of merging with the mother/carer and the adventure of feeling separate. During this stage, the parents need to support the child's individuation process and this includes fostering their capacity for empathy which is rooted in the experience of successful bonding and merging during the Oral phase.

- The dilemma of grandiosity versus vulnerability. These terms describe a paradoxical split between the innate potential for power and creativity in every human being and the intense physical and emotional vulnerability of being human. As the infant begins to have a sense of themselves as separate from their families they are confronted by this dilemma – the Vulnerable Child's awareness of their weakness and helplessness and the 'magical child' longing to create and embrace life. The parents and carers need to help the child develop confidence in their creativity and personal power alongside a healthy acceptance of human vulnerability.

Narcissistic wounding occurs when the parents and carers are unable to support the child in integrating either of these polarities.

### Story – Narcissus

In Greek mythology, Narcissus was a beautiful youth whose mother had never allowed him to see his own reflection. One day when he saw his image reflected in the surface of a mountain pool he became besotted with the face mirrored in the water. He lay gazing into the pool for days until he was overcome by the pain of his obsessive love and killed himself.

In the place where his young blood soaked into the earth, a flowering narcissus sprang up – symbol not so much of Narcissus's folly but of the human need for self-knowledge. The infant in the rapprochement phase needs the family to mirror back their unique individuated self and affirm their worth. Unfortunately, in many families the adults are not able to support the child's emerging individuality. They mock their vulnerability, criticize their mistakes and attempt to mould them to conform to the family values. In many families one or both parents demands that the child must excel, be brilliant or special in a way that reflects positively on the parent. The parents are blinded by their own defences and they fail to recognize the child's right to be different, to express their own essential nature.

The confused child becomes increasingly, obsessively bound up in the difficulties of finding their true sense of identity. In the myth, Narcissus is loved by a nymph called Echo, but Echo is unable to speak, she can only repeat what others say to her. Echo can be said to represent Narcissus's anima, the numinous voice of Essence – but the Narcissistically wounded child can no longer hear the inner voice of guidance.

The next three defences/character types emerge from the issues of Narcissistic wounding – when the parents/carers try to repress the nature of the child and impose their own ideals and codes of behaviour.

27

# THE BUDDING OR MASOCHIST STAGE

Reich named the third stage the Masochist stage, extending through the second and third year of life when the child develops mobility and speech and begins to assert their autonomy. Trauma in this stage comes when the parents or carers inappropriately block the will of the child who suffers from being dominated and humiliated and reacts with feelings of powerlessness and shame. The Masochist defence is associated with stubborn resistance and repeated experiences of defeat.

# 28

## The Budding or Masochist Stage

## The Psychological View: Wounding and Defence in the Masochist Stage

*Better to reign in Hell, than serve in Heaven*
John Milton, *Paradise Lost*

When they reach the rapprochement phase the infant gradually moves out of the state of total dependency. They begin to develop the awareness of being a separate individual with their own desires, urges, reactions and responses – their own 'Yes!' and their own 'No!' Experienced parents will smile as they recall the difficulties they encountered with their children during this phase (parents who are still in this phase with their children may be less inclined to see the funny side of the situation!) The young child wants freedom. They want to follow the impulses of the soul, feel their own power and ride the waves emanating from their Core Star instead of being carried passively down a road of their parent's choosing.

### Wounding

Problems in this stage occur when one or more of the adults in the child's life is unable to tolerate the uninhibited expression of the child. Instead, the adult aims to control the child by imposing their own ideas of what is best.

To return to *The Continuum Concept*, a remarkable aspect of Jean Liedloff's description of the Tauripan people is that they did absolutely nothing to interfere with the freedom of their children, even very young infants who had just learned to crawl. In their close-knit tribal groups, living in communion with Nature, the people allowed their children to explore their world (which included jungle creatures, rushing waterfalls, fire pits and sharp knives), without any intervention from the adults. My understanding of this is that this kind of tribal people must have a highly developed instinctual/intuitive connection to the flow of energy in Nature around them – natural Higher Sense Perception. Their whole survival is dependent on this intuitive awareness and so they trust that children are born with an innate sense that will guide them through the hazards of their jungle life.

Those kind of tribal societies are rapidly vanishing today and it seems that things like technology and urban dwelling are an inevitable, possibly an important, part of the future of the human race. Still, we can learn from the values of the tribal peoples and recognize the difficulties for children and families in civilized, urban societies. In this complex world, governed by reason rather than intuition, the newly autonomous child is quickly met with rules and interventions that can range from low-level nagging, through rigidly imposed discipline, to intimidation and outright physical abuse and domination. The extremes of dominant adults shouting and hitting little children are too often apparent on our city streets, yet in most tribal societies it is considered shocking for an adult to raise their voice to a child.

On a very unexceptional day-to-day basis, many good, kind parents fundamentally ignore the expressed wishes and the underlying nature of the child and impose their own world-view of what is safe and 'right'. This can be a very subtle process, I know, because, as a parent, I have done it! The control that an over-anxious parent imposes on their offspring is rooted in their own defences. The parent projects their unconscious fears onto a situation and their warnings, demands, instructions and reproofs impact on the child as an invasion of their delicate boundaries undermining their fragile certainty of self. To begin with, the child struggles to affirm their autonomy but the adults have all the power, so the will of the child is continually thwarted. If there has been earlier wounding in the Schizoid and/or Oral stages, the infant will already lack a healthy core of strength and resilience so that when demands are made of them they quickly collapse. In the Masochist stage, the feeling of inner weakness leaves them with no strength with which to withstand the onslaught of pressure from the adults.

The child in the Budding/Masochistic stage is tender, vulnerable and supersensitive to criticism, mockery, humiliation, impatience or repression. Over time, the effect of the constant thwarting of the child's free will begins to undermine their sense of self-worth. It leaves them doubting the validity of their own perceptions, uncertain in their choices, reluctant to bring forth their Essence for fear of attack and defeat. In place of self-confidence comes the notion of failure and the child develops shame, one of the most painful and restrictive of feelings. When a child knows shame they begin to doubt in the intrinsic goodness of their own Essence. They become increasingly inhibited by fear that the person that they truly are, even the beautiful light of their Core Star, is no good, unwanted or even dangerous.

**Defence**

The moment comes when the child caves in and submits to the demands of the adults. And if the experience of disempowerment is continually reinforced, the child's life develops into a shuffle between compliance and defiance as the child attempts to retain some vestige of personal power through resistance; sometimes extremely stubborn resistance. Over time, this dance becomes an ingrained pattern. With the discovery that their authentic self-expression is unwelcome, the child learns to control their spontaneous response to life and this process of inhibition becomes internalized in the form of resistance to their own creative flow. In adult life, spontaneous self-expression becomes a major struggle for the Masochist type as they battle with the frustration of their automatic compulsion to resist anything that risks revealing the self. The Masochist type will pursue tortuous, labyrinthine mental paths, overanalysing everything before they will make even quite simple requests or initiate anything that risks exposure.

When involved in acts of self-expression, whether it is composing a symphony or telling a joke, a person must believe that their creative efforts are valuable. Every creator, from a toddler with a crayon to a basket-weaver in an old people's home, is motivated by a highly unselfish form of self-love and delight in their own creativity, and it is painful when fear of criticism inhibits the freedom of self-expression.

## The Psychological View: Wounding and Defence in the Masochist Stage

It is one thing for an artist to be critical of their work in order to improve; it is quite another when a person fails to even pick up the paintbrush because of the anticipation of failure. So, the freedom to create, which is of central importance to the Budding /Masochist type, gets tangled up in self-doubt. This is the typical wounding of the Masochist defence, growing from the first moments of shame into stubborn resistance and on into creative paralysis.

In relationship, many Masochist types learn to avoid conflict by presenting a mask of compliance. However, buried behind the mask is the rage that was the child's original reaction to their feelings of disempowerment. Repressed fury turns into brooding resentment that is all the more frustrating because the anger is withheld in order to avoid the humiliation of further defeat. The Masochist type avoids confrontation but their negativity comes out in the form of passive aggression, spite and envy. Over time this generates a recurring pattern of defeat and humiliation in one form or another. The Masochist type may spend years lost in confused states of domination, bullying, manipulation, 'pleasing and appeasing', resistance, paralysis, victimization, extraordinary bad luck, intense frustration and shame.

### Recognizing the Masochist Defence

The physical body of the Masochist type is usually stocky and heavy. The weight they carry is a physical reflection, both of the need to pad and protect themselves from invasion and of the overloaded state of their inner world, congested with unexpressed feelings, unmanifest ideas and unfinished creations. They usually live in a degree of chaos, testament to the tortuous complications of their inner puzzling and inability to make their world clear.

There is something of the adolescent in the Masochist type, expressing their wounding through sullen withholding like a sulky teenager; a stubborn, morose, brooding figure ready to resist just about anything! Sometimes, their resentment leaks out in the form of whining that provokes others and leads to yet more experiences of attack and defeat, and they are often victims of bullying. Masochist types may protect themselves by becoming adept pleasers with uncanny abilities to sense atmosphere and mood. They may be intelligent and witty, sometimes cunning, highly perceptive with eyes that have hidden depths.

In their highest expression Masochist types are illustrious creators capable of intricate craft and skill. Beethoven, a classic Masochist type – stocky, heavy and notoriously sullen and difficult – was one of the greatest composers in history.

With a high degree of perception and understanding of human nature, Masochist types have great negotiation skills and, with their chameleon disguises and masks, they also shine in the world of theatre.

**Story – The Minotaur**

The classical story associated with the Masochist stage is the mythic tale of the Minotaur. The Minotaur was a monster with the body of a man and the head of a bull. He was the obscene offspring of Pasiphae, the queen of Knossos in Crete, who had mated with a bull. Pasiphae's husband King Minos had a labyrinth built in which to keep the Minotaur, hiding away his monstrosity and the shame of the queen. Every year, King Minos demanded that seven youths and seven maidens should be sent from Athens to be sacrificed by being thrust into the labyrinth and left to the Minotaur. Eventually, the hero Theseus came from Athens as a sacrificial victim. Ariadne, the daughter of King Minos, fell in love with Theseus and helped him to defeat the Minotaur. She gave Theseus a ball of twine which he unravelled as he descended deep into the heart of the labyrinth. There, Theseus battled with the Minotaur and killed him using a sword Ariadne had given him. Then he made his way back, following the twine through the dark labyrinth, found Ariadne and quickly sailed away in his ship.

The idea of a murdering monster living deep down in the dark heart of the labyrinth is an image of the repressed and concealed rage of the Masochist defence. In Voice Dialogue terms, when an aspect of self is disowned, denied a voice and cut off from the light of consciousness, it becomes demonic, i.e. hideously distorted in its expression. The image of the Minotaur symbolizes the Masochist type's belief that that they have something hidden in their Core which is hideously loathsome, shameful and dangerous. And the labyrinth itself is a key image of the Masochist wound representing the typical painstaking analysis and twisted and anxious over-thinking that is typical of the Masochist process.

In 2003 the director Ang Lee made *Hulk*, a film of the eponymous comic strip hero. This is a modern myth for the Masochist condition. Bruce Banner is a mild-mannered scientist, a pleaser and a bit of a doormat, whose girlfriend, Betty, has given up on him because he lacks emotional depth and passion. The parents and authority figures around Bruce Banner fit the Masochist model perfectly. When Bruce was a little child, his mad scientist father performed invasive experiments on him. One experiment went wrong and caused Bruce to mutate so that when he is finally triggered into anger he transforms into the raging, super-strong, green monster – The Hulk!

The Hulk has to deal with two distorted and hostile father figures. Betty's father is an army general, a cold, rigid workaholic who has lost touch with his humanity, while Bruce's father is insane, ruthless and manipulative. Both of them are out to control or destroy the loathly Hulk but all the might of the US Army cannot stop the Hulk once his rage is liberated. The only person who can reach him is Betty, whose gentle touch, love and acceptance return the Hulk to his human form. The Hulk embodies almost unlimited power but it is not available to Bruce because it is locked away in his disowned rage.

So, the Masochist type come to believe that what they have inside of them, their very Essence, is something monstrous, evil and loathsome. They fear that if they actually allowed themselves to free this caged and hidden thing it would turn out to be something very, very bad. Desperately ashamed and afraid of exposure, the Masochist type learns to conceal their thoughts and bottle up their emotions. But in this way they cut off from the spontaneous upwelling of their life force. Without the protection of their natural self-assertion and aggression, and unable to access their authentic voice, the Masochist type feels extremely vulnerable and seeks protection by learning to manipulate or to appear to comply. Because they do not feel powerful or lovable the Masochist approaches things indirectly, sabotaging their chances of success and developing a self-fulfilling belief in the inevitability of failure. Each new defeat contributes to the Masochist's profound fear that in their very Essence they are simply no good.

# 29

## The Budding or Masochist Stage

# The Healing Response to the Masochist Defence

For a healer or therapist the Masochist defence can be one of the hardest to work with. Very often the Masochist type is a 'nice' person who really dislikes conflict and it is extremely difficult for them to access their repressed feelings of anger. And the Masochist has learned to resist anything that comes towards them, even support offered with the best of intentions. So the Masochist type is notorious for their 'Yes, but…' response to helpful suggestions; a game that enables them to defeat a therapist, healer or anyone else who tries to support them.

Often the Masochist type seems to live by stumbling from one disaster to the next. It is as if they are at war with Fate and their hesitancy in following the life pulse continually backfires on them. The sheer force of their resistance, which looks like stubborn self-defeating defiance, comes from the view of a very hurt child and it needs great compassion and patience to reach this furious little being.

What the Masochist needs is space – a lot of it! A personal cathedral of space! From a very young age they have tried to hang onto some sense of personal power by resisting anything that feels like a demand. Because the Masochist is constantly tangled up in problems, people are always trying to sort them out by telling them what to do – but this is exactly how they became wounded in the first place. Even if a parent, a friend or a healer only wishes to help stop the suffering, the agenda they bring belongs to them and not to the Masochist individual.

The first thing the Masochist needs is unconditional acceptance of whoever they are, including whatever kind of mess they are in! In the story of the Hulk, the only person who can reach the monstrous Hulk is Betty, who does nothing to try to 'fix' him; she only reaches out to touch his face with the utmost gentleness and kindness. The keywords for healing the Masochist are acceptance and spaciousness.

On an energy level, the healer has to withdraw their own energy field and make it as small as they can so that the Masochist soul can fill the space with their own Essence without feeling that they are bumping up against someone else.

The Masochist specializes in problems that present insuperable difficulties and impossible choices. The healer/helper's job is actually very simple – they only have to remember that the choice is not theirs to make. The Masochist may be stuck with an impossible dilemma (and they usually are), but the only question is whether the healer has the patience and the compassion to simply remain present and sit with them in their dilemma while the Masochist soul finds their own, often highly unexpected, way out of the labyrinth. Healing for the Masochist is not to find the solution to any particular problem but to know that they are completely free to make their own choices, including their own mistakes.

Hopefully, into every Masochist life there comes a turning point. However complex the labyrinth, however dense the shadows, it is all just energy waiting to be returned to life. Over time, the individual learns to release the old stuck energy so that the field becomes ever more transparent and more and more of the light of the Core Star shines through. With the transformation of the old negativity a beautiful space of inner freedom opens up, bringing with it a sense of enormous creative potential.

# 30

## The Budding or Masochist Stage

## The Spiritual View: the Gifts of the Budding Stage

> *Hiding is a way of staying alive. Hiding is a way of holding ourselves until we are ready to come into the light. Even hiding the truth from ourselves can be a way to come to what we need in our own necessary time.*
> *Hiding is one of the brilliant and virtuoso practices of almost every part of the natural world: the protective quiet of an icy northern landscape, the held bud of a future summer rose, the snow-bound internal pulse of the hibernating bear.*
> David Whyte, *Consolations*

The Masochist defence emerges in the third stage of child development. If we refer back to the metaphor of the growth of a plant, the Masochist stage corresponds to the Budding phase when the plant first appears above the ground. The delicate shoots push up through the soil, seeking the light of the sun and, for the first time, feel the spaciousness of the sky. Just as the young plant is fragile but full of potential and ready to grow and flower, . Just like a shoot pushing up from the protective darkness of the earth, seeking nourishment from the radiant light of the sun, a child in the Budding phase needs to glow in the warmth of parental delight and family applause and feel free to experiment as they bring forth their first attempts at independence.

The life task in the Budding stage is for the young being to develop a strong sense of identity, self-awareness and personal power. This does not mean gaining power over others; it means taking responsibility for their own unique life force and bringing it forth into the world. This entails learning how to maintain healthy boundaries, feeling free to say 'No' as well as to say 'Yes'. Personal power is grounded in a healthy, balanced state of self-confidence that naturally supports asserting autonomy. Most of all, personal power allows us to access the raw life force that wells up in response to our longing to create.

Anything that a human being creates carries the distinctive stamp of their own Essence. This is what we love about art as we so clearly recognize the difference between the work of one artist and another. Nobody but Van Gogh could have painted his paintings, nobody but Beethoven could have composed his symphonies, nobody but Shakespeare could have written his plays. In a person's creative endeavours we clearly see the radiance of their unique Essence shining through. In the Budding stage the soul longs to allow their life force to flow out into their creations and see the beautiful light of their Essence reflected back to them.

### The Nature of the Incoming Soul

The soul in the Budding stage has come to explore the nature of their unique, individual identity. They want to be seen and their longing is to freely express their individuality through creativity. One step on from the Rooting stage, the learning for the Budding soul is to establish a clear sense of an individuated self within their boundaries. Who am I? Where does my energy field end and another person's begin? What do I want to express?

The Budding soul is not physically dominant individuals but with their sensitivity and intelligence they have highly developed communication skills. They bring the gift of humour, using wit to diffuse aggression and to laugh at the irony of the human predicament. They make excellent negotiators, using their communication skills, verbal dexterity and deep understanding of human nature to calm aggression and their 6th level intuition to sense the way through complex relationships.

The Budding soul has a questioning, analytical mind and their creations appear in their energy field and in the physical world as complex and intricate designs, demanding high levels of skill in their execution. When they have established a sense of their true power the Budding soul becomes the personification of creativity and freedom, sculpting matter and worldly events into beautiful forms and stories. The Budding soul is the ultimate alchemist, transforming lead into gold, illuminating the dense world of physical matter with the beautiful light of their unique Creative Essence.

### The Appearance of the Budding or Masochist Stage in the Human Energy Field

Unlike the Germination and Rooting souls, the Budding souls do not focus their energy upwards to the outer edges of the field, yearning for non-physical life. The Budding souls have incarnated specifically to engage with the experience of being human and they bring their focus down to the lower chakras of the field – meeting the challenges of the world of matter and human relationships. However, the Budding soul is highly sensitive, not far removed from the childlike receptivity of the Rooting stage, and they retain a strong focus on 6th chakra perception, giving them intuitive super sensitivity, alert to the shifting energies, thoughts and moods of people around them.

An area of great importance for the Budding soul is the 3rd chakra and the surrounding area of the field. The 3rd chakra is where we translate our creative impulse into plans for action in the physical world. This is a place of mental activity and the Budding soul uses a thoughtful, analytical approach when working out the best way to get a result. Most importantly, the 3rd chakra is where we locate the profound sense of our unique role in the unfolding of the universe, which is the source of our feelings of personal power. When there is wounding to a person's self-belief, when they doubt their ability to be effective, this undermines their self-esteem and they feel ashamed. Shame is the feeling most associated with Masochist wounding. Then the 3rd chakra becomes the home of the Inner Critic who finds fault with everything and paralyses the creative flow. For those with a strong Masochist Characterology, the Inner Critic can transform the 3rd chakra into a torture chamber where the mental gifts are turned on the self in a merciless analysis of failings, flaws, self-blame and shame.

The light of the Core Star wells up through the centre of a person's HEF from the infinite depths of the Universal Energy Field. When there is Masochist wounding the centre of the HEF becomes increasingly dense, occluded by the build-up of paralysed life force, and the light of the Core Star becomes shrouded by the withheld energy. Then large areas of the HEF lose transparency while depression and hopelessness cast a grey film over the entire field. In defence, the Masochist energy field has a resistant rubbery feel to it and may appear to be blotted with spongy, fungus-like masses where the creative impulse has turned to decay.

On the Haric level of the HEF, deep within the pelvic cradle is the Lower Tan T'ien, which appears as a red-gold centre of raw power, firmly anchored into the earth. The Lower Tan T'ien is our major source of grounding, power and presence. From the Lower Tan T'ien the Hara line connects upwards to the Middle Tan T'ien, which is situated in the upper chest. The Middle Tan T'ien appears as a beautiful soft light and it is where we hold our soul's longing for this life. The Middle Tan T'ien is closely related to a person's core Essence. And it is the raw life force welling up from the Lower Tan T'ien, flowing up the Hara line to the Middle Tan T'ien and out into the world, that provides the power and the energy that enables us to fulfil our life purpose.

When the area around the 3rd chakra is severely distorted by the blockages of the Masochist defence then, over time, the Hara line between the Lower and the Middle Tan T'ien gets pushed out of alignment or appears to splinter and break. When this happens the soul's creative impulse is unable to flow through and out into manifest form.

Eventually the Masochist soul will reclaim the liberation of their own spontaneous life impulse. They start figuring out how to get their needs met, learn how to assert themselves, hold firm boundaries and take responsibility for expressing with their own authentic voice. Then the old blockages start to dissolve and more and more life force is liberated into the creative expression of self that is the longing of the Budding/Masochist soul. When the Budding soul starts to heal and to release the Masochist blockages then they are able to free up the 3rd chakra, realign the Hara and open up the flow of their powerful, creative intention, which is their gift. When the Budding soul moves into their authentic creative flow then the HEF is lit up by a beautiful clear golden light, emerging as beautiful intricate patterns of light weaving through the HEF like golden threads.

# 31

# The Budding or Masochist Stage

## The Astrological View: the Astrology of the Budding or Masochist Type

The two planets associated with the Budding/Masochist phase are the Sun and Pluto. These are two very different, opposing energies. The Sun represents consciousness, creativity, warmth, radiance and the light of life. Pluto represents the dark of the unconscious, the dream world, the instincts of the body, the cycles of sexuality, procreation, birth and death.

The Sun brings feelings of joy in life, self-esteem, entitlement and creativity as we shine our unique individual light out into the world. Pluto connects us with the instinctual power of the body and the raw, unformed energy of the life force. As Uranus takes us out to the distant stars, Pluto takes us within to the unborn potential of the black velvety void. In the HEF, the energy of the Sun expands upwards and outwards while the energy of Pluto contracts inwards and downwards.

The gift of Pluto gives us access to the power and the wisdom of the body but we tend to value the rational heroism of the Sun and devalue the instinctual wisdom of Pluto. One way of looking at the problem of the child in the Masochist stage is that the rational Solar thinking of the parents continually overrides the instinctive Plutonian awareness of the child. It is hard to give voice, we barely even have the language to speak of Pluto's sacred knowledge, yet it is vitally important for both principles to find expression.

# 32

# The Budding or Masochist Stage
## The Sun, Ruler of Leo, When Afflicted

The Sun is the ruler of the fiery sign of Leo. The brooding, defeated, withholding Masochist type could not be further from the extrovert self-confidence of someone with the Sun in fiery Aries, Leo or Sagittarius. So in the horoscope of the Masochist type we will find challenges or "afflictions" to the Solar energy. Yet it is that uninhibited freedom of self-expression and certainty of personal power which is the Masochist longing; this is what they seek. It may be repressed but it is the Solar principle that the Budding/Masochist soul has come to develop in this life.

**Planetary Archetype – Essence**

Like the Sun in the solar system, the Sun is central to the dance of the planets in the chart. The placement of the Sun signifies the most important area of growth on the path that this person takes in life. The Sun is the symbol of our conscious mind; it is that which we clearly see and know in the light of day – our rational understanding. It represents the innate urge to create and it represents our faith in life supported by our self-love, self-belief and self-esteem. In itself, power is not an issue for the Sun; it simply is the symbol of the creative power at the heart of a person's life. But the zodiac signs and the planets found aspecting the Sun will tell us about the ease (or otherwise) of a person's access to their personal power and the freedom (or otherwise) with which they express their individuality.

The Sun is very closely related to the sense of Self. However, I think it is worth repeating that the Sun does not represent the totality of individual self or Essence. Our Essence comes from the Core Star, beyond the physical plane, and it is much, much greater than our human personality. The Core Star is the source of everything that we are and it is the light of the Core Star that illuminates the kaleidoscope of energies created by the planets in the HEF.

The nature of the Solar principle first comes to a child through their perception of their own father. Just as the Moon represents our perception of mother, including the Divine Mother, the Solar principle is a continuum which extends from our relationship with our personal father to the primal principle of the Masculine and our images around 'God the Father'. In the I Ching, the first of the sixty-four hexagrams is called Ch'ien, The Creative, and this is the archetype of the Sun.

> *Great indeed is the generating power of the Creative;*
> *All beings owe their beginning to it.*
> *This power permeates all Heaven.*
> Richard Wilhelm Translation, *I Ching* 1

**Wound**

In a perfect world the creative process would be an effortless flow from inspiration to manifestation. But when the shadows of fear and self-doubt block the light of the Sun then the natural flow from desire to accomplishment falters and becomes distorted.

The Sun needs to shine and it is painful for a person when they feel that their spontaneous expression of self is not seen or not welcome. A child loses faith in their budding sense of self when they find that the adults around them criticize their free expression and reject or try to control their creative endeavours. These difficulties will show up in the chart as aspects to the Sun from any of the outer planets but particularly from Pluto or Saturn. And when we are talking about the Sun, they will be experienced predominantly in the child's relationship with the father and other adults carrying the Masculine energy. (We will see later that Masochist wounding is also indicated in relationship with the mother when Pluto and other difficult planets are in aspect to the Moon.)

## Story – Perseus and the Gorgon

The Solar principle runs through all our myths, legends and fairy tales because developing and expanding the light of consciousness is the fundamental nature of human life. It is the universal story of every hero or heroine who sets off on a quest, meets adversity and sticks with it until the task is complete and they defeat the dragon or spin the flax into gold, return with the boon, marry the prince or princess and live happily ever after. This is a collective metaphor for the profound sense of purpose that is at the heart of every life, the feeling that we have come here for a reason with an inexpressible longing for fulfilment. The heroic urge inspires us to create our own unique life story, building and rebuilding our sense of self – this is the domain of the Sun where we shine the God-given light of our essence out into our beautiful and terrible world.

The Greek myth of Perseus and the Gorgon illustrates the Masochist issue: the Solar hero battling with an adversary who tries to destroy life through paralysis. King Acrisius of Argos was told by the oracle that his daughter, Danae, would have a son who would kill him. Trying to avoid his fate, Acrisius had Danae locked up in a bronze chamber to prevent her conceiving a child. However, when Zeus descended into the chamber in the form of a shower of gold, Danae became pregnant and gave birth to Perseus. Fearful for his life, Acrisius had Danae and Perseus placed in a wooden chest and cast out to sea, thinking that that would be the last of them. But the mother and child survived, washed up on the shores of the island of Seriphos where they were taken in by a fisherman called Dictys.

Perseus grew up to be a fine young man but Polydectes, the king of the island, fell in love with Danae and wanted to get rid of Perseus. Polydectes invited Perseus to a banquet and then publicly shamed him for, unlike all the other guests, Perseus arrived without a gift. Perseus promised that he would bring the king any gift he would name. Polydectes immediately demanded that Perseus bring him the head of Medusa, one of three monstrous sisters, the Gorgons. Anyone who looked into the dreadful faces of the Gorgons was instantly turned to stone and Polydectes had no doubt that Perseus would fail.

The Gorgons were hideous creatures whose bodies were covered in scales; they had talons like the Furies and hair that was a mane of venomous serpents. Two of the Gorgons were immortal and could not be slain but Medusa was mortal. Some versions of the myth say that Medusa was once a very beautiful woman. She had been raped by Poseidon in the sacred temple of Pallas Athena and it was Athena who had cursed her with her terrible form and the fate that anyone who looked upon her face would turn to stone. No mortal man could combat the Gorgons but Perseus was helped by the Olympian gods. Mercury gave him a sword of adamantine and lent him his winged sandals and Pluto lent him his helmet of invisibility. Most of all, he was helped and guided by Pallas Athene, who gave him her silver shield with a surface as smooth and fine as a mirror.

First Perseus flew beyond the edge of the world to the immortal realms where he tricked the three Fates into telling him how to find the lair of the Gorgons. Following their instructions he flew far to the north in the direction of night, until he came to the cold dark land of the Hyperboreans where the Sun only rose once a year. As Perseus walked through the silent land he saw the many frozen statues of those who had gone before him and had been turned to stone. At last he came to the cave of the Gorgons. Perseus drew his sword, strapped the shield to his arm, placed the helmet of invisibility on his head and vanished from sight. Then he advanced into the cave with his eyes fixed only on the image mirrored in the shield. Never once did he glance directly at his surroundings but soon in the reflection he saw the face of the sleeping Gorgon. As he hesitated, the baleful eyes of Medusa opened and the slithering snakes of her hair started up, hissing and spitting, sensing the presence of the invisible hero.

Swiftly Perseus brought down his sword, beheading Medusa in one mighty stroke. Still looking only in the mirror he seized the head and thrust it into a goatskin bag that Minerva had given him.

As he turned to leave a wondrous sight met his eyes, for from the severed neck of the cadaver emerged the magical winged horse Pegasus, who leaped away and soared up into the skies. Perseus' heart lifted at the sight of the beautiful creature but then he heard terrible shrieking as the two other Gorgons discovered the mutilated corpse of their sister. He rose into the air and fled under his helmet of invisibility, pursued by the vengeful Gorgons.

Perseus made his escape and flew back to Seriphos. On the way he rescued the beautiful princess Andromeda from a sea monster and took her back with him as his bride. On his return Perseus strode into the court of the king and pulled out the head of Medusa, thereby turning Polydectes to stone. Danae and Dictys, the fisherman who had first sheltered Perseus, now became the rulers of Seriphos.

Meanwhile, in Argos, King Acrisius had no idea that Danae and Perseus had survived. One day Perseus went to Argos to compete in some games. At the tournament Acrisius sat with the elders, unaware that the young man who came forward to throw the discus was his grandson. As Perseus ran up to make his throw, his foot slipped on the grass and the heavy silver discus flew from his grasp. It struck Acrisius on the head, killing him instantly and so, at last, the Oracle was fulfilled.

(In this myth, the destructive force comes from a representation of the feminine but in other stories the destructive force is masculine, e.g. in the simple tale of Jack and the Beanstalk it is a devouring, man-eating giant that Jack has to overcome.)

Perseus represents the young Solar consciousness struggling to find his place in the world. Before he can come into his rightful inheritance he must encounter the supernatural monsters that dwell in shadow – the frozen conglomerates of despair lodged in the unconscious. If Perseus had identified only with rational thinking nothing would have changed. But Perseus has the capacity to open to the non-rational, numinous world of the gods. Jupiter, his father, sends magical gifts and the three Fates guide him to meet his destiny. Minerva (or Pallas Athena), the goddess of wisdom, represents the feminine aspect of the Solar principle. She shows Perseus that the dread inhabitants of the shadow can be transformed in the mirror world that represents the power of reflection – our capacity to Witness.

The capacity to Witness, to simply observe without judgement, is of vital importance in psychotherapy and healing. The shield of Minerva is the symbol of the Witness – our ability to put a distance between ourselves and our conflict and to look compassionately but dispassionately at both sides and see the dilemma. When we enter a state of Witnessing we open a doorway to guidance from a greater aspect of self. Like Perseus receiving the gifts from the gods, in the Witness state we are able to gain understanding and awareness from a Universal Intelligence that shows the way to retrieve the life force that has become frozen. When Perseus destroyed Medusa, magical Pegasus was liberated from the accumulation of trapped suffering and hatred that she the Gorgon had become.

Perseus' story speaks of the journey through Masochist wounding because his adversary is a power that paralyses the life force. The face of Medusa is associated with a negative aspect of the mother – an archetypal representation of feminine outrage and fury. Very often the tender Budding child lives with this terrifying face hidden in the heart of the family and the life force gets turned to stone and becomes a paralysing weight on the energy field.

The noble story of Perseus is *not* the typical life path of the Masochist type! A person stuck in the Masochist defence is not heroic – they are constantly defeated, know very little of triumph and they either try to wriggle out of a fight or run away and hide. If Minerva handed them the Sword of Truth they would drop it like a hot potato! Instead of standing up for themselves and fighting the good fight, they please and appease but they hold grudges for years and their resentment comes out in the form of spite, passive aggression and manipulation. They lack integrity and lie when they should tell the truth, and when they experiment with telling the truth it gets them into trouble. They weakly submit to domination and bullying when they are in the right and they stubbornly cling to untenable positions when they are wrong. I wonder if you feel a tiny sense of relief when you read this? The Masochists are not noble archetypes, they are very messy and they are human!

The path of the Sun is at the heart of every life but for the Masochist there are many twists and turns in the labyrinth, years of hiding, inertia and resignation before something enables them to withdraw their rabbit's gaze from the face of Medusa. Hopefully, the day comes when they pick up Minerva's shield and gaze into the reflection so that they can, at last, Witness the image that first terrorized them, without succumbing to its paralysis.

## In the Human Energy Field

Of all the planets, the light of Sun is the closest to that of the Core Star and when the energy of the Sun is strong then it fills the HEF with a warm, golden light radiating upwards and outwards from the centre of the body. The sign of the zodiac which the Sun occupies creates a specific ambience in the HEF. When the Sun is in its own sign of Leo it radiates a hot gold, like the August sun, sometimes overwhelmingly powerful. When the Sun is in the sign of Aries it is said to be in its 'exaltation' (meaning the sign where the Sun is most easily able to be expressed) then the Solar light is charged with a fiery red glow that can swiftly burst forth into the ferocious burning heat of the warrior. When the Sun is in its 'detriment', in February's sign of Aquarius (i.e. opposite to the sign of Leo which is ruled by the Sun), then the Solar light is diffuse, pale and remote like the sun in winter.

We have seen that, for the Germination/Schizoid and Rooting/Oral souls, the light in the HEF is more transparent, drawn upwards towards the high vibrations of the outer levels of the field. With the Budding/Masochist soul the HEF is denser and has a slower vibration. The field does not have the cosmic brilliance of the earlier stages but shines with a softer, warmer glow.

When a person is running the Masochist defence the energy contracts away from any sense of invasion or pressure and the HEF takes on resistance with a spongy, rubbery feeling. Within the HEF there are areas of tangled dark energy obscuring the light of the Core Star – the Masochist labyrinth of blocked energy.

However, when the individual connects to the support of their alignment on the Haric level they are able to bring through the gifts of the Budding soul. Their HEF expands and becomes immensely spacious, their energy quietly radiates outwards from an inner core of stillness and the Solar light streams effortlessly through the emptiness. The Masochist labyrinth of distortion is transformed into beautiful, intricate golden patterns that are characteristic and the gift of the Budding soul.

## The Sun in Aspect to the Ascendant, the Planets and in the Houses

The Sun in aspect to the Ascendant is not an indication of Masochist wounding but is associated with the Flowering/Psychopathic type. However, when the Sun is above the Ascendant in the 12th house this is a prime indication of Masochist wounding.

### The Sun in the 12th House

The 12th house is the most difficult placement for the Sun. Often, the Sun in the 12th is an indication that the glory and radiance of the Solar light has been suppressed and lost somewhere down the ancestral line. In some way the family is not able to welcome and celebrate the spontaneous creative self-expression of this child. For example, this can happen in a very rigid conformist family, a very religious family or in a very impoverished family where there is no time or money for Solar playtime. Growing up in such an atmosphere, this individual will never feel that they are special, worthwhile and important. People with the Sun in the 12th house feel that they were not 'seen' in childhood. In keeping with the Masochist template, this child will end up with a confused sense of identity, self-doubt and uncertainty even about their right to exist.

The affairs of the 12th house are closer to the depths of Pluto's domain than to the Solar light of everyday, worldly activity. The 12th house is the house of the unconscious and our connection to the non-physical world. When the Sun falls in this house the Solar principle expresses in ways that range between extreme Masochist withholding and the refined awareness of one who brings the light of consciousness into the unseen worlds. The Solar energy of a person with the Sun in the 12th connects us to the vast numinous world of Spirit. Planets in the 12th house are paradoxical in that, although the individual finds it hard to access the energy in their personal life, they represents something about a person's Essence that is their gift to the collective. Though they may struggle all their lives with self-doubt, the person with the Sun in the 12th brings a larger-than-life Solar radiance into the world which is inspiring to others, often in the fields of spirituality and healing.

### The Sun in the 4th and 8th Houses

Another indication of the Budding/Masochist energy is when the Sun falls in the 4th or 8th house. The focus of both these houses turns inward – the 4th to the inner life of the family and the 8th to the private world of intimate relationships.

Planets in the 4th house, at the nadir of the chart, are difficult to bring into conscious awareness (like a milder version of planets in the 12th house). When the Sun is in the 4th house a person may shine their Solar light within the security of the family but feel more introverted, vulnerable and cautious out in the world. Similarly when the Sun is in the 8th house the focus of attention is internal and the nature of communication deeply sensitive so that in larger groups the person may suffer from Masochist wounding and withholding. The 8th house is about intimacy and sexual relationship so the movement of energy is inward towards the feelings and sensations stirred up in the depths of the relationship and we find that planets in the 8th house struggle to find spontaneous expression away from the intimacy and sensitivity of deep contact.

### The Sun in Aspect to Saturn, Pluto and Chiron

In itself the Sun symbolizes personal power, confidence and spontaneity – the exact opposite of Masochist wounding. The Masochist wound is only indicated when the Sun is involved with difficult planets which interfere with its natural expression. When Pluto, Saturn or Chiron are found in aspect to the Sun this is a sign of the Masochist wound.

### Pluto in Aspect to the Sun

Pluto in aspect to the Sun is a sign of power issues associated with the father. When there is Masochist wounding, the father may have been extremely overpowering, threatening, domineering or abusive. He may also have been more covertly manipulative but the child still feels invaded and controlled so that freedom and self-expression are replaced by power struggles and resistance. In its positive expression Pluto in aspect to the Sun may indicate a very deep committed relationship with the father and it is a sign of tremendous personal power tempered by compassionate understanding of human flaws. Though Pluto is one of the most difficult of all the planets, in its Essence it seeks change, transformation and healing and many healers and psychotherapists will have a Sun-Pluto aspect.

### Saturn in Aspect to the Sun

A negative Saturn operates through criticism, rigid discipline and control. An aspect between Saturn and the Sun indicates that, in childhood, the radiance and spontaneity of the Sun has been undermined by the expectation that the child must adhere to some kind of family or tribal code of behaviour. These rules can be blatant or subtle but the child lives with a constant fear of judgement and criticism, which can lead to deeply ingrained feelings of failure and shame – of not being 'good enough' for the father. Though there is usually some difficulty, a Sun-Saturn aspect is not as painful as a Moon-Saturn aspect; the Sun has more resilience in the face of Saturn's judgements. The positive expression of Saturn aspecting the Sun is a very loyal and reliable father and an individual with the capacity to manifest results as the creative impulse is supported by healthy discipline, stamina, structure and purpose.

### Chiron in Aspect to the Sun

A Sun-Chiron aspect indicates the presence of something painful in the relationship with the father. In the worst cases it can indicate serious issues like abuse or violence from the father. It may also indicate a father who had some kind of illness or disability that impacted the relationship with the child. Whatever the cause, the child's self-confidence is undermined and at worst they may be permanently damaged. As always, these aspects can open the door to wisdom, tolerance and compassion – the ability to surrender to whatever is arising and remain open-hearted.

The quest for the bright, heroic, creative freedom of the Solar principle is the story of the Budding/Masochist soul. Much as they may try to resist the pressure to take up the heroic quest, it is the central issue of the Budding life to discover who they really are, follow their own free choice and find the courage and power that liberates them to shine their Solar light.

# 33

## The Budding or Masochist Stage
## **Pluto, Ruler of Scorpio**

> *Pluto draws things in and down to his hidden realm, and is in some ways an image of the introversion of libido or psychic energy.*
>
> Liz Greene, *The Astrology of Fate*

Pluto is the ruler of Scorpio, traditionally the darkest of the signs. Pluto symbolizes raw power. It is associated with all processes of transformation, including the cycle of pregnancy, birth and death, images arising from the realm of the unconscious and all issues around power. Pluto was discovered, i.e. emerged into the collective consciousness, in 1930, synchronous with the splitting of the atom, the rise of Nazism and the flowering of psychotherapy. Pluto is the planet at the core of the Budding/Masochist phase.

In the solar system, tiny frozen Pluto is the most remote of all the planets. It is so far away that, if you could stand on the surface of Pluto, the Sun would only look like a very big star. Pluto is a 'trans-Neptunian object', a planetoid from the Kuiper Belt, which is an area of debris at the outer edge of the solar system held in the gravitational field of the Sun. If we regard the solar system as a macrocosm of human consciousness then the Kuiper Belt is like the first edge of the unconscious, a repository of karma and disowned aspects of the self hovering on the fringes of consciousness. The work of the newly discovered planetoids, such as Pluto and Chiron, is to show us the pathways into issues waiting to be brought into the light of consciousness.

## Planetary Archetype – Essence

In mythology Pluto is the fearful Lord of the Dead, the god of the Underworld. Pluto's domain is hidden deep under the ground and never sees the light of the Sun. Psychologically, the Underworld represents the unconscious and the name Pluto means 'riches', so this realm contains hidden treasure. Whenever he appeared in the upper world Pluto wore a helmet of invisibility because Pluto rules aspects of the self that are not eager to be exposed. Pluto does not appear in the light of the rational mind but comes to us in dreams, through gut reactions, through the instinctive wisdom of the body.

For an animal living in the wild, Pluto, in the form of death, waits around every corner; but it is also Pluto, in the form of the instinctive reactions of the body, that will save a life. When we are in touch with Pluto we are aware of the presence of death but this helps us feel the power of the life force more acutely.

In Carlos Castaneda's book, *Journey to Ixtlan*, the sorcerer Don Juan says:

> *A warrior knows that his death is waiting, and the act he is performing now may well be his last on earth.*

Pluto rules the miraculous functioning of all the cells and the systems of the body. In particular, Pluto and the sign of Scorpio are associated with sexuality, procreation, pregnancy and birth. Pluto's realm is the domain of deep sexual union and the heat of intense animal desire and passion. In Pluto's instinctual animal depths comes the moment when two separate individuals unite in passion as the Masculine penetrates and the Feminine receives. From this sacred union new life is created and our whole world is born from this. In that moment of conception Pluto is the raw energy that initiates the processes of cell division, the spark that animates the biological cells. While the Solar principle initiates creativity from the light of consciousness and the mind, Pluto's raw power arises from unconscious processes in the body. The Sun acts through reason; Pluto acts through instinct. The mind is illuminated by the light of the Sun but the power of Pluto arises in the unknowable depths of the body.

The unconscious is the repository of many aspects of our being that we fear and repress. In Greek mythology five rivers run through the Underworld: the River Styx (meaning 'hatred'), the River Acheron (meaning 'sorrow'), the River Cocytus (meaning 'lamentation'), the River Phlegethon (meaning 'fire') and the River Lethe (meaning 'oblivion'). The souls of the dead were required to drink from the waters of Lethe in order to forget their earthly life and to remain unconscious. In our everyday lives we do not talk about things like hatred and lamentation and we are ashamed when our vulnerability and dark feelings are exposed. In order to gain access to Pluto's realm we must travel, like Perseus, beyond the comfortable routines of our everyday life and sink down into a subterranean world that lies beneath our habitual level of consciousness. There is nothing trivial in this descent and this is no place for superficial judgements or delusions. But it is in those moments, when we really know the raw truth of our mortality and powerlessness in the face of birth and death, that we learn both to surrender to a greater power and to take responsibility for the creative power that is ours.

In the HEF, the Lower Tan T'ien represents the root source of the life force. Meditators and practitioners of martial arts learn to shift their attention away from the chatter of the mind, focus on the breath and the rhythms of the body and sink their consciousness down into the Lower Tan T'ien within the pelvic cradle. The Lower Tan T'ien is Pluto's home. When a person's actions arise from this centre they are capable of extraordinary feats. When our words arise from the Tan T'ien we speak with a power and a truth that is unknown to the Little Mind. When our intention arises from the Lower Tan T'ien we are unstoppable.

### Wound

Ideally, human life might be conducted as a dance between the Solar light of the mind and the Plutonian instincts of the body. But humankind usually worships the light of the Sun and fears the power of Pluto. We go happily towards the shining Sun but we run from dark Pluto. And so Pluto always evokes difficulty and suffering and, as with Chiron, our first meeting with Pluto is likely to come through wounding. Pluto is notoriously one of the most difficult planets in the horoscope. The Sun radiates warmth and light in whatever house it occupies, but Pluto's house feels dark and fearful, a place where we are required, however unwillingly, to journey into the Underworld. Wherever Pluto is placed in the chart indicates an area of life in which we may repeatedly encounter challenges to our sense of personal power. Pluto is at the heart of the Masochist defence. If a child is too much dominated and controlled then the instinctual impulse arising from Pluto's realm gets blocked, festers and becomes unhealthy. In Voice Dialogue we recognize that disowned aspects of the self that are left for too long in the darkness become distorted and we refer to them as 'demonic' energies. The monsters of mythology – the Gorgons, the Minotaurs and the Furies – are the images of that paralysed and imprisoned life force. For the Masochist it is impotent fury that lies buried under the weight of years of pleasing and appeasing.

For all of us, it is a difficult labyrinthine path to unravel our tangled beliefs and images around what might be our authentic nature. But, often, the things that we reject, repress and deem unacceptable in ourselves contain treasure that remains lost to us all the while we deny them. We all have aspects of ourselves that make us feel desperately ashamed but these are part of our life force and they cannot be eradicated, only transformed, and this is the work of personal growth, psychotherapy and healing. The healing of Pluto's distortions comes when, like Perseus, we bring the light of Solar consciousness into the shadows of the Underworld. Here we find old forgotten wounds and memories that have held us back for years. When these issues are allowed to emerge into consciousness, the whole HEF shifts. When we retrieve any previously denied aspect of self, a wave of liberated life force surges through, like Pegasus rising from Medusa's corpse, invigorating our whole energy field. Then we can start to re-connect to the warmth of the Sun that restores our faith that we are worthy and deserving of love and reminds us that we have come to this life with the sacred task of expressing our own unique Essence in a way that no one else in the universe can do.

**Story – Ereshkigal and Inanna**

One of the most important stories associated with the feminine deities of the Underworld – and one of the most psychologically meaningful stories for the Masochist – is the ancient Sumerian myth of Ereshkigal and Inanna.

Ereshkigal and Inanna were sister goddesses. Inanna, Queen of Heaven, was a Solar deity, beautiful and charming, known as 'the Lady of the Sky'. She had a much happier life than Ereshkigal who was Queen of the Underworld, 'Lady of the Great Place Below'. Ereshkigal had been abducted, ravished and abandoned in the Underworld, left alone with the souls of the dead. Ereshkigal could never again ascend to the heavens and she was utterly miserable.

One day Inanna decided to visit her sister down in the Underworld. It was guarded by seven gates and at each of the gates Innana was required to strip off an item of clothing. By the time she came in front of Ereshkigal's throne Innana was completely naked. Ereshkigal was a seething mass of outrage, bitterness and fury and the sight of her more fortunate sister acted as a fan to the flames. She immediately killed Inanna and had her body hung up on a meat hook and left to rot.

Before she left for the Underworld, Inanna had given a message to her servant, Ninshubur, instructing her to let the gods know where she was if she did not return safely. When Innana did not return, Ninshubur went to the gods and told them what had happened. The gods were dismayed but not at all eager to confront Ereshkigal. However, Enki, the god of magic (an earlier version of Mercury), decided to help. Enki took the humble dirt from beneath his fingernails, fashioned it into two little figures, called 'the Mourners', and breathed life into them. The Mourners had no real identity of their own; they had no independent power of speech but could only repeat whatever another person said to them. Enki sent the Mourners down into the Underworld to parlay. When the Mourners met Ereshkigal she proceeded to bewail her terrible fate, listing all her misfortunes and pain. The Mourners repeated every word, obediently reflecting her sad situation without any kind of judgement. Ereshkigal was so pleased to feel that someone had finally listened to her that her mood softened and she allowed Inanna to be brought back to life and return to the heavens.

This story is another illustration of Masochist wounding. Ereshkigal has been violated, abused and rejected. She has no access to the light of the heavens but lives out her days in darkness amongst the souls of the dead. Here we see the image of one who has experienced great pain and suffering but still goes unheard. Ereshkigal is denied access to the upper world – to the light of consciousness – and her emotions have turned into a mass of resentment, bitterness and vengefulness. Ereshkigal represents the unvoiced outrage that turns to spite in the oppressed heart of the Masochist. Few people willingly undertake the journey to this realm of suffering and self-pity. When Pluto becomes active in the chart and pushes us down the descent to the Underworld, like Inanna losing her clothing we are stripped of everything that belongs to the Solar world. We must arrive naked and defenceless like Innana, and we must listen without judgement like the Mourners when we come into the presence of our abandoned, impotent fury.

Inanna is an earlier version of Venus, the feminine representative of the Solar principle. She has lived a life in the sun and has no experience of Ereskigal's pain, but she is a lesser being because of her ignorance. Before her journey to the depths, charming Inanna is associated with the mask of the 'pleaser'. When she returns to the upper world the first thing Inanna does is dispose of her unsupportive husband who failed to come to her rescue when she was trapped. She has given up on 'pleasing' and become a more powerful being.

For a person with a strong Masochist defence, nothing ever really works out for them as long as they are still running from Ereshkigal. The Solar energy of Inanna will remain weak and ineffectual until Ereshkigal is given a place in consciousness.

In the life of the Budding/Masochist soul there may be repeated episodes of domination, violation and defeat and it is notoriously one of the most difficult of the Character defences to heal. There may be many failed attempts to confront the Gorgon and unfinished journeys to the Underworld before the Masochist individual is able to step out from behind their chameleon disguises and begin to exchange the inner turmoil of frustration and resentment for stillness, depth and power.

### In the Human Energy Field

In the HEF a negative or unconscious Pluto creates darkness with a density that obscures the translucence of the aura and feels extremely threatening and unyielding. In the journey of consciousness the archetype of Pluto leads us into the deep stillness of the level of the Hara and the Lower Tan T'ien, the root of the life force.

Radiating out from the Lower Tan T'ien, the energy of Pluto appears as a glow of weighty, red-gold light like the heart of a volcano. When a person is aligned with the positive expression of Pluto their field opens out into vast spaciousness with a core of profound stillness and willingness to embrace all of life without judgement. Energy wells up from the Tan T'ien and flows effortlessly into the Haric level, the level of Intention, and the HEF feels immensely strong and safe. This state of presence is the gift of Pluto. It gives us the strength to live through times of adversity with the capacity to accept whatever life presents us with and it is also the power that fuels our personal creative drive and enables us to fulfil our longing and purpose.

### Pluto in Aspect to the Ascendant, the Moon and the Sun

There's no doubt about it, the energy of Pluto is dark. It takes us away from the light of consciousness into the instinctual realms and the raw power of the life force. Pluto represents issues of power and control but it is also one of the planets most associated with healing and transformation. When Pluto is in aspect to the Ascendant, Sun or Moon, the depth and power of Pluto will be a tangible presence in a person's HEF. Pluto brings the possibility of Masochist wounding in childhood as well as the gifts of the Budding stage coming through one of the parents or as a notable presence in the family dynamics. (For astrologers, the hard aspects – squares, conjunctions, oppositions and inconjuncts – are more likely to indicate wounding and the softer aspects – trines, sextiles and quintiles – are more likely to indicate the gifts of the Budding soul.)

### Pluto in Aspect to the Ascendant

When Pluto is in aspect to the Ascendant, issues concerning power, depression, danger, death and transformation will have been some kind of presence around the birth and/or early days in the life of the child. When Pluto is found close to the Ascendant (which is called a conjunction), it often indicates that there was some threat of death during the gestation period (when Pluto is in the 12th house), at the time of birth (Pluto near the Ascendant) or in the early days of life (Pluto in the 1st house). For people who have this aspect, the power of Pluto can be felt as a palpable force in the way they express their identity and their sense of self.

### Pluto in the 12th House

This is a sign of a dark energy lodged in the unconscious, something from Pluto's realm that has been handed down through the ancestral line. There may be a history of violent power struggles or feminine outrage or any experiences of invasion, persecution and defeat that have left a long shadow on the ancestral inheritance. Pluto in the 12th is often seen when there was some threat of death to the foetus during pregnancy, sometimes even a question about terminating the pregnancy.

### Pluto in the 1st House

Similarly, Pluto in the 1st house is often a sign of something gloomy or dangerous hanging in the air in the child's early days – often an invasive or depressed parent. Whatever it is, this threat or shadow makes a heavy imprint on the baby's fluid and open energy field.

Planets and the sign on the Ascendant and in the 1st house give a picture of a person's sense of identity and Pluto's presence here often signals some form of oppression. The individual may communicate with a negative expression of Pluto: so guarded as to be inscrutable, covertly manipulative, resentful, spiteful, stubborn or ruthlessly domineering.

The positive expression of Pluto is a person with great understanding of human nature, and Pluto in these placements will be found in the charts of psychotherapists and healers or practitioners of martial arts and leaders in any field requiring the ability to take responsibility for great power. When the expression of Pluto is clear these individuals have a magnetic presence, radiating a tangible sense of strength and power.

Individuals with Pluto in aspect to the Ascendant or in the 12th or 1st house may have more than one run-in with death; however, they have tremendous resources of stamina, endurance and courage. They may also experience several cycles of death and rebirth in their sense of identity, and their lives demonstrate the alchemy of transformation.

## Pluto in Aspect to the Moon

When Pluto is in aspect to the Moon, or when the Moon is in Scorpio, this often indicates wounding at a deep level because the Moon represents the early years when our preverbal experience is emotionally intense and the baby's energy field is open and unshielded. When there has been wounding in this stage, the pain of a Moon-Pluto aspect can congeal into a formless, instinctive dread of helplessness – a powerful urge to hide our vulnerability. People with Pluto aspects to the Sun, Moon or Mercury, or an emphasis on Scorpio, can be the most heavily controlled and defended individuals. They have a partially conscious dread that an undisguised, spontaneous response will lead to the exposure of their vulnerability and a repeat experience of invasion, defeat and humiliation.

Historically, Pluto is referred to as a male god and has a strong association with martial arts and the archetype of the warrior. However, Pluto is the ruler of Scorpio, which is a feminine sign. So, it could also be said that the energy that Pluto represents is feminine in Essence as it has to do with the instincts of the body and the emotions. This is confusing but, perhaps, all the archetypes defy rigid categorization and have both a masculine and feminine expression.

In *The Power of Now*, Eckhart Tolle describes what he calls 'the collective female pain-body':

> *The accumulated pain suffered by women through male subjugation of the female over thousands of years.*

We can recognize the female pain-body in the image of Plutonian figures like Ereshkigal and Medusa – burning with the fury of a woman who has been violated. With the idea of reincarnation, we have all had lives as both men and women and so we all share the imprint of these memories (whether consciously or not), so a Moon-Pluto aspect is a prime indication of the presence of the collective female pain-body (in both women and men). With the negative expression of a Moon-Pluto aspect the mother carries the energy of the Medusa – the fearful, paralysing face of feminine outrage. Often, within the family, the mother is entangled in depression and despair emanating from her experience of violation or disempowerment. A woman with these issues may distort into domineering or manipulative control of the family or she may sink into depression and be unavailable to the family.

The positive expression of a Moon-Pluto aspect is a mother who is deeply rooted in her true power with access to the instinctual wisdom of her body. This placement could signify a mother with a fierce commitment to her family and who fosters deep loving relationships; a tower of strength capable of holding the family together in the face of adversity. A Moon-Pluto aspect could be a mother who is a powerful figure out in the world or she could be a quietly unseen alchemist and healer, a woman with authentic understanding and acceptance of human nature and the ability to ride the waves of whichever changes life brings.

### Pluto in Aspect to the Sun

With the wounded expression of Pluto in aspect to the Sun there is a shadow cast over the face of the Solar light. We have already seen that this is a prime indicator of Masochist wounding. A Sun-Pluto aspect indicates some kind of Plutonian energy found in the father, which spills out as a heaviness or an unnamed threat that hangs in the ether of the family. This is often something dark, such as depression, or it can be an excessive need for control and domination, and it can indicate issues around sexuality. In extreme cases this placement indicates sexual abuse, criminality, violence or murder. Consciously or unconsciously, the light of the Sun is caught in a web of darkness, A father struggling to avoid the dread of his own inner Minotaur cannot celebrate the untrammelled life force of the child.

The child grows up into an adult with a sense of self that is not whole; instead, they live as if someone else has the power. The child's unmet need for validation of the self and the right to autonomy resurfaces again and again in a repeat pattern of issues around power with anyone who appears to be in the role of authority. The underlying issue is usually highly unconscious, but as long as a person is in the grip of the illusion of an external authority, like a child waiting for permission, they remain frustrated and disempowered.

The positive expression of Pluto in aspect to the Sun is a father who has a deep understanding of relationship and is in touch with his own personal power. A person who has a positive Sun-Pluto expression will be an individual with tremendous stamina, persistence and creative drive. When the Solar energy of the creative mind is combined with the raw power of the instinctive Pluto, this person is very likely to make their mark on the world.

34

# The Budding or Masochist Stage

# The Houses: Where to Look for the Budding/Masochist Stage in the Chart

The core issue for the Budding or Masochist stage is freedom of self-expression and the exploration of individuality through creativity. The houses associated with these issues are the 1st house, which has to do with a person's sense of identity; the 3rd house, which concerns issues of communication; and the 5th, which is the house to do with spontaneous playfulness and creativity. The 4th and 10th houses are also relevant as they show the influence of the parents on the Budding child.

**The Ascendant and the 1st House**

The Ascendant and the 1st house, as we have seen, depict the earliest phase of life. Planets in aspect to the Ascendant and in the 1st house describe a person's sense of identity.

The Sun in the 1st house is a powerful placement and is often an indication of the Flowering/Psychopathic Characterology. However, it can also be an indication of the Budding/Masochist soul – a person who is learning, in this lifetime, to build the radiance of the Solar principle into their sense of identity.

When Pluto or either of the challenging outer planets of Saturn or Chiron appear in the 1st house this is commonly an indication of wounding and the need for transformational work to be done on establishing a strong, clear sense of identity. However, as always in astrology, as well as presenting a challenge and the need for healing the planets bring their own gifts that are part of that healing and become the strengths of the transformed sense of identity.

## The 3rd House

The 3rd house is one of the keys to the Budding/Masochist stage. It is during the Budding/Masochist stage that the child learns to speak – probably the single most important tool of self-expression – and it is the 3rd house that represents the development of speech and verbal communication. Positive planets here emphasize the importance of communication and self-expression, the gift of the Budding/Masochist soul; challenging planets here indicate blocks and restrictions on the fluency of communication and the need for transformation.

### Pluto in the 3rd House

The 3rd is the house of communication, networks and the local environment. It is also the house of siblings. Pluto in the 3rd often indicates a sibling who carried some aspect of the energy of Pluto. It can sometimes be a sign of a sibling who died, but more often shows a sibling who was invasive and controlling or one who was very deep and powerful.

When Pluto is in the 3rd house there may be issues of resistance or control around communication. A person with Pluto in the 3rd may be drawn, quite obsessively, into writing or some other form of artistic communication but they may find themselves often stuck with creative blocks or can get entangled in power struggles with editors or other powerful people. Pluto in the 3rd could be associated with secretive, underground networks, communication that is hidden behind Pluto's helmet of invisibility. As always with Pluto, this individual is required to dig deep and learn to communicate from the deeper truth of the instinctual level.

### Saturn in the 3rd House

Very often Saturn indicates the presence of the Inner Critic, and here fear of failure is linked to difficulty with self-expression and communication. Over time, this may be transformed through hard work and self-mastery, and this placement can also indicate a person whose profession is built around networking and communication.

## The Houses:
## Where to Look for the Budding/Masochist Stage in the Chart

### Chiron in the 3rd House

Chiron is always associated with wounding and healing and Chiron in the 3rd house may be a sign of a disability associated with communication. The 3rd house is the house of siblings and this placement can sometimes indicate a sibling with a disability that has an impact on the whole area of life to do with communication, networking and self-expression. This placement can also indicate someone who brings the light of healing into the area of communication or who communicates about healing, e.g. some kind of therapist.

### The 5th House

The 5th is the house of creativity – the spontaneous, playful, creativity of childhood. This is the world of the Magical Child, an energy that is very dear to the Budding soul. The 5th house is one of the most beautiful houses in the horoscope because as well as a child's joy of being in the physical world – curiosity, exploration, playfulness and wonder – it is also the house of love affairs and romance. The 5th house is where we shine. It describes the nature of our creativity and indicates the qualities we can expect our own children to bring into our lives.

The Sun is most at home in the 5th house, and when the Sun, Moon or a stellium of planets is found here it is a sign that creativity is very important in this person's life. However, these placements are not an indication of the Budding/Masochist stage but of the Flowering/Psychopathic stage.

### Pluto in the 5th House

Pluto in the 5th house is often a clear indication of Masochist wounding. A person with Pluto here may be extremely controlled in their creative expression. Self-doubt and resistance block their spontaneous impulses so that they repeatedly find disappointment in their creative endeavours and in their hopes of romance. However, even with these kind of challenges,, people are often obsessively attracted to Pluto's house, continually drawn into the Masochist struggle as they sense the life force there, waiting to be released. Individuals with Pluto in the 5th will find their creative path entails the journey to the Underworld. Here Pluto demands transformation and re-generation. When creative expression is rooted in an authentic sense of self and creative power, Pluto in the 5th can be a powerhouse of creativity.

### Saturn in the 5th House

Saturn is the planet most associated with the voice of the Inner Critic and with the formation of the Superego – a set of 'rules' for success (which is explored at length in the Harvest/Rigid stage). The negative expression of Saturn in the 5th is a sign of the Budding/Masochist type as it indicates a childhood marred by cold, harsh discipline and criticism, leading to painful feelings of failure in the area of creative self-expression. As always with challenging planets, over time the person can learn to use Saturn's gifts of discipline, structure and persistence to support them in becoming powerful creators.

### Chiron in the 5th House

This can indicate a person with the Masochist fear that their Essence contains something toxic, like a kind of poison. Chiron in the 5th can also indicate injuries and disabilities that block the ease of creative expression. A positive expression of this placement might be someone who works through artistic expression to transform their wound and bring about healing.

## The Parental Axis – the 4th and 10th Houses

The 4th and 10th houses represent the parental axis and, again, the nature of the planets found here show the influence of the parents in supporting or obstructing the development of the child. Saturn or Pluto in these houses indicates issues of control coming from one or both of the parents. Mars or Jupiter here can indicate a fiery or dominating parent who left the child feeling invaded and overwhelmed.

## The Houses:
## Where to Look for the Budding/Masochist Stage in the Chart

### Pluto in the 4th and 10th Houses

The 4th house represents a person's overall experience in the family home in childhood as well as the family life they create as adults. When Pluto is here we find Pluto's energy, danger, power struggles, sexuality and death as a presence in the family home. This can be a direct indication of a dominant, controlling and invasive father and this placement may be seen when the child suffers sexual abuse or where there is violence or a power struggle in the sexual relationship between the parents. The positive expression of Pluto in the 4th house could be a family capable of deep, powerful, close, committed and loving relationships.

When Pluto is in the 10th house it often indicates issues of domination, control and manipulation – blatant or subtle – in the relationship with the mother. The 10th house is also the house of career and aspiration and in adulthood the person may remain trapped in the grip of the internalized mother, continually encountering power struggles, defeat and domination in their attempts to forge a life and bring their aspirations into manifestation. The positive expression of Pluto in the 10th could be a mother with deep feelings, who is charismatic and at ease with her power. The person's own aspirations might be towards deep relationships and they may find themselves in positions of power in the world.

### Saturn in the 4th and 10th Houses

Saturn in either of the houses associated with the parents is a likely indication of critical, controlling behaviour from one or both parents. This kind of parenting leads to Masochist wounding but is compounded and overlaid by the Rigid wound of conformity and control.

### Summary

Indications of emphasis on the issues of the Budding/Masochist stage:

- Pluto in aspect to the Ascendant, the Sun or Moon
- Saturn or Chiron in aspect to the Sun
- The Ascendant, Sun or Moon in the sign of Scorpio

- Pluto in the 1st, 3rd, 4th, 5th, 10th or 12th house
- The Sun in the 4th, 8th or 12th house
- The North Node in the 1st, 3rd or 5th house

## The Sun and Pluto

Pluto and the Sun are a strange pairing yet they are two sides of the same coin, for without access to the deeps of the Underworld the Solar principle will fail. Without the magical depths of Pluto's world the Solar principle turns into the shallow rationality of the patriarchy, which we shall meet in the Rigid defence. And it is the Solar principle that heals the wounded Masochist type by bringing the light of consciousness into the dark of the labyrinth. We cannot truly live until we bring consciousness into the shadows of our inner world but every time that journey is made the light of Essence shines brighter. In our soul's journey through incarnation, the Budding stage brings the turning point when we find the personal power that frees us to radiate our Solar light into the world.

35

# THE FLOWERING OR PSYCHOPATHIC STAGE

In the fourth stage, the development of the Psychopathic type is associated with the older child, aged three to five, who is ready to focus on the area of relationship. The child develops gender awareness and begins to explore their sexual identity in relationship to the parent of the opposite sex. Wounding in this stage occurs when a parent, to a greater or lesser degree, transgresses the child's boundaries leading to the breakdown of trust in relationship and the fear of betrayal. The child reacts by developing the Psychopathic defence of aggression but they have a repeating pattern round issues of betrayal in relationship.

# 36

## The Flowering or Psychopathic Stage

## The Psychological View: Wounding and Defence in the Psychopathic Stage

The next developmental stage after the Budding/Masochist stage begins around the age of three and carries on until around the age of five. The child has now established a degree of autonomy and becomes increasingly aware of the people around them. In the Budding/Masochist stage the issue is establishing a clear sense of self. In the Flowering/Psychopathic stage the issue is the self in relationship with another.

This is the age when the child develops gender awareness by learning to distinguish between the sexes and the different feelings and responses evoked by one or the other. They discover that they are either a girl or a boy and observe that their parents and siblings are also members of one of these two teams. With a growing awareness of their sexual identity, the child takes the first step on the path of romance by falling in love with the parent of the opposite sex. Radiating their shiny new sense of self, the child seeks the approval of the adored parent. This is a very important stage in the development of self-belief. The child needs to have their Essence mirrored back to them – to feel validated by their 'beloved', confident that their individuality, beauty and prowess are recognized and appreciated.

What happens next has much to do with the quality of the relationship between the parents. Sometimes, the two parents have a well-balanced adult relationship in which their needs for intimacy and sexual fulfilment are met. In this case it is not too difficult for the parent of the opposite sex to welcome and validate the adoration of the child without transgressing their fragile sexual boundaries. This is a delicate task because the parent has to affirm and celebrate the child, including their sexual beauty, while holding the boundary that makes it clear that that their own romantic interest is directed towards their adult partner, not the child.

## Wounding

In the first place, the risk of Psychopathic wounding in the child begins when there are problems in the relationship between the parents, i.e. when the parents have reached a point where various aspects of their need for intimacy are not being met in their adult relationship. Then, instead of holding a boundary that protects the child, the adored parent of the opposite sex, consciously or unconsciously, starts meeting their own romantic/sexual needs through the unconditional love of the child. This does not necessarily imply the extremes of incest and child abuse. Without going to anything like those lengths a parent can subtly seduce the child, leading them to believe that they are secretly the chosen one, embodying all the special qualities that their partner, the other parent, lacks.

Meanwhile, the parent of the same sex is not enjoying this situation at all. They too are suffering from unmet needs for intimacy and this sense of lack turns to envy when they see that the child is now the recipient of the love and attention of which they feel they are deprived. We are back to Oral wounding here. The adults (however irrationally – because the defences are not rational) are still waiting for someone to meet their unrequited infantile needs. One parent seeks to get the love they never had through the unconditional adoration of the child; the other becomes envious when they see the infant getting the attention they feel they never got.

Parental envy of the child of the same sex is a very common thing. It is the psychological basis for all our fairy tales about wicked stepmothers and evil kings attempting to dispose of their children by sending them off on impossible quests and it is the foundation of the universal human experience of the 'eternal triangle'.

Unfortunately, in many families the incest taboo is broken, leading to actual sexual abuse of the child. In other families, although physical sexual abuse does not occur, nevertheless the difficult boundaries around sexuality and co-dependency can become very weak and distorted even though the whole issue remains mostly unconscious. Unconscious or overt seduction by one parent, and envy from the other, creates tension and anxiety for the child who is still very young and feels that their very survival is at stake when it comes to parental love. It is sad and quite terrifying for them to find themselves in competition with the parent of the same sex. At the same time the 'seduction' by the parent of the opposite sex leaves the child with an uneasy sense of the lack of boundaries and an unnamed fear of the parent's adult sexuality. So the child's budding sexual identity is split by the dysfunctional dynamics of the parental relationship. The infant's delightful, innocent wish to be seen to be brilliant, beautiful and adorable has to contend with seduction from one parent and rivalry from the other; a double-bind which the child lacks the resources to untangle.

Betrayal is built into the dynamics of this situation and betrayal is the primary wound in the Psychopathic defence. In the child's very first romantic relationship the seductive parent makes a promise that can never be kept. The child can never become the partner of the adored parent but they get seduced into the illusion that if they can demonstrate just how brilliant, beautiful and wonderful they are then they will defeat the competition and finally win the heart of the 'beloved'. The demand for the child to be exceptionally brilliant is a version of Narcissistic wounding – the demand is actually a reflection of the parent's own feelings of inadequacy but the child internalizes this as an expectation, which they must fulfil.

When a child grows up in a family in which dysfunctional relationships are the norm this becomes the mould for their expectations of relationship. From their perception of the parental relationship the child creates a template of beliefs about the nature of sexual partnerships. Coming so early in life when everything is still unformed, the impossible triangle and the inevitability of betrayal gets wired into the energy field of the young being and does untold damage to their ability to trust.

## The Psychological View:
## Wounding and Defence in the Psychopathic Stage

### Defence

In early childhood an infant will die if the parent abandons them. The child in the Psychopathic stage is still very young and the danger of death through abandonment feels real, so the quest for approval takes on the intensity of an issue of survival as the child struggles to match up to the parent's expectations. They project an inflated, 'grandiose', idealized self-image out into the world in an attempt to meet the parent's expectations/demands. But behind the grandiose displays the child holds a hidden fear that in their Essence they are worthless. The worthlessness sometimes takes the form of extreme self-loathing in the child, who comes to feel that their true nature is intolerably flawed. Their apparent bravado conceals the desperate need to hide their vulnerability and shame. Their inflamed urge to excel becomes an obsession with achieving some kind of conquest, domination or glory that will, at last, match up to the requirements of the 'beloved' and assuage their feelings of worthlessness.

Psychopathic wounding is the classic form of Narcissistic wounding. The parents demand that the child be 'special' and this is the next stage of issues around the Solar principle first encountered in the Masochist stage. The Masochist tries to hold on to a sense of self by resistance and withdrawal but the Psychopathic type comes out fighting. The natural longing to shine becomes overcharged with anxiety from the underlying fear of betrayal and the tension escapes in fiery emotional outbursts as the child tries to conquer and dominate by assertion of the will. Despite their aggression, and the fact that they often win their fights, the person in a Psychopathic defence operates from a place of profound victim consciousness, as deep as the Masochist's and possibly even harder to see because, for the Psychopathic type, it is more disguised.

It is in the nature of healing that wherever we are holding distortions in our energy field becomes an area of life where we repeat negative experiences over and over again until we find a way to release the pattern. People with Psychopathic wounding become trapped in a world of fantasy, addicted to doomed relationships, wildly stimulated by the love of the 'chase' but unable to follow through and sustain an intimate relationship. Both the quest for brilliance and the search for romance are caught up in the distorted belief that there is a battle that must be won, an adversary to be overcome before they can be worthy of love.

The core issue for the Psychopathic Characterology is betrayal and always, at the very earliest stage in any of their relationships or projects, there is deception. Before they take the first step on the journey a promise has been made that can never be kept and sooner or later the lie will become clear. Lovers, best friends, father- and mother-figures, bosses and colleagues, someone always sabotages them and makes off with the prize – the money, the girl, the job, the medal, the credit, the promotion, and so on. The brave, heroic persona of these individuals disguises their hopeless double-bind that underpins everything, the tension between the desperate attempt to match up to the parental idealization and their fierce denial of their vulnerability. One of the hardest things for the adult Psychopathic type to realize is that the first betrayal is always a self-betrayal.

**Recognizing the Psychopathic Defence**

In adult life, the individual with Psychopathic wounding stumbles through repeating cycles of seduction, rivalry, triangular relationships, false promises and betrayal. It may take many years for them to discover that it is possible to relate in any other way. When we see adults lurching from one abusive or disappointing relationship to the next we understand the power of these deep-rooted patterns, probably brought in from previous incarnations and reinforced by childhood experience. No matter how painful, their energy keeps flowing down the same well-worn path – never underestimate the difficulty we humans have with change!

The Psychopathic type develops into a 'heroic' individual, always ready to take action and confront something, rescue someone, deal with some miscarriage of justice or initiate some project. This defence is found in people who take up just causes (and lost causes), fighting for the underdog, continually moving on to the next honourable quest, certain that, this time, they will prevail. They are usually found in positions of initiative and leadership because they have ferocious drive and ambition. With their fiery temperament the Psychopathic type will easily offend other people and they are inclined to tread on a lot of toes on their way to being toppled off the top. They intimidate people and do not easily empathize with the hurt feelings of those they offend. However, they do not waste time holding grudges or brooding over past injuries, so although they are quick to anger they are equally quick to release their emotion and move on, leaving those around them to recover from the passing storm.

With their addiction to triangular relationships they repeatedly end up caught in one or more corners of the triangle of 'victim', 'persecutor' and 'rescuer'. While they like to identify themselves as the 'rescuer', the Psychopathic type can easily turn into a bully or persecutor. The strength of their identification as a champion of justice and truth makes it very nearly impossible for the Psychopathic type to see that their own behaviour might be at fault. They find it extraordinarily difficult to apologize or to accept responsibility for their mistakes because deep inside everything feels like a life and death battle for survival – 'I have to be right or I will die.'

Anyone who has worked with young offenders will recognize the type of person who cannot admit to having done wrong, even when they have just perpetrated a violent act or committed a crime. They will refuse to acknowledge even minor mistakes and are very likely to erupt into an outburst of rage when pressed to take responsibility for their behaviour. And as these situations play themselves out and betrayal strikes, they end up yet again back in the corner of the 'victim'.

## Physical Appearance

The physical appearance of the Psychopathic type is the exact opposite of Oral spinelessness! The back is held very erect, chest thrown out and shoulders stiff and square like a soldier's, head held high, with glowing eyes. They have a proud and fearless gaze, inspiring to others, they are direct and outspoken, and scornful of those who are not. With such immense vision and courage they are charismatic, natural leaders and fearless competitors, hard-working to the point of being fanatically driven so that they suffer from periodic episodes of burn-out. They are top-heavy in build with an over-large chest cavity, a reflection of the passionate and overheated heart beating within. The legs of the Psychopathic type are often surprisingly thin and even rather weak, revealing that despite their fiery willpower they are not steady on the ground. Their passion is coloured by illusion and perhaps those little legs know that sooner or later someone is going to pull the rug out from under them.

### Story – King Arthur and the Knights of the Round Table

We have already looked at the idea that many myths and fairy tales are versions of the story of the Sun – the journey of the development of consciousness enacted by the archetypes of the hero or heroine. The stories are romantic in that they seek a happy-ever-after union of the Masculine and the Feminine and they are based around the idea of testing and proving the worth of the hero or heroine through ordeals. The heroic male is sent off on a white horse to look for something to conquer while the heroine is required to demonstrate her exceptional virtue by getting stuck into some impossible task such as spinning flax into gold. The story of the hero or heroine is the Essence of the romantic path of the Flowering/Psychopath soul. The Psychopathic type is spurred on in the hope that their tremendous achievements will finally make them worthy of love. In the distortions of their wounding their aim is to defeat the wicked kings, queens, usurpers, step-mothers, ogres and witches (that represent the parent of the same sex), finally gain the love of the beloved (parent of the opposite sex) and take up their rightful place as ruler of the kingdom (family).

The romantic epic of King Arthur and the Knights of the Round Table is built around the issues of the Flowering/Psychopathic stage. The most important of all the quests of the Knights of the Round Table was the quest for the Holy Grail. The Holy Grail is a symbol of the sacred Feminine and the Grail Quest represented the highest ideals of chivalry – the strength and valour of the Masculine offered in sacred service of the gentleness and wisdom of the Feminine. A classic example of the tragedy of Psychopathic wounding is the poignant tale of one of the greatest knights of all, Sir Lancelot of the Lake.

**Story – Sir Lancelot of the Lake**

King Arthur's vision of chivalry brought the best of knights to sit at the Round Table at Camelot. When Sir Lancelot arrived he appeared to be the perfect knight with healing powers as well as unequalled courage and skill in battle. But on the day that he arrived in Camelot, Lancelot fell in love with Guinevere, Arthur's queen; his noble heart was compromised and he never gave his love to another woman. For many years Lancelot served his queen as a good knight should, seeking only to bring her honour through his mighty deeds. But Lancelot's passion for Guinevere tarnished everything that he did and cost him his dearest dream, to win the quest for the Holy Grail. Only the best and the purest of all the knights ever came within sight of the Holy Grail but Sir Lancelot was one of them.

In his youth Lancelot travelled through a desolate wasteland and came to the mysterious Castle Carbonek, where the Grail was held in the care of the wounded King Pelles. Lancelot remained for a time at Castle Carbonek, where he was privileged to witness the procession of the Holy Grail. The king's daughter, Elaine, fell in love with Lancelot but he could not return her love. Then Elaine resorted to sorcery to make herself look like Guinevere and Lancelot was seduced into spending the night with her. When he awoke and saw what he had done Lancelot was overcome with madness and ran naked into the forest. Elaine gave birth to Galahad, who was the purest knight of all, the one who eventually achieved the quest of the Holy Grail, but Elaine died of a broken heart.

Years later, still locked in his forbidden love for Guinevere, Lancelot, with his friend Sir Gawain, came once more to Castle Carbonek. When the procession of the Holy Grail appeared Gawain and Lancelot followed it through the castle and up to the Chapel of the Holy Grail. Gawain was admitted into the chapel but when Lancelot stepped forward the door slammed in his face. Lancelot fell to the floor and prayed to God saying, 'If ever I did anything that was pleasing to You, let me be allowed to see at least something of what I seek.'

Then the door opened and inside Lancelot saw Sir Gawain standing in front of the altar with the Grail Maiden and the Hermit of the Grail. The Hermit of the Grail removed the cloth that covered the Grail but a mighty voice cried, 'Lancelot, come not here for you are not worthy. Behold the light of the Holy Grail but from it you may not drink.'

Sir Lancelot and Sir Gawain went back to Camelot and told of their adventure. But all too soon Lancelot's eyes returned to Queen Guinevere and he forgot how he had failed when he had come so near to achieving the quest of the Holy Grail. The day came when Guinevere finally spoke to Lancelot of her love for him. They spent the night together but King Arthur's treacherous son Sir Mordred made sure that they were discovered. Lancelot escaped but Guinevere was imprisoned and sentenced to be burned at the stake. At the last moment Sir Lancelot rescued Guinevere from the flames but great divisions had opened up amongst the knights, who had been forced to choose between Sir Lancelot and the king. The tragic Battle of Camlann followed and thus came the fall of Camelot. King Arthur was mortally wounded and was carried away to the magic Isles of Avalon.

Lancelot and Guinevere both survived the battle. They said their last goodbyes and Lancelot promised that he would never be unfaithful; Guinevere became a nun and Lancelot became a monk. Years passed and, one night, Lancelot dreamed that he heard Guinevere calling out to him. Soon the news came that she had died. Lancelot brought her body to Glastonbury and pronounced the sermon over her grave. Within a few weeks he, too, was dead. Over his grave his brother, Sir Hector, stood and declared, 'There will never be any knight to rival you, Sir Lancelot, the greatest knight who ever lived.'

And so the last light of the realm of Logres was extinguished, for soon the Saxons conquered Britain and the Dark Ages descended on the western world.

## The Psychological View: Wounding and Defence in the Psychopathic Stage

King Arthur's vision of chivalry shines down through the centuries – the ideal of offering masculine physical prowess in service of Divine feminine wisdom. The quest for the Holy Grail symbolizes the union of Spirit and Matter, the sacred heart of relationship between man and woman, and this is the Essence that the Flowering soul longs to bring through into the world.

True to the Psychopathic template, Lancelot was unable to fulfil his highest ambition because right at the very beginning he betrayed his true Essence and everything most dear to him by clinging to his obsessive love for the queen. The fact that he was never able to release the destructive fantasy of his love for Guinevere perfectly illustrates the wound of the Psychopathic type's unconscious choice of betrayal.

# 37

## The Flowering or Psychopathic Stage

# The Healing Response to the Psychopathic Defence

The child with Psychopathic wounding has experienced seduction and betrayal. Trust in unconditional love has gone, while competing and winning have taken on a life and death significance. In childhood they came to believe that great things were required of them so now they need a healer's help to relinquish the grip of the illusion of the demands of grandiosity. The healing response to an individual with Psychopathic wounding is to hold a state of unconditionally loving acceptance. It is a transforming experience for the Psychopathic type to be in the presence of someone who has no requirement, no expectation that they should be anything at all. The keywords are 'No demand' and the healer needs to maintain well-grounded steadiness and trustworthiness that comfort and hold out hope to the confused and frightened child at the heart of the defence.

When they are in their defence, the Psychopathic type forces energy up through their spine and the back of their HEF, throwing energy upwards and forwards in an effort to use their willpower to dominate. A healer can help by quietly grounding: bringing their energy right down and holding the vibration of a deep connection with the earth. Working with an individual with Psychopathic wounding can be extremely challenging because at first they are aggressive, domineering and controlling, so as to deny their vulnerability. The healer needs to avoid getting entangled in any kind of combat by holding a calm state of mind that simply says 'No contest'. Held in the stillness of quiet grounding and unconditional acceptance, it finally becomes possible for the Psychopathic type to discover that hidden in the vulnerability that they came to despise is their true self and their authentic human goodness.

## The Healing Response to the Psychopathic Defence

Like all the defences, the Psychopathic type suffers from a human being's primal fear that they are not loved; always the central issue, the universal human delusion that we lack love. Yet on the level of Spirit and Soul it is clear that we are made of love, it is our Essence. No other being can give love to us, nor can they take it away. But in the little egoic mind, the Psychopathic type starts from a false premise and searches for love in all the wrong places, battling away, down through the ages until a turning point comes. In a moment of surrender – sometimes a very dark and hopeless moment – the first light dawns as they begin to remember that there is nowhere to go to look for love because it is already here.

Love is the primary state of existence and the life force of the Universe. In the non-physical realm it is not difficult to love; in fact, anything else is impossible. Something happens to us in the process of entering into the physical world that causes us to become afraid. The newborn baby sits in terrified judgement on life and splits existence into heaven and hell. The nursing infant lives in terror that there is just not enough love to go round. The autonomous child builds themselves a cage in which to hide the horror of their self-loathing. And the romantic child becomes paranoid and turns their longing to shine into the capacity to kill.

Many of our greatest romances are tragedies in which the hero and heroine never get into the nitty-gritty of a real relationship to deal with whatever shadows arise in the pursuit of intimacy. The Psychopathic soul has everything to learn about real flesh and blood relationships. Hopefully, the Psychopathic type reaches the point when they are able to break away from the doomed fantasy of the parental triangle and choose the less dramatic but much more meaningful path of authentic human relationship.

# 38

## The Flowering or Psychopathic Stage

## The Spiritual View: the Gifts of the Flowering Stage

*Anger is the roar of a lion, the cry of a universe longing to be born.*
*It reminds you, when you have forgotten,*
*That the power of life moves through you.*
*That you have a voice.*

*Do not push your anger away, or label it 'negative' or 'unspiritual'.*
*Do not pretend it is not there.*
*No need to act it out, either.*

*Feel its pounding, its vibrations, its longing to be acknowledged, held.*
*At its burning core, discover courage.*

Jeff Foster, *Be Gentle With Anger*

From the spiritual viewpoint, the incoming soul is not merely at the mercy of the environment into which they are born. This soul has had lifetimes of experience in relationship, in both male and female bodies. A newborn baby comes with a set of unformed tendencies and the current family scenario is a mirror of the inner patterns of relationship that they have come here to celebrate or to heal.

## The Stage of the Creative Process

In the creative process, the fourth stage is the phase of Flowering, which corresponds to the Psychopathic stage. This is the most strikingly active stage of growth as the flowers put forth a radiant display of colour and scent, attracting insects to fertilize them and birds to scatter their seeds ready for the miracle of the procreation of life.

The Flowering soul is seeking relationship, sexual union, fertility and procreation. Like a sperm racing towards an ovum, competition is an innate element of this quest and in their search to attract a mate the Flowering soul reaches the pinnacle of their strength, beauty and allure. The Flowering soul becomes a radiant star, desirable and desiring, bursting with youthful strength and vigour. This is not the time for reflection, meditation or analysis but for action, challenge and adventure!

In the Budding stage the individual discovered the power to express their individuated self. In the Flowering stage their life task is to discover what it takes for one brilliant and beautiful individual to be in loving relationship with another. They are learning how to balance the energies of the Masculine and the Feminine, the most delicate and skilful dance of how to give and how to receive.

This is the stage of the creative process that we love and celebrate the most but the Flowering soul can only manifest their beautiful dream of romantic love when they learn to trust and open to their vulnerability. As well as being beautiful and courageous they also have the difficult task of doing the thing they are most afraid of – to surrender! It is clear that in the collective consciousness of the human race there is profound confusion, pain and distortion around the relationship between the Masculine and the Feminine. This confusion is present in all cultures and it has manifested throughout history as painful, often appalling acts of persecution and abuse, and in everyday life we constantly deal with issues of rejection and betrayal, domination and control in our relationships. It can be said that war itself, the greatest affliction in human history, is the outcome of the distortion of the Psychopathic defence when the urge to attract a mate becomes a perverted drive to gain prowess through acts of domination and violence.

Yet we all love a hero and we admire and are uplifted by those whose star shines bright in any field – all the great figures who capture the imagination with their marvellous achievements and heroic stories. These are the Flowering souls who inspire us to live and love to the full and be the greatest that we can in this life.

## The Nature of the Incoming Soul

People with an emphasis on the energy of the Flowering soul are natural leaders. They focus on the power of the will – the capacity to take action in the world in response to the desire welling up from within. They are full of fire and passion and are a source of inspiration, imagination and initiative, carrying many others with them on a wave of energetic creativity. They have a natural star quality and they illuminate the human condition with courage, beauty, honour and truth.

A major part of the Flowering soul's life purpose is to bring truth and justice to their communities but they will not succeed in their quest while they continue to attempt to win by forcing their will onto others. Once they are able to stabilize their energy field and allow the light of their Core Star to illuminate their path with compassion and understanding, they bring warmth, hope and inspiration to all. The Flowering souls love the drama and adventure of life on earth and embody the archetype of the romantic hero and heroine. They live out the ultimate human dream of noble conquest, triumph, sexual love and fertility, and they create glorious lives that light up the world like shooting stars soaring across the sky.

## The Appearance of the Flowering or Psychopathic Stage in the Human Energy Field

The HEF of the Flowering soul is brilliant, colourful and dynamic. There is a lot of activity in the area of the field around the heart chakra, also known as the astral plane. Shamans believe that the astral plane is created from human consciousness, thus here we find every imaginable kind of story and every kind of being covering the whole spectrum from demons to angels. This is the place of dreams and nightmares, past lives and emotional experiences ranging from the utmost horror to the utmost bliss. This area of the field is dramatically beautiful, lit up with brilliant colour and deep shadows, and it is here that the Flowering soul is drawn into the kaleidoscope of human stories.

With their drive, enthusiasm and passion for life, the Flowering soul's energy field appears highly charged, with the energy flowing upwards and outwards like a fountain and quite often like a firework, flickering, crackling and sparkling with fire. They quickly attract attention and are often surrounded by a little group of low-energy souls coming to warm themselves in the radiant fire.

In the HEF, the Flowering/Psychopathic soul sends energy streaming up and radiating out from the central vertical power current. When they feel thwarted or threatened their whole energy field pushes forwards while a wave of energy surges up the spine and gathers over their head like a thunder cloud, from where they hurl bolts and blasts of energy at whatever or whoever they think is getting in their way.

However, hidden beneath the external brilliance of a person with Psychopathic wounding is the confused, frightened energy of the Narcissistically wounded child. The split between grandiose radiance and repressed vulnerability can be seen in their HEF; the energy field is not well grounded and the bottom half of the field is weak and lacking in energy. The upward and outward energy comes from the heart, but if the central vertical power current is not sufficiently anchored into the earth this puts a strain on the heart, causing the Psychopathic type to repeatedly suffer from burn-out (and eventually from heart problems).

The Flowering soul has a big, generous heart and the 4th chakra is hot and bright. The 2nd chakra – the sensual, sexual centre in the pelvic cradle – is also active, celebrating joy in the life of the body. However, when there is Psychopathic wounding the 3rd chakra is shadowed by the person's underlying self-doubt and fear of betrayal, and this obstructs the flow of energy between the 2nd and 4th chakras. When the heart centre is disconnected from the 2nd chakra, sexuality is disconnected from love: the classic split between images of the

Feminine as Madonna/whore, the person you marry versus the person you desire. While this disconnection remains in place the individual will have a split between lust and love, going through serial sexual adventures but unable to make the commitment to deep and sustained intimacy.

When the Flowering soul makes the connection between the 2nd chakra and the heart then they are the most beautiful and colourful of souls. When their HEF is grounded and aligned, it perfectly illustrates the creative process as the life force wells up in the Lower Tan T'ien, flows up the central vertical power current and streams out into the aura, radiant and inspiring. All great performers demonstrate the light of the Flowering soul – filling theatres, studios, political platforms, boardrooms, lecture theatres and concert halls with the shining light of their Creative Essence.

39

# The Flowering or Psychopathic Stage

## The Astrological View: the Astrology of the Flowering/Psychopathic Type

The planets associated with the Flowering/Psychopathic stage are Mars, the Sun and Jupiter, the planets that rule the trinity of Fire signs in the zodiac. We have seen that the Sun represents the warm light of consciousness and creativity. Mars is hot and red and represents raw physical energy, drive, passion and aggression. Royal Jupiter symbolizes the principle of expansion, enthusiasm, adventure and opportunity. All three planets are associated with the extrovert energy of initiative, action, leadership and creativity. They are three different ways of expressing the life force. Mars is raw physical energy bursting forth into action, the Sun moulds the life force into creative expression, while Jupiter represents vision and a wisdom that sees beyond the horizons of everyday living. Mars is like untrammelled, adolescent energy, quite likely to get out of control! The Sun is the adult immersed in the heroic struggle to master the creative drive. Jupiter is the more mature expression of the Fire principle – inspiring, commanding and far-seeing.

# 40

## The Flowering or Psychopathic Stage

## Mars, Ruler of Aries (and Scorpio)

Mars is the ruling planet of the sign of Aries, a masculine, positive sign – the first sign of the Zodiac following the time of the spring equinox. Aries has a similar energy to the Ascendant and the 1st house as it represents new life, the first raw breath, undifferentiated life force surging through the body of a newly incarnated being. Before the discovery of Pluto, Mars was also the ruler of Scorpio – a feminine, negative sign – where it is associated with sexual passion and the instinctual drives of the body.

### Planetary Archetype – Essence

Mars is associated with the colour red; with fire, action, leadership, rivalry, anger, violence, iron, weapons, martial arts, penetration, blood, muscle, desire, passion and sex. More than any other planet, Mars represents the Essence of the Psychopathic/Flowering stage.

Our whole biological existence begins with the union of Masculine and Feminine that occurs when a sperm fertilizes an egg. In the sexual act, millions of sperm compete in a life and death race to be the first to reach the ova, penetrate the egg wall and initiate growth. Only one succeeds. This is how all life begins and this is the function of Mars – competition, penetration and initiation.

Mars embodies the will that goes out into the world to achieve a desired result. It is connected to both the Sun and to Pluto because the desire to act is either born from the conscious will of the Sun or wells up from the deep instinctual urges of Pluto. Mars goes into action, takes the creative impulse and propels it through into the manifest world. The symbol for Mars is ♂ , which is the symbol for the phallic energy of the Masculine. Venus, whose symbol is ♀, represents the Feminine principle of relationship and Mars represents the urge to separate and individuate. It is the exact opposite of Neptune's longing to merge and the two planets have a lot to learn from each other. In *The Astrological Neptune and the Quest for Redemption*, Liz Greene says:

> *Asking for what one wants is a function of Mars in the horoscope; and Mars, like Saturn, is a natural polar opposite of Neptune, because it represents the assertion of individual desires. This means the end of fusion.*

The focus of Mars is on the needs of the self, not on the needs of others, and the willpower of Mars turns to aggression if it is thwarted. Mars represents the archetype of the warrior and has the capacity for ruthlessness, the capacity to kill and the capacity for cruelty. Often we fear the energy of Mars, both in others and in ourselves. However, we are very drawn to the part of the horoscope in which Mars appears.

Minerva, the goddess of wisdom, was said to have been born directly from the head of Jupiter, the king of the gods. Jupiter's wife, Juno, was furious that her husband had had a child without her. In revenge, she managed to give birth to a child herself, without recourse to Jupiter, and that child was Mars, born out of spite. This perfectly illustrates the conflicted parental relationships that bring about the Psychopathic wounding: Mars, the god of war, born out of a bitter power struggle between the king and queen of the gods; not loved for his own sake but used to get even with his father.

In traditional astrology Mars was known as the Lesser Malefic and regarded as a planet that brought trouble. To the Greeks he was known as Ares and the Greeks hated him, because to them he was nothing but a war-mongering bully. Ares had two squires named Deimos (Fear) and Phobos (Fright) who accompanied him as he went around causing strife, conflict, fights and battles and leaving a trail of bloody carnage behind him. However, the Romans had more respect for Mars. He was believed to be the father of Romulus and Remus who built the city of Rome and so he represents one of the founding principles of the great Roman Empire. To the Romans, as well as being the god of war he was also the god of agriculture and the god of the spring, associated with fertility and growth. He was sometimes called Mars Gradivus, which means 'to become big' or, simply, 'to grow'. In Roman mythology the two squires of Mars were known as Honos (honour) and Virtus (virtue). In *Dynamics of the Unconscious* Howard Sasportas says:

> *The Roman Mars was accompanied by honour and virtue. It is honourable to stand your ground, to value who you are, to grow into that which you were meant to become. It is virtuous to realize your destiny.*

This sums up the gifts of the Flowering stage. Between Greek Ares and Roman Mars we find the entire spectrum of the expression of the Psychopathic/Flowering stage.

### Wound

Mars is not at all altruistic or lofty and otherworldly like Neptune or Uranus. Mars is the principle of individuality and it is not the province of Mars to be polite or try to see the other person's point of view. Mars is practical and active, angry and blunt, healthy and sporty, passionate, sexual and all about visceral life on Planet Earth! Mars is lusty, hungry and urgent and he does not like the idea of deferred gratification. When this streaming energy gets blocked, it builds up behind the blockage like molten lava in a volcano until it soon bursts through.

Problems occur when the natural flow of this hot stream of energy becomes disconnected from guidance – from the patience, presence and wisdom of the Source. When there is Psychopathic wounding the individual loses their basic trust in life. Their fundamental belief, conscious or unconscious, is that betrayal is just around the corner. This creates tension, impatience and greed, almost a panic – 'I want what I want and I want it NOW!'

If Mars is not tempered by something else in the chart then it easily goes out of control. The person is swept along by emotion and the energy becomes a forcing current driven by the egoic power of the will. In this situation, when something gets in the way the energy of Mars changes from being the flow of the life force to the force of aggression, with the wish to destroy whatever is seen as the enemy. When Mars is out of control a person is barely conscious of what they are doing – they 'see red' and are carried along by their blood lust, just as the noble warrior turns into a frenzied killing machine capable of the most bloodthirsty acts, such as murder, torture, rape and genocide. In *Star Warrior,* the biography of the shaman, Harley Swiftdeer, he describes some of the worst moments of his experiences in the Vietnam War.

> *The deepest horror of war is when you start enjoying it and don't have a way to let go of the complications from that. There is a power in taking human life. It's so simple to kill. You pull a trigger or snap a neck, and life is gone – it's gone forever. One day in Vietnam I realized that I enjoyed killing.*

One of the most difficult questions for people on a spiritual path is, 'How does the Divine Power let this happen?' This question is unanswerable but death and destruction are an inevitable part of human existence. And always we have free will. Our divinity is not an external force; it lives within us and the authority to choose the path of peace or the path of war is ours and ours alone.

The mighty and terrifying goddess Kali represents the feminine aspect of Mars. If Mars is associated with the force of Aries, Kali is associated with the power of Scorpio. Like Mars, she is capable of destruction, bloody conflict, war and death. In Hindu mythology Kali is described destroying the evil demon Raktabija by sucking the blood from his body. Kali then dances on the field of battle, stamping on the corpses of the slain. But Kali is considered one of the greatest, if not the greatest, of all the Hindu deities representing the outpouring of unbridled, instinctive life force.

### Story – Jason and the Argonauts

The story that is often associated with Mars and the zodiac sign of Aries is the Greek myth of Jason and the Argonauts.

Jason was another fatherless boy, the rightful heir to throne of Iolcus in Thessaly. His uncle, King Pelias, had usurped the throne but, when Jason discovered the secret of his birth and went angrily to Pelias to demand the return of his kingdom, Pelias agreed to give Jason his rightful inheritance if he could fulfil a quest to bring the fabled Golden Fleece of Colchis back to Iolcus. Jason was happy to take up the challenge and set about building his ship, the *Argo*, and gathering a crew of heroes to accompany him. He and the Argonauts set sail and had many adventures before they came to the land of Colchis where the magical fleece was kept. Aeetes, the sorcerer king of Colchis, had no intention of giving up the fleece. He told Jason he could have the fleece if he could fulfil certain tasks; tasks which Aeetes secretly knew to be impossible. He told Jason that he must catch two fire-breathing, brazen-hooved bulls, harness them to a plough and till the earth in the Field of Ares, then sow the field with dragons' teeth which he gave to Jason in a bronze helmet.

Jason thoughtlessly agreed to everything the king said. The headstrong hero might easily have fallen at the first hurdle but Aeetes' daughter Medea had fallen in love with Jason and decided to help him. Medea knew that no ordinary man could tame the bulls because the fire that came from their nostrils scorched everything that came near them. Like her father, Medea had magic powers and she made Jason a protective ointment which he smeared all over his body. The ointment prevented the bull's fire from touching Jason, who was able to harness them and plough the field. Then, when Jason started sowing the dragons' teeth a regiment of armed fighting men sprang up from the ground where the teeth had fallen and advanced upon the Argonauts. However, Medea had warned Jason and instructed him to throw the bronze helmet which had held the dragons' teeth in among the attacking warriors. At once the warriors turned and started fighting each other and soon they had all perished.

One of the Argonauts was the musician Orpheus. When Jason set out to get the fleece, Medea asked Orpheus to accompany them. They came to the sacred grove where the fleece was hung among the trees and saw that it was guarded by a massive dragon. Jason bravely prepared to do battle but Medea turned to Orpheus and asked him to play music on the lyre that he had with him. When Orpheus started to play, the beauty of the music enchanted the dragon and soon it fell asleep. Jason crept past the beast, pulled down the Golden Fleece and the three of them quickly made their way to the port where the *Argo* and her crew were ready and waiting. Medea accompanied Jason on board and brought her young half-brother with her. Swiftly they sailed away from Colchis.

King Aeetes was furious and determined to retrieve the Golden Fleece. He set off in pursuit in his own ship, using his magic to give him speed so he was soon gaining on the *Argo*. As the angry king's ship neared them, Medea took drastic action. In an instant she stabbed and killed her brother, Aeetes' young son. Then she hacked his body to pieces and threw them overboard. The king's ship slowed to a halt to gather up the pieces of the body so that the boy could have a proper burial. The *Argo* sped on her way and they returned to Iolcus, triumphant. Pelias gave up the crown and Jason became king in his place.

Jason married Medea, who bore him two children. But as the years passed Jason tired of her and started courting the daughter of the wealthy and powerful King of Corinth. This was a serious mistake! Medea was not a woman to be taken lightly and in her fury she killed their own two children as well as Jason's new bride. She cursed Jason then flew into the sky in a chariot drawn by winged dragons.

Jason's life descended into misery. Ageing and depressed, he often walked on the seashore where the *Argo* now lay beached. One day, Jason was sitting in the shade of the boat, dreaming of his former glory, when the mighty figurehead, originally a gift from the gods, tumbled from the rotting timbers and struck him on the head, killing him. And thus, one of the greatest heroes came to an ignominious end.

The beginning of this story has all the youthful honour, courage and adventure of the Flowering Stage, though already there is treachery – Pelias trying to cheat his nephew of the throne and the sorcery of King Aeetes.

Medea is a powerful figure, the feminine counterpart of Jason – his anima. Medea, like Kali, represents many of the qualities of Scorpio: magical, single-minded, powerful and ruthless. Jason's headstrong courage, physical strength and willpower alone would not have defeated Aeetes' magical beasts and warriors. He needs Medea's magic, which represents the creative power of intuition; the need to connect with supernatural power in order to deal with the challenge. Mars rules blood and muscle, he is the raw masculine energy of the physical body and Medea represents the magical feminine, instinctual wisdom that comes from listening to the body-mind rather than relying on linear intelligence.

In keeping with the Psychopathic defence, the moment when Jason betrays Medea is the moment when he betrays himself. Unfaithful to Medea, his magical intuitive self, he chooses instead the political power that comes through marriage to the daughter of a wealthy king. Medea's revenge is relentless and complete, and anyone with Mars or Aries strong in the chart will find that the cost to their soul is great indeed if they ever try to bargain their life force for security. Caught in the Psychopathic wounding, Jason's ill-considered selfishness costs him everything in the end. He betrays himself and those he loves, and his foolish death is brought about by the decaying, neglected hulk of his once glorious ship.

### In the Human Energy Field

In the HEF Mars is slightly different to the other planets in that the energy of Mars focuses both inwards and outwards. As the principle of action and the god of war, Mars directs energy out into the world through initiation, assertion and aggression. However, as the ruler of blood and muscle, sexuality and the immune system, Mars also focuses energy inwards into the biological processes of the body and the animal power of the instincts.

In the HEF Mars gives off a vibrant red light. In warrior mode, Mars can light up the entire HEF – sometimes raging out of control like a forest fire, sometimes fiercely controlled with the precision of a martial artist. In the aura the energy of Mars arises from low down in the HEF: from the genitals, the 2nd and 1st chakras in the pelvic cradle. When a person is centred and grounded, Mars also connects inwards to the deep level of the Hara and the root power of the Lower Tan T'ien. When pure intention wells up from the Tan T'ien it is the red light of Mars that initiates action, streaming forth into the HEF like blood surging through the veins.

When there is Psychopathic wounding, the person loses faith in their connection to the earth and the lower half of the field becomes weak. The whole of the HEF is thrust out of alignment, pushing forwards, and the hot Mars energy is pulled upwards, gathering around the chest and overstimulating the heart or accumulating as pressure under the top of the skull. When the Psychopathic type gets angry the Mars energy surges up the spine and out of the top of the head to gather in a menacing cloud from which erupts the explosive fire of Mars enraged. The Psychopathic type lives in the moment and they do not bear grudges. Once the storm has passed their energy field clears, and the individual goes on their way feeling much better for their discharge and quite oblivious to the havoc they have wreaked in the HEF of anyone unlucky enough to get in their way!

### Mars in Aspect to the Ascendant, Sun and Moon

Like Pluto, Mars has to do with the instincts and impulses of the body and the upwelling power of the life force. But, where Pluto hides, Mars comes out fighting! Mars is raw red energy that goes straight into action and if it is blocked it turns to anger and aggression. A person with Mars in aspect to the Ascendant, Sun or Moon radiates the hot energy of courage and readiness to leap into action and, beyond that, the threat of aggression. So Mars brings the heroic gifts of the Flowering stage as well as the possibility of Psychopathic wounding in childhood coming through one of the parents or as a notable presence in the family dynamics.

### Mars in Aspect to the Ascendant

This can be quite a positive placement when the ease of access to the life force is at the foundation of the person's identity and their way of relating to the world. These individuals are competitive, highly assertive, sometimes bad-tempered and aggressive, but they have obvious qualities of leadership, initiative and integrity – a person with a strong Mars has an innate love of the truth, they have no truck with deceit. Their high levels of energy make them restless, impatient, and they need to be active a lot of the time. Often they are sporty and enjoy taking risks. A person with Mars in aspect to the Ascendant knows what they want and will go directly after it, like a hunter, and this capacity for direct action gives them heroic charisma. Mars is associated with desire, sexuality and the love of the chase, and this will be a major factor in their way of relating.

### Mars in Aspect to the Moon

Mars in aspect to the Moon is a more difficult placement. By nature, the Moon is sensitive and gentle, and we have seen that she symbolizes the nurturing relationship between a mother and child. Mars does not sit easily in this tender environment.

Mars in aspect to the Moon is usually indicative of a mother with some of the qualities of Mars – restless, self-centred, competitive and quick to anger. This can often be a secondary indication of Oral wounding when the anger or even violence of the mother undermines the baby's need for gentleness, or when anger was a major disturbing presence in the family. Similarly it can indicate Masochist wounding when the infant feels threatened and invaded by the angry or violent outbursts from the mother or other family members. Aspects between Mars and the Moon can be an indication of the mother's rivalry with her daughter and seduction of her son.

A Moon-Mars aspect can also indicate a mother in touch with the positive expression of Mars and this is also found when the Moon is in the sign of Aries. This can be a mother who is highly energised, active and creative and who supports a healthy directness, authentic integrity and ease with anger and assertiveness within the family.

A Moon-Mars contact is a symbol of the archetypal energy of Diana the huntress and goddess of the Moon. Diana was the sister of Apollo, the Sun god. Apollo was very much associated with civilization and the arts but Diana lived wild and free in the forests and mountains. Diana symbolizes the wild, instinctual side of the Feminine principle.

### Mars in Aspect to the Sun

This can be an extremely positive aspect, a sign of honourable heroic qualities, leadership and creativity. This person is likely to be an unstoppable force with huge resources of stamina and energy. The positive expression of Mars in aspect to the Sun is a father with the qualities of Mars – energy, initiative, integrity, honour, desire, ambition, assertiveness and aggression. The negative expression of this placement is an angry father: selfish, insensitive and aggressive to the point of violence and cruelty. Aspects between Mars and the Sun are a powerful indication of Psychopthic wounding in the form of the father's envy and rivalry of the son and seduction of the daughter.

Mars, the Lesser Malefic of ancient astrology, is not an easy planet. Notwithstanding their considerable intelligence and access to the gut-feeling intuition of the physical body, people with a strong Mars are frequently overpowered by the hot, obsessive urgency of their will. An individual with a strong Mars or emphasis on Aries brings tremendous gifts of courage, initiative and leadership. They are charismatic and sexual, passionate and exciting, and they shine a noble and brilliant light in this world.

# 41

# The Flowering or Psychopathic Stage
## The Sun, Ruler of Leo

The Sun represents the creative principle and the energy of the father. We have seen it as the symbol of the Solar qualities of authentic self-expression that the Budding/Masochist soul is seeking. When the Sun in the chart is 'afflicted' – in aspect to Saturn, Pluto or Chiron or lost in the 12th house – this is a sign of Masochist wounding and the need for transformation and healing of the Solar principle. When the energy of the Sun is unfettered and strong in the chart, it is a sign of the fiery outgoing nature of the Flowering or Psychopathic type.

**Planetary Archetype – Essence**

The god associated with the Sun is Apollo; son of Jupiter and twin brother of Diana, the goddess of the Moon. Apollo brought the most refined and creative aspects of culture – music, poetry, drama and knowledge – to mankind, and so the Sun is often a strong influence in the charts of musicians, artists and performers.

Apollo was very important in the culture of ancient Greece, the birthplace of western civilization. He was served by the priestess in the shrine of Delphi who was the oracle of Apollo. One of his names was Apollo Longsight; his vision and oracular power symbolize the human capacity to see the bigger picture. Apollo brings the light of reason, understanding and the ability to interpret the meaning of events. Apollo is a symbol of the light of human consciousness that comes, like the dawn, to dispel the terrors of the night. In *The Mythic Tarot* Liz Greene says:

> *Apollo is the dispeller of fear and his bright light casts away shadows.*

When the Sun is strong in the chart it gives the person faith, self-confidence, self-belief, generosity and a love of life. With the vigour of the life force expressing through romance, sexuality, creativity and play, the Sun is at its happiest in the Flowering stage.

### Wound

Some people find it hard to understand how there can be a wounded, negative expression of the Sun. In the western world we tend to value the Solar domain – light, expansion, the rational mind, logic, reason, activity and achievement – and to devalue the Lunar domain – darkness, contraction, feelings, instincts, receptivity and stillness. When the active principle of the light is not balanced with the patience and stillness of the dark, both areas are diminished. When there is no welcome for the dark of the inner world, then the light of the Sun becomes relentless. The burning heat of the Sun can scorch and destroy, and many young and vulnerable aspects of life that need to gestate in darkness are destroyed if they are prematurely exposed to the light. When the Solar principle becomes all-powerful, the life and joy go out of it and it degenerates into the dry, rational control of the patriarchy.

Like a child in the Flowering stage the Sun needs to shine and to be seen and appreciated. But Narcissistic Psychopathic wounding distorts this into a grandiose need for glory which has a charge, a heat, a demand, that oppresses and alienates people. When there is Psychopathic wounding the Solar energy becomes too hot – the individual will become self-obsessed and power-hungry, dominating conversations and creating dramas, insensitive to the needs of other people.

### Story – Sir Percival

The legend of King Arthur and the Knights of the Round Table is, in itself, a heroic, Solar tale and we have seen how the story of Sir Lancelot illustrates the wounding of the Psychopathic type. Unlike Lancelot, Sir Percival was one of the few knights to succeed in the quest for the Holy Grail and so his story illustrates the positive path of the Sun.

Percival grew up rough and wild, living alone with his mother in the depths of the forests of Wales. He had no contact at all with the outside world until one day Percival came across a group of knights hunting in the forest. The leader of the knights was Sir Lancelot, who spoke kindly to the wild young man who was clad only in the skins of wild animals. Lancelot invited Percival to come to Camelot to serve King Arthur. After that, there was no turning Percival; he said goodbye to his weeping mother and set off to meet his destiny.

On his journey he came across a pavilion where a beautiful damsel lay. In a dreamlike state, Percival bent and kissed the sleeping maiden. He took a ruby ring from her finger and replaced it with his own gold ring set with a diamond. Then he stumbled from the magical place and continued his journey to Camelot.

Here he was given a position as a servant at the court of King Arthur. Many of the knights scorned this uncultivated young man who they mocked for his crude manners and lack of grace. But Percival proved himself in combat and earned his knighthood by defeating the Red Knight who had insulted King Arthur. Percival was still ignorant and clumsy but Sir Gonemans, a kind old knight, took him home and trained him in the skills of knighthood.

Eventually Percival set out on his travels. He was one of the very few knights to come upon the Wasteland, find his way to Castle Carbonek and have sight of the Holy Grail. When he arrived at the magical castle, Percival was overjoyed to discover the maiden from the enchanted pavilion. She was Lady Blanchefleur, the daughter of the wounded King Pelles. Blanchefleur recognized Percival from her dreams and she still wore his ring on her finger. However, she said that it was not yet time to speak of their love.

When Percival sat at dinner, the great door to the chamber suddenly flew open and the miraculous procession of the Holy Grail entered. The light that shone from within the Holy Grail was so bright that none could look on it and Percival sank to his knees. He longed to speak and ask the meaning of these events but he remembered how he had been criticized for his ignorance and rudeness so he choked back his words and knelt in silence.

When the doors closed behind the procession Lady Blanchefleur told Percival that it was not yet his time to claim the discovery of the Grail and when that time came, only the most worthy of knights would be able to approach it. The impetuous Percival leaped up, crying, 'None but I shall achieve the quest of the Grail!' and, ignoring Blanchefleur's cries, he ran out into the night. In the morning when he awoke, the castle had vanished.

Percival searched for many days but to no avail. In great sorrow he decided to return to his mother in Wales and, before long, he met a wise old crone who took him in. She informed him that he had failed an important test. If, when the Grail Procession passed he had stepped forward and asked the right question, King Pelles would, at last, have been healed and the ruined Carbonek returned to its former glory. She also told him that his journey home was for nothing; soon after he had left her his mother had died from a broken heart.

Filled with remorse, Percival returned to Camelot where he performed great deeds but always he longed for Blanchefleur and searched for the Grail Castle. After many years Sir Galahad, the purest knight that ever lived, arrived at the court of King Arthur. On that day the Grail Procession came to Camelot and so began the final quest for the Holy Grail. Sir Percival rode with Sir Galahad and Sir Bors de Gannis and the Grail Knights came once more to Castle Carbonek where the old, wounded king still languished in his suffering.

When the knights sat down to dine, everything was just as before: the doors flew open and the procession of the Holy Grail passed through. Percival's heart lifted to see that the maiden carrying the Holy Grail was his beloved Blanchefleur. This time, older and wiser, with the wisdom of experience, Percival stepped forward and humbly asked the question, 'Whom does the Grail serve?'

Instantly a great transformation occurred. The wound of King Pelles was healed and the castle and all the land miraculously restored. Sir Galahad was, indeed, the only knight pure enough to achieve the quest and drink from the light of the Holy Grail but it was Sir Percival who brought healing to Carbonek. In time he married Blanchefleur and became king of Castle Carbonek. Together they reigned for many years and Carbonek remained a beacon of chivalry and hope in the dark days after the defeat of King Arthur.

Percival's road is the path of the Sun – a quest for glory, full of mistakes, humbling lessons and redemption through the hard-won wisdom of experience. Right from the start there is an issue with the father who he never knew and so the young Percival is unformed: a diamond in the rough, full of raw courage but naive, arrogant, impetuous, ignorant and clumsy. He is a classic adolescent, self-centred, inconsiderate, hot-headed and thoughtless, and this has tragic consequences for his mother who dies of a broken heart after his precipitate departure. But Percival is driven by the powerful Solar consciousness of his life purpose – to find his manhood in becoming one of the best of all knights and serving the luminous Solar figure of King Arthur. His fundamental intention is to be of service and because he remains pure of heart he succeeds in the end and brings a great good into the world.

In the beginning the young Percival acts impulsively and instinctively, without reflection. The kind Sir Gonemans teaches him a little more awareness but this has the unfortunate (and typical) effect of making him self-conscious so that when he sees the Grail for the first time he does the Masochist thing – withholds his authentic impulse, chokes back his questions and loses a great opportunity. Following this his Psychopathic lust for glory becomes his undoing. Percival's wish to be the one who triumphs in the quest for the Grail is selfish and egoistic, and in his haste he runs out and loses his connection to the wise and gentle Blanchefleur and his access to the Grail Castle. Then Percival realizes what his thoughtlessness has cost him – his mother, Blanchefleur, the healing of King Pelles and his realm. Such moments of remorse come as painful awakenings which prompt us to relinquish old habits and, out of the death of the old, a new awareness is born.

Then follow the long years of atonement. Percival fights innumerable fights, is tempted by at least two witches disguised as damsels in distress and is befriended by a lion (emblem of the instinctive aspect of the Sun) whom he saves from a serpent. But Percival does not give up on his dream.

Whenever he is in trouble he prays to God the Father for guidance and, ultimately, he never loses faith. When he finally gets his second chance he is ready, he has become wise and humble. He has learned that there are greater things in life than personal gratification and so he asks, 'Whom does the Grail serve?' Percival recognizes that his courage and strength are gifts, not designed for personal glorification but to be given in service of humanity. In the spirit of service he, at last, achieves his Solar purpose and his light shines long into the world.

### In the Human Energy Field

In the HEF, the Sun acts as a channel for the light of Essence, the light of the Source. The Solar light expressing through the Flowering/Psychopathic energy is very different to the Solar light in the Budding/Masochist stage. When the energy of the Sun is strong, the warm golden light of the Sun shines from the centre of the body like the light emanating from the Holy Grail, giving the person a large energy field full of movement and radiating vibrant golden light. The Sun focuses the light upwards towards the heart and the head and outwards into creative action in the world.

The Sun is happiest in Aries, Leo or Sagittarius, the three Fire signs associated with the Flowering/Psychopathic stage. When the Sun is in Aries, the Solar light feels almost tangible, a constant presence of aliveness with a red glow that can easily flame forth into the fierce burning light of the warrior. When the Sun is in its own sign of Leo it radiates a hot golden light like the August sun, which is often charismatic and commands attention but can also be too self-centred and overwhelming. In Sagittarius, the Solar light is a deeper autumnal gold, just as warm as in Aries or Leo but less demanding, sweetened by wisdom and laughter.

### The Sun in Aspect to the Ascendant or the Moon

The Sun represents the light of consciousness and the connection to self, which supports individual creativity. It is not aggressive like Mars but gives off a warm golden light of self-confidence and when in aspect to the Ascendant or the Moon it brings through that radiance. It can sometimes be difficult if the Ascendant or the Moon is in a more sensitive or retiring sign that is uncomfortable with the Sun's need to shine. The Sun can be an indication of narcissism and Psychopathic wounding or of the creativity and leadership of the Flowering stage.

### The Sun in Aspect to the Ascendant

This is almost invariably positive because the Solar self-confidence is the foundation of the person's sense of identity. Then their way of relating is filled with the warmth of the Sun and their faith in life.

### The Sun in Aspect to the Moon

Aspects between the Sun and Moon vary significantly according to the nature of the aspect. If the aspect is harmonious, then this is a sign of a healthy balance between the Masculine and Feminine principles – often a sign of a harmonious loving relationship between the parents. When the Sun and Moon are in a challenging aspect this can indicate conflict in the parental relationship and some kind of struggle between the Masculine and Feminine. The more negative version of a powerful Sun-Moon aspect is a person who is Narcissistically self-centred: obsessed with the importance of meeting their own needs through the two major principles most associated with the self – the Sun (consciousness) and the Moon (feeling). The positive expression is a balance between the emotional intelligence of the Moon and the rational creativity of the Sun.

The Solar principle represents the quest to bring the light of Essence into Conscious Awareness. The process of awakening and expressing our unique, authentic nature lies at the heart of every life, although the challenges will vary according to the energy patterns the individual is here to express or to heal. We humans have not yet got the knack of learning through joy – we tend to learn the hard way and some of us spend many, many years in the Wasteland. Many people become cynical and lock away the memory of the Holy Grail along with Santa Claus and Peter Pan. But the light of Spirit is eternal and, sooner or later, in this life or another, we can reawaken to the realization of who we really are.

# 42

## The Flowering or Psychopathic Stage
## Jupiter, Ruler of Sagittarius (and Pisces)

In traditional astrology Jupiter was known as the Greater Benefic, the bringer of good fortune. Jupiter represents the principle of expansion, a visionary who looks beyond the horizon to see new, previously unimagined possibilities. Jupiter represents the amazing human capacity to bring some completely new idea out from the void, and in this way Jupiter resembles Uranus but is much less abstract. Jupiter brings good luck, opportunity, inspiration, enthusiasm and joy. Before the discovery of Neptune, Jupiter was also the ruler of Pisces and shares Neptune's visionary spirituality and love of the world of the imagination.

Like Mars and the Sun, Jupiter belongs to the element of Fire: dynamic, creative and regal. Whereas Mars and the Sun can be pushy or domineering, Jupiter attracts attention in a way that seems more natural and effortless. Mars, the Sun and Jupiter all like to get attention but Jupiter does it more gracefully, with ease and humour! The Sun and Mars can both feel oppressive and demanding in their attention-seeking, but larger-than-life Jupiter has star quality, easily takes the space and inspires its listeners with wisdom, hope and laughter.

In the horoscope, Jupiter brings a powerful, expansive, uplifting energy into the part of the chart in which it falls and to any planets that it touches. Jupiter represents such a positive energy that wherever it appears in the chart will always feel like 'the answer'!

### Planetary Archetype – Essence

Jupiter was the king of the gods, the god of the sky and thunder. He was omnipotent, and looking down from on high on Mount Olympus he guided the destiny of mortals. One of the emblems of Jupiter is the eagle, and Jupiter brings the capacity to see far.

Jupiter was not a bad king. He was not such a megalomaniac that he felt compelled to reject or eat his children like his father Saturn and grandfather Uranus. In fact, Jupiter was addicted to having children! Jupiter had a roving eye and, as well as fathering several of the gods and goddesses, many of the well-known heroes and heroines were the children of his illicit affairs; Jupiter never missed an opportunity to sow his seed! The psychological significance of Jupiter's many children is unlimited creativity, the love of possibility, potential and growth. In the style of his grandfather, Uranus, but with much more warmth and joy, Jupiter represents the moment of conception, the birth of a possible future as he plants his seed, fertilizes the egg and moves on.

A person with a strong Jupiter is never, ever short of an idea. They rise to any creative challenge with a flood of possible routes, pathways, schemes and projects, which can be overwhelming for the individual as well as those around them. But, like a flower scattering its seed into the wind, Jupiter does not plan where his seeds will fall and, unless some structured, earthy or maternal energy fosters them, most of the seeds will never grow. Jupiter does not destroy his children with perfectionism, as Uranus did, but it is not his job to stay around and get his hands dirty in the nitty-gritty of parenting. The work of manifestation is left to planets more at home with grounding and structure, and particularly Jupiter's complete opposite Saturn, which carries the principle of limitation.

Jupiter represents the archetype of the High Priest and Priestess, the quest for higher knowledge, the philosopher, the cleric and the law-maker. In his search for meaning he is an adventurer, a traveller in many worlds, journeying in his quest to the four corners of the physical world as well as to the inner world of the psyche. Jupiter is associated with Jung's theory that human beings have an innate psychological urge to seek for spiritual meaning, for a relationship with the Divine. Jupiter is a spiritual leader, a guide and teacher of higher knowledge. Like Moses bringing down the Ten Commandments, Jupiter works with religious law – the moral and philosophical codes that underpin civilization.

## Wound

Just as it is not in the nature of Mars to consider other people's feelings, so it is not in the nature of immortal Jupiter to consider the limitations of life on earth. Jupiterian inspiration is like a beautiful hot-air balloon rising into the sky, lifting the heart and raising the hopes of anyone who watches. But if Jupiter is not backed up by a more grounded energy then, like the balloon, his beautiful promise of hope can turn out to be nothing but hot air and the balloon will vanish into the heavens or plummet out of the skies.

Jupiter is the principle of expansion and optimism but when there has been Psychopathic wounding his visionary enthusiasm turns into a life-defeating attachment to grandiosity and illusion. It is not Jupiter's role to have his feet on the ground but when energies in the chart stack up to make the realm of the imagination too powerful then overheated Jupiter can defeat any hope of completing a project. This kind of inflated Jupiter has no understanding of patience and structure and he wants to move on even before the planning stage is complete.

The keyword here is 'inflation', thus a negative expression of Jupiter will be found in the charts of individuals gripped by a grandiose, idealized view of the self; extreme cases suffer from bipolar disorder and any other form of mania. One minute they are flying high – singled out by the Divine because they are so special – the next moment, reality hits and, grandiose even in despair, they crash into the deepest, blackest depression.

Somewhere back in childhood, the Jupiter type concluded that reality (in the form of Narcissistic expectations from one or both of the parents) was too dangerous to cope with; Jupiter is one of the planets most associated with the wounding of the *puer aeternus*. The Jupiter type subsequently spends years on the run, living in a dangerous fantasy world – gamblers, con men, cult leaders and impossible dreamers. This kind of person does not need to be encouraged to listen for their inner voice because they probably already think they are hearing it, though I doubt if it is the still quiet voice of the Higher Self that has got their attention! When the fire is out of control and expansion has turned to inflation, healing means finding a way to bring Jupiter's hot air balloon down to earth to give reality a chance.

Jupiter was the law-maker and immensely powerful. Though he was often wise and more likeable than Mars (the word 'jovial' is derived from his name), in his negative expression he represents an inflated sense of God-given self-righteousness. The danger is that a person with a strong Jupiter will buy into their feelings of omnipotence and channel their power into a vision that has become fanatical. Eve Jackson, author of *Jupiter: An Astrologer's Guide,* made the disturbing discovery that Jupiter was prominent in the charts of nearly all of the Nazi leaders. Jupiter's charisma can disguise megalomania, which was very much the case with the rise of Nazism.

At the darkest end of the spectrum, Jupiter's self-righteousness leads to religious bigotry and all kinds of blind, fanatical fundamentalism. The medieval inquisitors, the Gestapo torturers, the Ku Klux Klan lynch mobs and the terrorist bombers – these are the representatives of the dark face of Jupiter, making the simple raw aggression of Mars seem relatively harmless. Stan Lee's superhero Spider Man says:

> *With great power comes great responsibility*

though I think he heard it first from Jesus, who said:

> *For unto whomsoever much is given, of him shall be much required: and to whom men have committed much, of him they will ask the more.*

**Story – A Christmas Carol**

In Charles Dickens's famous tale of *A Christmas Carol*, the three spirits of Christmas illustrate the Essence of Jupiter as the bringer of insight, wisdom and renewal.

Scrooge is a bitter, avaricious old man who has lost his way. He has completely shut down on compassion, morality or hope and lives a miserable existence, an empty husk of a life in which nothing matters but work. Jupiter connects us to Divine grace and so Scrooge is blessed with a night of visitations from beyond the grave and the chance to transform his life.

First comes Marley's ghost, the spectre of Scrooge's deceased business partner, who shows him the terrible consequences of a life lived for nothing but greed. Then, with the three spirits, the Ghost of Christmas Past, the Ghost of Christmas Present and the Ghost of Christmas Yet to Come, Scrooge is taken on a journey of awakening.

The spirit of Christmas Past shows significant turning points in Scrooge's life. First we see him as a boy with his loving sister Fan and we hear of the difficulties in his relationship with his father. We see the pain of his childhood, we begin to understand how Scrooge has been wounded and how that eventually led him to close his heart. We move on to the next phase of Scrooge's youth when his life seemed promising, with a benevolent employer and a fiancée named Belle. But time passes and we come to an older Scrooge whose grim attachment to work and money has caused Belle to leave him. The ghost then forces the unhappy Scrooge to witness a vision of Belle as she is now: a mature woman with a husband and family, the happy life that might once have been his.

In his second visitation Scrooge meets the Ghost of Christmas Present – a wonderful illustration of Jupiter as the Greater Benefic. We find the ghost magically surrounded by all the fruits of the earth, the bringer of unlimited abundance. But he is much more than a jovial Father Christmas: he also represents the moral aspects of free will, and Scrooge discovers that this benevolent spirit is only able to leave his blessings in homes where his generosity is recognized and welcomed. The ghost shows Scrooge the home of his clerk, Bob Cratchit, where the family is merry despite having very few material comforts. Scrooge is also told that the young Tiny Tim, who is ill, will die unless he receives help. The spirit also takes Scrooge on a walk through the streets of the city and shows him the moral consequences of greed. He reveals the terrifying presence of two wretched, starving children, Ignorance and Want – the victims of human lack of compassion.

The third ghost, the fearful Ghost of Christmas Yet to Come, reveals the future, the terrible consequences that will come about if

Scrooge does not change his ways. Scrooge witnesses his own meaningless and un-mourned death contrasted with the sorrowful passing of the beloved invalid child Tiny Tim. But Scrooge has understood. He is appalled and begs for the chance to mend his ways and bring about a better future. That opportunity is, of course, granted him. The final scene where Scrooge emerges as a new man, ready to embrace the world in the true spirit of Christmas, is a perfect illustration of the joy, excitement and expansion of Jupiter. With his renewed vision, so many possibilities arise for Scrooge to re-engage with his humanity and compassion.

This story is about our intention, the choices we make in life. It illuminates the possibility that while a person's history can be blighted by difficult circumstances it is also created by the nature of the decisions they make along the way. Scrooge's awakening is a Jupiterian revelation that we are always free to change: the future is not fixed and in every moment new possibilities arise. The journey through past, present and future is a psycho-spiritual reckoning with Scrooge's life and a renewal of love and hope.

The Ghost of Christmas Present is the embodiment of Jupiter. He is huge and merry, the soul of generosity, and when they walk through the streets of London the spirit is ready to offer his gifts to any person who will receive him. He is also far-seeing and wise and he understands that Scrooge's compassion for the fate of Tiny Tim is the key to unlocking his hardened heart. Reminiscent of the magic of the Snow Child, the bounteous Ghost of Christmas Present lives only for a short while, but long enough to re-awaken Scrooge's humanity.

Jupiter brings vision, meaning and purpose in life. The ghosts of *A Christmas Carol* embody the wisdom of Jupiter and remind us to take a look at our lives and be aware of the choices we are making. The past, the present and the future all belong to us and Jupiter reminds us that we are free: we are the makers of our own lives and our creative potential is vast.

## In The Human Energy Field

Once, I was on a plane coming in to land through a towering mass of clouds. The Jumbo Jet felt quite puny amongst the huge white thunderclouds. As we made a bumpy and scary descent, a beautiful shifting green and gold light filtered through the awesome clouds, somehow combining the qualities of tremendous beauty with danger, power and exhilaration. This is the light of Jupiter, the God of Thunder. When a person's Jupiter is fully active their energy field takes on precisely that thrilling, towering presence, giving us the sense that we are in the presence of the king of the gods.

Jupiter is by far the largest of the planets of the solar system and one of the key indications of a strong influence from Jupiter is a person with a big, golden, radiant energy field; very charismatic and giving a sense of something that is larger than life. No other planet, not even the Sun, makes the HEF so expanded, so magnetic and somehow combining the qualities of great charm with effortless power. A positive expression of Jupiter gives us the feeling of an ideal father: strong, charming, lovable, humorous, generous and benevolent.

Before the discovery of Uranus and Neptune, Jupiter was the planet that represented our link to the transpersonal dimension, to the realms of Spirit. In his role as our connection to the Mind of God, Jupiter often focuses energy up to the vision of the 6th chakra and to the 'direct knowing' of the 7th chakra. However, unlike Uranus and Neptune, Jupiter is also very concerned with human issues; the quest for meaning and purpose, justice and morality. It is the inspiration and faith of Jupiter that gives us the sense of our life purpose and in this role Jupiter connects to the deep level of the Hara.

The powerful central Hara line anchors a human being into the heart of the Earth and also rises up to the stars – 'To infinity and beyond' says that highly Jupiterian hero, Buzz Lightyear. The Hara line carries the energy of our life purpose; the developmental path of the Soul. On the Hara line, around 3 feet above the head, there is an energy centre like a star, which is the place of our connection to the Divine, to the Mind of God. This star holds the energy of Jupiter. When we raise our awareness up to the star we come into contact with the benevolent power and wisdom of the Universal Mind; the consciousness of the Universal Energy Field from which we are born and to which we shall return. In this place we have no doubt of our Divine inheritance; we find faith that all is well and receive guidance to inform our choices from the highest, most spiritual level. So Jupiter is our connection to the benevolent goodwill of the Divine, bringing us a constant source of inspiration and faith in life.

When there is wounding and a lack of grounding in the HEF, the energy of Jupiter turns to grandiosity, becomes inflamed, over-expanded, manic and the Haric connection to the Earth is weakened and eventually broken. Then, with the desperation of a drug addict getting a 'fix', the exhilaration of the upward and outward surge takes on a powerful forcing current and the HEF feels dangerously overheated and out of control.

### Jupiter in Aspect to the Ascendant, the Moon and the Sun

Jupiter represents the principle of expansion and when it is in aspect to the Ascendant, Sun or Moon, the joyful qualities of optimism and enthusiasm will shine through a person's HEF. Jupiter can also be over-expansive, overpowering and fanatical so it brings the possibility of Psychopathic wounding in childhood as well as the gifts of the Flowering stage coming through one of the parents or as a notable presence in the family dynamics.

### Jupiter in Aspect to the Ascendant

When Jupiter makes an aspect to the Ascendant, or the Ascendant is in Sagittarius, the joviality, humour, warmth and charisma of Jupiter becomes a major part of the person's identity and of the way in which they present themselves to the world. These charismatic individuals will never be short of an idea, can easily 'think outside the box' and see possibilities beyond the ideas of more methodical thinkers. They are full of laughter and optimism and they often have many followers who are drawn to their effortless bonhomie and warmth.

## Jupiter in Aspect to the Moon

Jupiter in aspect to the Moon can indicate a very positive relationship with an inspiring mother who radiates warmth, creativity, enthusiasm and optimism. With Jupiter's love of travel and seeking out new experiences, the mother or other ancestors may have originated from a different country or the family may go on to make their home in a foreign country. The mother may be a philosophical, spiritual or religious seeker or the family may be part of a strong spiritual community.

As always, the negative possibilities of this planet are that the fire of Jupiter turns into blinkered, God-given righteousness, fanaticism, mania and difficulty in coming to terms with reality. When Jupiter aspects the Moon, or when the Moon is in Sagittarius, the mother can be a very overpowering, dogmatic individual and this placement is often a secondary indication of Masochist wounding.

## Jupiter in Aspect to the Sun

Of all the fiery planets, Jupiter is the least contentious; Jupiter has natural star quality, authority and wisdom and does not have to fight as hard as the Sun and Mars to get attention. Jupiter in aspect to the Sun is often very positive and can be a sign of a warm, powerful, charismatic and inspiring father.

Again, the negative expression of Jupiter in aspect to the Sun is religious fundamentalism and someone who is fanatically attached to some moral or political ideology. The fiery nature of Jupiter and the Sun make them overly subjective in their thinking, blind to other people's right to a different point of view. In childhood, the negative expression of a Sun-Jupiter aspect is an extremely dominant father who imposes his world view on the family.

A negative Jupiter is also associated with bipolar disorder, individuals who swing between wild inflated visions and dark despair and this, or a version of this, may be an issue with the father. Individuals with a strong Jupiter or an emphasis on Sagittarius love to show a bright face to the world but they often have great difficulty in coping with grim realities, the dark moments in life. When there is a death or when something fails and their optimism deserts them, the Jupiterian soul can fall into deep depression. This is not the face they wish to show to the world but it is symptomatic of the tendency of Jupiter/Sagittarius types towards manic behaviour and bipolar disorder.

Jupiter represents the human search for something greater, for meaning – questions of spiritual purpose and religion. A Sun-Jupiter aspect is often found in the charts of community leaders, teachers of higher knowledge and wisdom, priests and shamans. Jupiter also has to do with moral questions and the making of law – the archetype of the Judgement of Solomon – and so it is associated with judges, lawyers and solicitors.

Larger-than-life Jupiter is highly likely to be a dominant feature of the charts of actors, all kinds of performers, celebrities and anyone who looms large on the world stage. The origins of theatre connect back to ancient spiritual rituals and mystery plays and bring us the Jupiterian experiences of inspiration, enlightenment and expansion – as well as the joy of comedy. Jupiter in aspect to the Sun is also common in the charts of great voyagers, explorers, mountaineers and travellers of all kinds. The energy that drives the explorer to seek what is over the horizon also fuels inner journeys of spiritual discovery.

Jupiter brings us wonderful feelings of possibility, meaning and purpose; the phoenix eternally rising from the ashes bringing hope into our darkest hours. Jupiter is also associated with the grandiosity and illusions of omnipotence emerging from the damaged child who believed they were required to be 'special'. The Jupiterian soul has to navigate the tricky waters between the adrenalin rush of an ungrounded fantasy of glory and the action of a true visionary moving with an authentic inner connection to Divine wisdom.

# 43

## The Flowering or Psychopathic Stage

## The Houses: Where to Look for the Flowering/Psychopathic Stage in the Chart

In the Flowering stage, the individual wants to come forth and light up the world with their creative fire. So, to begin with, the houses associated with this stage are the Fire trinity – the 1st, 5th and 9th houses. I also associate the 11th house with the heroic aspect of the Flowering/Psychopathic type as champions of social justice, community leaders energetically working towards a vision of a better world.

### The Ascendant and the 1st House

When any of the 'fiery' planets – the Sun, Mars and Jupiter and their signs of Leo, Aries and Sagittarius respectively – are found aspecting the Ascendant or in the 1st house this indicates that the energy and courage of the Flowering/Psychopathic stage are a major part of the individual's sense of identity and their way of presenting themselves to the world.

### The 5th House

This house is where the light of the self shines in playful creativity and love affairs, and is the heart of the Flowering stage. A gathering of planets here indicates an emphasis on the Flowering stage. However, Saturn, Pluto or Chiron in the 5th are indications of Masochist wounding.

### The 9th House

The 9th house is associated with travel and journeys, including journeys of the mind and our search to find meaning in life. This house is associated with religion, philosophy and spiritual, moral and political systems of thinking. It is in the 9th house that we make the moral code by which we live and the laws of our societies. It is also the house associated with teachers of higher knowledge, the archetype of the High Priest or Priestess. Planets here show the Flowering/Psychopathic type out on their quests, bringing all their courage, integrity, vision and wisdom to their communities.

### The 11th House

Like those of the 12th house, the traditional descriptions of the affairs of the 11th house can be hard to grasp, and appear confusing or slightly insubstantial unless placed in a spiritual context. Traditionally the 11th house is the house of friendship and it describes our relationship to all kinds of networks, from local social clubs to the World Wide Web and Facebook. However, there is more to the 11th house than social success. While the 10th house represents the pinnacle of achievement in human society, the 11th house begins to focus beyond the limitations of the world of matter, expanding out towards the non-physical realms of the 12th house. The 11th house can be seen as the bridge between the concrete cultural forms of the 10th house and the diffuse, non-physical world of Spirit and the Collective Unconscious which is the 12th house.

Traditionally, the 11th house is the house of hopes and dreams. The 5th house (opposite the 11th) has to do with personal creativity and the 11th house also has to do with creative vision but in the context of a group or a network. The 11th house is where we can explore human creative potential as a group, including the wider vision of where the human race might be heading. And this brings me to the ideas of the twentieth-century spiritual philosopher, Teilhard de Chardin (the final case study in Part III of this book). Teilhard de Chardin was one of the great palaeontologists of the early twentieth century and a world authority on the theory of evolution. He was also a Christian mystic and he introduced the idea of evolution as a drive that carries the human race towards a global expansion of consciousness and an ultimate moment of complete re-unification with the Divine (and these ideas have been taken up by many subsequent thinkers including Peter Russell, author of *The Global Brain Awakens*). Teilhard believed that the human race is in the process of becoming a unified collective mind, with each individual contributing their Essence to the development of the Soul of the World. Even back in the mid-twentieth century Teilhard saw the development of the new technologies, communication networks and computers as part of the move towards collective union and the Divine awakening of the consciousness of the human race.

Like King Arthur's ideal of chivalry, Teilhard's idea of the spiritual evolution of the human collective gives a role of cosmic importance to the 11th house. This leads me to class the affairs of the 11th house with the pioneering vision of the Flowering/Psychopathic soul (with emphasis on planets like Jupiter and Mars, and also Uranus and Mercury) rather than with the Harvest/Rigid planets (Saturn and Venus) whose role emphasizes physical world limitations, stability and harmony rather than the unpredictable disturbances of spiritual growth.

From this view we can regard planets in the 11th house as representing the individual's creative contribution to the awakening of the collective. People with a strong emphasis on the 11th house are those who recognize the oneness, the unity, of all life and have come here to induct a bigger picture, a new vision for the human race.

## The Parental Axis – the 4th and 10th Houses

The 4th and 10th houses, as we have previously seen, represent the parental axis, and fiery planets found here will indicate that one or both parents brought the Flowering/Psychopathic fire into the family dynamic. Mars, the Sun or Jupiter in the 4th house is often an indication of Flowering/Psychopathic fire in the father that impacts the family; in the 10th house this indicates the Flowering/Psychopathic energy coming from the mother. These placements can also be an indication of Masochist wounding when the child experiences the fiery nature of the parent as invasive or overwhelming.

## Summary

Indications of emphasis on the issues of the Flowering/Psychopathic stage:

## The Houses:
## Where to Look for the Flowering/Psychopathic Stage in the Chart

- Mars, the Sun or Jupiter in aspect to the Ascendant, the Sun or the Moon
- The Sun, Moon or Ascendant in Aries, Leo or Sagittarius
- Mars, the Sun or Jupiter in the 1st, 4th, 5th, 9th, 10th or 11th house
- The North Node and any other emphasis of positive planets in the 1st, 5th, 9th or 11th house

The gods of fire – Mars, Jupiter and the Sun – represent the exhilarating power of the life force, the raw energy that wells up into the Core and out of which we create our being and our life stories. They represent three aspects of the Flowering stage – energetic, playful and inspiring with courage, creativity and vision. The Flowering soul has come to enjoy sexuality, fertility, union and creation. Their longing is to find the ecstasy of relationship between the gentle receptive wisdom of the Feminine and the active power and purpose of the Masculine.

44

# THE HARVEST OR RIGID STAGE

The fifth stage, the Rigid stage, is associated with the older child aged between four and seven years old. The child is learning the social rules of how to fit in with their family, their peers, their tribe and their community. Trauma in this stage comes from the experience of being judged, criticized and controlled leading to the fear of failure and the fear of rejection. The child develops the Rigid defence, which is associated with issues of extreme control and judgement and the need to adhere to recognised standards of behaviour and achievement.

# 45

## The Harvest or Rigid Stage

## The Psychological View: Wounding and Defence in the Rigid Stage

The fifth stage occurs between the ages of four and seven as the child continues to explore what it is to be in relationship – with their parents, their family and the world at large. The child is no longer merged, they feel more like a separate individual and they are learning about the demands, the expectations and the responsibilities of being a member of this tribe in which they have landed! The older, more self-conscious child becomes increasingly aware of the ways in which different behaviours evoke differing responses – approval or disapproval from their parents and extended family.

Ideally, a parent will be supportive in allowing the child's own inclinations and values to unfold but it is also inevitable that the pliable personality of the child is stamped with a template of the parent's making. And to a large extent this is exactly what the child wants. The child in the Rigid stage is eager to learn what it takes to be accepted, how to fit in and belong in the family and in society. They intuitively detect coldness and withdrawal of contact from a parent who disapproves of their actions, just as they recognize the warmth and sense of belonging when the parent welcomes their behaviour.

All families operate within some system of beliefs, which serve a kind of tribal instinct to keep the community united. Sometimes the code is very obvious and oppressive, as with families who are fanatical followers of a religion or have a fierce allegiance to a political ideology. There are also less threatening codes of behaviour – intellectual families, sporty families, families who must look good, food and drink families, medical families, aristocratic families, working class families, and so on. Each family will have its own unique book of rules for belonging. Some are bearably light, some are soul-destroyingly heavy.

So the Rigid stage can become a minefield of demands and judgements as the child tries to figure out the rules. They try hard to comply with the expectations of the older generation but the Rigid wound is another version of Narcissistic wounding because the child is not seen and valued for their own individuality. The child with a Masochist defence tries to resist, the child with a Psychopathic defence reacts with aggression and the child in the Rigid stage becomes rational and controlled. 'Control' is the keyword for the Rigid type.

## Wounding

Trauma occurs in the Rigid stage when, exactly as the name suggests, the family edict is rigid, unyielding, set in stone. Doing the 'right' thing is paramount and the code of conduct is of more importance than the wellbeing of the child. Anything in the child that threatens the system is rejected, sometimes in extreme ways such as beatings and other punishments but often much more subtly. The child finds out that much of their natural spontaneous way of being is not welcome and they learn to repress the aspects of their nature that get them into trouble. In effect, they create trouble for themselves in order to stay out of trouble!

Most Rigid wounding happens in families that have the appearance of conformity rather than in an obviously fanatical family where the wounding is more likely to be Psychopathic or Masochistic. In a more 'normal' family there are subtle but very powerful rules in place that quietly punish transgressions and enforce the correct standards of behaviour. The classic Rigid manifesto is usually some version of – go to a good school, get a good job, own some property, be rich, be heterosexual, get married, have well- behaved children, be clean, be thin, look good, be healthy, be sociably acceptable, go to church/mosque/temple/synagogue, be polite but know your boundaries and don't hang out with people who are the wrong colour or religion or who are poor, weird, chaotic, eccentric or who threaten to rock the boat in any other way! Whatever form the family template of beliefs takes, it makes a judgement on the right and wrong ways to do life and this becomes the yardstick of success.

Rigid wounding occurs in the moment when the child abandons their own inner sense of direction and replaces it with an externally imposed view of what is 'right'. Even the most beautiful spiritual truths can be internalized as an oppressive rule. Whether we are listening to Moses speaking from the mountain or the Buddha telling us to let go of our cravings, the voice that is telling us how to behave is not our own. When there is Rigid wounding the child's life force gets channelled into an unremitting struggle to match up to an acquired set of standards. They learn to conform to an ideal and in doing so they give up a part of their soul. Their locus of attention is external instead of internal and the question changes from 'Who am I?' to 'Who do they want me to be?'

At the heart of the Rigid wound is a profound loss of faith. From infancy onwards, the child's accumulating experiences of trauma obscure their connection to the Core Star. After all their encounters with fear, deprivation, oppression and betrayal it can feel as though their inner light was a fairy tale that never really existed. More than any of the other Character types, the Rigid type has lost their connection to their Core Star. Instead, they fear that what they have inside of them is nothing at all.

During the Psychopathic stage the individual is still driven by a passionate romantic belief in love and honour. But when there have been too many experiences of betrayal and too many disappointments then that naive heroic faith is lost. A person with Rigid wounding has an entrenched and much more cynical version of the Psychopthic hope that love can be 'won'. They are gripped by a deeply held belief that love is totally conditional.

For many people with Rigid wounding, the material world is the only reality. For others, their internal sense of spiritual or creative purpose has been ensnared by a Rigid agenda, so they are driven by anxiety to match up to the criteria of a religious creed or formula for how to be 'good'! Whether their rule book is based on a material or a spiritual formula, the Rigid wound creates a script that effectively blocks the individual from connection to their Essence.

### Defence

For the child in the Rigid stage, their understanding of what does and does not meet with approval becomes internalized as a powerful code of conduct, known as the Superego. The Superego's rules can feel like the Ten Commandments, carved on tablets of stone. Once in place, these laws are enforced by the Superego's executioner, the Inner Critic.

We have seen that the Inner Critic is a voice that is born very early in life, in reaction to pain and terror in infancy. The Critic comes from a place of irrational dread, concerned only with fear and defence, and it knows nothing of joy or creativity or truth. It is surprising to realize that the Critic's original intention was to protect the terrified infant. And the distorted belief that runs the Critic is that its job is to figure out what is wrong with us and tell us about it so that we can fix it. The Critic may have originated from the need for protection but its effect is to reinforce the conviction that there is something badly wrong with us. It speaks with the voice of someone who loathes and despises us and it becomes our own Inner Terrorist.

The voice of the Inner Critic is a major component of the Rigid defence and it brings us agonising shame. The Superego sets up a book of rules to match up to the family expectations and the Critic delivers a merciless attack on any failure to meet those standards. The voice of the Critic runs like an endless loop, relentlessly telling us what we have done wrong, focusing on every way in which we have failed and anticipating further disappointment. The tricky thing is that there is always a tiny kernel of truth in the Inner Critic's attacks. The Critic hooks into any aspect of the self which suffers from self-doubt and it makes no allowances for natural human flaws.

When looked at objectively, the judgements of the Inner Critic are ludicrously out of proportion to the reality of a situation. From the detached position of the Witness, listening to the relentless attacks of the Critic is like listening to child abuse, yet still we give it our attention and become lost in the misery of self-loathing and despair that the

Critic brings. The Inner Critic causes us more pain than any other aspect of our being; the bigger the Critic the younger the age of the terrorized child who first brought it into being. The Inner Critic is a major component of the majority of mental health problems; an extreme version is the 'Killer Critic' who will drive a person to suicide.

### Recognizing the Rigid Defence

The Rigid defence presents in two major ways – the Materialist Rigid and the Perfectionist Rigid.

### The Materialistic Rigid Type

For the Materialist Rigid type, success is measured in terms of worldly things such as income, possessions, lifestyle and status, with an emphasis on stability, tradition and maintaining the status quo. Conforming to the standards set by their culture, these people are the backbone of society: responsible, hard-working and conscientious, bringing high standards of organization, efficiency and practical common sense to their work. They often rise to positions of authority because their high moral standards and 'work ethic' make them a good choice for promotion to any role that requires responsibility and hard work. Professional people, such as doctors, lawyers, accountants, administrators, secretaries, schoolteachers, soldiers and policemen have this kind of Rigid defence; certain about the need for discipline, procedure and sticking to the correct moral and legal codes. They create stable families of law-abiding citizens and impressive family dynasties of successful progeny who often follow similar career paths to their parents and grandparents.

The Materialist Rigid type holds strong boundaries and exudes a smooth harmony that repulses any excessive expression of vulnerability. The collapsing Oral type and the ineffectual Masochist type will find themselves suffering from insidious feelings of inferiority in the presence of the Rigid type. The Rigid type politely despises the eccentricity of the Schizoid type, the neediness of the Oral type, the failures of the Masochist type and the melodrama of the Psychopathic type, and they radiate a subtle air of superiority. They do not appreciate the beauty of human diversity; instead, people who are 'different' are seen as a problem. They are judgemental of individuals who threaten the status quo and the end of this road is fascism – the rejection of those they consider undesirable on grounds of race, religion or politics.

## Physical Appearance

The Materialistic Rigid type usually looks good, with a pleasant face, even features and a well-proportioned body. They maintain a clean, healthy appearance with regular exercise and a balanced diet. They work hard to ensure that their sleek exterior reflects the image they wish to project, and these days they will resort to cosmetic surgery to correct any mistakes that Nature left them with. They have clean, nicely decorated homes, neat gardens and shining cars. They usually have good health, though they often suffer from back problems and chronic muscular tension resulting from excessive control. The more intense Rigid type becomes over-anxious, obsessive and inflexible; people with Obsessive Compulsive Disorder suffer from an extreme version of Materialistic Rigid wounding.

The Materialist Rigid type focuses on external things; they give their attention to detail, to the periphery of things and avoid going into the heart of the matter. They are calm and reasonable and avoid displays of emotion. When they encounter any kind of emotional upset the typical Rigid reaction is to try to 'fix' the problem by proposing logical solutions, analysis and explanation, but if the emotional outburst persists they will soon remove themselves from the scene. They regard displays of feelings and vulnerability as a weakness but the price they pay is the absence of authentic human contact. When the only things that matter are the things of the material world then the inner life of the soul becomes hard to reach. As the years go by these individuals start to suffer from loss of meaning. Things that were once joyful lose their sparkle and life becomes monotonous and predictable. Though they may appear to have 'made it', with all the trappings of comfort and stability, their lives begin to feel increasingly disappointing and empty. Beneath the conventional Rigid type's appearance of stability is the fear that there is no life beyond material existence, so that they themselves only amount to the sum of their mortal legacy. This fear is the driving force behind their worldly ambition as they anaesthetize themselves by fortifying their little castle of security, dreading to look over the parapet in case there is absolutely nothing out there.

**Story – American Beauty**

In the Greek creation myth, we have seen that Ouranos (Uranus), the sky god, destroyed all his progeny because he saw ugliness in the children of Matter. Eventually, Gaia, the earth goddess, hid her son Cronus (Saturn), and when Cronus was fully grown he attacked Ouranos and castrated him. Cronus then became king but, in his dying breath, Ouranos prophesied that Cronus himself would be dethroned by one of his own sons.

Cronus married the earth goddess Rhea but, mindful of the prophecy, he followed in his father's footsteps and destroyed all his progeny by swallowing them whole as soon as Rhea had given birth to them. True to form, Rhea objected to this treatment of her children, concealed her third child, Zeus (Jupiter), and gave Cronus a stone wrapped in swaddling cloth, which he duly swallowed. Then Zeus was reared in secret and when he grew to manhood he went to Cronus disguised as a cup-bearer. Zeus gave Cronus an emetic to drink which caused him to vomit up all the children he had swallowed: Hestia, Demeter, Hera, Hades and Poseidon. These were the Olympian gods and goddesses who immediately joined forces with Zeus. They overthrew Cronus and he was imprisoned in Tartarus along with most of the other rejected or defeated children of the earth.

In this brief summary of the myth we see how Ouranos rejected his children and flung them away from him whereas Cronus swallowed them and kept them inside of him. Great parents! The children are symbols of creation, of new manifestations of the life force. Ouranos and Cronus represent aspects of the psyche unable to cope with the free flow of the life force. For Ouranos the issue is perfection, for Cronus the issue is control. Cronus (as Saturn in western astrology) represents that aspect of the Rigid defence which blocks the spontaneous upwelling of the creative impulse and represses it in order to maintain control.

The Oscar-winning movie *American Beauty* beautifully illustrates a story about the breakdown of the Materialist Rigid defence. The film follows the progress of Lester Burnham, a middle-aged, middle-class American whose life is beginning to come apart. His relationship with his wife, Carolyn, is a loveless sham, their communication made up of her meaningless platitudes and controlling demands and his resentful submission. Both his wife and his teenage daughter, Jane, despise him, though his wife makes every effort to keep up appearances in public. In the narrative we hear Lester say:

> *They think I'm a loser. They're right, I have lost something. I don't know what it is but I didn't always feel this sedated.*

When Lester finds that he is being fired from the firm where he has worked for twenty years, it is the last straw. Now that he has nothing to lose he begins to break out of the pretence of his phoney existence, this time saying:

> *I feel like I've been in a coma for about twenty years and now I'm waking up.*

Lester has a showdown with his wife, he makes the effort to form a better relationship with his daughter and falls obsessively in love with her beautiful best friend, Angela.

A new family has moved in next door: the fascistic Colonel Frank Fitts (a classic portrayal of the Rigid patriarch) his oppressed and depressed wife and their teenage son, Rickie. Rickie maintains the appearance of total compliance with his father's rigid and violently enforced regimen, but actually he has a secret life of his own, making money as a drug dealer. Rickie is a photographer and also a mystic who sees beauty everywhere. Rickie has managed to remain in contact with his Creative Essence whereas his father has lost his inner connection.

As the film progresses all the characters – Lester, his wife, his daughter and even Colonel Fitts – are challenged in their old patterns of behaviour and all find themselves thrown into exposure of their deeper selves as the outer shell breaks open. New levels of truth are found, eventually with tragic results for Lester, while hope of redemption is carried by his young daughter and Rickie, who escape to the city and refuse to conform.

One of the themes of *American Beauty* is the distorted sexuality underlying the polite facade of middle-class American life. This is a feature of the Materialist Rigid wound when there is a pronounced split between love and lust. Lester comes extremely close to making love to the doll-like Angela. At the last minute, he restrains himself as reality breaks though his fantasy and he realizes that, beneath her highly groomed and sophisticated veneer, she is just a child. His wife, Carolyn, has a comical but passionate affair with her boss. Something inside the daughter, Jane, is courageous and authentic enough to respond to the 'weird' Rickie's interest in her and to leave the suburban life behind to go away with him to New York. The most warped character is 'faggot- hating' Colonel Fitts who is appalled to discover that he has homosexual feelings for Lester, and he deals with the unbearable complexity of his situation by killing Lester with one of his many guns.

At the beginning of the film, all the characters are living a lie; a routine, daily grind of keeping up appearances and maintaining control. But the life force breaks through when Lester realizes he has nothing to lose, living for the moment as the facade crumbles around them all and he rediscovers the beauty of life.

### The Perfectionist Rigid Type

The Perfectionist Rigid defence does not appear to be conformist or materialistic. Whereas the Materialistic Rigid defence is an overlay of Masochistic repression, the Perfectionist Rigid defence is an overlay of Schizoid splitting. This version of the Rigid defence is found in an individual who is driven by an internalized agenda of perfection. It shows up in any kind of excessive or obsessive activity that has become inhuman in its demands – the self-flagellating monk or the dancer with blood oozing through her *pointe* shoes, and it is often a major factor in the development of eating disorders.

The Perfectionist Rigid wound is very commonly found among people on some kind of a spiritual path. These are the spiritual seekers who cannot forgive themselves for being anything less than perfectly saintly – relentlessly charitable, merciful and forgiving – and are at war with all their 'selfish' human desires that keep them from union with God. This is sometimes referred to as a 'spiritual bypass' – when a person uses their vision of spiritual sweetness to avoid the challenges of messy but authentic human relationships.

The Perfectionist Rigid wound has done much to shape the history of the world. It is the drive at the heart of the split between mind and body that has caused so much suffering through the negative interpretation of religions, particularly Judaism, Christianity and Islam. The Perfectionist Rigid enters into a tragic struggle to overcome their natural bodily urges and human instincts, frantically clinging to the belief that avoiding the 'sins of the flesh' will buy them a place in Heaven. Whatever creed they follow, the root of their Rigid defence is fear of the uncontrolled fire of emotion and desire and the ultimate vulnerability of the body.

### Story – *Turandot*

The Perfectionist Rigid defence is connected to early Schizoid terror and the inability to tolerate the reality of the essentially flawed nature of human life. The fairy tale story of Puccini's opera *Turandot* illustrates the archetypal wound of perfectionism.

*Turandot* is set in ancient China. In the opening scene a stranger, the deposed Prince of Tartary, arrives in Peking and is unexpectedly reunited with his blind and aged father Timur and his faithful slave-girl Liu. Liu reveals that years ago she fell in love with the prince and this love has kept her with the old king and sustained her through all their trials.

Turandot is an exquisitely beautiful Chinese princess and suitors came from far and wide to seek her hand in marriage. But Turandot is cruel, with a heart of ice. She sets her suitors three impossible riddles and when they fail to solve them she has them executed. When the prince catches a glimpse of Turandot he falls under the spell of her beauty and declares himself a suitor. Turandot appears and tells the story behind her cruelty. She reveals that long ago her ancestress, Princess Lo-u-Ling, was ravished and murdered by an invading foreign prince. Turandot declares that Lo-u-Ling has been born again in her and she will never let any man possess her. She warns the prince to withdraw, but he remains committed.

Turandot sets the prince three riddles but to her great distress he finds the solution to each one. Turandot begs her father not to allow the prince to marry her but the Emperor insists that her oath is sacred and she must wed the prince. Turandot cries out in anguish but the prince announces that he has a proposal for her. He tells Turandot that if she can discover his name before sunrise then he will forfeit his life.

Merciless Turandot decrees that there will be mass executions if the stranger's name is not discovered by sunrise and the unhappy people desperately search to find his name. At last a group of soldiers drag in the slave-girl Liu but she faithfully refuses to reveal the prince's name, even under torture. Turandot cannot understand Liu and demands to know what gives her the courage to withstand her torment. Liu simply replies, 'Princess, it is Love.' Then Liu seizes a soldier's sword and kills herself.

As the crowd and the grieving Timur carry Liu's body, away the prince and Turandot are left alone. He reproaches Turandot for her cruelty, calling her 'The Princess of Death' but then he takes her in his arms and kisses her. The kiss awakens an unknown passion in the princess. Shaken and bewildered, she begs the prince to leave and ask nothing more of her, taking his mystery with him. Instead the prince reveals his name – 'Calaf, son of Timur' – and puts his life in her hands. Turandot and Calaf approach the throne of the Emperor and Turandot declares that she knows the stranger's name. 'His name is Love', she declares, and so, at last, Turandot releases the fury of her ancestress and opens to love.

Like so many fairy tales, the story of Turandot makes no sense as an adult human drama. But when it is interpreted as a symbolic representation of an archetypal process it illustrates the issue of the Perfectionist Rigid type. Turandot represents an unachievable ideal of perfection that destroys the capacity for authentic human relationship – the belief that only when we are perfect will we be good enough to be worthy of love. Like a Killer Critic she sets unattainable standards and impossible riddles overhung with the threat of death. She is implacably merciless and she cannot comprehend the love of humble Liu. Warm-hearted Liu represents the archetype of the gentle, ever-loving, vulnerable Inner Child who is tortured to death by the relentless cruelty of the Perfectionist Critic.

We learn that, in the first place, it was the historic outrage of the violated Princess Lo-u-Ling that became the drive behind Turandot's ruthlessness. And so we see how the Perfectionist Critic originates from an experience of trauma. Somewhere in the history of this defence, whether in childhood or in a previous existence, something terrifying has occurred. The horror of the original wounding gets channelled into the building of an impregnable fortress, 'perfection = protection', in the attempt to make sure that it doesn't happen again.

Calaf represents the need for change: the struggle to bring the issue into consciousness and break the grip of the ancestral curse. We can regard the search for the name of the stranger as that stage of self-exploration when we struggle to name – to witness – the distorted beliefs that drive our defences. When the nature of the original trauma comes into awareness it becomes possible to release the paralysing grip of the demand for perfection and to learn compassion and tolerance for the inevitable mistakes and blunders of human life. It was Calaf's kiss, the stirring of the non-rational instincts of the body, that finally awakened Turandot's humanity and melted her frozen heart.

46

# The Harvest or Rigid Stage
## The Healing Response to the Rigid Defence

With regard to wounding and defence we can see the journey through the developmental stages as instalments of separation from our Essence – our beautiful Core Star that goes unseen in our families and societies. By the time we get to the Rigid wound the inner connection with the light of Essence is completely lost.

The Materialist Rigid type experience life only on the outside, for they have forgotten that they ever had an inner being to express. They run their energy field efficiently and well, holding very strong boundaries. But often the HEF of the Rigid type feels cold and impenetrable, and beneath the cool, smooth surface of the aura there is a sense of a gap – a strange, empty gulf in which the movement of the life force gets lost.

It is extremely hard for the Materialist Rigid type to recognize this hollow place in their life. In the eyes of the world these people have 'made it' and they have no need to question their superior status. It takes quite a jolt to shake the materially successful person into awareness that something terribly important is missing from their life. The challenge often comes in the form of a personal tragedy – anything from an unexpected redundancy or divorce to the death of a family member or the diagnosis of a dread disease. The Rigid type is shocked to find, as their world tumbles around them, that their material wealth and achievements have not taught them how to cope with failure and loss. Their show of religious conformity has not given them access to a faith that can help them in a crisis and the individual often goes through a bleak period, sinking into severe depression and despair.

Then the healing response to the Rigid is to help them to find a way to reach back through the emptiness and find a deeper level of experience. The healer will need to welcome any expression of feeling and vulnerability that gets past the Rigid armouring and keep affirming the person's Core qualities that are longing for expression. The healer needs to expand their own Core Star to vibrationally connect to the Core Star of the client. Making this vibrational connection supports the person with Rigid wounding to have a tangible experience of the warmth and radiance of this inner light that they had forgotten how to feel.

The healing response to the Perfectionist Rigid type is to encourage tolerance for mistakes and imperfections. As always, the deepest level of transformation requires going beyond rational mental understanding into the emotional experience at the heart of the wound. Somewhere in childhood, or in a previous existence, this soul took on the struggle for perfection as a way of escaping from feelings that, as a child, they could not tolerate. Now, with an adult consciousness and good support, the individual needs to reclaim those lost emotions and make a different choice – the choice to be human, get messy and to accept all aspects of the self, including vulnerability.

Experiences of vulnerability and loss of control bring up feelings of great shame for the Rigid type but human beings learn their most important lessons through adversity. When life pushes the Rigid type out of their safety zone they fall into what they fear will be a bottomless pit of failure. Instead, the void turns out to be the place of the Core Star and an opportunity for reconnection with the warmth of human relationships and the life of the soul. In the defencelessness of their darkest hour the individual rediscovers the sincerity of heartfelt communication and the beauty of human vulnerability, compassion and empathy.

When all their careful plans have stopped working the Rigid soul has the chance to start again. They have not lost their worldly skills but they have acquired a priceless new wisdom and now they can step out on to a fresh path, not dictated to them by others but following the longing of their soul. They are able to move out from the bleak emptiness of the Rigid defence and embrace their soul's longing to bring though the gifts of the Harvest soul.

# 47

## The Harvest or Rigid Stage

## The Spiritual View: the Gifts of the Harvest Stage

> *I have walked that long road to freedom. I have tried not to falter; I have made missteps along the way. But I have discovered the secret that after climbing a great hill, one only finds that there are many more hills to climb. I have taken a moment here to rest, to steal a view of the glorious vista that surrounds me, to look back on the distance I have come. But I can only rest for a moment, for with freedom come responsibilities, and I dare not linger, for my long walk is not ended.*
>
> Nelson Mandela

From the perspective of creative consciousness the soul in the Harvest stage has the ultimate skill. They have gained mastery of the laws of the physical world and they are able to take the creative process to its final conclusion and bring vision through into manifest form.

The stage corresponds to the Harvest phase in the life of a plant when all the work of Germination, Rooting, Budding and Flowering comes to fruition and the creative cycle is completed. The leaves and flowers that have served their purpose die back, leaving fruits, seeds, grains, nuts and berries to ripen into fullness in the last of the summer sun. The richness and colour of the autumn are a mirror to the fruitfulness of the mature soul having brought their work to completion.

## The Nature of the Incoming Soul

At the other end of the spectrum from the Germination and Rooting souls, the Harvest soul is focused on life in the physical realm. They have come to create order and harmony and they embody the energy of the elder: wisdom, patience, stability and the persistence to see things through. Whereas the soul in the Flowering stage is fiery and fast-moving, the Harvest soul has the qualities of patience and calm.

When the Harvest soul is aligned with their power, they are beautiful to see as their central vertical power current drops deep down into the core of the Earth beneath them and extends high above them to the stars. A human being in this state is like a deeply rooted tree of light, a bridge between heaven and earth. The Harvest soul understands the principles that underpin the world of matter and they have developed all the skills required to bring about growth in the physical world. They work in harmony with the laws of time and space, expertly directing their energy and attention while also maintaining connection to the non-physical realms and the integrity of their vision.

To be able to hold this energy state requires maturity and wisdom. The Harvest soul has an unshakeable loyalty to Essence and their energy field reflects their steady alignment of vision, purpose and presence. Neither the fragile, visionary children of the Germination and Rooting stages, nor the identity-seeking adolescents of the Budding and Flowering stages, have the deeply grounded strength that the Harvest soul brings. These are the law-makers, the leaders and teachers, with a palpable inner authority. The soul in this stage has grace and timing born from the wisdom of experience, and their longing is to be of service, both to humanity and to the Divine. These are the souls who have learned to dance to the rhythm of time and sculpt the density of matter into the forms of their dreams.

## Appearance in the Human Energy Field

When they are in their Rigid defence the HEF feels exactly as the name suggests – rigid, hard and impenetrable. The HEF of the Oral type feels liquid, floppy and clammy to touch, but the HEF of the Rigid type, the exact opposite of the Oral type, gives off the sensation of armour, steely and unyielding. The Rigid type may have a softer veneer of politeness and charm but there is a lack of real contact. Instead, they give off a subtle feeling of indifference and disdain and beneath the surface there is a feeling of coldness and emptiness.

When the Harvest soul is connected to Essence the hardness of the Rigid defence shifts into a feeling of tremendous strength and trustworthiness as they connect into the deep level of the Hara. When a person's Hara is aligned they are unshakeably rooted into the ground of their being, with the life force flowing like a river along the path of their intention. This supports the flow of energy through the aura, with emphasis on the structured levels of the field where the individual focuses on the process of manifesting events in the material world. Whatever the project they first access the ideal blueprint for construction, held in the quiet stillness of the 5th chakra, then draw it down to the mental analytical energy of the 3rd chakra. With a good feeling about their worldly competence, the Harvest soul is comfortable on the third level of the HEF. Here they mentally plan the steps towards manifestation and this comes through as effective clear structures held in the 1st chakra. As the physical matter and/or events of the material world gather around the 1st chakra structures, the energy of the vision flows through and finally manifests in the world of form.

# 48

## The Harvest or Rigid Stage

## The Astrological View: the Astrology of the Harvest/Rigid Type

The planets associated with the Harvest/Rigid stage are Venus, the goddess of love and beauty, and Saturn, who represents the principle of limitation. We have already met Saturn in battle with his father, Uranus. Saturn castrated Uranus and threw the discarded genitals into the ocean, and Venus arose from the waves there. Venus emerges from the archaic conflict between Uranus's cosmic idealism and Saturn's rigid realism and her arrival symbolizes the birth of the ideals of peace and co-operation as the founding principles of civilization.

# 49

## The Harvest or Rigid Stage
# Venus, Ruler of Taurus and Libra

Venus was the goddess of love. She was beautiful, desirable, self-centred and fickle and liked to do exactly what she wanted. She was married to Vulcan, the blacksmith god, who was ugly and lame. Vulcan was the son of Jupiter and Juno, and when he was born he was so ugly that Juno hurled the tiny baby off the top of Mount Olympus. He was rescued and had a happy childhood growing up underwater with dolphins but he probably had a lot of issues around rejection! Venus and Vulcan did not have a happy marriage and ugly, hard-working Vulcan represents the shadow of Venus – that which she rejects. Venus was constantly having affairs, most notably with Mars, and in this aspect she also relates to the love triangles and betrayals of the Psychopathic wound. Venus was not rude and aggressive like Mars but she was manipulative, using charm and seduction to get her way.

### Planetary Archetype – Essence

The Essence of Venus is happiness! She is charming, playful, arousing, alluring, sexual, sensual and she represents the Harvest soul's delight in the joy of loving and being loved and the sensual pleasures of the body. Venus was one of the most important and powerful of all the Olympian gods and in traditional astrology she was known as the 'Lesser Benefic', the bringer of good fortune, love and happiness. In terms of astronomy, Venus is the brightest star in the sky, always close to the Sun, and she is a 'Solar' goddess in that she is shining, visible and associated with conscious Awareness. (The aspects of relationship associated with more instinctive and unconscious feelings are the province of the Moon and Neptune.)

The symbol of Venus, ♀, is the symbol of the Feminine and Venus represents the principle of relationship. Venus forms a duality with Mars, ♂. Like Mars, Venus has to do with desire but while Mars represents the urge to separate and act as an individual, Venus represents the urge to relate with another and find communion. Venus, particularly in the sign of Libra, is concerned with the issue of choice, and people with a strong Venus often find themselves challenged by a split between their wish to please others and their more selfish and instinctual desires.

Venus is the ruler of two signs – Taurus and Libra – and she expresses different qualities in the different signs. Taurus belongs to the element of Earth, and Venus in Taurus is associated with the sensual pleasures of the body. Libra belongs to the element of Air, and Venus in Libra is associated with the ideals of romance, marriage and all kinds of partnerships. In Taurus, Venus relates to the 'cornucopia', the symbol of earthy abundance associated with Saturn. In Libra, Venus relates to the Airy idealism and perfectionism of Uranus.

**Taurus**

Like Eve, naked in the Garden of Eden, Venus in the Earth sign of Taurus is a sensual, earthy love goddess, delighting and revelling in the beauty of the earth and the pleasures of the body. Venus in Taurus loves nature, all the birds and the beasts, the fruits and the flowers, the gardens and the wildernesses of our beautiful planet.

Venus in Taurus is artistic and creative. Taurus is symbolized by the Bull and it is interesting to note that Pablo Picasso, who constantly returned to the theme of the bull in his art, had five of the eleven planets in Taurus as well as Venus in Libra! Venus loves the sensuality of making beautiful things – prints, ceramics, textiles – and Taurus is associated with music and song.

Venus in Taurus is also associated with financial matters and wealth. Pleasure-loving Venus wants a life in the sun – beautiful surroundings, good food and wine, money, jewellery, *objets d'art*, music, poetry, sensual touch, bathing, massaging, stroking and blissful sexual union. Venus in Taurus is a symbol of the gifts of the Harvest phase.

## Libra

Venus in Libra also appreciates wealth and beauty, although Venus in Libra is more idealistic and less sensual than Venus in Taurus. Venus in Libra is a hostess, a conversationalist, a patron of the arts and a lover of music. Venus in Libra loves culture but, above all, Libra is the sign of relationship and seeks the ideal of romantic, harmonious, loving relationships.

Libra belongs to the element of Air, which has to do with the mind, ideas and ideals, concepts and communication. Libra is symbolized by a set of scales and is the only sign of the zodiac whose symbol is an inanimate, man-made object. The scales of Libra are an abstract symbol of the ideal of balance and fairness in relationship. Libra represents the ideals of justice and the law as the means of keeping the peace in a civilized, humane society. The scales of Libra also symbolize the question of choice: weighing up a decision and choosing one thing over another. Making choices that are aligned with our soul's longing and purpose is a major part of the creative process and the gift of the Harvest soul.

## Wound – Venus in Taurus

The negative expression of planets in Taurus is the Materialist Rigid defence – people for whom the allure of the pleasures of the physical world has become all-consuming. They live life on the surface, focused on wealth, status, keeping up appearances and avoiding anything that threatens their stability. Taurus is the sign of the Bull, and Taureans can be obsessively single-minded. In her demand for pleasure, Taurean Venus can descend into selfishness, greed, gluttony and lust, capable of extravagant and decadent behaviour in pursuit of personal gratification. The sensual pleasures bring us delight, ecstasy and bliss; they are our Garden of Eden and life is joyless without them. But when the inner connection to the Core is missing the wonder of life is lost and what remains is a shell of acquisitive seeking after gratification, money and status while a gnawing feeling tells us that something is missing; the fire has gone out and life has lost its meaning.

## Story – King Midas

The story for Venus in Taurus is the myth of foolish King Midas. When Midas was a baby, a procession of ants appeared one day, carrying grains of wheat up the side of his cradle and depositing them around the sleeping child. This was considered to be a very good omen and a portent of the great wealth he was to accrue in his life.

Midas grew up and became a good king, and when Silenus the satyr appeared at his doors, Midas made him welcome and gave him food and shelter. Silenus was the tutor of Bacchus, the god of the vine, and when Silenus told the story of King Midas's kindness, Bacchus rewarded King Midas by granting him a wish. King Midas loved wealth and he immediately asked that everything he touched would turn to gold. Midas was delighted to think that he would become the wealthiest man in the world. He danced around touching everything and soon his palace was gleaming like the sun.

But, as always, a gift from the gods brings a whole new set of problems. King Midas soon discovered that he was unable to eat or drink because food and water turned to solid gold in his hands. Midas wandered through his garden, no longer delighted as the delicate flowers turned to sculptures of gold. Suddenly he came upon his youngest daughter, who ran to him and seized his hand before he could stop her. Instantly his beloved child was turned into a perfect little gold statue. Even King Midas's tears turned to gold as they fell from his eyes. His only solution was to make his way to the temple of the Oracle where he prayed and begged for help. Bacchus was merciful and when the Oracle spoke it told Midas that in order to be released from the consequences of his wish he should go to the source of the River Pactolus and bathe. Midas followed his instructions and flung himself into the river. His terrible gift was removed from him and taken in to the River Pactolus, whose sands turned to gold while Midas returned to his palace, humbled but a much wiser man.

This well-known tale speaks for itself. Humanity and love are lost when the pursuit of wealth outweighs everything else. People with an emphasis on Taurus in the chart are often drawn into just this kind of mistake, the Materialist Rigid wound – so consumed by greed that all other values are discarded for the sake of the acquisition of wealth and status.

### Venus in Libra

Libran Venus is more controlled and avoids the sensual overindulgence of Taurus. Libra likes things to be nice, harmonious, sweet and lovely. Libra dislikes conflict and in order to keep the peace they will often give way to others and be over-anxious to please. The persona of the 'Pleaser' is always a sign of a powerful Inner Critic, so there is an iron hand inside the velvet glove. Venus in Libra has inherited the idealism of Uranus, from whose seed she sprang. In this role, her love of beauty and harmony turns to cold idealism. Libra's judgemental codes of behaviour give her a Superego of steel and this, more than any other sign, is an indication of the Perfectionist Rigid wound.

From the Libran view everything is measured against the stern criteria of the Superego's rules for perfection. In this world people are 'in' or 'out', right or wrong, above or below in a hierarchy, measured by status, success, wealth, accomplishment, fashion, beauty and talent. Like the Libran 'Iron Lady', Margaret Thatcher, Libra can bring Rigid standards and judgements into any form, whether it is politics, business, religion or art.

Individuals with the Ascendant, the Sun or the Moon in Libra suffer greatly from an inhuman demand for perfection, which can lead to an obsession with looking good and such problems as eating disorders, and the self-loathing that even highly attractive people can suffer from when they look in the mirror. The sweetness and charm of Libra is not false and they are too graceful to be rudely critical of others. But inside they often harbour one of the most merciless of Critics. Whatever beauty, gifts and talents they have are judged under the harshest light and nothing is ever good enough.

Librans are attracted to the arts but an emphasis on Libra can indicate a perfectionism that can paralyse the artistic impulse before they even pick up the paintbrush. Art, like life, is a question of going with the flow but the wounded Libran approaches everything with a pre-conceived agenda, with a fixed idea of how things ought to be. When the individual is constantly looking over their shoulder to figure out what some eternal authority requires of them, their authentic creative self cannot be expressed! The other side of this demon of judgement is the capacity for highly refined discernment that brings greatness to human achievements, and this is the gift of the idealism of Libran Venus.

**Story – Pallas Athena**

The figure that illustrates the archetypal nature of Venus in Libra is the Greek goddess of Wisdom, Pallas Athena (known to the Romans as Minerva).

Pallas Athena bypassed the biological process of birth and emerged whole and fully armed from the head of Jupiter and, like Venus, she is a feminine representative of the Solar principle. Athena was a warrior goddess but she was not a bloodthirsty killer like Mars. She was wise and thoughtful; a civilizing force bringing many skills and crafts to mankind.

At the end of the Battle of Troy a terrible marital dispute took place when King Agamemnon returned home to his wife Clytemnestra. While he was away at war, Agamemnon sent for their daughter Iphigenia and had her killed as a sacrifice to appease the gods. Clytemnestra was outraged. She took a lover, Aegisthus, and together they plotted revenge. When Agamemnon returned, Clytemnestra and Aegisthus murdered him in his bath.

Before Agamemnon arrived, Clytemnestra sent their son Orestes away to prevent him from interfering. But Orestes was visited by the god Apollo who told him of the crime and insisted that Orestes had no choice but to avenge his father's death by killing his mother. This put Orestes in an impossible situation for to commit matricide would bring down retribution from the Furies but Apollo threatened him with equally terrible punishments if he did not obey his command. Eventually Orestes obeyed Apollo and killed both Aegisthus and his mother. Then, indeed, the Furies tormented him, hounding him throughout Greece until, maddened and exhausted, Orestes finally sought sanctuary at the shrine of Pallas Athena.

Athena took pity on the young man who was caught, through no fault of his own, between the implacable forces of the matriarchal Furies and the patriarchal Apollo. Athena set up a court with twelve human judges to hear Orestes' case but, when the evidence was heard, the jury was split! Six of the jurors sided with Apollo, who asserted that the father's was the most important life, and six sided with the Furies, who believed the mother's life was more important. Athena was left with the deciding vote and chose to side with Apollo and deliver Orestes from the curse of the Furies. As usual, Athena administered justice with wisdom and grace, because she diplomatically placated the Furies by offering to set up a shrine in their honour. And so, at last, peace was restored and Orestes was released from the curse.

Here we see Pallas Athena representing the civilizing energy of Libra – setting up the first jury, bringing justice, an end to violence and a resolution that serves everyone. Without Athena's wise intervention Orestes would have died and the curse, with its unfair feuding and bloodletting, would have continued down the ancestral line. Athena does not simply rush in with her sword and do battle, she sets up a jury to debate the situation in a calm and reasonable way. The goddess holds the balance and has to make a difficult decision but, in the end, nobody else has to die. Athena recognizes that the Furies have a legitimate place in life and honours them with a shrine. The Furies are placated and the curse is lifted.

In the resolution of the conflict in Northern Ireland, a lot of spiritual and practical work was done by groups of dedicated women who were committed to bringing about an end to the violence, and they might well have felt the beneficial presence of Pallas Athene. This capacity to come between warring factions and negotiate some kind of truce and a way forward is the gift of Libra. People with an emphasis on Libra make the greatest diplomats, with balanced understanding of both sides of the conflict and the lofty vision to see the third way.

## In the Human Energy Field

There is something lovable and alluring in the energy of Venus, which gives a person a shimmer and a grace that flows through the energy field like a beautiful scent, a ripple of music, the touch of silk or the sound of laughter. The energy of Venus flows and ripples through the 2nd, 4th and 6th chakras and the colour of Venus energy ranges from sky colours of blue and lilac associated with the celestial love and vision of the 6th chakra to the gentlest pink light radiating from a tender heart of the 4th chakra through to the hot rose or peachy orange associated with the sensual sexual pleasures of the 2nd chakra. On the higher levels of the field Venus has a sound like the singing of angels and on the lower levels her sound is like the purring of a cat and her touch like velvet or fur. Venus in the HEF is felt as joy and pleasure.

A classic sign of Rigid wounding is when the 2nd and 4th chakras are disconnected, which means that sexuality is split off from love. Many men split the archetype of the Feminine into the Madonna and the whore. Similarly, a woman with a Rigid defence may marry a good, steady man who reminds her of her father and then rock the boat by falling for a 'bad' man who carries the dark, disowned energies; wild, passionate and out-of-control! When Venus is expressing negatively there may be too much focus on the pleasures of the body so the 2nd chakra gets overcharged and overindulgent, or there may be too much focus on the idealism of the 6th chakra and the sweetness and light of the 'spiritual bypass'.

## The Heart Tan T'ien

The Haric level is the deep, inner level of the field where we hold our intention to live and fulfil our life purpose. The Hara line appears as a column of light running vertically through the centre of the body, connecting three vital points of light – the Lower, Middle and Upper Tan T'iens. The Middle Tan T'ien is situated in the upper chest, a little above the heart, and it radiates an exquisite light connected to the energy of the soul. This is the place where we hold the longing to fulfil our life purpose and this is the highest expression of the energy of

Venus, the joy we find in being who we came to be, living our lives in honour of both our humanity and our Divinity. The Middle Tan T'ien is one of the most beautiful and inspiring places in the HEF as our heart's longing generates an exquisite light that guides us through life.

## Venus in Aspect to the Ascendant, the Moon and the Sun

When Venus is in aspect to the Ascendant, Sun or Moon, beauty, charm and a lovable quality will be a tangible presence in a person's HEF. Venus looks for peace and harmony but sometimes this comes with a hidden agenda of perfectionism and a set of 'rules' about how to behave. So Venus brings the possibility of Rigid wounding in childhood as well as the gifts of the Harvest stage coming through one of the parents or as a notable presence in the family dynamics.

## Venus in Aspect to the Ascendant

When Venus aspects the Ascendant or is in the 1st house, the charm and allure of Venus becomes a major factor in this person's identity and way of presenting themselves. The Ascendant and the 1st house say a lot about a person's appearance and when Venus is here a person will look good and radiate the seductive allure of Venus in the 1st house. People with this placement are often very lovable and affectionate, bringing sweetness and life-affirming happiness into their relationships. The presence of Venus in the 1st house also indicates that idealism and perfectionism were a factor in this person's infancy. It can be a sign of Narcissistic wounding when one or both parents have an expectation or a demand that this child should be beautiful and adorable or even perfect. Often, the person is born into a family with the Rigid goal of harmonious living, and the Venusian child takes on the responsibility of being the oil on troubled waters, thereby finding it difficult to assert their own needs. We have seen that Venus goes with the persona of the 'Pleaser', underpinned by an extremely demanding version of the Inner Critic.

## Venus in Aspect to the Moon

This brings the two principles of relationship together and in its positive expression it is a sign of a gentle, affectionate and sensitive soul. There is often a close, loving relationship with the mother, which gives these individuals inner radiance as well as outer beauty. The Moon represents the body and a positive Moon-Venus contact goes with people who are sensual and attractive and feel happy in their bodies.

However, if Venus is in a challenging aspect to the Moon and expressing negatively then, unfortunately, the very opposite can also be true. Negative Venus brings the Perfectionist Inner Critic and negative Moon-Venus contacts go with eating disorders, cosmetic surgery and people who are obsessed with the flaws and imperfections of the body. Venus was a vain goddess and highly competitive about her beauty, and in this role she plays a part in the love triangles of the Psychopathic defence. In a woman's chart, Venus in aspect to the Moon can indicate rivalry with the mother who may feel threatened by the youthful charm of her daughter. In a man's chart, Moon-Venus aspects can indicate a seductive mother who manipulates her son to be on her side in her battle with the father.

Venus loves the arts and a Moon-Venus contact is very common in the charts of all kinds of artists as well as patrons of the arts. Negatively expressed, there is a risk that the perfectionism of Venus inhibits a person's attempts at artistic expression.

## Venus in Aspect to the Sun

Venus was a Solar goddess, brilliant and shining and powerful. Venus never appears further than 48° from the Sun and contact between Venus and the Sun is normally a radiant and happy placement. Apollo, the god of the Sun, was associated with the arts and Sun-Venus contacts give a great love of the arts and all aspects of culture.

Venus in aspect to the Sun often indicates a happy, loving relationship with the father and a father who embodies the Venusian qualities of charm and grace. With the negative expression the father is only interested in what is sweet and easy about the child and is not available when the child is in difficulties. This can be an indication of Narcissistic wounding when the father needs the child to be beautiful as a kind of trophy or testament of his success.

Venus, the goddess of love, was born from the bloody conflict between Uranus and Saturn. Venus is the principle of relationship and she represents the possibility of happiness, beauty, romance and the sensual pleasures of the body that arise from finding the balance between the Uranian principle of cosmic idealism and the Saturnian principle of earthly reality.

# 50

## The Harvest or Rigid Stage
## Saturn, Ruler of Capricorn (and Aquarius)

Saturn is the ruling planet of the sign of Capricorn and, before the discovery of Uranus, it was also the ruler of the sign of Aquarius. Saturn is one of the most powerful of all the planets, for he represents the laws and the structures of physical reality.

Before the discovery of Uranus, Neptune, Pluto and Chiron, Saturn was thought to be the outermost planet of the solar system and he was known as the 'Gatekeeper'. The planets beyond Saturn's orbit are referred to as transpersonal planets because they are not concerned with individual human stories but represent archetypal forces of change. As the Gatekeeper, Saturn holds the boundaries of existence in the material world. In the Uranian and Neptunian realms our souls can fly free but in human life we are bound by the laws of the world of matter. Saturn brings order out of chaos and he is the principle of form and structure. He rules the skeleton – the bones are the underlying structures of the body and the skin – the physical boundary of the body. In traditional astrology Saturn was also known as the 'Great Malefic', the harbinger of misfortune. Saturn is the most feared of all the planets for he often presents us with grim, unwelcome paths to follow. Whereas joyful Jupiter represents the principle of expansion, Saturn represents the principle of contraction and unyielding limitation.

### Planetary Archetype – Essence

Saturn rules the structures that underpin the functioning of the physical realm: the laws of physics, chemistry, biology and all the unbreachable laws that give consistency to life in the material world. Saturn is the Lord of Time – the inexorable coming of old age, the passing of the wave of life and the inevitability of death.

Saturn also represents the rule of law in human societies. He administers 'karmic law', delivering inevitable consequences that follow the choices we make, and Saturn embodies the archetype of the Judge – penalizing irresponsible behaviour and rewarding diligence.

People, especially young people, tend to experience the limitations of Saturn in a negative way and, like Pluto and Chiron, we first meet Saturn through wounding. Wherever Saturn falls in the chart is an area of life where we feel innately inadequate, as though we missed out in our education – this is something we just don't know how to do! In Saturn's house we feel clumsy and inept, dogged by the fear of failure. In youth we try to cover up by copying how other people do it but that usually doesn't work and we end up in trouble, again! Eventually, in time, something, at last, goes right. Slowly and painstakingly, one step at a time, we start to gain mastery of this area of life. As the years pass, we gradually build our own tried and tested way of operating in this area and develop a quiet new confidence with knowledge based on our own direct experience.

One way of understanding Saturn is to think of the process of crystallization. Originally, a crystal starts off in a liquid state, still fluid and capable of changing shape. As the process of crystallization proceeds, more and more of the liquid settles into a crystalline state until, eventually, all the liquid has taken on a permanent, unchanging crystalline form – it has become a rock! This is the way that Saturn operates over a lifetime. At the beginning of life our Essence flows out into the physical world, fluid and unformed, open to many possibilities. And as the years pass, more and more of our being crystallizes into a strong, stable form because, through our lived experience, something has become realized. At the end, the experiences of a lifetime have formed into a beautiful crystal of Essence – the distillation of the soul's work in this life. This crystal is the mystical lapis, which was the end result of the processes of alchemy. Wherever Saturn is active in the chart, some aspect of self that is still liquid and changeable is taking on form, crystallizing into something concrete, clear and permanent.

The process of bringing Essence into form usually involves a struggle and, for much of life, things touched by Saturn do not work out easily. Saturn feels like a harsh disciplinarian, demanding that we dig deep to find the courage, stamina, resilience and persistence to keep going when the road is rough. Often we feel daunted and crushed by the burden of hard work and struggle, and Saturn is associated with depression, oppression and a punitive feeling of bondage, of being chained to grim, inescapable hardship.

However, there is another way of looking on the challenges of hard work and responsibility. Robert Fritz said 'Discipline means doing what you want!' When we are focused and aligned with what we truly want, then the necessary steps, the discipline, come easily to us and this is the power of intention. When we leave fantasy behind and embrace reality, when we balance the books and have relationships of integrity, when we put in the effort and stick to our truth, then Saturn presents us with rewards, with the fruits of our labours.

Saturn helps us to make things happen, to manifest measurable, tangible results in the physical world. A person with a strong Saturn will be ambitious and want to build a career or a dynasty or some kind of edifice out in the world that will be a lasting testimony to their achievements. Saturn also brings the quality of loyalty; a person with a strong Saturn will not let you down. This loyalty is a quality of Essence for it arises from a deep inner knowing of what must be done.

Above all, beyond the ephemeral issues of worldly ambition, Saturn is about presence. By this I mean the ability to be fully present with whatever is arising – when we are grounded into the earth and the body; when we are able to be in the moment and feel the stillness that is beyond all of life, no matter what else we are experiencing.

When we are connected to Essence and rooted in presence, Saturn brings the steadfastness of a mighty oak and a certainty that will withstand the force of a hurricane. In mythology, the reign of Saturn was known as the Golden Age when he introduced civilization, agriculture and the calendar to mankind. The cornucopia, or horn of plenty, is the highest expression of the sign of Capricorn and this symbol relates to the fruits of the Harvest stage.

### The Patriarch and the Crone

Astrologers refer to Saturn, in the traditional way, as a masculine figure. Saturn often appears as a tyrannical father figure, a negative distortion of the archetype of the Patriarch. The Patriarch is an older man, a powerful authority figure, but in distortion he becomes controlling, judgemental, cold and cruel. He is authoritative and effective in a disciplined, mental, analytical way but he dislikes feelings and despises vulnerability, and he considers displays of emotion to be a contemptible, feminine weakness. This version of the Patriarch is the negative voice of the Masculine that has split away from relationship with the Feminine and he is very misogynistic. He regards young women as sex objects, trophies and playthings, and he is threatened by the power of mature women and tries to belittle their intuitive wisdom.

The destructive voice of the Inner Patriarch does not only belong to men, it is equally powerful in women. In women the voice of the Patriarch is hidden beneath their identification with being female but it can create an unconscious but immensely destructive sense of worthlessness and self-loathing. (Any woman who takes her daughter for female genital mutilation is following the instructions of her Inner Patriarch.)

In astrology, it is easy to see a negative Saturn operating as the cold, authoritarian, Masculine archetype of the Patriarch. But, in Essence, Saturn is a feminine principle because it has to do with the earth and the body and it is the ruling planet of Capricorn, which is a feminine sign. It is the feminine principle, the Yin energy, that rules the world of Matter. Like Mary giving birth to Jesus, like the Holy Grail containing the light of Spirit, it is the Feminine which gives form to the formless. The raw creativity of the Masculine principle begins in the realm of Uranus where vision has yet to become realized. As guardian of the laws of matter, Saturn rules the Feminine process of manifestation and it is the patience and the persistence of Saturn, the ability to work in harmony within the laws of Nature, that brings the archetypes of ideas into physical form.

Saturn's Greek name was Cronus, which is the root of the word 'crone' – an old woman in the final stage of life. The Crone is often feared and loathed, like the witches in *Macbeth*, but in her highest expression she represents the serene kindness and wisdom of the elders. The great gift of Saturn is an understanding born of experience, the profound insight and acumen distilled from having lived a life. Saturn brings us the calm patience of the sage, the grandmothers and grandfathers, with knowledge gleaned from the passing of the years. The fruitfulness of the Harvest stage is the product of the union of Masculine and Feminine and when we can honour the authority, wisdom and compassion of the Crone and the Patriarch, side by side, then we inherit the cornucopia of Saturn.

**Wound**

Traditionally, Saturn is linked with the sign of the cross, which is an archaic symbol for the material realm. In the holy story of the Crucifixion, the Cross is the ultimate image of the suffering of human life. The symbolism of the Crucifixion is that of the immortal soul transfixed in time and space by the laws of incarnation. The light of Jesus is the light of Essence held in every human being and Saturn represents the immutable structures that bind every soul as they descend into the beautiful and terrible world of matter.

On earth, death walks with us from the beginning to the end of life and from the traumas of the Schizoid stage onwards the threat of annihilation never leaves us. All our defences come into being as an attempt to find protection from the terror of existence, whether natural disasters or man-made catastrophes. As the keeper of the laws of physical life, it is Saturn that most activates our fear – anything from annihilation and abandonment to rejection, failure, shame, hopelessness and despair.

**The Superego**

The origin of the Superego is the voice of the parents giving the child instructions on what is acceptable and unacceptable behaviour. This voice becomes internalized as a set of rules for success and failure. Different families, religions and cultures will have different codes for success but, whatever it is, frightened humanity clings to their book of rules in an attempt to find safety. In this way the laws of nature become mixed up with the fear-based laws of the Superego and this is the negative expression of Saturn. Saturn is the planet most associated with the distortions and judgements of the Superego.

The positive expression of Saturn is the power of our intention to live a human life aligned with our sense of purpose. But when a person has lost touch with their Essence they substitute the promptings of the Superego for the authentic longings of the soul. Life becomes all about conformity, responsibility, discipline and obedience but it loses all meaning – it is all form and no substance. The anxieties about avoiding emotional turmoil drive a person into an excessive attachment to order and discipline. They find security in methodical, repetitive working activities and, like Scrooge, work and the amassing of wealth fill the days leaving no room for uncomfortable feelings. But when our goals belong to our parents, or to our spouse or to some other false god, sooner or later Saturn will come along and knock down our misguided constructions. If we have made choices that lead us away from our soul's purpose then Saturn will let us find out the hard way.

Into every life there comes a moment when the cross is hard to bear. The weight of our burdens is too great, our obedience has received no reward, the road is too long and there is no sign of deliverance, no light at the end of the tunnel. These phases of life are characterized by some kind of fate that seems inescapable – children to bring up, people depending on us for care, money that must be earned in dreary employment, debts that must be paid, promises we must fulfil, relationships from which we cannot escape, declining health with no hope of a cure. In these times we can feel horribly trapped with no possibility of freedom or joy. The grim days when we feel caught between a rock and a hard place are the days of Saturn. In traditional astrology Saturn rules the knees and very often, like Jesus stumbling under the weight of the Cross, Saturn brings us to our knees.

Saturn rules the passage of time, and when Saturn is active in the chart time seems to slow right down. Like a schoolchild watching the clock in unutterable desolation, the days of suffering drag past, relentlessly unchanging in their demands, and each exhausting hour seems like a day. Traditionally, our grim lessons with Saturn are about developing endurance and strength so that when Saturn finally moves on and we are released from our prisons we are much stronger than before.

In the western world there is new learning arising from wisdom of ancient mysticism that brings another way of understanding the role of Saturn. We can regard what happens to us in times of adversity as alchemy for the soul when our suffering prompts us to find a different way of being and a different relationship with time. Eckhart Tolle, author of *The Power of Now*, talks about the 'pain-body', an aspect of our little egoic mind that holds an accumulation of memories of suffering. The pain-body, best buddy of the Inner Critic, feeds on torment and misses no opportunity to dwell on affliction – recalling it, anticipating it and searching it out in every possible way.

Eckhart Tolle had an epiphany one night in the midst of a crisis of despair when he shifted into a completely different state of being which he describes as:

> *My true nature as the ever-present I am: consciousness in its pure state prior to identification with form.*

By centring his consciousness fully into the present moment, Tolle shifted into a state of awareness where he was completely free of the pain-body. Maintaining a conscious focus in the vast spaciousness of the present moment liberated him from the distortions of the pain-body and connected him to the formlessness that lies beyond the physical world.

Saturn is the Lord of Time. Could it be that when the days drag and the hands of the clock seem to move in slow motion that Saturn is presenting us with an opportunity to shift into a different awareness?; into Eckhart Tolle's 'ever-present I am? When our lives feel unbearable, we torment ourselves by dwelling on the fantasy of what should be happening, of how our lives ought to be, from our blameful memories of how it all went wrong to our anticipation of how bad it is going to get. In this painful anxiety of attachment to the past or the future we completely obliterate the undying wonder of the life that is here right now.

I have no wish to offend anyone whose life circumstances are very bad by trivializing their feelings or suggesting that shifting to a different kind of perception is easy – it's not. The idea of shifting into the spaciousness of the present moment is simple but remarkably hard to do. But when, through some kind of grace, we are able to make the transition into the 'now' – through focusing on the breath, by noticing what is happening in the body, by really experiencing the world around us – then we may be released from suffering and even a veritable tornado of pain can be gently held in the light of Presence. It seems to me that the human ability to enter into an awakened state of Presence is the beginning of the shift of consciousness that I have been searching for since 1976.

**Story – Jack and Jill**

The story that follows describes the workings of Saturn as the Inner Critic. It is an old English fairy tale, the original story of Jack and Jill.

Jack and Jill were a brother and sister who lived with their mother in a tumble-down cottage at the foot of a great mountain. They were kind and helpful children, yet no matter how hard they tried to please their mother she was constantly harsh with them. Nothing they did was ever good enough; she criticized everything they did and at their slightest protest she would fly into a rage and punish them, beating them with a stick or sending them to bed without supper.

One day when they were out in the woods, the children heard cries for help and ran to the rescue of a stranger who was being attacked by a bear. Jack fired an arrow at the bear, which ran off into the forest. The children took the stranger home and persuaded their surly mother to give him shelter for the night.

The next morning the stranger spoke to the children and revealed that he was a wizard who knew all about their difficult lives. He told them that when they were very young their mother had been a kind and gentle woman. After their father died an evil sorcerer had tried to force their mother to marry him but she had refused his offer saying that now she lived only for the love of her children. At this the sorcerer fell into a rage and pronounced a terrible curse.

'You shall indeed live only for your children, from this day forward their lives are totally in your hands. If you should ever utter one word of love or encouragement to your precious brats, they will instantly die. One act of kindness, one word of praise and they will be lost to you forever.'

Then the wicked sorcerer had waved his magic wand and the widow and her children were swept into the air and deposited in the wretched hovel which was now their home.

In great excitement Jack and Jill asked if there was a way to break the evil spell. The stranger told them they must climb to the top of the great mountain that rose behind their cottage and there they would find a spring of water with magical healing properties. They should collect a pitcher of water and bring it to their mother. If she drank of the water before the sun went down the spell would be broken forever.

The children set off at once but the mountain was peopled with goblins who played tricks on them and prevented them from succeeding in their quest. In the end they were helped by the King of the Rabbits who told them that they must carry a branch of the magical rowan tree, which would ward off all evil attacks. Protected by the magic of the rowan the children at last managed to get to the top of the mountain and collect a pitcher of the healing water.

Quickly they returned to home and took the water to their mother. When she drank it a miracle occurred. The world spun round and, when they opened their eyes, instead of their miserable hovel they were standing beside a large comfortable house. Best of all, their mother was transformed into a beautiful, happy woman. She gathered the children into her arms, overjoyed that at last she was free to give them the words of love and praise that they deserved and that she had longed to speak for so many years.

This story is about the Inner Critic. It is useful to have it as the final story in the book as the Critic's belief that there is something fundamentally wrong with us is the outcome of the distortions of all the defences.

In Voice Dialogue, we find that all the inner selves are motivated, in the first place, by the urge to protect the individual. The Inner Critic aims to find safety for the individual by goading them to be perfect. In the story the mother thinks that she is saving her children's lives by criticizing them. Nothing Jack and Jill do can ever be good enough for this mother, no matter how hard they try. She believes that they will die if she ever lets them know that they are good, and this is the belief that drives the Critic.

The Critic is the source of endless misery for human beings. In its controlling coldness it is at the other end of the spectrum from the poisonous fury of Medusa but it has the same effect – it paralyses the life force with dread. We become afraid that in our very Essence we are flawed and unwanted. This lack of self-belief sabotages all our efforts, creating a self-perpetuating cycle of failure and self-loathing. The voice of the Critic can drive us to complete despair and at its worst it takes on the role of the Killer Critic who believes that the person might be better off dead and drives them to suicide. This is the most extreme expression of a negative Saturn and astrologers see that these kinds of tragedies often occur at a time when Saturn is active in the chart. But just as the life force trapped in Medusa was transformed into Pegasus, the spirit of freedom, the Essence of Saturn – clear intention, purpose and presence – is exactly that which will enable us to achieve our hopes and dreams and bring us the cornucopia.

### In the Human Energy Field

In traditional astrology Saturn rules the skeleton, the framework on which our body is built, and it has a similar function in the Human Energy Field. Saturn connects to the energy of the Hara, the energy of intention. At the centre of the HEF is the Hara line, a powerful line of energy descending down into the centre of the earth, anchoring and grounding the soul here in physical incarnation. It also extends upwards, reaching beyond the physical world into the non-physical dimensions. This central column of living light and energy is the soul's bridge between Heaven and earth. When the Hara line is strong, clear and flowing it plays a major part in the creative process because it holds the individual's authentic intention to create, to manifest. This is the energy of Saturn.

In the Rigid defence, negative Saturn operates through fear: fear of failure, fear of judgement and, perhaps the ultimate fear, the fear of shame. In fear the individual doubts the safety of the earth and the anchoring root of the Hara becomes weak. The Hara runs at a deeper level than the shifting kaleidoscope of human emotions but if there is a continuous vibration of fear and shame in the aura then the Hara line starts to break up. If the Hara is weak, broken or pushed out of alignment, it becomes impossible to manifest a creative result.

The energy of the Hara is based in Presence, our ability to trust in the Divine and surrender to the moment. When the individual has lost that faith then Saturn operates on the auric level as the Superego and the Critic aiming to keep control. When Saturn is operating in this negative way, whatever it touches hardens and takes on the Rigid inflexibility. Meeting a person with a strong Rigid/Saturn energy can feel like walking into a door: there is something so stiff, tightly held and unyielding in their HEF.

Saturn, the principle of contraction, and Jupiter, the principle of expansion, form a duality. In the beginning of *A Christmas Carol* Scrooge epitomizes the negative expression of Saturn while Jupiter, embodied in the wisdom of the three ghosts, brings insight, vision and the freedom to change. On the level of Hara, Jupiter represents the visionary energy connecting to the Divine through a star above the head. When Saturn is operating negatively a person's Hara line becomes distorted and they lose their connection with their life purpose, which only increases the despair. Then what is needed is the energy of Jupiter, our connection to the Godhead through the star, which gives us the vision and inspiration to realign the Hara, reconnect to the power of the Lower Tan T'ien and the delight of the Middle Tan T'ien (Venus). When Saturn comes out of the Rigid defence and operates through the Harvest energy then the Hara line is magnificent, deeply anchored in the earth, soaring up to the skies and raining a fountain of golden energy into the field.

Saturn is the hardest taskmaster. In the Germination and Rooting stages we still like to believe that life is just a dream, that we are just a membrane away from the effortless creativity of the gods. But Saturn is not hooked by illusion, no matter how beautiful it seems. Saturn's constant demand is that we get real, remain present, align our intention and courageously work with the limitations of this world. In this great mystery of incarnation we struggle to become lucid dreamers and master every level of the creative process. In the fullness of time and experience we become wise, ready to take up our responsibilities as the elders who guide humanity towards the harvest of the fruits of life on earth.

### Saturn in Aspect to the Ascendant, the Moon and the Sun

Saturn represents the principle of contraction and the energy of Saturn has a heaviness, like the experience of gravity, a quality which can be immediately felt when it is in aspect to the Ascendant, Sun or Moon. This downward pull of Saturn can be experienced as an oppressive weight on the personality but it can also be experienced as a core of unshakeable strength and trustworthiness. Saturn is often an indication of Rigid wounding in childhood but it can also indicate the gifts of the Harvest stage coming through one of the parents or as a notable presence in the family dynamics.

### Saturn in Aspect to the Ascendant

The presence of Saturn in aspect to the Ascendant is often an indication of a difficult birth. Saturn is associated with science so this can also be a sign of medical intervention during labour and childbirth. A negative Saturn tries to keep control but labour and childbirth require surrender, not control. A more positive expression of a Saturn aspect to the Ascendant would be the presence of a spiritual midwife who brings through the wisdom of the grandmothers.

With this placement the Saturnian energy becomes a major factor in this person's identity. When they go out into the world, the energy of Saturn will be a palpable presence in the way they present themselves in relationship to others. A positive Saturn will give a person a powerful, authoritative persona. However, the more common, negative expression of Saturn on the Ascendant or in the 1st house is someone who appears, at first meeting, awkward, clumsy and often painfully shy. Saturn here goes with feelings of inadequacy, of not being welcome, and there is often some version of a story about unwanted pregnancy that goes with this placement. Saturn acting as the Judge undermines the person's self-confidence and years may go by before the individual learns to build a more confident way of relating.

**Saturn in Aspect to the Moon**

This is one of the most painful placements and it is one of the clearest indications of Oral wounding. The Moon symbolizes the archetype of the Vulnerable Child, a young and tender energy, who is completely bewildered by the Superego's demands and devastated by the attacks of the Critic. The Moon is full of waxing and waning emotions and is hurt and sometimes terrorized by Saturn's coldness and demand for discipline and self-control. A person with Saturn in aspect to the Moon is extremely likely to develop the 'caretaking' reaction to Oral wounding – a brave little soldier trying to support everyone else, living in denial of their own needs and ashamed of anything they construe as weakness. The Moon represents everything to do with the family, and contact between the Moon and Saturn can indicate issues of judgement and control coming down the ancestral line. However, it can also be a sign of a powerful central core to the family or dynasty and unshakeable loyalty to family ties.

When Saturn is in aspect to the Moon, the individual often radiates an energy which is an awkward mixture of Saturnian control and Lunar vulnerability. Hopefully, with the passage of time, the individual will find ways to integrate the strengths of both the Moon and Saturn. The positive expression of this combination would be a person who, over the years, moves from the collapsing and caretaking of the Oral defence into the authentic inner strength which is the ultimate gift of Saturn.

## Saturn in Aspect to the Sun

The warmth of the Sun is more robust than the fragile, vulnerable Moon, and Sun-Saturn aspects often have a more positive expression. The worst kind of Sun-Saturn contacts are a sign of a tyrannical and despotic father, a cold and distant father or an absent father. The positive expression is a strong and authoritative father, wise and well grounded.

Aspects between Saturn and the Sun are one of the clearest indications of Masochist wounding because the spontaneous expression of the Sun is inhibited by the control of the Superego and sabotaged by the cruelty of the Inner Critic. Often a person with this aspect may have complex layers of defence – the outer mask of the Rigid overlaying significant Masochist withholding, which is also an overlay to a Solar energy made fragile by early Schizoid or Oral wounding.

The positive expression of this aspect, one which is commonly seen in later life, is the authentic wisdom and authority of the elder. Sun-Saturn contacts indicate individuals with a lot of 'backbone', capable of achieving great results though diligence and patience.

# 51

## The Harvest or Rigid Stage

## The Houses – Where to Look for the Harvest/Rigid Stage in the Chart

Souls in the Harvest stage have come to work in the world of form, to create harmony and order and bring things to fruition. The houses associated with this stage are the 2nd and the 7th houses, associated with Venus, and the 10th house which is associated with Saturn.

### The 2nd House

Planets in the 2nd house tell us about a person's issues around receiving any kind of nourishment and abundance, which includes their relationship with money. When any of the outer planets – Chiron, Uranus, Neptune or Pluto – are found in the 2nd house it is an indication of Oral wounding and issues around deprivation. However, when Saturn or Venus fall in the 2nd house it indicates a Rigid overlay to the original Oral wounding. Thus a person with Venus in the 2nd may become greedily obsessed with material possessions and a person with Saturn in the 2nd house may become avaricious or Rigidly controlling about money in reaction to the underlying fear of Oral lack. The positive expression of Venus or Saturn in the 2nd house is a person who brings the Venusian gifts of the Harvest soul. Venus here can be someone who manifests a deep, committed, loving relationship or one who gains nourishment from the beauty of Nature or has an ease of access to abundance, whether money or beautiful things or any of the fruits of the earth. Saturn in the 2nd house is less likely than Venus to express positively. Saturn is typically associated with our work and so this might be someone who makes a living as an authority figure, such as a lawyer. It could be someone who is an authority on money and works in a bank or someone who works with the body as a fitness instructor. Our experience of Saturn gets better with time so this might be a mature person with valuable experience and understanding around abundance and the laws of manifestation.

The Sun, the Moon or any gathering of personal planets in the 2nd house indicates that much of this person's energy is focused on the sensual experience of living in a body and creating material satisfaction and stability in the manifest world – the gift of the Harvest/Rigid soul.

### The 7th House

The 7th house is associated with all kinds of partnerships and relationships. Whereas the 2nd house has the vibration of Venus in Taurus, the 7th house has the vibration of Venus in Libra and the civilizing aspiration of Pallas Athena. The 7th house represents the moment when the individual steps out into the world to meet the 'other' and explore the sense of self in relationship. So the 7th house is more than the house of marriage and romance – it is also where we learn about negotiation, exchange, protocol, respect and co-operation. Pallas Athena introduced the idea of a jury and brought peace to the bloodlust in the house of Orestes. This ideal of peaceful cooperation brought about through communication, negotiation and respect for the law is the expression of 7th house and this is fundamental to the work of the Harvest/Rigid soul.

### The 10th House

The Midheaven, or MC, is the zenith, the highest point in the chart The MC is an important point in the chart, symbolizing our aspirations in life, our hopes for the highest expression of our soul's intention and purpose. The MC and the 10th house are connected to our choice of career in the world of work and on a deeper level they show the Essence of what it is that we have come to build, the kind of life we want to manifest in the physical world. The Midheaven and the 10th house are the areas of the chart most relevant to the Harvest/Rigid stage as they describe our aspirations and represent worldly achievements. Planets here are the strongest indication of the Harvest/Rigid stage.

**Summary**

Indications of emphasis on the issues of the Rigid/Harvest stage are:

- Venus or Saturn in aspect to the Ascendant, the Sun, the Moon or the North Node
- The Sun, Moon, Ascendant or North Node of the Moon in the sign of Taurus, Libra or Capricorn
- Venus or Saturn in the 1st, 2nd, 4th, 7th or 10th house
- The North Node and any other emphasis, e.g. a large group of planets in the 2nd, 7th or 10th house

Venus and Saturn are two planets not normally associated with one another. Venus is sweet and light, associated with pleasure, beauty, love and happiness, Saturn is grim and severe, associated with discipline, duty, responsibility, oppression and depression.

What they have in common is that in their negative expression both planets can be dangerously demanding – the idealism of Venus can bring on crippling perfectionism and Saturn as Judge activates the Inner Critic. However, they are not cosmic idealists like Uranus and Neptune because both planets are focused on the unfolding of our human lives, here on Planet Earth. In their highest expression Venus and Saturn bring through the gifts of the Harvest stage as Venus connects to the longing of the soul to make life on earth beautiful and Saturn gives us the strength, the wisdom and the patience to make it happen.

47

# Conclusion

Every human being on the planet has been through all the developmental stages; every one of us has been wounded and each one of us has all the defences.

Every person has an immortal soul and each one of us has the potential for all the gifts of all the stages of the creative process.

Wounding in the first two stages, the Schizoid and Oral, is universal. For the non-physical soul the impact of incarnation in a physical body is huge. Even in the best of circumstances there are still many challenges for the new infant. At worst, the impact on the baby is shattering and the soul may spend much of this life trying to separate from the terrifying vulnerability of physical existence. Defences formed in the Masochist, Psychopathic and Rigid stages are always an overlay – a second layer of defence in an attempt to compensate for the primary distortions of infantile terror.

The defences are not who we are, they are the way we stop ourselves from being who we are. But when we are in the grip of our defences we get lost in them. We totally believe that they are real, that this is the way it is. Our defences cause us immense pain – so much pain that people are driven to commit violent acts, such as suicide and murder, or to drug addiction or to life cycles of defeat and suffering.

But our defences are part of us, made of our own energy, a mess of tangled up, thorny life force that has not yet been allowed to be expressed – almost like a bud that has not yet unfurled its petals.

When I look at a person's energy field I see the unstoppable light of their Essence pouring forth, breaking up into rivulets as the energy streams around their energy blocks, like a great river through a swampy delta. And no matter how much anguish they cause us, these blocks are made of our own consciousness and no one can take them away. As we grow in awareness, as our souls evolve, piece by piece, miracle by miracle, we dissolve our tangles and return our life force to the flow. And often the darkest hour comes just before dawn.

The five developmental stages that I have talked about are a simplistic breakdown of the development of a human personality, something that is so immensely complex that it defies categorization. But understanding the five defences can help us to understand why we are the way we are. Understanding, witnessing and Awareness are the keys, the first steps towards transformation.

Nobody IS a Schizoid or a Masochist. Even though people who understand Characterology sometimes talk that way, this is only a shorthand for a reality that is infinitely bigger than any label we apply. Each individual expresses their own unique balance of whatever wounds and gifts they bring from every stage of life, including past lives. Similarly, nobody IS a Taurus or a Pisces, although everyone, including professional astrologers, talks that way. Nobody expresses only Neptune or only Mars, but a chart will reveal which are the planets this soul is most drawn to explore and develop this life. The planets are symbols of archetypal patterns of energy flowing through our lives. Like the defences, each planet can express as a painful knotted distortion or in its luminous exaltation.

Many people cannot find their way through the vast amount of information held in a natal chart, yet how could a chart be anything less than complex when it is the representation of a human life? There comes a point where all our little systems of thinking and analysing break down because, in the end, the soul is so much bigger than any description we can give it. Words really cannot describe the miracle of creation that is a person – a vast being of light made up of millions of cells given the breath of life by a consciousness that is a unique expression of the Divine.

So everything I have written is inadequate – both too complicated and too simple. We are back to Lao Tzu:

*The Tao that can be named is not the Tao.*

Not to mention the elephant and the blind men! Yet words are all we have. As Eckhart Tolle says, words are not the way but they can point us towards the way.

# Conclusion

The defences are our teachers. Our wounds are the grit in the pearl, our allies on the path of awakening, and the gift of astrology and healing is to understand that in our suffering something is seeking to emerge, like the shell of an egg breaking open at last. Every human being on the planet is flawed. Human beings are messy – we are not designed to be perfect! The purpose of this book is to support a new understanding of how you came to be the way you are and the awareness that, whoever you are, it is not a mistake, only something real and tender and very beautiful, struggling to be born.

The one thing that is not shown in a person's natal chart is their Essence. Our Essence arises from our Core Star, our Divine home, the place where we are born from the Universal Energy Field. The Essence of every being has a light that transcends any kind of earthly limitation but it is that beautiful light which shines through and illuminates our little human lives for our one brief moment on the stage of the world.

# PART III

# THE ASTROLOGY OF CHARACTEROLOGY

This part of the book contains five case studies of individuals whose horoscopes and life stories illustrate the five different Character types. This section will only be fully comprehensible to readers with at least a minimal knowledge of the language of astrology.

- The rock guitarist **Jimi Hendrix** as an example of the Germination/Schizoid soul
- Hollywood legend **Marilyn Monroe** as an example of the Rooting/Oral soul
- Film director, actor and playwright **Orson Welles** as an example of the Budding/Masochist soul
- Mexican painter **Frida Kahlo** as an example of the Flowering/Psychopathic soul
- Spiritual philosopher **Teilhard de Chardin** as an example of the Harvest/Rigid soul

This book is about Characterology and so my aim in these case studies is to illustrate how the placement of the planets in the chart point to the person's character structure.

My focus is on the archetypal nature of each of the planets and the effect they have on each other through the aspects. The way that a planet expresses the sign it occupies can be profoundly altered by the influence of a strong aspect from another planet. Because I am also aiming to show a horoscope as a kind of 'energy read-out' I have tried to simplify the aspects with a 10° orb for conjunctions, oppositions, trines and squares between any planets, 6° orb for sextiles and 2° orb for any minor aspects.

In each of the five cases I have the sense of one particular planet that speaks most strongly of the Essence of that person. With Jimi Hendrix it is Uranus; with Marilyn Monroe it is Neptune; with Orson

Welles it is Pluto; with Frida Kahlo it is Mars; and with Teilhard de Chardin it is Saturn. All five were famous and so Jupiter is also strong in each of their charts.

Clearly, a person's life cannot be summarized in a few pages. So, when writing my mini-biographies, my aim has been to search out the themes relevant to the exploration of the five Character types and to demonstrate the link between the planets and a person's Characterology. Please regard these case studies in the light of an exploration, perhaps a moment to see astrology or psychology or the Human Energy Field in a new way.

52

# THE GERMINATION OR SCHIZOID SOUL: Jimi Hendrix

> *When I entered his presence it was like stepping into a field of electricity.*
> Thomas Lopez

Jimi Hendrix was one of the greatest electric guitarists in the history of rock music and one of the most influential pop musicians of the twentieth century. In the 1960s he was a pioneer in exploring the possibilities of the electric guitar and he became the supreme innovator, experimenting with electronic feedback and controlled distortion to create a new musical form. In 2003 the magazine *Rolling Stone* named Hendrix the top guitarist on its list of the 100 Greatest Guitarists of All Time. Yet Jimi Hendrix came from an extremely impoverished background, he was unable to read music, and mastered the guitar in his teens by playing along to music on the radio.

Jimi Hendrix was born on 27 November 1942, a few weeks after Neptune entered the sign of Libra. He was among the first of the generation born with Pluto in Leo and Neptune in Libra; the generation that brought the astonishing wave of creativity and innovation that swept through popular culture in the 1960s. Even among the guitar giants of his time, Jimi Hendrix stands head and shoulders above the crowd as one of the most brilliant and innovative of all.

## Characterology

The music of Hendrix is so original that I see him as a classic example of the Germination/Schizoid type: a genius with a mind capable of taking great leaps into the unknown to bring back music, sounds, techniques, poetry and performance that were lifetimes ahead of what had gone before.

## Childhood

Jimi was born in Seattle, Washington, an African-American also of European, Cherokee and Mexican descent. His mother, Lucille, was sixteen, little more than a child when she fell pregnant with Jimi, and he did not have an easy start in life. These were the war years and Jimi's father, Al Hendrix, was drafted into the army and left a few days after his marriage to Lucille. At the time of Jimi's birth, Al was stationed at an army base in Oklahoma and he was not allowed leave of absence to visit his wife and child. Al did not meet his son until Jimi was three years old.

Lucille named her son Johnny Allen Hendrix. but life was hard. Money and work were hard to come by for African-Americans and the young woman could not cope. She had help from various family members but eventually she left her baby in the temporary care of friends in California. So we see a classic case of Schizoid wounding – from the moment of his conception Jimi's family was fragmented and his young mother was in trouble.

When his father, Al, was discharged from the army he took custody of his son and changed the boy's name to James Marshall Hendrix. Al was reunited with Lucille and, at the age of three, Jimi found himself in the same room with both his parents for the first time in his life. Jimi's parents tried to make a life together but they were extremely poor, times were hard and both turned to drink. Al became an abusive husband and father, and the relationship was marred with conflict and violence. Jimi was often sent to stay with relatives who reported that even at the age of four he was sometimes sad and withdrawn, and when asked about it he said 'Mom and Dad are always fighting, I wish they'd stop.'

Hendrix had two brothers, Leon and Joseph, and two sisters, Kathy and Pamela. Joseph, Kathy and Pamela were all born with health complications. Kathy and Pamela were taken into care soon after their birth but Jo stayed with the family until he was three. Jo was born with a disabled leg and Lucille lived in hope that he could have surgery. But Al was afraid of the cost of medical bills and, against Lucille's wishes, he insisted that Joe was given away into state care. This may have been the last straw for Lucille and when Jimi was nine his parents divorced. Al won the custody of the children but Jimi always worshipped his mother in her absence. Eventually Leon was also taken into care but Jimi managed to dodge the welfare workers and remained living with his father in dire poverty.

Jimi sometimes spent weekends with Lucille and her extended family, and he idolized and adored his mother. But Lucille died when Jimi was fifteen. This was at the time when he got his first real guitar, so Jimi's music became a channel for his grieving for his mother and his feelings about his fractured childhood. From that time on, his guitar never left his side. Music became the refuge for this impoverished young man with the soul of a genius. 'Castles Made of Sand' is the song that Hendrix wrote recalling memories of his childhood and his parent's relationship that could provide no more containment and protection for the family than a sandcastle at the edge of the ocean.

**Career**

Jimi was expelled from school when he was sixteen, possibly for holding the hand of a white girl. At seventeen he joined the army but after fourteen months he was discharged, either because he was too rebellious for the army or because he was injured in a parachute jump. From then on, all through the early 1960s Jimi worked as an electric guitarist playing back-up guitar for various R&B bands. However, with his radical approach to music he needed more freedom of expression than he could find as a back-up guitarist and he was soon drawn into the ground breaking music scene of New York's Greenwich Village. In 1965 he formed his first band, Jimmy James and the Blue Flames, and he was seen by other musicians who quickly recognized his talent. Among them was the English bass guitarist Chas Chandler who persuaded Jimi to come to England. England in 1966 was at the cutting edge of a revolution of artistic innovation and here Jimi's radical virtuoso guitar playing was instantly recognized; he quickly rose to success and stardom and a legend was born.

Jimi was left-handed and, being self-taught, he had invented his own unique way of playing. He used right-handed guitars, turned upside-down for left-hand playing, and restrung so that the heavier strings were in their standard position at the top of the neck. This is a marvellous expression of quirky Uranus who doesn't even notice that there is a rule but simply invents a new way of doing things, and Jimi has been described as 'A master at breaking conventions.'

Jimi had big, beautiful hands, capable of executing extraordinary feats on the guitar, characteristically using his thumb to fret bass notes, leaving his fingers free to play melodic fills on top, so he could play lead and rhythm parts simultaneously. His performance on stage was skilful and astonishing, as he produced his amazing sounds playing the guitar with his teeth, behind his back and sometimes setting the guitar on fire.

For four years Jimi produced a stream of highly successful recordings and performances and became world-famous. On 18 September 1970, soon after achieving enormous success playing at the Isle of Wight Festival in England, Jimi Hendrix died tragically, choking on his own vomit while he was unconscious after imbibing a cocktail of drugs and alcohol.

# 53

## The Germination or Schizoid Soul

# Interpreting the Horoscope of Jimi Hendrix

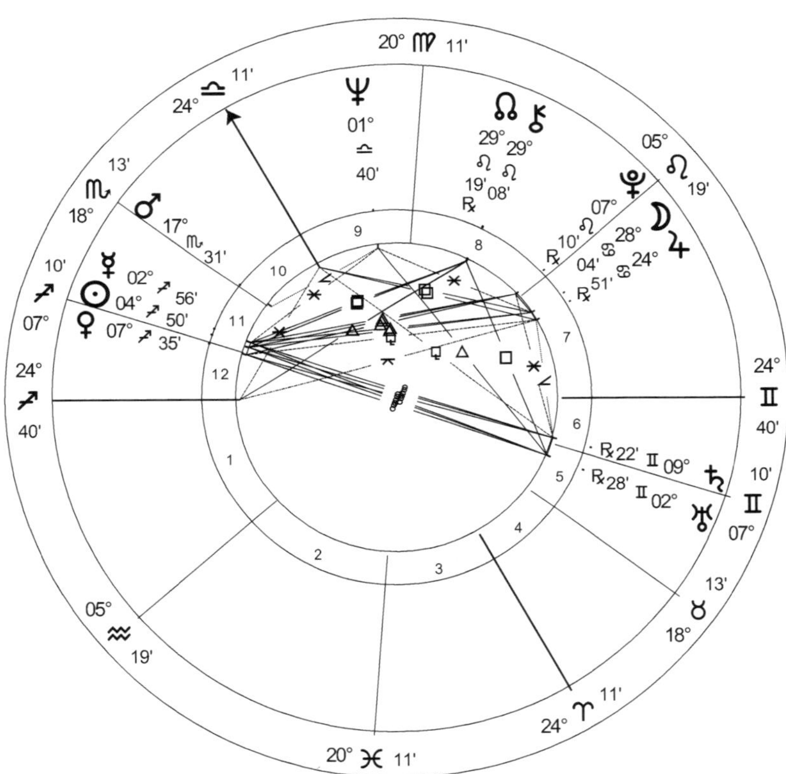


**Jimi Hendrix**

10.15 am Friday 27 November 1942, Seattle Washington USA

Placidus House System

Chart from Solar Fire version 7 Astrolabe, www.alabe.com.

## Dominant Planets and Themes

There are two themes that stand out in the chart of Jimi Hendrix. One is the intensity of the expansive, electric Germination energy represented in the opposition between Uranus in Gemini and the Mercury-Sun-Venus stellium in Sagittarius. The second is the sensitive, dark, contracting Rooting and Budding energy of the Cancer Moon conjuncting Pluto in the 8th house

### Germination/Schizoid Energy – Uranus and Mercury

I had always suspected that Hendrix, such an electric artist in every sense of the word, was likely to have a strong influence from Uranus. Even so, when I first opened up his chart I was astonished to see the intensity of Jimi's Germination/Schizoid energy represented by Uranus opposing the Sun and Mercury, which is almost exact. Looking at the multiple lines of opposition zinging across the chart between the stellium in Sagittarius and the Uranus-Saturn conjunction in Gemini I felt I was looking at the strings of Jimi's guitar, with Uranus at one end channelling unheard-of sounds from the cosmos across the chart into Mercury expressing through his skilful hands and long fingers to bring through his amazing music.

This electric opposition fires up the artistic conjunction of the Sun, Mercury and Venus. Saturn gave Jimi the persistence and discipline needed to channel his creativity and give his music a form that could be heard in the physical world. And with Uranus conjuncting Saturn, Jimi's music takes a form that is completely original.

### Flowering/Psychopathic Energy – Jupiter and the Sun

The energies of the Sun, Mercury and Jupiter are written all over Jimi's chart – creativity, communication and vision. His whole chart is illuminated by the light of the Sun, which is in aspect to every planet except Mars, while Jupiter, the chart ruler, is exactly inconjunct the Ascendant, conjunct the Moon and the ruler of the creative stellium in Sagittarius. The creative flame in this chart surges upwards to the heavens through the revolutionary genius of Uranus and the visionary nature of Jupiter. We have seen that Uranus takes the life force out through the crown chakra to the 7th level of the field – out into the cosmos, like a bolt of lightning channelling pure innovation from the heavens. Jupiter is a warmer, less impersonal, planet but he also lifts us heavenwards, up through the Upper Tan T'ien, to bring inspiration and vision from the Universal Mind.

**Bowl Chart Shape**

The planets in Jimi's chart form a Bowl shape: all, apart from the Saturn-Uranus conjunction, fall in the southern hemisphere of the chart (i.e. above the horizon). The southern hemisphere represents issues of the collective, which is, of course, where Jimi fulfilled his destiny, out on the world stage. Most of the planets are gathered in conjunctions and small groups and these are all in aspect to each other (sometimes across the signs).

So Jimi's chart appears as half a star, founded on the powerful opposition between the planets in Gemini and Sagittarius, and everything else being in a sextile, a trine or a square to the opposition. (The only planet not involved in this half-star is Mars.) This rare aspect pattern is a strange mixture of the harmony of the trines and sextiles and the intensity of the close involvement of all the planets. This combination of harmony and intensity seems to fit with the one-pointed artistic creativity of Jimi's life. Jimi's chart does not have a single planet in Earth – even the angles are in Fire and Air. The only anchor for this fountain of creativity comes from Saturn in Gemini in opposition to the Sagittarius planets. So here we see Saturn in a positive role holding the alignment of Life Purpose and manifestation.

**The Moon, Pluto, Neptune and Chiron**

The Watery energy of the Moon, conjunct Pluto and sextile Neptune, has a deepening influence on Jimi's chart. Chart ruler Jupiter is in Cancer, also conjunct the Moon, connecting the planets in visionary Sagittarius with the oceanic dream world of the Lunar principle. Jimi's Chiron is exactly conjunct the North Node in Leo (orb 0° 11'). Joy in creativity is the Essence of Leo and this was a large part of the driving force behind the wave of artistic innovation that the post-war children of the 1940s brought through. Jimi's Chiron in Leo signifies the pain of his childhood but it also signifies a very soulful part of his nature, which was an important element in his artistic expression. Beneath the golden fire that radiates upwards and outwards in his energy field is the very different energy flow of Chiron, Pluto and the Moon forming a pool of softer darker energy that sinks inwards – the wounding of his childhood opening to the depth of Jimi's human feelings.

Maybe it is not surprising that with such an intense streaming of energy Jimi's star soared high into the sky but only burned there for four years before he was gone.

# 54

## Indications of Characterology in Jimi Hendrix's Chart

## **Germination/Schizoid Energy**

### URANUS

- *Uranus exactly opposition Mercury (orb 0° 28')*
- *Uranus opposition the Sun (orb 2° 22')*
- *Uranus opposition Venus(orb 5° 07')*
- *Uranus sextile the Moon (orb 4° 24')*
- *Uranus trine Neptune (orb 0° 48')*
- *Uranus square Chiron (3° 09')*
- *Uranus square the North Node (orb 2° 36')*
- *Uranus in Gemini*

### MERCURY

- *Mercury conjunct the Sun (orb 1° 54')*
- *Mercury conjunct Venus (orb 4° 39')*
- *Mercury trine the Moon (orb 4° 52')*
- *Mercury trine chart ruler Jupiter (orb 8° 05')*
- *Mercury sextile Neptune (orb 1° 16')*
- *Mercury square Chiron (orb 4° 13')*
- *Mercury square the North Node (orb 3° 48')*

### CHIRON

- *Chiron trine the Ascendant (orb 4° 28')*

The Germination/Schizoid stage begins with the very earliest moments of life so we start by looking around the Ascendant, which represents the time of birth.

### The Ascendant

The major aspects to Jimi's Ascendant are a trine from Chiron, a square from Neptune and there is also has an inconjunct from Jupiter. Neptune speaks of the Rooting/Oral energy and Jupiter of the Flowering/Psychopathic energy but Chiron in aspect to the Ascendant is a clear indication of Schizoid wounding. The energy of a trine is harmonious and not so dynamic but it describes the pain and fragmentation in Jimi's family as a fundamental reality woven into his entry into this world.

### The 12th House

This house represents the gestation period. Jimi has Venus here, a sign of a golden time in utero. Probably Lucille and Al were very much in love to begin with but the tension of an unplanned pregnancy is indicated by the shock of the opposition from Uranus and Saturn and the square from Chiron.

In the Placidus house system Jimi's Sun is just at the end of the 11th house. Planets in this position, 2 degrees away from going over the cusp of a house more often express through the affairs of the house they are entering than the one they are leaving. The affairs of both the 11th and the12th house are transpersonal i.e. looking beyond the successes and failures of the ego to the issues of the collective but I feel that Jimi's Sun expresses very much as a $12^{th}$ house Sun.

Planets in the 12th house have a paradoxical role in that they represent the gifts that a person brings to the collective but at the same time they represent qualities that have been lost in the ancestral heritage and are difficult for the person to own in consciousness. Thus, Al was not able to offer Jimi a reflection of the golden creative radiance of his Solar nature; Al could not give to Jimi that which he was unable to recognize in himself. Instead, Al took on the role of Saturn as critic – he was sometimes brutal, discouraged his son's passion for music and wanted him to go out and get a 'proper' job. But the 12th house is the house of the dream world and this is where Jimi went to escape the harsh reality of his young life. The 12th house is the place where we can open out into the vastness of the imaginal realms and it was here that Jimi was free to bring through the Essence of creativity and artistry represented by a Mercury-Sun-Venus conjunction in the 12th house.

### The Moon

Jimi romanticized his memory of his beautiful young mother and the complexity of his feelings are shown by the many planets involved with the Moon. The Moon is sextiled by Uranus and trined by Mercury, both the major indicators of Germination/Schizoid energy. Here we see again the fragmentation of Jimi's childhood and his teenage mother who put him into care, fracturing the luminous container of the Moon. However, although Uranus and Mercury are in Air and Fire respectively, the Moon is strong in its own Water sign of Cancer and the aspects are trines and sextiles, not squares or oppositions. This aspect formation of a mini-triangle with the Moon and two such intensely creative planets is an indication of artistic talent. So, as much as this configuration is an indication of Schizoid wounding, it is also a powerful indication of the gifts of the Germination soul.

### Uranus

The gift of Uranus is genius, brilliance, originality and radical leaps of creative innovation. The wound of Uranus is shock and shattering of the sense of safety and containment in physical form. Uranus is the Essence of the Germination/Schizoid soul.

Jimi's Uranus almost exactly opposes Mercury (orb 0° 28') and also the Sun and Venus. It almost exactly trines Neptune (orb 0° 48'), it sextiles the Moon and squares the conjunction of the North Node and Chiron, so the impact of Uranus is everywhere in this chart. Uranus rules electricity and there is no clearer expression of the combination of Uranus-Neptune and Mercury than the inspired, electric music of Jimi Hendrix.

Uranus brings freedom, change, rebellion and revolution. It is an exciting and sometimes (not always) a joyful energy and it is, by nature, adolescent and idealistic. Uranus is sometimes described as the higher octave of Mercury and both planets have a quality of youthfulness which can be playful but also destructive. In Jimi's chart the combination of juvenile Uranus and Mercury with the Sun and Saturn evokes the archetype of the *puer aeternus*, the eternal youth.

### Eternal Youth

*Puer aeternus* is a term used in Transpersonal Psychology for an aspect of masculine energy – a youth who cannot escape adolescence and cross the threshold into maturity. Liz Greene says:

> *The puer is antithetical to the Father [principle]. He is flighty, airy, aesthetic, spirited, youthful, brilliant, but incapable of establishing loyalty or permanence in relationship.*

When there have been difficulties in the relationship with the father, a young man can become trapped in a Peter Pan world – unable to move on to develop the mature qualities of responsibility, self-respect, self-discipline and persistence, which the father did not model. Jimi's chart so clearly illustrates this split in the opposition to the Sun from the Saturn-Uranus conjunction. The Sun represents the child's image of the father; Jimi's father was violent and abusive and Saturn opposing the Sun is the image of the tyrannical father from whom the *puer* takes flight. The shattering effect on the young Jimi appears as experiences of shock coming from the opposition from Uranus. However, it is worth noting that, in his own way, Al stuck by his son. He kept Jimi with him and it was he who bought him his first real guitar, so we also see Al and Saturn as the only available anchors in Jimi's impoverished childhood.

Chiron is square to the Mercury-Sun/ Saturn-Uranus opposition. At the apex of the T-square Chiron is the dynamo that drives this configuration: a sign of the impossible hurt of his relationship with his father but also of the light of Chiron that takes us to another place – the pain that opened Jimi to the depth of feeling he brought to his music.

## Mercury

When I look at this chart I keep coming back to Mercury. In its negative expression, Mercury brings polarization and splitting, and the opposition to Uranus and trine to the Moon reinforce all the indications of Schizoid wounding – the shattering impact of Jimi's experience in his family. However, in mythology it was Mercury who introduced music to the human race – he invented the first lyre by stringing cow gut across a tortoise shell. So, above all, Jimi's Mercury was a powerful indication of the verbal and musical gifts of the Germination soul. Like the Sun, Jimi's Mercury was in aspect to everything in the chart except Mars and it was even more closely in orb than the Sun – in other words, more closely trining the Moon and Jupiter, more closely squaring Chiron, more closely sextiling Neptune and exactly opposing Uranus.

Mercury is also opposed by Saturn from the 6th house. The combination of Saturn and Uranus is never easy – we are back with the mythological war between Uranus, the cosmic idealist, and Saturn, the lord of limitation. So Uranus in Gemini demands perfection and Saturn becomes the obsessive drive and self-discipline required to reach the astonishing level of skill that Jimi achieved (Mercury and the 6th house are both associated with skills). Mercury rules the hands, the nervous system and all expressions of the mind – music, speech, wit and poetry, words, numbers and the ability to see patterns and make connections. Any combination of Mercury with the feminine planets – the Moon, Venus and Neptune – is often an indication of artistic ability. Jimi's Mercury, so strongly emphasized in his chart, channelling through the cosmic innovations of Uranus signifies the Essence of a great communicator, an immensely skilled musician and poet.

> *As close as human hands can come to the hands of the Lord in Heaven and still remain human.*
> Kevin Burshstein, *A Rare Jimi Hendrix Interview*

### The Sun

The Sun's conjunction with Mercury and Venus, the sextile from Neptune and the trine from the Moon only add to our understanding of Jimi as an inspired artist, poet and musician. And it is in the opposition from electric Uranus that Jimi's untutored and unrestricted mind was free to create a new form of electronic guitar music, inventing sounds that had never been heard before – bringing through the innovation that is the gift of the Germination soul. Saturn at one end of the opposition and Venus at the other helped to ground Jimi's creativity and enabled him to achieve the technical brilliance needed to express the sounds that he wanted to make.

A free-flying Uranian, Mercurial, Peter Pan soul like Jimi's did not cope well with the limitations of life in the physical world and the radiance of the Sun and Jupiter gave no real grounding to this Lost Boy. Nothing in his childhood had brought Jimi a sense of earthly containment and nothing in Jimi's chart could help to bring him down from his visionary heights and show him how it would be possible for him to live on in the physical world and grow old. Jimi Hendrix is celebrated as one of the '27 Club', a group of highly talented musicians – Brian Jones, Janis Joplin, Jim Morrison and Jimi Hendrix – who all died within a two-year period, all at the age of 27, thus avoiding the challenges of the Saturn return; immortalized by fame and remaining forever young.

The life and the horoscope of Jimi Hendrix perfectly illustrate the wounds and the gifts of the Germination/Schizoid soul. He had the skills of a genius, with the electric brilliance of Uranus pouring through his music. In his mind Jimi could walk among the stars but he never learned to cope with the limitations of life on earth.

# 55

# Indications of Characterology in Jimi Hendrix's Chart

## Rooting/Oral Energy

### THE MOON

- *The Moon in its own sign of Cancer*
- *Chart ruler Jupiter conjunct the Moon (orb 3° 13')*
- *Chart ruler Jupiter in Cancer*
- *The Moon trine the Sun (orb 6° 46')*

### NEPTUNE

- *Neptune square the Ascendant (orb 7° 00')*
- *Neptune sextile the Moon (orb 3° 36')*
- *Neptune sextile the Sun (orb 3° 10')*
- *Neptune sextile Venus (orb 5° 55')*

### TWELFTH HOUSE

- *Venus in the 12th house (conjunct the Sun)*

### The Moon

With the Sun, Mercury, Venus and the Ascendant in Sagittarius, the first impression of Jimi was the expansive golden fire of Sagittarius electrified by the brilliance of Uranus flowing through in opposition to the planets in Sagittarius. But behind this radiant exterior the Lunar influence is equally strong.

The Moon trines the Sun and chart ruler Jupiter is conjunct the Moon in the Moon's own sign of Cancer. All the transformational outer planets are in aspect to the Moon. Pluto conjuncts the Moon and Neptune and Uranus sextile the Moon. So this Moon speaks of many things.

In the first place, the Moon describes the difficulties that beset Jimi's relationship with his mother, the break-up of the family and the

Oral wound of deprivation and abandonment. However, because the Moon is strong, in its own sign and not in aspect to either Saturn or Chiron, I feel that there was a way in which Jimi was able to receive love from his mother and so this Moon speaks of more than maternal deprivation. Into his experience of a devastating lack of family support, the conjunction from Jupiter and the sextiles from cosmic Uranus and mystical Neptune gave Jimi an outlet – an escape into the world of the imagination. The Moon also represents the archetype of the Muse – that elusive, non-rational light of inspiration. The Moon is strongly associated with artistic creativity but in a very different way to the energy of Fire. With the soft light of the Moon we gain access to the dream world and non-rational intuitive knowing. With the sextile from sensitive, spiritual Neptune and in its own sign of Cancer, Jimi's Moon represents an ocean of feeling; a powerful emphasis on the element of Water. The conjunction with Pluto emphasizes the dark realms of the psyche and it is a classic indication of childhood pain – the violence that cast a shadow over Jimi's family and his mother's depression and early death. But the Moon and Pluto both operate on the level of feelings. Pluto comes with drive and passion and this conjunction was another factor that enabled Jimi to express a profound depth of emotion in his music. So the influence of the Moon in Jimi's chart draws the energy inwards to heart and soul. This deep well of feeling was what made Jimi's music great, just as much as his electric innovations.

### Neptune

Neptune is another strong influence on Jimi's chart, on the midpoint of the wide trine between the Sun and Moon and square to the Ascendant. Neptune brings sensitivity and mysticism and Jimi's family spoke of him as a wise and gentle child with a spiritually questing mind. But Neptune is the key signature of Oral wounding; Jimi grew up in abject poverty and his Neptune recalls the story of the Little Match Girl adrift on the streets with nothing in this world to hold on to.

Neptune is a prime indication of musical and artistic ability, and the little triangle formed between Neptune sextiling the Sun-Moon trine is yet another indication of artistic talent. Neptune gives ease of access to the non-physical realms, channelling music through the creativity of the Sun and imagination of the Moon. Musical Venus conjuncting the Sun is also included in this very beautiful and harmonious configuration. In general, people writing about the relationship between Jimi's parents (indicated by the Sun and the Moon) emphasize the conflict, violence, abuse and alcoholism that destroyed the relationship. But this very sweet aspect pattern makes me think of the romantic love that originally drew the couple together. Racism, war and poverty proved to be afflictions that the fragile relationship could not survive but it seems that, initially, Jimi Hendrix was born from a big romance.

Jimi's Ascendant has only two major aspects and the most important is the square from Neptune. The Ascendant represents the threshold between our inner awareness, arising from our vast internal world and our perception, and our way of self-expression in the exterior world. Signs and planets aspecting the Ascendant describe both the way in which we express a sense of our unique identity as well as the lens through which we perceive life. The influence of Neptune here points to an issue with boundaries – one of the biggest challenges for the Oral type. With no Earth in the chart, the Sun in the 12th house, a watery Lunar presence and the square to the Ascendant from Neptune, it would have been difficult for Jimi to find a grounded, focused sense of his own boundaries.

There are two antidotes to help a Neptunian individual get to grips with life on earth. One is the realism and toughness that can come from a strong Saturn; the other is the self-assertiveness coming from a strong Mars. Jimi's Saturn is the only thing that helps to ground the immense creativity in the chart but its influence is undercut by the other-world energy of the conjunction from Uranus. Jimi's Mars is strong in its own sign of Scorpio, trining Jupiter and the Moon, and this combination of planets will have given him the core of powerful raw energy that drove his career and gave him tremendous sexual charisma. However, Mars is semi-squared by Neptune so, again, the instinctual power of Mars is diverted into the ethereal realms of

Neptune and we see the expression of that raw power coming through Jimi's music. Neptune brings the tendency to fly from the harshness of life into the world of the imagination but it is also associated with more destructive forms of escapism. The mythic figure of Dionysus, the Greek god of wine, is one of the archetypes linked with Neptune. Dionysus led wild drunken orgies seeking Divine communion through sensual ecstasy. Jimi was a prime example of the stars of the sex, drugs and rock and roll generation; notorious for his sexual adventures and the unrestrained experimentation with drugs and alcohol which eventually brought about his death.

**Secondary Progressions of the Moon**

The secondary progressions of the Moon during Jimi's first year of life paint a picture of his troubled infancy. However, these progressions can also be seen as the signature of his innovative and artistic Essence flowing through his unformed energy field.

- At three months, the sextile of the progressed Moon to his natal Neptune became exact
- At four months, the sextile to Uranus and the trine to Mercury became exact
- At six months, the progressed Moon trine to his natal Sun became exact
- At ten months, the progressed Moon exactly trined natal Venus and simultaneously conjuncted natal Pluto in Leo. The conjunction of the progressed Moon to Pluto, before Jimi's first birthday, would have set the seal on the break-up of the Lunar container in his energy field
- At one year, the sextile of the progressed Moon to Saturn became exact

Looking at this series of transits I can almost hear the notes of a scale or the plucking of the strings of a guitar as, one by one, each of the archetypes was activated in Jimi's chart, bringing their gifts as in a fairy tale christening.

56

# Indications of Characterology in Jimi Hendrix's Chart

## Budding/Masochist Energy

### THE SUN

- *The Sun moving into the 12th house*
- *The Sun square Chiron (orb 5° 42')*
- *The Sun opposite Saturn (orb 4° 32')*

### PLUTO

- *Pluto conjunct the Moon (orb 9° 06')*
- *Pluto trine the Sun (orb 2° 20')*
- *Pluto exactly trine Venus (orb 0° 25')*
- *Pluto (wide) square Mars (orb 10° 21')*

### EIGHTH HOUSE STELLIUM

#### Pluto

Pluto is the prime indicator of the Budding/Masochist energy. Jimi has Pluto conjunct the Moon and it exactly trines Venus and also the Sun and Mercury. Pluto is in a wide square to Jimi's Mars, and so Pluto touches every one of Jimi's personal planets. Pluto is associated with instinctual drives; the aspects to Venus and Mars gives sexual magnetism, which Jimi had in abundance. This passionate sexual intensity is shown again by the placement of Pluto in the 8th House.

Pluto here speaks of the dark shadows of Jimi's childhood, the break-up of his parent's relationship, beatings from his father and his mother's early death. Pluto's aspects to Venus and Mars both represent issues of power and abuse in the parental relationship and the fact that little Jimi was a witness to domestic violence. The Moon-Pluto conjunction describes disempowerment and depression in Jimi's mother and difficulty and despair in both parents, unable to find a way to make their lives work. All this would have impacted heavily on Jimi with the unshielded energy field of a child, causing him to withdraw and put a block on outward displays of his vulnerability. Like the shell of the Cancerian Crab, people with an emphasis on Water in their charts are often the most emotionally defended – their sensitivity causes them to feel in need of extra armour. Pluto conjuncting a Cancer Moon is always likely to be emotionally defended and this aspect, as well as the trine from Pluto to the Sun, is an indication of Masochist wounding and introversion.

A person with Masochist wounding withholds from spontaneous expression for fear of the overpowering domination and abuse they experienced in childhood. But the path of the Budding/Masochist soul is to seek to find their authentic sense of self through creativity. So it was through his music that Jimi was able to find his inner light. In Essence, Pluto is associated with the raw power of the Lower Tan T'ien and the Hara – the energy that drives us to fulfil our Life's Purpose. We can see how Jimi's Pluto came through the personal planets with a power that propelled him unimaginably far from his roots with a force that took him all the way to the top and out onto the world stage.

### Sun-Venus Conjunction in the 12th House

Jimi's Venus fall in the 12th house and I have said that I feel the Sun also expresses through the 12th. Personal planets in the 12th house are a classic indication of Masochist wounding where the child's radiance is not celebrated, and Jimi's Essence and his artistry were definitely not seen in his childhood. The Sun's T-square with Saturn and Chiron describe classic Masochist wounding through the bullying and violence, as well as the work ethic, of his father. In his teens his father did not take Jimi's guitar playing seriously but wanted him to go out and get a job. Eventually, when Jimi tried to stand up to Al, his father punched him and that was the moment when Jimi left home, left Seattle, jumped train and set off to find the music.

The 12th house is the place of our connection to the non-physical realms and also shows us ancestral issues. It is likely that Jimi was at the end of many generations in which the creative and artistic energy of the conjunction of Venus, the Sun and Mercury was repressed, lost, not allowed to shine or to be brought fully into consciousness. Like a perfect illustration of planets in the 12th house, Jimi brought through his musical Essence, gave it to the world and, like so many gifted artists, sacrificed his own life on the altar of fame

# 57

# Indications of Characterology in Jimi Hendrix's Chart
## Flowering/Psychopathic Energy

### JUPITER

- *Sagittarius Ascendant*
- *Jupiter conjunct the Moon (orb 3° 13')*
- *Jupiter square MC (orb 0° 40')*
- *Jupiter exactly inconjunct Ascendant (orb 0° 11')*
- *Jupiter trine Mars (orb 7° 20')*

### THE SUN

- *Sun in Sagittarius*
- *North Node in Leo*

### MARS

- *Mars in wide trine the Moon (orb 10° 33')*

Jupiter has a dominant influence on this chart, with the Ascendant, Sun, Venus and Mercury in Sagittarius and Jupiter conjunct the Moon. Jupiter is one of the planets of Fire associated with the heroism, romance and charisma of the Flowering/Psychopathic type. A strong Jupiter is often found in the charts of famous performers whose expansive energy can inspire many and fill theatres. We see the power of Jupiter and the gifts of the Flowering soul in Jimi's commanding stage presence, and he is notorious for the occasions on which he set his guitar alight – when he literally played with fire! But in his personal relationships Jimi was not prone to the pugnacious aggression typical of the more Martian Psychopathic type. Instead, his family remembered him as a quiet boy, a wise and gentle soul.

### Jupiter in Cancer

There were a number of reasons why Jimi, with all his Fire, did not come across as the classic aggressive Psychopathic type. To begin with, planets in Sagittarius always express with less aggression than planets in Aries or Leo. Jovial Jupiter was the king of the gods and Jupiter/Sagittarius people don't have to try so hard to get attention; they are not so driven and they are more effortlessly inspiring. One of the keywords for Sagittarius is 'wisdom' and one of the key images is of the High Priest. But, more than this, away from the stage Jimi was often described as a shy person, the opposite of the extroverted Flowering/Psychopathic type. Here we see the dominant influence of gentle Watery Cancer, with Jupiter conjunct the Moon in Cancer, softening and sensitizing the Jupiterian Fire. A chart with the ruling planet in Cancer, conjunct the Moon and in the 8th house is introspective and this is echoed by the placement of the Sun in the 12th house. This emphasis on two of the Water houses – the 12th and the 8th houses – signifies the energies of the Rooting/Oral and Budding/Masochist stages, where there is great sensitivity and much of the self is withheld, focused on the inner world.

### Harmonious Aspects

The square is the aspect that I associate with the drive of the Flowering/Psychopathic soul. Jimi had four squares in his chart. However, none of them was likely to bring through the typical extrovert aggression of the Flowering/Psychopathic type. Jupiter exactly squared the MC but the MC is in peace-loving Libra. Neptune squared his Sagittarius Ascendant but Neptune only repeats the theme of gentleness and sensitivity. This emphasis on harmony is repeated when we look at the predominance of trines, sextiles and conjunctions forming a half star. Jimi's Mercury-Sun-Venus conjunction trines the Jupiter-Moon-Pluto group and sextiles Neptune. The Uranus-Saturn conjunction trines Neptune and sextiles Pluto and the Moon. Nine of the planets in the chart are drawn into this harmonious formation – no wonder Jimi expressed himself through music.

The most difficult square came from Chiron in Leo making a T-square to the opposition between the planets in Sagittarius and Gemini. Chiron here represented a powerful driving force in the chart, the wounding that was the dynamic motor behind Jimi's creativity. But again, Chiron is not a typical Psychopathic extroverted energy; it takes the life force inward to a place of reflection, seeking solace from connection to the Divine. Similarly, the wide square between Mars and Pluto is dark and powerful but the energy goes inward down to the Lower Tan T'ien; it is a classic indication of Masochist withholding. The opposition between the planets in Sagittarius and Gemini was the central creative channel in Jimi's chart. But with Chiron squaring it, and Pluto trining the Sagittarius planets and sextiling the Gemini planets, the inward-moving energy of the Budding/Masochist type was an equal and opposite force to the outward-flowing drive of the Flowering/Psychopathic soul – giving depth and soul to his creative fire.

**Mars in Scorpio**

Mars is the planet most associated with the aggression of the Psychopathic type. Mars in Scorpio widely squaring Pluto in Leo gives a powerful internal drive but not an extrovert energy. The other aspects to Jimi's Mars are from the visionary planets of Neptune semi-squaring from Libra, and Jupiter trining from watery Cancer and conjunct the Moon. Once again, the energies of Neptune, Libra and Cancer all serve to soften and diffuse the force and aggression of Mars. Everything pulled the energy inwards, holding Jimi back from the more typically Psychopathic, aggressive expression of Mars. To many people, Jimi was a hero but he was not a bully.

# 58

# Indications of Characterology in Jimi Hendrix's Chart

## Harvest/Rigid Energy

### VENUS

- *Venus in the 12th house*
- *Venus conjunct the Sun (orb 2° 45')*
- *Libra MC*

### SATURN

- *Saturn opposite the Sun (orb 4° 32')*
- *Saturn opposite Venus (orb 1° 47')*
- *Saturn opposite Mercury (or 6° 26')*
- *Saturn semi-square chart ruler Jupiter (orb 0° 21')*

Clearly, Jimi was never motivated by the typical Rigid/Harvest need to follow a steady, long-term strategy to achieve a stable life in the material world. He was not goal-oriented in the Rigid style and he didn't have much of a plan! Jimi was much more simply driven by his overwhelming need to make music. Nevertheless, Jimi had motivation that took him to the pinnacle of achievement and that one-pointed determination is a quality I associate with the Harvest/Rigid stage.

### Venus in the 12th House

Jimi has Venus rising in the 12th house, conjuncting the Sun and Mercury and the ruler of his Libra MC – a strong placement and Venus is well integrated into the rest of the chart. Planets in the 12th describe the unborn child's time in utero, so the energies of the 12th house are pre-verbal, deeply embedded in the newly forming cells of the embryo. Though strong during the time in utero, planets in the 12th house sink into the unconscious after birth, like the memory of a dream. It is not easy for the individual to integrate the energy of these planets into their personal everyday life but they operate as an unconscious yet compelling drive. We see this not only in Jimi's musicality (music is strongly associated with Venus) but also in a kind of sweetness and charm that seemed to have been a widely recognized part of his personality.

Venus is about happiness – peace, harmony, beauty, romance, abundance and all the sensual joys of the body. So Venus in the 12th house, closely opposing Saturn and exactly trining Pluto, goes with a childhood in which this kind of Earthly happiness is not easily found. We can see, in such a bleak childhood, how easy it was for Jimi to channel all his life force into the one-pointed urge to express himself through music. Venus in aspect to Saturn is a strong indication of a Superego message that love is highly conditional – an internal belief that love and happiness (Venus) are dependent on some kind of achievement or good behaviour (Saturn). Venus can be very idealistic and so this aspect can easily develop into a Perfectionist Inner Critic The exact trine between Venus and Pluto only reinforces the sense of gloom so that the only possibility of happiness or escape comes through the Saturnian self-discipline of daily practice on the guitar. So Jimi's Venus in the 12th describes the way that his artistic Essence was not recognized or fostered in childhood but rose up in his soul from a place that transcended his personal circumstances. His soul's drive to make music is echoed by his Libra MC and his Venus rising brings the qualities that were the hallmark of the Neptune in Libra generation – peace and love and music. And, as is so often the case with planets in the 12th, the beauty of his art and music was his gift to the world.

## Saturn

We have seen that Jimi had Saturn opposite the Sun. This placement describes the brutality he often experienced in relationship with his father, very much like Jack and Jill in the fairy tale who could not earn praise or even acceptance from their mother, no matter how hard they tried. But this placement, with a retrograde Saturn in Gemini in the 6th house, opposing Mercury, the Sun and Venus, and conjuncting Uranus (the higher octave of Mercury), also represents the talent and the persistence that helped young Jimi to teach himself to play guitar. Gemini, Mercury and the 6th house all speak of the potential for the development of tremendous skill. And it was the self-discipline of Saturn that enabled Jimi to follow his star and become a virtuoso artist excelled by none.

When we look at how this appears in Jimi's energy field we see Saturn working as the power of intention running like a river through Jimi's central Hara line – connecting to the vision of the upper chakras and flowing down through arms, hands and fingers – to bring through the Harvest gift of manifestation in the world of form.

59

# Jimi Hendrix's Human Energy Field

An astrologer connecting Jimi's chart with his HEF can easily perceive the electric brilliance of Uranus, the starlight shimmer of Neptune and the golden glow of the Sun arcing across the chart with the quicksilver light of Mercury channelling the energy into musical patterns of precision and clarity.

**The Auric Level**

Jimi's upper chakras were dynamic, highly charged and brilliant. The 7th chakra vibrates with the cosmic energy of Uranus, while Jupiter and Mercury create a stream of inspired mental energy flowing from the 5th chakra (the chakra of the voice and higher creativity) up to the 7th to access the mind of God. The energy of Neptune ripples through the silvery celestial light of the 6th chakra, which opens to express through music and poetry. Mercury is connected with the 5th chakra, the throat centre, and brings the artistic creativity of the opposition to Uranus and the sextile to Neptune streaming through the nervous system and out through Jimi's hands.

When Jimi was performing everyone could feel the electricity of his Flowering and Germination energy radiating out from his energy field. Playing his guitar, working with feedback to make his unearthly sounds, his Solar energy would fill the stage with a glow that was shot through with the electric light of the exact Mercury-Uranus opposition. At other times, when singing his soulful lyrics, Jimi's field would shift to the inward flow of the Rooting energy connected to the soft heart of his Cancer Moon, lit up by golden Jupiter but deepened and shadowed by the presence of Pluto.

With the Moon conjunct Pluto in the 8th house, Jimi's Lunar energy feels very different to his Solar radiance. In the heart of Jimi's HEF the Lunar light appears liquid, sad, soft and dark; the light of regal Jupiter glows through as if seen through deep water; while Pluto gives a feeling of tremendous depth and stillness. But the silvery light of the container of Lunar energy is fractured like glass broken by the impact of the shocks of childhood. The Moon is the main anchoring force in Jimi's HEF but, with no planets in Earth, the Lunar energy could not sufficiently hold the life force or root the energy field down into the earth.

So the overall energy of Jimi's energy on the auric level moves two ways – in dynamic, fiery electric waves of the Uranian and Solar energy radiating out to the cosmos, and the Lunar energy moving inward into the deep feeling heart of his being.

## The Haric Level

Often, on the auric level of the HEF we experience Saturn and Pluto as painful destructive energies. But if we look to the deeper level of the Hara then we feel Saturn and Pluto as the strength of Jimi's soul's intention to bring great music into this world. Deep in the core of his energy field Jimi's Hara line is strong, as if on a soul level he had only one purpose in coming to the Earth and this he unswervingly achieved with total dedication to his music. We can sense the raw power of Pluto welling up through the belly into the root of the Lower Tan T'ien and charging the Hara line with an unstoppable drive.

Jimi's Venus is almost exactly trine to Pluto, and on the level of the Hara Venus represents the longing held in the Middle Tan T'ien; an exquisite light shining from above the heart representing his soul's yearning. Saturn brings the strength of the central Hara line, rising from the Root Tan T'ien, connecting up through the Middle and Upper Tan T'ien and extending out into the beyond, holding the life path and the structures that would allow Jimi's music to become manifest in the world. At the deep centre of Jimi's energy field is the light of the Core Star, the magnificent light of a musician who changed history and was an inspiration to millions. The Essence of Jimi Hendrix's chart and HEF is a beautiful kaleidoscope of revolutionary fire and creativity rising from a deep well of emotion. And like the Fire that fills his chart, he burned out very quickly and his like will not been seen again in my lifetime.

60

# THE ROOTING OR ORAL SOUL: Marilyn Monroe

> *She was a whirling light to me then, all paradox and enticing mystery, street-tough one moment, then lifted by a lyrical and poetic sensitivity that few retain past early adolescence.*
>
> Arthur Miller, *Timebends: A Life*

Marilyn Monroe is a Hollywood legend. In her time she was considered to be one of the most beautiful and alluring women in the world. She ranks high in various lists of the top movie stars of all time and in numerous polls she was voted some version of the sexiest star of the 20th century. Yet, just like Jimi Hendrix, Marilyn was born into exceptionally difficult circumstances. Her life was a true Cinderella story, going from a lonely childhood living in foster care to international recognition as a star of the silver screen.

Marilyn was born on 1 June 1926, when Neptune was transiting through Leo – the era which saw the birth of the film industry (Neptune is associated with photography and the glamour of the movies, Leo associated with stardom, performance and theatre). With a Leo Ascendant and Neptune rising in the 1st house, Marilyn seemed to embody the magic of the movies and she became the personification of Hollywood glamour. To the public Marilyn was more than an actress. Carried by the wave of the ever-expanding influence of cinema and the media, Marilyn was everybody's sweetheart and she became the object of a mass projection of the 1950s' archetypal image of womanly beauty.

### Characterology

Neptune, like Uranus, connects us to the perfection of the world of Spirit. Anyone with Neptune rising is going to bring through some of the stardust from Neptune's realm, and in the eyes of the public Marilyn became identified with the archetype of the Goddess. But Neptune is also the major significator of Oral wounding. Marilyn was repeatedly abandoned in childhood; she suffered from profound Oral wounding and the fragile orphan girl was psychologically ill-equipped to deal with the pressures of fame. She had a childlike quality of vulnerability, like the Little Match Girl eternally waiting for someone to take care of her.

Everyone who got close to Marilyn became drawn into trying to reach this sweet lost child. Almost without exception, people tried to rescue her by trying to take control of her life: instructing her, directing her, trying to mould her malleable fluid Neptunian persona into some kind of order. But this is the exact opposite of the healing response for the Oral wound; anyone with strong Orality needs to be given the space, time and support to develop their own inner strength and authority.

True to the Oral/Neptune dynamic, Marilyn oscillated between times of sweet compliance when she would try so hard to be what people wanted her to be and then, sooner or later, break out into hysterical panic attacks. As long as Marilyn remained divorced from her own inner authority she was always going to cycle back into the Oral state of collapse.

## Childhood

Marilyn Monroe was born Norma Jeane Mortenson. The daughter of Gladys Baker, she was never certain of the identity of her father. Gladys Baker was an unstable young woman who had already abandoned her first two children and walked out of two marriages. She knew that she was not able to take on the responsibilities of motherhood and two weeks after Norma Jeane was born Gladys gave her up into foster care. Immediately we see Marilyn's Schizoid and Oral wounding as a fatherless infant abandoned by her mother.

Norma Jeane's mother Gladys and grandmother Della were restless, brittle women. It helps to understand Marilyn's Characterology when we see the history of dysfunctional relationships and mental health problems that were Marilyn's inheritance coming down the ancestral line.

When Gladys was a child her father developed severe dementia caused by syphilis of the brain. After several months in a mental hospital he died a harrowing death leaving Gladys with a lifelong fear that her family was blighted with a tendency towards madness. After that, Gladys's mother Della went from one troubled relationship to the next until eventually she had the chance of a more lasting relationship with a man named Charles Grainger. Della wanted to move in with Grainger but 14-year-old Gladys was a sulky teenager who made no effort to please the latest man to come into her mother's life. Della's way of resolving the situation was to get Gladys out of the way; she lied about her age and married her off to a 26-year-old man named John Baker.

Gladys had two children with John Baker. Still only a teenager, she frequently left the children in the care of neighbours and carried on going out like any other young girl. After a few years she left John Baker, returned to live with her mother and had almost no further contact with her children. Gladys got herself a job working on the fringes of the movie industry and became a good-time girl. She followed in her mother's footsteps, lurching from one relationship to the next, and was married and separated for the second time before she fell pregnant with Norma Jeane. Gladys recognized that she could not cope with looking after her baby so she gave Norma Jeane into the care of a foster family named Bolender.

For the next seven years Ida and Adam Bolender gave Norma Jeane a stable home, and whatever psychological strength she developed must be down to the foundation of care she received from them. But the Bolenders had rigid, moralistic, puritanical Christian views and Marilyn recalled that, as a child, she felt she continually failed to live up to their standards.

During these years Gladys visited her daughter from time to time but she remained a shadowy figure on the periphery of Norma Jeane's life. But when Marilyn was seven, Gladys bought a house of her own and took her daughter back to live with her. This marked the end of any kind of stable home life for Norma Jeane.

A few years previously, Gladys's mother Della had died of a heart condition which had brought on a state of manic depression during her last months, compounding Gladys's fear of inherited madness. Then, not long after taking Norma Jeane to live with her, Gladys heard that her grandfather had committed suicide. To Gladys, this appeared as damming evidence of her family inheritance of mental instability. With transiting Chiron 2° from her Gemini Sun, Gladys descended into a severe and prolonged depression from which she never recovered. She was prescribed medication, which is likely to have caused her additional problems, and by the time the Chiron transit became exact, Gladys had suffered a complete mental breakdown and was admitted to a mental institution. Norma Jeane was declared a ward of the state and Gladys's best friend, Grace McKee, became her legal guardian.

Grace McKee was a dominant figure in Norma Jeane's development. In stark contrast to the Bolenders she was a hedonistic woman, obsessed with the glamorous world of the movies. She filled Norma Jeane's head with the idea that she would grow up to be a movie star and took the pre-pubescent Norma Jeane for hair-dos and make-up sessions in beauty parlours, grooming her for her glamorous future.

But Grace McKee could not provide the stability that Norma Jeane had known with the Bolenders and for the rest of her childhood Norma Jeane was continually moved from place to place. When Grace got married, Norma Jeane was sent to live in the Los Angeles Orphans Home and then to a series of foster parents. Opportunities arose for Norma to be adopted but Grace blocked them all. A couple of years later, Norma Jeane moved back in with Grace but this proved to be disastrous as her husband tried to sexually assault her. Grace sent her away to live with relatives but here she was assaulted again.

Eventually she had a period of stability living with an older woman, Grace's Aunt Ana. When Ana became ill, Norma returned to live with Grace once more. Finally, when Grace and her husband moved away to the East Coast in 1942, Norma Jeane was given two options: return to the orphanage or get married. In a situation very like her mother's at the same age, 16-year-old Norma Jeane married James Dougherty, the boy she was dating.

**Career**

Norma Jean's marriage did not last long. At work she was noticed by an army photographer who encouraged her to take up modelling. Attractive and naturally photogenic, Norma Jeane joined the Blue Book modelling agency and quickly became a successful model, appearing on dozens of magazine covers. Jim Dougherty was not happy about this and demanded that Norma Jeane chose between her marriage and her career. But Norma Jeane could see the real possibility of a future in modelling and acting, so she divorced Dougherty.

In her twenties, Norma Jeane went from modelling to acting in the movies and rose quite swiftly to stardom, changing her name to Marilyn Monroe. It is a little hard to understand how the girl from such an emotionally impoverished background found the grit and determination to make it in such a challenging profession. Many people who knew her commented that alongside her very real fragility she had an inner steeliness of ambition. Perhaps the inner steel came from the fact that in her beauty Marilyn had found the one thing she could use to get the love and attention she craved.

During her early school years Marilyn was described as an unremarkable, shy and lonely girl, but all that changed when she went through puberty. As Marilyn's body developed she started to attract notice and this was her turning point. Marilyn said of that time:

> *Suddenly, everything seemed to open up. Even the girls paid a little attention to me just because they thought, 'Hmmm, she's to be dealt with.'*

Norma Jeane came to realize that in her sexual allure she had, at last, found a way of getting attention.

For a young woman in the repressive 1940s and 1950s, Marilyn was surprisingly uninhibited and unashamed of her body. With the memory of Grace McKee's years of coaching for her role as a movie star, Marilyn's sensual beauty became her lifeline, the thing she had that everybody wanted. So Marilyn fell in love with the camera and she was always at her best in photographic sessions away from the pressures of acting. One of the early photographers she worked with commented:

> *Suddenly, everything seemed to open up. Even the girls paid a little attention to me just because they thought, 'Hmmm, she's to be dealt with.'*

Modelling was almost the only thing in her life that came easily to Marilyn. Her childhood history of abandonment and rejection left her psychologically fragile and she was dogged by mental health issues right up until her death from an overdose of sleeping pills. Throughout her life Norma Jeane went from one mother figure to the next, but each one ended up pushing her away. Even during the years she spent with the Bolenders, Ida Bolender never allowed Norma Jeane to call her 'Mother'. It could not be a more poignant illustration of the Oral wound – the longing for welcome and containment in the arms of a mother, a longing that was never met.

Marilyn's beauty and screen presence made her noticeable in all her films and after a few years she landed a contract with Twentieth Century Fox. But, true to the Oral template, the vulnerable young Marilyn was exploited by the movie companies. At the time when her films became major box office attractions she was still under contract as a stock actor and received a salary less than that of the technicians working on the film. Tied to a seven-year contract with Twentieth Century Fox, she was continually cast in roles as some version of a dumb blonde, a stereotype which became increasingly unacceptable to her.

Many of those who knew her remarked on her intelligence; one statistic gives her an IQ of 168, significantly higher than that of President John F Kennedy with whose name she was sometimes linked. She had not been well educated and this contributed to her lifelong feelings of inadequacy but, with the Sun in Gemini, she read widely, had a love of poetry and Russian literature and accrued a large personal library. Marilyn longed to be taken seriously as an actress and in 1955 (the year of her Saturn return), she moved to New York City to study Method acting under Lee Strasberg at his Actors Studio. Although Marilyn was plagued throughout her career by her profound lack of self-confidence, Lee Strasberg considered her to be one of the two greatest actors he coached (the other was Marlon Brando).

Eventually, after years of struggle with the big Hollywood film companies, she formed her own motion picture company, Marilyn Monroe Productions. This was quite an achievement as Marilyn was among the first of the big movie stars to break away from the power of the movie moguls. Her company went ahead to produce *Bus Stop* and *The Prince and the Showgirl*, films which allowed her to demonstrate the extent of her ability as an actress.

During her acting career Marilyn was notorious for being difficult to work with. She habitually turned up hours late for filming and often forgot her lines. The truth was that Marilyn's low self-esteem gave her acute stage fright. She had a Perfectionist Inner Critic that gripped her with the belief that she was not good enough even in the face of overwhelming evidence to the contrary. She struggled constantly with insomnia and her tardiness was the result of both nervousness from her excessive fear of failure and her erratic sleep patterns.

Marilyn looked for support in every direction. She employed a series of drama coaches who she relied on heavily, insisting that they remain on set when she was filming, often to the dismay of her directors. She had psychotherapy with a number of therapists on whom she became extremely dependent. Her therapists regularly broke the boundaries of the profession by becoming far too involved in her life and prescribing a variety of drugs that were probably addictive and had dubious side-effects.

Last, but not least, Marilyn searched for security through her relationships. She had numerous sexual liaisons and almost certainly made her entrance to the movies via the casting couch. With at least two episodes of sexual abuse in her childhood, Marilyn would have had no chance to develop a sense of her woman's right to sexual boundaries. There are some theories that Marilyn suffered from bipolar disorder that included hyper-sexuality.

Marilyn's two most significant relationships were with the famous baseball player Joe DiMaggio, and the left-wing playwright Arthur Miller. She married Joe DiMaggio in 1954 but the marriage lasted less than a year as Joe could not cope with his wife's success and he became violent with her. In 1956 Marilyn married Arthur Miller but this marriage was even more disastrous because the cool, intellectual Miller found that he could not tolerate Marilyn's neurotic behaviour. After her divorce from Miller in 1961, Marilyn's relationship with Joe DiMaggio was revived. He became increasingly concerned about the people she had around her and was ready to try again with their marriage. Before that could happen, Marilyn came to a tragic end when, on 5 August 1962 she died from an overdose of sleeping pills. There has been a lot of speculation about her death, ranging from conspiracy theories about her murder due to her connection with the Kennedys to the irresponsible administration of drugs by her psychotherapist. The romantic Joe DiMaggio had half a dozen red roses delivered to her crypt every week for twenty years after her death.

# 61

## The Rooting or Oral Soul

# Interpreting the Horoscope of Marilyn Monroe

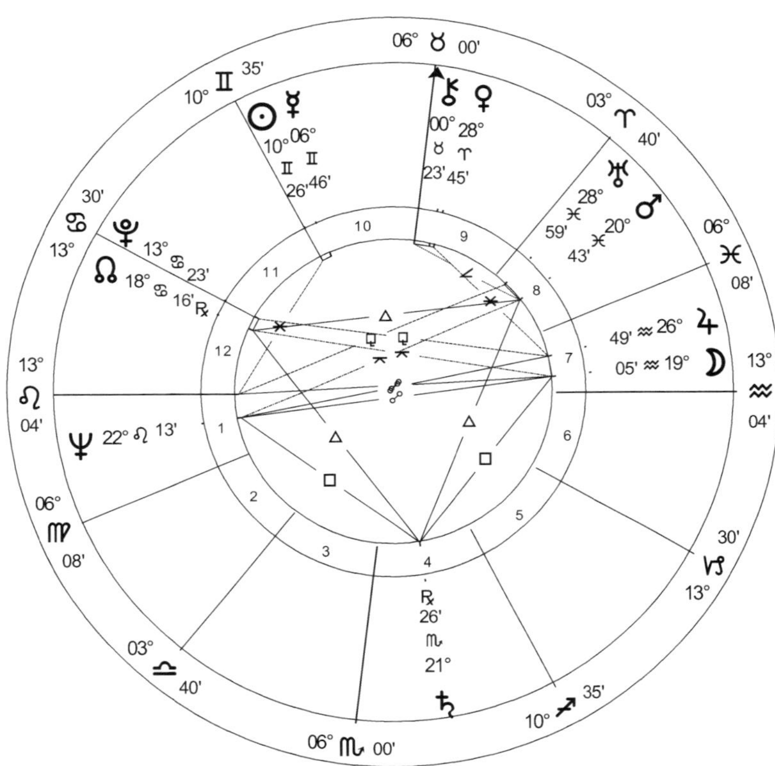


**Marilyn Monroe**

9.30 am Tuesday 1 June 1926, Los Angeles California USA

Placidus House System

Chart from Solar Fire version 7 Astrolabe, www.alabe.com.

## Dominant Planets and Themes

> *Moon-Neptune, more than any other planetary contact, understands most deeply the tragedy of human loneliness.*
> Liz Greene, *The Astrological Neptune and the Quest for Redemption*

**The Sun and Venus**

There are two main themes in Marilyn's chart. Firstly, Marilyn as star of the silver screen is clearly visible in a combination of placements that were full of light. Her Leo Ascendant is ruled by the sparkling 10th house Gemini Sun trining the Aquarius Moon, and with Venus shining out from the MC and glamorous Neptune rising we recognize the well-known image of Marilyn that was so radiant and alluring.

**Fixed T-square**

The second theme is represented by the Fixed T-square between the Aquarius Moon in opposition to Neptune and squaring Saturn – a difficult combination of planets that perfectly describes the energy of the Rooting/Oral soul and shows Marilyn's lifelong struggle with Oral wounding. Marilyn's deprived childhood was a classic example of Oral and Schizoid wounding and these themes dominate in her chart.

**Saturn**

Marilyn's chart has a Bucket configuration and Saturn is given extra prominence as the handle of the Bucket. Other than Neptune rising, Saturn is the only planet in the northern hemisphere of the chart. Saturn is also involved in the Grand Trine in Water and it is the apex of the T-square. The energy of Saturn is not what we associate with Marilyn Monroe but, hidden away in the 4th house, Saturn is an extremely powerful force in her chart. Similar to planets in the 12th house, those in the 4th are not easily brought into consciousness, but Marilyn's Saturn is the signature of the ambition that took her to the very top of her profession. With Chiron being the only planet in the chart in an Earth sign, Marilyn's main access to any kind of grounding and structure came from her Saturn. This was her legacy from her childhood years with the Bolenders, echoed by the South Node in Capricorn. However, Marilyn never quite reached the point where her Saturn could function as an authentic sense of inner authority. Instead, Saturn operated negatively in the form of a relentless Inner Critic that fuelled her mental health issues and made her desperate for approval.

### Neptune

Even more than her prominent Sun, the most instantly recognizable key to Marilyn is her Neptune in Leo, in the 1st house, trining Venus on the Midheaven. A strong Neptune is often a factor in the charts of the stars of the silver screen; individuals who seem larger than life, embodying some archetypal quality which they carry for the collective. Neptune is the bringer of celestial vision, that which takes us beyond our human limitations, connecting us to the dream of an ideal world – a longing for the beauty and perfection of the non-physical realms. And, like Uranus, Neptune has a distaste for the imperfections of human life. Marilyn's Neptune in the house of identity would have equalled Saturn in driving her Inner Critic with an obsessive demand for perfection.

Neptune transcends boundaries and seeks oneness, union and communion. Neptune in the 1st house endows a person with exquisite sensitivity and grace but it also gives us a sense of an individual with not enough skin – lacking in boundaries and open to every wind that blows – truly the 'Candle in the Wind'. With Neptune in the 1st house it was easy for Marilyn to abandon her true sense of self and become a shape-shifter, able to camouflage herself with whatever mask would be most pleasing to the people around her. And, of course, Neptune's ability to merge and empathize was also the foundation of her great talent for acting.

The archetype of Neptune is associated with beauty, glamour, magic, fantasy and imagination, and it is likely to be strong in the chart of any kind of artist. Neptune is also associated with surrender to the wildness and ecstasy of sexual union, and Marilyn's Neptune in the 1st house endowed her with sexual allure; for many, she seemed to embody a vision of transcendent female loveliness. She personified many aspects of the archetype of the Goddess and it is possible to regard her life story as a mirror to the difficulties besetting the feminine principle in western culture of the mid-twentieth century.

### The Puella

We have spoken of the powerful archetype of the Patriarch – the negative aspect of the masculine principle, an energy which dominated the collective culture of the twentieth century. We see the judgemental voice of the Patriarch coming through Marilyn's Saturn, which squares her Neptune. Caught up in polarity with the Patriarch is the archetype of the *puella*, a young woman, the female version of the *puer aeternus*. The *puella* tries to please and appease her way out from the criticism and control coming at her from the Patriarch, but she never grows up to achieve the authority, status and dignity of a mature woman. Neptune is one of the prime significators of the adolescent energy of the *puella* and Marilyn was very much identified with this image. To the Patriarch, the *puella* is the ideal woman – young, beautiful, girlish, foolish, dependent, helpless and sexually available. Much of Marilyn's screen persona fits the Patriarchal image of the *puella* and Marilyn was celebrated for her vulnerability, a feature that was as much her signature as her sex appeal. Despite her considerable intelligence she was continually cast in the role of a dumb blonde. For many women of that era, it was difficult even to conceive of the idea of a woman as sufficient unto herself or to fully embrace the possibility of living as the power and authority in her own life.

The two signs that most represent the true power of the feminine principle are Taurus and Cancer. In these signs we see the archetypal feminine as a goddess of the earth, the powerful creator of form, the mother that births the light of Spirit. Marilyn has the North Node in Cancer and her MC is in Taurus so we see that this Goddess energy is what she seeks, it is what she aspires to. However, Chiron falls right in the middle of the conjunction between her Taurus Midheaven and her Venus in Aries. This placement of Chiron says it all, representing deep archetypal wounding to the Goddess energy.

# 62

# Indications of Characterology in Marilyn Monroe's Chart

## Germination/Schizoid Energy

### THE SUN

- *The Sun, chart ruler, in Gemini*

### MERCURY

- *Mercury in Gemini*
- *Mercury conjunct the Sun (orb 1° 40')*

### URANUS

- *The Moon in Aquarius*
- *Uranus quintile the Sun (orb 0° 33')*
- *Uranus sesquiquadrate the Ascendant (orb 0° 55')*

### Gemini Sun

Marilyn's Sun conjunct Mercury in Gemini is immediately a sign of Germination/Schizoid energy. Gemini is a beautifully light sign but fragile, always ready to break up, split and polarize. As the ruler of the Ascendant, the Gemini Sun conjunct Mercury describes the fractured energy around at the time of her birth when her mother (another *puella*) removed herself from the responsibilities of parenthood and gave her away.

Marilyn had all the charm, wit, intelligence and the typical mercurial fluidity of a Gemini, and this was a major source of her brilliance as a comedienne. But Gemini is always inclined to suffer from mood swings and in Marilyn these were so severe as to be a likely indication of bipolar disorder. The energies of Mercury and Gemini are often a sign of a hypervigilant, anxious, overactive mind, making it difficult for Marilyn to get her feet on the ground and find the stillness and strength of her inner core.

### Aquarius Moon

All this is compounded by the Moon in Aquarius. An Aquarius Moon is always somewhat detached. This can be a sign of spaced out, Schizoid disassociation but it can also bring a valuable ability to regard a situation objectively, to witness without judgement. With both the Sun and the Moon in Air, there is a double emphasis on the activity of the mind, bringing the lightness, understanding, intelligence and wit which are the gifts of the Air signs. But, again, this also speaks of a relentlessly active mind – the tendency to overthink things, trying to get control through mental analysis, list-making and planning – all of which fuels the tendency towards anxiety.

An Aquarius Moon square Saturn in the 4th house has a very cold feel to it: an indication of something bleak in childhood. The Moon represents our images of 'Mother' and the positive expression of an Aquarius Moon speaks of a mother who is friendly, intelligent, free-thinking and ahead of her time. But Gladys expressed more negative Aquarian qualities – ungrounded, emotionally disconnected, unpredictable and unable to offer any consistency of care. The square between Saturn and the Aquarius Moon represents the split between the unconventional path (Aquarius) that Gladys took and the responsibilities of parenthood (Saturn) that she avoided. The coldness of this placement also speaks of the austerity of Marilyn's early years with the Bolenders.

The typical Schizoid often has a wild, disjointed appearance. However, Marilyn loved her beautiful body, she occupied a lot of her time with grooming her appearance and was sexually uninhibited. But the Airy nature of her Aquarius Moon and the Gemini Sun relates to the ideal of the body beautiful rather than to the ability to simply be present and accepting of the body as it is. In the same way, her unrestrained sexuality (which has more to do with her Neptune rising) also speaks of a disconnection with a more embodied sense of boundaries.

## Jupiter Conjunct the Moon

Marilyn has Jupiter conjunct her Aquarius Moon (another indication of the possibility of bipolar disorder). Wilful and fun-loving Jupiter reinforces the picture of Gladys as a freedom-loving, pleasure-seeking 'good-time girl', a 'flapper' of the 1920s, unable to anchor herself in a sustained relationship or commit to parenthood. It is interesting to note that, like her daughter, Gladys had the Sun in Gemini and the Moon and Jupiter in Aquarius, conjunct Saturn in Capricorn. Gladys's mother, Della, also had the Moon conjunct Jupiter with a square from Uranus. Marilyn's female ancestors were all struggling with an issue around the feminine principle represented by aspects from Jupiter and Uranus to the Moon.

There are two ways that I interpret a Moon-Jupiter conjunction. One is the archetype of Juno, the queen of the gods, wife of Jupiter. This speaks of an identification with the role of a wife and mother – the sense of pride in family and dynasty and marriage takes on great significance and these things will be at the core of a person's life. This would be the likely expression of Moon-Jupiter found in the Earth or Water signs and also in the sign of Libra.

The second interpretation is the archetype of the Moon goddess Diana the Huntress – wild and free, a rule unto herself – living beyond the limitations of any patriarchal control. This version of Moon-Jupiter would be found in the Air and Fire signs. In the charts of Della, Gladys and Marilyn, the Moon is either in Aquarius or in aspect to Uranus, and so it is the freedom of the archetype of Diana that is trying to come through. However, the expression of Diana requires a core of inner certainty and ego strength that is not easy to access, particularly for the women in the twentieth century. Instead, all three woman were trapped in the adolescent fragmentation of the *puella* – the restlessness and recklessness of Gemini and Aquarius, Jupiter and Uranus, polarized in conflict with the demands and responsibilities of Saturn – a conflict that none of them was able to resolve. The energy of Aquarius is always about change and, above all, it is about freedom. On a deeper level, in Marilyn's Aquarius Moon we see the ideal of Diana, a vision of a woman as a powerful, free, self-determined and sexually liberated individual – the vision that was struggling to come through down the line of her female ancestors.

### Saturn Squaring the Moon

Saturn in the 4th house often indicates something difficult and bleak in the family, and its square to the Moon emphasizes the lack of maternal warmth and care in Marilyn's childhood. So we see that for Marilyn, right from the start, the Moon as the container of life was painful and fractured and unable to hold and anchor the brittle energy of the Sun in Gemini. We will see later how the pain of Saturn in the 4th house played a major part in providing the drive and ambition that took Marilyn so far from her roots.

### Essence – Uranus and Neptune Quintile the Sun

The gifts of the Germination/Schizoid soul are genius, brilliance, creativity and innovation. The Sun in Marilyn's chart is in a very beautiful configuration: a close quintile from both Uranus and Neptune and the two bi-quintiled planets reflect the true nature of Marilyn's gifts. In its negative expression, Marilyn's Uranus brought her numerous experiences of shock and disruption and often operated as a jarring lack of coherence, instability and mental health problems. Similarly, negative Neptune shows up in her persona of victim, her overwhelming vulnerability, her difficulty with time and structure and her dependency on tranquillizers. But the quintile is a delicate aspect, signifying potential talent. The refined quality of these aspects, as well as the nature of the two planets, speaks of creative genius and exquisite sensitivity and these are the qualities of her Essence that were struggling to emerge in the life of this intelligent and talented woman.

63

# Indications of Characterology in Marilyn Monroe's Chart

## Rooting/Oral Energy

### THE MOON

- *The Moon opposition Neptune (orb 3° 08')*
- *The Moon square Saturn (orb 2° 21')*
- *North Node in Cancer*

### NEPTUNE

- *Neptune rising in the 1st house (orb 8° 09' from the Ascendant)*
- *Neptune trine Venus (orb 6° 32')*
- *Neptune quintile the Sun (orb 0° 13')*

### SATURN

- *Saturn in the 4th house*

Marilyn's chart shows so many signs of Oral wounding that it is hard to know where to begin and this was her dominant characterology. We have seen that one of the most important energy patterns in her chart is her fixed T-square with Neptune in Leo opposition the Moon in Aquarius, both square to Saturn in Scorpio. The Moon and Neptune are the two signifiers of Oral/Rooting Characterology and when bound together with Saturn they represent a complete picture of the Oral wound of deprivation of nourishment and care.

**Saturn in the 4th House**

Marilyn's 4th house Saturn squaring her Aquarius Moon is a classic indication of Oral wounding. At its best, Saturn in the 4th house can indicate a parent who brings the qualities of the Harvest soul: steadfast and loyal, providing a family life that is stable and ordered. However, Saturn in the 4th is often a sign of a cold, critical parent; sometimes a cruel disciplinarian; a sign of something harsh in the family home. Saturn in the 4th house goes with children who doubt that they are welcome in their family, and Marilyn's Saturn gives the feeling of her years with her foster parents who were reliable and consistent but puritanical, austere and judgemental.

Saturn squaring the Moon is a notoriously painful placement. The energy of the Vulnerable Child, represented by the Moon, is caught in a painful relationship in which Saturn takes on the role of the Critic. Insecurity in infancy is the basis for the development of the Inner Critic. The aim of the Inner Critic is to find strategies that will shield and hide the vulnerability of the infant, but this sets up a dangerous vicious cycle in which the dictates of the Inner Critic only serve to compound the terror of the Inner Child. In Marilyn's case, Saturn in the 4th represents a bedrock belief that she was unwanted and would always be rejected. Out of this she developed a powerful Pleaser – a desperate drive to seek approval that would take her all the way to international stardom. The Moon opposing Neptune indicates exquisite sensitivity but Neptune also brings intense idealism. In combination with the square from Saturn, this is the configuration of a Perfectionist Inner Critic, very likely a Killer Critic, and we know that Marilyn was often depressed and suicidal.

### Neptune in the 1st House – Opposing the Moon, Squaring Saturn

Planets in the 1st house are powerful, at the core of a person's sense of identity. Here, Neptune speaks of Marilyn's profound longing for union, for the possibility of loving and being loved. Gentle, hypersensitive Neptune in the 1st house has enormous difficulties with boundaries. Individuals with this placement find it very hard to assert their rights and needs, or even to know that they have rights and needs. So in childhood, the unprotected Norma Jeane became the victim of sexual abuse and this alone would have been enough to trigger her lifelong mental health problems. Like the abused and abandoned child that she carried inside her, Marilyn suffered from a chronic anxiety disorder and she became pathologically clinging and needy. Tragically, in a classic expression of Neptune and the Oral wound, Marilyn's longing for love always became distorted into a state of merging and dependency.

As the third arm of the Fixed T-square, Neptune represents Marilyn's reaction to the pain of the Moon-Saturn square by escaping into fantasy and the illusions of glamour and the movies. But Neptune here also represents everything that we know and love about Marilyn Monroe. It is Neptune, rising in the 1st house, trining Venus (orb 6° 32'), that gives her tremendous feminine beauty, sexuality, sensuality and allure. Neptune is opposition Jupiter, two of the planets most associated with acting, and Neptune, in particular, with the cinema. Neptune gives Marilyn the magical quality of the shape-shifter who can take on any role, the music, the poetry and the artistry of a dream-weaver, a story-teller and a great performer.

### Jupiter Conjunct the Moon

In Marilyn's chart, Jupiter conjunct the Moon and in opposition to Neptune re-emphasizes the tendency to fantasy. However, it is Jupiter that brings the larger-than-life quality of a performer who could captivate her audience and bring laughter and joy to millions.

Wherever we have Jupiter in the chart feels like 'the answer', it feels like this is the place where we will solve all our problems! The 7th house represents partnerships and how we perceive the 'other' in relationship. With a Moon-Jupiter conjunction in the 7th house, Marilyn constantly sought from others the mothering she lacked. Over and again in her life she became heavily dependent on the people who got close to her. Her desperate Oral demands were too much for her husbands and lovers but also for her mentors – the drama coaches on whom she was heavily reliant, and a series of psychotherapists, nearly all of whom became unprofessionally enmeshed with her.

The negative expression of Oral wounding is victim consciousness, difficulty holding boundaries, chronic feelings of weakness and the tendency to collapse and escape the harshness of the world through drugs, alcohol, fantasy and romantic illusions. The healing response for a person with Oral wounding is to be supported in finding their power; to discover their own authentic strength instead of seeking it in others. In her final years, following her Saturn return, Marilyn began taking steps towards greater autonomy by forming her own company and taking more control of her career.

But for most of her life, almost without exception, the people closely involved with Marilyn were caught up in the powerful Neptunian delusion that Marilyn needed rescuing. This is everybody's first reaction to the Oral wound, and time and time again her lovers, friends and mentors tried to rescue her by trying to control her. It is hard to understand the actions of her last psychotherapist, a doctor who not only prescribed excessive amounts of tranquillizers but broke some of the basic tents of psychotherapy by treating her in his family home and allowing her to become involved in the life of his own family. It may be that he was trying to remedy the deprivation of her childhood but Marilyn became pathologically dependent on him, unable to make a decision without consulting him – the exact opposite of learning, at last, to have faith in herself.

# 64

# Indications of Characterology in Marilyn Monroe's Chart

## Budding/Masochist Energy

### PLUTO

- ***Grand Trine in Water – Pluto trine Saturn (orb 8° 03') and Mars (orb 7° 20')***

With her light Gemini Sun, Mercury shining from the 10th and the grace and artistry of Neptune in the 1st, Marilyn had few obvious signs of the dense vibration of Masochist wounding. But with her identification with super-sensitive, anxious-to-please Neptune, Marilyn lacked access to an authentic sense of personal power. Grace McKee indoctrinated the young Norma Jeane with the idea that she was going to be the next Jean Harlow. Grace was projecting her own fantasies onto Norma Jeane who was not seen and valued for herself. This was Narcissistic wounding, which is the issue for the Masochist stage. The Masochist soul seeks to regain their sense of Essence through acts of creativity, and many performers are working out their Masochist wounding through their art.

### Grand Trine in Water, the 4th, 8th and 12th Houses

In his book *Astrology, Karma and Transformation*, Stephen Arroyo refers to the 4th, 8th and 12th houses as those most associated with karma and the most difficult for planets there to find expression. The 4th, 8th and 12th are the three houses whose affairs are most private, most hidden from the world. In terms of the Human Energy Field, the nature of these houses pulls the energy inwards into contraction. The 4th house has to do with home, family, roots and ancestors – the place we go when we are away from the world in the private heart of the family. The 8th house has to do with the intimacy, the deepest levels of emotional and sexual communion between two people. The 12th is the house of our connection to Spirit, the dream-world and the unconscious, far removed from everyday living. Marilyn has Saturn in Scorpio in the 4th house, Mars in Pisces in the 8th house and Pluto in Cancer on the cusp of the 12th, and the three planets form a Grand Trine in Water. Water is the element of feelings so this repeats the sense of energy focusing inwards to connect with the inner world. This configuration of planets, in Water, in the karmic houses is an indication of the withheld energy of the Budding/Masochist energy. In particular, we see the naturally outgoing fire of Mars restrained by the weight of Pluto and Saturn.

**Mars in Pisces in the 8th House**

Marilyn has Mars conjunct Uranus in Pisces in the 8th house. Mars brings passionate sexuality and with the wild Dionysian abandon of Pisces and the 8th house this contributed to her fantastic sexual allure.

Mars rules desire, willpower, assertion and aggression. Direct, outspoken Mars has no problem with boundaries, he is the principle of autonomy and individuation, and Mars is exactly that which we need to cultivate as the antidote to Oral wounding represented by all-surrendering Neptune.

*Asking for what one wants is a function of Mars in the horoscope; and Mars ,like Saturn, is a natural polar opposite of Neptune, because it represents the assertion of individual desires.*

Liz Greene, *The Astrological Neptune and the Quest for Redemption*

But Marilyn's Mars is hidden away in the 8th house in gentle, Watery Pisces. Mars is also conjunct cool, dispassionate Uranus. In a different sign and house Uranus and Mars can make an electric and warrior-like energy, but in Pisces, in the 8th house, Marilyn has very restricted access to the clear, clean, forthright self-assertion of Mars. In addition to this, her Mars is bound up with Pluto and Saturn, the two most repressive planets in the zodiac. This configuration is the basis of Marilyn's Masochist/Budding energy and we can also see that her wild

Piscean Mars-Uranus energy would not have been welcomed during her formative years in foster care with the Saturnian Bolenders.

**Pluto in Cancer in the 12th House**

Marilyn's Pluto is exactly on the cusp of the 12th house and I feel it belongs in the 12th. Planets found in the 12th represent ancestral and genetic issues, often an aspect of the psyche that has become disowned by succeeding generations of the family, and we have already seen the fragmentation of the feminine principle coming down Marilyn's ancestral line

Although Pluto was a male god, in my view Pluto represents a feminine energy: the deep stirring of the life force within the body and the ruthless instinctual power of archetypes such as Medea the Sorceress and Kali the Destroyer. So Marilyn's 12th house Pluto reveals that in her ancestral inheritance to access the power of Pluto is not functioning well. Instead it is the negative face of Pluto – the bitter energy of Ereshkigal – the pain-body of the Feminine – that occupies the 12th house. This creates a classic Gemini split – the *puella* represented by the light planets in Air and Fire running to escape the gloomy energy of Pluto. Again we see Marilyn divorced from a sense of authentic Plutonian power and so she is thrown back, again, into the fantasy world of Neptune.

**Saturn in Scorpio in the 4th House**

Lastly, in the third point of the Grand Trine, we come back to Marilyn's Saturn in Scorpio in the 4th house. Saturn and Mars, the Greater and Lesser Malefics, in combination with Pluto make for a very difficult, potentially violent and even life-threatening combination and there have been various conspiracy theories that Marilyn was murdered.

We have talked about Saturn as the Patriarch: a rigid male authority figure and a controlling disciplinarian. However, like Pluto, Saturn, the ruler of Earthy Capricorn, in Essence represents a feminine principle associated with the physical structures of the world of matter and the body. A more benevolent way of seeing Saturn is in the archetype of the Crone, an old woman who offers wisdom born of experience. Once again, the energy of the Crone, the mature, wise, compassionate authority of the Feminine, is that which is disowned in Marilyn's chart. It would be foolish to say that Saturn is ever an easy planet but, as much as Mars, Saturn could have been the antidote to Marilyn's extreme Oral wounding. But Marilyn was not able to access the wisdom and authority of the Crone. Instead what we see is Saturn appearing as her foster family's Rigid moralistic regime and distorting into its fear-based, negative role as the Inner Critic.

I have focused very much on the Masochist wounding here, largely because I see so much wounding in Marilyn's childhood. But it is one of the main contentions of this book that we are all greater than our human stories and wherever there is wounding there is also a gift and the light of Essence that is struggling to emerge. Marilyn's Grand Trine in Water, even with Saturn included, expresses her fluidity with feelings – a vital part of her talent as an actress. Had she lived into middle age she might have found more and more ways to access and express that deep flowing channel of feeling.

# 65

# Indications of Characterology in Marilyn Monroe's Chart

## Flowering/Psychopathic Energy

**THE SUN**

- *Leo Ascendant*
- *Sun trine to the Moon (orb 8 ° 39')*
- *Sun sextile the Ascendant (orb 2 ° 38')*
- *Sun in the 11th house*

**JUPITER**

- *Jupiter conjunct the Moon (orb 7 ° 44')*
- *Jupiter opposition Neptune (orb 4 ° 36')*
- *Jupiter sextile the MC (orb 3 ° 17')*

Marilyn's childhood was so chaotic that she does not fit into the classic Psychopathic scenario of a child caught between two warring parents. Nevertheless, the concerns of the Flowering/Psychopathic soul – both the longing to shine and the wound of betrayal of trust – are among the dominant issues of her life.

In childhood, Marilyn was let down, rejected or pushed away by every one of the women she ever hoped she might call 'Mother'. This left her with a profound mistrust of women. In adult life Marilyn formed several intense relationships with women who came into her life in the role of drama coaches or psychotherapists. But the pattern was that Marilyn did not sustain these relationships. With the fickleness of Gemini she eventually took on someone new in the position and had little more to do with the previous incumbent. So, in adulthood, the boot was on the other foot – this time it was Marilyn who rejected the mother figure. Years after her original breakdown, Marilyn's mother Gladys was released from mental hospital, a broken woman.

Many times she made pathetic requests to come and live with Marilyn, but though Marilyn always took care of her mother financially she never re-established a full relationship with her. Similarly, Grace McKee, who had been so instrumental in setting Marilyn on the road to stardom, was never part of her protégée's glamorous life once Marilyn made it; Marilyn had been rejected by Grace too often.

In childhood, Marilyn had almost no experience of a father figure and Grace McKee's husband and another male relative had sexually assaulted her. Nevertheless, Marilyn was more trusting of men than she was of women, which is common among women lost in the dynamic of abuse and typical of the Psychopathic wound. In childhood she had known repeated experiences of betrayal by mother figures she had hoped she could trust while the father figure remained in the realms of fantasy, and we can see that so many of the difficulties in her chart come back to the Moon.

## Leo Ascendant and the Sun

Marilyn has a Leo Ascendant with the Sun as the chart ruler prominent in the 10th house. The Sun also sextiles the Ascendant, doubly intensifying her Solar star quality, and we can see that the Flowering/Psychopathic soul's need to shine was a dominant factor in Marilyn's sense of identity; one of the most powerful drives in her chart.

The Sun is also in a wide trine to the Moon, with two delicate quintiles from Uranus and Neptune. We have seen that the quintile is traditionally a sign of nascent talent, and Neptune and Uranus here contribute to the Gemini gifts of speech, communication, verbal expression, drama, music and wit.

Other than these aspects and the conjunction with Mercury, the Sun is not involved in the rest of the chart and escapes any major entanglements with Saturn or the outer planets. So Marilyn was drawn to the Solar side of her chart – her golden Leo Ascendant or her light Gemini Sun in preference to the complex challenges of her Moon.

## Jupiter Opposition Neptune

Radiant Jupiter brings a lot of his larger-than-life charisma to Marilyn's chart – conjuncting the Moon, opposing Neptune and sextiling Venus and the Taurus Midheaven. Jupiter and Neptune are the two planets most associated with acting and cinema. Neptune gave Marilyn the actor's ability to merge and identify with a character; Jupiter gave her eye-catching stage presence; and the two planets in combination with her Leo Ascendant gave her exceptional star quality. But the square between Jupiter and Saturn is another sign of Marilyn's difficulty with Saturn, which polarized into the negative expression of Saturn as Patriarch and Critic and Jupiter as *puella* and fantasy.

The 7th house is the house of relationships and partnerships and 'the other'. Psychologically we can interpret Marilyn's Moon-Jupiter conjunction in the 7th house as a representation of her quest to find the mothering she lacked through the adoration of her public and in her marriages. But Jupiter, especially in Aquarius, is not a stabilizing force for grounding and is likely to bring Psychopathic inflation and betrayal. So the close relationships that Marilyn hoped would be 'the answer' turned out to be a further recycling of her childhood experience of control, manipulation and abandonment.

## Mars, Venus, Jupiter and Neptune

We have seen that Marilyn had Mars hidden away in Pisces in the 8th house and so she would not have come across as the classic, fiery, pugnacious Psychopathic type. But when the Flowering/Psychopathic type is an overlay to Oral wounding they take the indirect Pleaser's course of gaining power and attention through seduction, and in this Marilyn was second to none! In itself, her Neptune in the 1st was an extremely seductive placement and her Mars in Pisces in the 8th house was wildly erotic (Mars was also inconjunct Neptune). Added to this, Marilyn had Venus in hot Aries trining Neptune and sextiling Jupiter. And so her whole sexual nature was lit up by shimmering Neptune and expansive Jupiter, giving her a magical allure.

But betrayal is the signature of the Psychopathic wound. No matter how desperately attracted to her they were in the first place, all the significant men in her life eventually backed away from her. Her marriage to the baseball star Joe DiMaggio lasted less than a year as he could not cope with Marilyn's fame as a sex goddess. The intellectual Arthur Miller wrote that when he first met her 'The air around her was charged' and he spoke about her as a vital force lighting up the darkness. But like everyone else, Miller responded to Marilyn's patent vulnerability by trying to control her. This only had the effect of undermining her, and by the end of their marriage Miller came to think of her as 'a mere child, an abused little girl'.

# 66

## Indications of Characterology in Marilyn Monroe's Chart

## Harvest/Rigid Energy

**VENUS**

- *Venus conjunct the MC (orb 1° 21')*
- *Taurus MC*
- *Venus trine Neptune (orb 6° 32')*
- *Venus sextile Jupiter (orb 1° 56')*

**SATURN**

- *Saturn square the Ascendant (orb 8° 22')*
- *Saturn square the Moon (orb 2° 21')*
- *Saturn in the 4th house*

**TENTH HOUSE**

- *Sun-Mercury conjunction in the 10th house*

**SEVENTH HOUSE**

- *Moon-Jupiter conjunction in the 7th house*

**Venus conjunct Taurus MC**

Marilyn's wounding was predominantly Oral and in much of her life she was driven to seek for an elusive sense of security and containment. But though she was not an obvious Rigid type, something in her was ambitious, dedicated and steely enough to make it to the pinnacle of her profession. The Midheaven represents that which we aspire to in life and the 10th House represents the urge to manifest something tangible – ambitions and career paths that structure our lives out in the world. These are the areas of life associated with the gifts of the Harvest stage. With the Sun, the ruler of the chart, in the 10th house and the Taurus Midheaven conjuncted by Venus in Aries we see that Marilyn was strongly motivated by the Harvest/Rigid energy – perhaps, above all, by the longing to find harmony and stability represented by Venus and the Taurus MC. Whatever else was going on in her life, Marilyn was able to bring her bright Sun-Mercury conjunction in through the 10th house of achievement and manifest a brilliant career as a great actress.

### Saturn in the 4th House

Part of the drive that enabled Marilyn to meet the challenges of a very tough and competitive career came from her Saturn in the 4th. From birth onwards, so many things conspired to make Marilyn feel unwanted and not good enough but, by the same token, she was highly motivated to seek some place where she would feel valuable. Unfortunately, we have seen that Marilyn's drive was exacerbated in a negative way by Saturn in the 4th operating as a deeply ingrained Inner Critic.

Saturn in the 4th house, square to the Moon, often represents the energy of a frightened child for whom gaining approval has become the main issue in life. This intensely vulnerable child energy – lurching from Schizoid splitting to Oral clinging – is the basis of the Inner Critic; the younger the terrorized infant, the bigger the Critic that emerges from the fear. With idealistic Neptune squaring her Saturn and with beauty-loving Venus on the MC, Marilyn's Critic developed into a Perfectionist Inner Critic, which is the negative expression of the Rigid defence. Marilyn suffered from terrifying stage fright and her fear of not being good enough gave her chronic insomnia and caused her to have difficulty in remembering her lines, and her failure to cope with the stress often made her hours, if not days, late for work.

If she had lived, her midlife transits from the outer planets might have brought about a reckoning and some major transformation and healing for Marilyn. She had certainly started on the path of claiming her inner authority after her Saturn return. But Marilyn died when she was only beginning to integrate the energies of her own adult authority and strength.

**Venus**

Marilyn had Venus in Aries shining out from her Taurus Midheaven and this was how the public saw her – as the embodiment of the goddess of love and beauty. From puberty onwards, once she recognized the power of her feminine allure Marilyn learned to work hard on her appearance. Even as a young girl she started exercising and sometimes wore clothes that were a size too small for her – clinging, revealing and provocative. As a star she spent hours on her hair and make-up, dedicated to preserving her image as America's sweetheart. But Chiron closely conjuncting both Venus and the MC reveal the deep wounding that, just as much as her loveliness and artistry, became her signature. Alongside her loveliness, always there was pain – the quest for healing, which is the hallmark of Chiron.

67

# Marilyn Monroe's Human Energy Field

When we think of a natal chart as a pattern of energies that will also appear in the HEF then we immediately sense a connection between the planets in the upper half of Marilyn's chart and the dazzling light that many people would associate with Marilyn Monroe.

With her Leo Ascendant, sextiled by the Sun in the 10th house, there is a tremendous amount of Solar radiance in Marilyn's chart and an overall emphasis on the light of the positive signs. The Ascendant and all the personal planets except Mars are in positive signs, and the quicksilver Gemini Sun is conjunct Mercury, quintiled by electrical Uranus and starlit Neptune and trined by the silvery light of the Aquarius Moon. Beautiful Venus shines from the zenith of the chart and the ethereal loveliness and glamour of Neptune illuminates the core of Marilyn's identity from the 1st house – light, light, light, shining light! And amidst this shimmering radiance is the energy of Chiron, high on the Midheaven – the wounding that was her signature, just as much as her beauty.

Lower down the HEF, in the area of the pelvic cradle, the energy changes and here we can feel the presence of Saturn which sits at the root of her chart. There is fracturing and coldness from the pain of the Moon's T-square with Saturn and a dark but flowing river of feeling from Pluto and Mars trining Saturn.

### The Auric Level

The auric level is the more apparent level of the field where the seven chakras express the psycho-spiritual activity of the personality reacting and responding to life in the physical world.

On the auric level in Marilyn's HEF we easily perceive the shining light of her Neptune rising, trining Venus on the MC, both also in aspect to the Moon and Jupiter. The minute we approach Marilyn's HEF we can sense the silvery radiance of Neptune and on into the vibrant loving rose light of Venus. Neptune and Venus are both connected to the energy of the Heart chakra, which opens to radiate the warmth of Leo and the passion of Aries and the Middle Tan T'ien is lit up with her tender longing for love.

Also very prominent and accessible in the upper part of Marilyn's HEF is the quicksilver lightness of Mercury in Gemini, fluttering, singing, laughing and dancing around her heart, throat and head. Mercury and Neptune activate the vision and perception of Marilyn's 6th chakra which is large, often overcharged with the hyper-vigilant sensitivity of a fearful child, yet also giving her exquisite sensitivity and the empathic skill of her acting.

Deeper into the auric level, closer to the central vertical power current the roots of the 5th and 4th chakras are darkened with the shadows of old pain which appears as fracture lines in the chakras and accumulations of dark jelly-like mucus or dust. Further down, the area in the centre of the HEF around the 3rd chakra is heavily blocked and constricted by the negative judgements of the Inner Critic, the fear of failure and rejection. This paralysing vibration of fear blocks the flow of energy down into the lower chakras, which are weakened, shot through with her experiences of neglect and abandonment.

In the pelvic cradle, the planets involved in Marilyn's Grand Trine in Water – Pluto, Saturn and Mars – form a current of dark energy emanating from within the 2nd chakra. In this current is the bitter toxic energy of sexual exploitation and abuse. This, combined with the harsh aspects to the Moon (the Moon is associated with the womb), links to Marilyn's lifelong physical suffering from endometriosis and her difficulty in conceiving a child. The 2nd chakra is very full and active, often overheated but glowing with liquid orange light lit up and intensified by the passionate red light of Mars and at other times deepening into the dark inner spaces of the instinctual power and passion of Pluto.

Marilyn's Saturn falls right at the nadir of her chart and in its negative expression Saturn has a damaging impact on her base chakra. The base chakra supports the most fundamental level of survival in the physical world – the immune system, our overall state of health and all issues of physical and emotional security. Marilyn's Saturn operates as a cold, constricting energy that freezes the root connection between the base chakra and the ground and blocks her ability to feel the support of the earth. The confusing cocktail of medication which she took to relieve her psychological problems would only have weakened the strength of her base chakra (Saturn square Neptune).

### The Haric Level

Marilyn experienced a lot of pain in her life and this shows up as darkness and damage and weakness on the auric level of her field. But in her soul Marilyn was so much greater than her Oral wounding and we see that something more is happening when we look deeper into the Haric level of her energy field. The level of the Hara underpins the auric level of the field and this is where we hold our soul's longing and life purpose. Any figure who appears so large in the history of the world is one with a mighty soul and whatever difficulties she encountered in life were all part of the unfolding of Marilyn's soul's journey. On the Haric level, Marilyn's powerful Saturn gave her tremendous strength of purpose. Pluto conjuncting the North Node gives a similar indication of a powerful upwelling of the life force from the Lower Tan T'ien, which is the root of the Haric level. Higher up, in the Middle Tan T'ien situated above the heart, we feel the energies of Neptune and Venus and her tender longing for love.

On a soul level Marilyn came with a major task to complete and which she accomplished out on the world stage. Marilyn encountered all the traps and blockages of the Patriarchal culture of the US as exemplified by Hollywood and the movie industry. But she followed the path of her soul's intention to complete her destiny and reveal the energy of the goddess, the feminine principle struggling for transformation, self-expression, freedom and love.

68

# THE BUDDING OR MASOCHIST SOUL:

## Orson Welles

> *The word 'genius' was whispered into my ear, the first thing I ever heard, while I was still mewling in my crib. So it never occurred to me that I wasn't, until middle age.*
> Orson Welles, *This is Orson Welles*

When Orson Welles was less than two years old, a doctor told his parents that their child was a genius. Orson was raised as a child prodigy and his immense talent for drama flowered in his teens when he acted, wrote and directed plays while other students were still only thinking of their exams.

At the age of sixteen he went backstage at the Gate Theatre in Dublin, was spotted by one of the directors and offered a major role for which he received excellent reviews. Back in America he spent the next few years feverishly acting, writing and directing in theatre and radio; his unfettered imagination and creative drive filled every hour of the day. Hollywood was quick to pick up on this extraordinarily talented young man and at the age of twenty-five he directed *Citizen Kane*, still considered by many to be the greatest movie ever made.

### Citizen Kane

*Citizen Kane* is undoubtedly a work of genius. But though its brilliance was never questioned, right from the start *Citizen Kane* came under attack. Firstly there was a dispute over who should be credited for the screenplay, which was actually a collaboration between the young Welles and writer Herman Mankiewicz. Most controversially, it was widely recognized that the character of Kane was based on press tycoon William Randolph Hearst who threatened to take legal action, blocked the release of the movie and instructed all his newspapers to refuse to advertise the film.

## The Magnificent Ambersons

*Citizen Kane* was produced for RKO under a contract that included an unprecedented arrangement that gave Orson creative carte blanche; the company was not allowed to make a single change without his approval. Such creative freedom was never to be repeated. Instead, Orson's second big film, *The Magnificent Ambersons*, is notorious for the fact that the final edit of the film was taken out of Welles's hands. An hour of his original version was cut and destroyed and in Orson's eyes it was ruined.

For Orson, this was the start of a recurring lifelong pattern of struggle to get his movies and other projects finished and out into the world. With astonishing consistency he fell foul of producers and film companies, who failed to back him, fund him or leave him with editorial control of his work. Over and over again events conspired to block him from completing his projects and so many of his films ended up, like *The Magnificent Ambersons*, in the hands of editors who could not replicate his genius and mangled his work.

Orson had a reputation for having a big ego, not finishing his projects and for going over budget, yet by Hollywood standards his budgets were not that extravagant. Nevertheless, in later years he found it impossible to get backing for his films. He struggled on by financing his later projects through his own fundraising activities and used the fees he received from his acting roles to finance his own films.

In 1975, Orson was given a Lifetime Achievement Award by the American Film Institute. Welles, still only sixty, ended his acceptance speech with a request for one of the movie producers present to back him to complete another film, but to no avail. It is hard not to reflect on what films his extraordinary genius/talent might have produced had he been able to get the funding he needed.

## Characterology

There was little that was straightforward about Orson Welles; he was a big-hearted, complicated man who had a chequered career and in the course of his life his youthful promise turned into something of a tragedy. In his very complexity and the difficulties that beset his immoderate creativity I regard Orson Welles as a prime example of the Budding/Masochist type.

## Childhood

George Orson Welles was born on 6 May 1915, the son of Richard Welles and Beatrice Ives. Richard Welles was an inventor who had made a fortune manufacturing automobile lamps and he was a man who valued money and status. Orson later referred to his father's wealthy friends as 'aristocratic philistines', men who actively cultivated a dislike of the arts.

It came as a surprise then when Dick fell in love and married Beatrice Ives, an intellectual, cultured, musical and forward-thinking woman. The couple were temperamentally different and their unresolved conflict of values between art and money manifested as a major issue in Orson's career.

After they were married, despite her husband's contempt for the arts, Beatrice threw herself into her studies of classical music. She was a powerful, charismatic woman from whom Orson inherited much of his talent as well as his beautiful voice. She established herself in Chicago's artistic bohemian circles while Dick returned to his musical halls and taverns, each disapproving of the other's choice of company.

Among Beatrice's circle of admirers was Dr Maurice Bernstein, the man who first 'discovered' the genius of Orson Welles. When Orson was less than two years old Bernstein came from the nursery in great excitement and told Beatrice and Dick that their infant had just spoken to him in fully formed sentences. After that Dr Bernstein became increasingly involved in Orson's life, monitoring his progress and nurturing the child prodigy with educational gifts. Dr Bernstein seems to have been equally obsessed with Beatrice and Orson. He became a permanent fixture in the Welles's family life – a close admirer of Beatrice and the mentor of Orson, and he was known to the young Orson as 'Dadda'.

The gap between Dick and Beatrice Welles continued to widen. Beatrice's friendship with Dr Bernstein further alienated Dick, who began to drink heavily. Dick went travelling but when he returned the situation only worsened and when Orson was six years old Dick and Beatrice separated. Orson went to live with his mother in Chicago and visited and often went travelling with his father. Orson continued to be reared as a child prodigy. He became accustomed to mingling with adults and was quite an attraction at Beatrice's cultured salons. Orson recalled:

*Children could be treated as adults as long as they were amusing. The moment you became boring you were off to the nursery.*

Beatrice had suffered for some time from failing health and four days after Orson's ninth birthday his mother died. Dick came and took the bereft Orson travelling. When they returned a struggle ensued, with Dick and Dadda fighting over Orson. Dadda was now even more obsessed with Orson as a relict of Beatrice and each man wanted to determine the course of Orson's future in the next chapter of the battle between art and commerce. As a strange kind of compromise Dadda arranged to send Orson to stay with an eminent German psychologist who specialized in unusual children. However, the psychologist's interest in Orson threatened to become sexual and Orson ran away. The pendulum then swung the other way and Orson went to stay with his father who was living a big hotel with a variety of people including the cast of several vaudeville acts. It was here that Orson learned to do magic tricks, which remained a lifelong interest. Dadda did not approve of this company and eventually Dick and Dadda agreed to send Orson to the Todd School for Boys, both of them thinking that this was a way to rid Orson of the bad influence of the other.

At the Todd School Orson met Roger Hill, a dynamic and charismatic sports teacher. Hill became Orson's new mentor and was one of the most important men in his life. At Todd, Orson had access to the school's theatre and its printing press became an outlet for his many talents. Encouraged and nurtured by Roger Hill and his wife, Orson's creativity blossomed as he wrote, directed and performed in the school's plays.

In the summer of 1930, Orson, now fifteen, went on a rather difficult trip to the Orient with his father. Dick's health was declining due to the dissipated lifestyle he had led since the marriage break-up. Dick was saddened because he felt that Orson had 'passed from him'. Orson could feel the truth of this and also realized that his father was now an alcoholic. When Orson returned to Todd, Roger and Hortense Hill persuaded him to take a stand with his father. Following their advice Orson told Dick he wouldn't see him again unless he stopped drinking. But on 28 December Dick died from heart and kidney failure. Orson was tormented with guilt, feeling he had betrayed his father when he needed him. He believed that his father's feeling of having lost the tug-of-war for Orson, followed by Orson's refusal to see him, had killed him.

## Career

After his father's death Orson went on a walking and painting tour of Ireland. In Dublin, he decided to go backstage after seeing a play at the Gate Theatre. In a story straight from Hollywood, 16-year-old Orson was noticed by the directors, given an on-the-spot audition and landed a major role. The directors of the theatre, Micheál MacLiammóir and Hilton Edwards, were captivated by Orson's big personality and exceptional talent. They formed a lifelong connection and joined the list of Orson's mentors.

Back in New York, Orson was disappointed that he did not so easily land a part on Broadway. However, his creative drive did not flag instead he went into the most inventive and productive period of his life. He returned to Todd, working as a drama coach, and wrote the highly successful *Everybody's Shakespeare*. When he found his way back on to the Broadway stage he was noticed by the director John Houseman who recognized his genius. Houseman and Welles went into partnership working for the Federal Theatre Project. Here Welles directed an innovative *Macbeth* with the Negro Theatre Project and directed the controversial operatic musical *The Cradle Will Rock*. *The Cradle Will Rock* was too left-wing for the establishment who tried to shut the play down and padlocked the theatre on the opening night. Not to be defeated, Welles and Houseman shepherded the audience to a different theatre where the cast spontaneously improvised a performance, singing across the theatre to one another from the audience. Many who attended described it as one of the most moving theatrical experiences of their lives.

Following this, Welles and Houseman went on to found the much-acclaimed Mercury Theatre. With his relentless creative drive, Orson was simultaneously involved in a multitude of projects – acting writing and directing for theatre and radio. In 1938 The Mercury Theatre on Air hit the headlines with the notorious radio production of HG Wells's frightening science fiction novel, *The War of the Worlds*. This was presented in the style of a radio news broadcast, so realistic that it caused a nationwide panic. It was the shocking impact of this episode that brought Orson to the attention of George Schaefer, the president of RKO Pictures in Hollywood. Schaefer offered Welles what generally is considered the greatest contract ever offered to an untried director, including complete artistic control. For the one and only time in his career, Welles had financial backing and artistic control over his movie and from this came *Citizen Kane*.

*Citizen Kane* is played out through the eyes of a journalist on a quest to understand the life of deceased media mogul Charles Foster Kane. The journalist fails to unlock the key to the great man, and only in the closing shots of the film do we discover that the dearest thing to Kane's heart was a symbol of his boyhood that came to an abrupt end when his family inherited money. Orson Welles's first love was painting and with his artist's eye he worked closely with cinematographer Gregg Toland to create a film that is visually stunning; the dark brooding cinematography beautifully conveys the sinister world of Kane. Welles's directorial mastery is particularly evident in the editing of the film where he makes unexpected and imaginative cuts, juxtaposing one image with another, jolting the viewer away from the chronological passage of time and creating a kaleidoscope of views of the mysterious Kane. This innovative approach to film, born from Welles's years of working in live theatre, became a major influence on the art of movie-making which, in 1941, was still relatively young.

But Welles's relentless creative drive now prompted him to bite off more than he could chew. Before he had completed his second film, *The Magnificent Ambersons*, Welles accepted a commission to film a documentary about South America, part of a wartime propaganda effort designed to prevent Latin America from allying with the Nazis. Orson flew off to Brazil leaving *The Magnificent Ambersons* still unfinished. Nervous after the controversy over *Citizen Kane* and unhappy with the delay on the completion of *The Magnificent Ambersons*, RKO formed a committee to take over editorial control of the film. A large part of the impact of Orson Welles's directing comes from the extraordinary and disturbing visual awareness that he brought to his shooting and editing; there was not another editor who could see with his eyes. While Orson was still away filming in South America *The Magnificent Ambersons* was cut to pieces and a new happy ending tacked on.

From *The Cradle Will Rock*, through to *The War of the Worlds*, *Citizen Kane* and *The Magnificent Ambersons*, all of Welles's creations got into trouble. The real issue was that his work was ahead of its time and his ideas – political, literary and visual – were too radical for the theatre and film companies who wanted a safe return on their money. Welles was too innovative and too controversial as a director. All the Hollywood film companies withdrew from him and for the rest of his life he was involved in one struggle after another to find backing to direct his films. And so Orson continued to live out the original conflict between his parents – art versus commerce – over and over again.

## Decline

*Citizen Kane* appears as the zenith in the trajectory of Orson Welles's creative light, with the rest of his career becoming increasingly mired in the complications and difficulties of finding funding. It is quite painful to catalogue his descent from the early flowering of his multi-talented genius into the final years of his life when he made a living from advertising cheap wines and doing voice-overs for children's cartoons.

From time to time Welles succeeded in finding backing to direct another film and he made several more masterpieces. But, over and again, the final edit was taken out of his hands and hours of his original filming ended up on the cutting room floor. In 1947 he directed *The Lady from Shanghai* for Columbia Pictures who did not like Welles's rough cut and, against his wishes, edited out an hour of the original filming. In 1955 he directed *Mr Arkadin* and again the producer became frustrated by his slow progress, removed Welles from the project and finished the film without him. In 1956, Welles returned to Hollywood, appearing in a variety of radio and TV shows. Here Orson had another chance to direct when he was hired to act in Universal Studio's film *Touch of Evil.* On the insistence of the star, Charlton Heston, Welles was promoted to director. Filming proceeded smoothly, with Welles finishing on schedule and within the budget, and the studio bosses praising the daily rushes. But after the end of production, the studio re-edited the film, reshot scenes and shot new exposition scenes to clarify the plot. Welles wrote a 58-page memo outlining suggestions and objections. The studio followed a few of the ideas, but cut another 30 minutes from the film before they released it. Like much of Welles's work, film lovers have since tried to reconstruct the film according to his original intentions.

Welles attempted to solve his problems by funding his own films using the large fees he collected from acting in other people's movies, including the smash hit *The Third Man.* After getting into trouble over his American taxes Welles lived in Europe for nearly a decade. Here he patched together his own finances to direct and star in *Othello*, which won the Palme d'Or at the 1952 Cannes Film Festival. In 1962 Welles filmed *The Trial* and, in 1965, *Chimes at Midnight*, his two personal favourites of his films. In 1967 Welles began directing *The Deep* but, true to form, the backers ran out of money and the project was never finished. In 1970 Welles returned to Hollywood, where he continued to self-finance his own film and television projects. While offers to act, narrate and host chat shows continued, his primary focus in this period was filming *The Other Side of the Wind*, a project that lasted for six years and ran into legal and financial difficulties. In 1975, the American Film Institute presented Welles with a Lifetime Achievement Award. At the ceremony, Welles screened two scenes from *The Other Side of the Wind* in the hope of raising money to complete the film. Written by Welles, the story told of a destructive old film director looking for funds to complete his final film. The film remains unfinished and unreleased.

In the late 1970s, Welles began to appear in a series of famous television commercials, including the long-running Carlsberg advert with the catchphrase 'Probably the best lager in the world.' In a BBC comedy series he was pilloried with the line 'Orson Welles – advertising Carlsberg, probably the only job he can get nowadays.' His last film roles were voice-overs for two animated films. His last television appearance was on the TV show *Moonlighting*, which was aired five days after his death and was dedicated to his memory.

Welles was married three times, most famously to the beautiful star Rita Hayworth. He had a daughter by each of his wives but he was never faithful until his later years and his relationship with Oja Kodar which lasted nearly twenty years from 1961 until his death. Though he sometimes said that he was not particularly sexual, Welles adored beautiful women and had multiple love affairs including several with famous Hollywood stars. He loved to live the high life and enjoyed staying at the best hotels, wining and dining at the most expensive restaurants, and making extravagant and expensive gestures towards the cast of his films regardless of what state his finances were in.

He suffered from asthma and was never a sporting man. In the second half of his life his health deteriorated and he became seriously overweight. Orson Welles died from a heart attack on 10 October 1985.

# 69

## The Budding or Masochist Soul

# Interpreting the Horoscope of Orson Welles

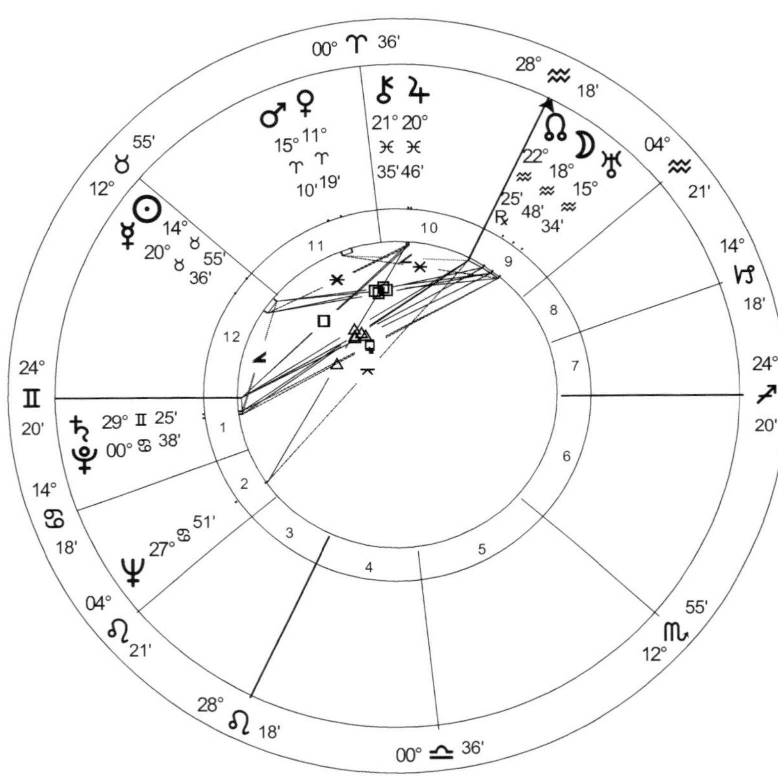


**Orson Welles**

7.00 am Thursday 6 May 1915, Kenosha Wisconsin USA

Placidus House System

Chart from Solar Fire version 7 Astrolabe, www.alabe.com.

# Dominant Planets and Themes

There were two things that stood out about the life of Orson Welles: his astonishing creative genius and his recurring struggle to get money and editorial freedom for his projects.

## Uranus and Mercury

The conjunction of Uranus with the Moon, the North Node and the Midheaven, all in Aquarius, creates an intense revolutionary Uranian/Aquarian energy which dominates Orson's chart. The influence of Uranus is doubly emphasized by the close square to the Sun (orb 0° 34') and to Mercury, the ruler of the Gemini Ascendant. These are clear indications of the Germination/Schizoid soul.

## Saturn and Pluto

When we look away from the electric brilliance of the Aquarius group at the zenith of the chart we find the dark and powerful energy of a close conjunction of Pluto, Saturn and the Ascendant, prominent in the 1st house. This conjunction creates an equal and opposite energy to that of Uranus and Mercury. In their highest expression Saturn and Pluto express qualities of patience, stillness, contact with the earth and with the instinctual power of the body. But to the Airy, electric energies of Uranus and Mercury, Saturn and Pluto can feel like forces of restriction, bondage and control. So we are looking at a chart split between the free-flowing, fast-moving energy of Uranus and Mercury and the issues of power and restraint represented by Pluto and Saturn. The polarity brings us, once more, to the scenario of the *puer aeternus*.

## *Puer Aeternus*

I have spoken before about the figure of the *puer aeternus*, an image from Transpersonal Psychology describing those who find it difficult to make the transition from adolescence into the authority and responsibilities of adulthood. We look to the masculine principle, often the energy of the father, to help us cut loose from the dependency of childhood. But when there is Narcissistic wounding and the influence of either parent is too domineering, a young person can become trapped in the world of the *puer*, a Peter Pan figure with gifts of vision and creativity but pathologically unable to grow up and embark on mature responsibilities and relationships. Experiences in the early years of life show up in the 1st house, and in Orson's chart the presence of Saturn and Pluto here suggests something very oppressive coming from one or both parents. Both planets represent issues of control; negative Saturn brings the 'rules' of the Superego and the Rigid attachment to ambition, status and success, while negative Pluto brings the covert or overt issues of domination and manipulation. The two planets represent the impact that the power struggle between Orson's parents had in his early years and their position in the 1st house indicates the difficulty for Orson in establishing his own authentic sense of identity. In particular, this conjunction represents the impact of the control of his mother and Dr Bernstein with their exalted expectations of him, and this is a clear indication of Masochist wounding.

The Sun is strong in Taurus, with the power of a Fixed sign, and larger-than-life Orson made his presence felt wherever he went. But the Sun's placement in the 12th house meant that behind the bravura and extravagant gestures Orson suffered from a lack of certainty about his own authentic identity. Again we meet the strange paradox of the 12th house: the radiance of his creative light seemed the most obvious thing about him and yet he remained uncertain of it in himself. His inner self-doubt meant that he lacked a strong sense of Solar power with which to hold back the oppressive weight of Saturn and Pluto. Orson has a Gemini Ascendant, and brittle Gemini is one of the signs most associated with the *puer aeternus*. The *puer* is terrified of the devouring, controlling energy represented by negative Saturn and Pluto, and Orson had the typical *puer*'s reaction which was to escape into the world of imagination. And so we see that behind the Gemini kaleidoscope of creativity and grandiosity that Orson displayed to the world lay his doubt about his true nature and identity – hence his comment that it was not until he reached middle age that he considered the possibility that perhaps he was not a genius. Orson's

Germination/Schizoid and Budding/Masochist Characterologies are the central themes in this chart.

Like Jimi Hendrix, Orson's chart has a Bowl configuration with most of the planets gathered in the southern hemisphere. The planets are divided into five sets of couplets with Uranus emphasised as the leading or 'cannonball planet'. This is quite an unusual pattern with several close squares and sextiles between the couplets. The intense energy coming through these five couplets was the basis of the multitude of talents that Orson brought to his creativity.

# 70

## Indications of Characterology in Orson Welles's Chart

### Germination/Schizoid Energy

**URANUS**

- *Uranus conjunct the Moon (orb 3° 14')*
- *Aquarius Moon*
- *Uranus square the Sun (orb 0° 39')*
- *North Node in Aquarius*
- *MC in Aquarius*
- *North Node conjunct the MC in Aquarius (orb 5° 35'), conjunct the Moon (orb 3° 37') and Uranus (orb 6° 51')*

**MERCURY**

- *Gemini Ascendant*
- *Mercury conjunct the Sun (orb 5° 41')*
- *Mercury square the Moon (orb 1° 48')*
- *Mercury square Uranus (orb 5° 02')*
- *Mercury square the North Node (orb 1° 49')*
- *Mercury square the MC (orb 7° 42')*

Orson has multiple indications of Germination/Schizoid energy, with Uranus and Mercury square to each other and closely involved with some of the key features of the chart.

**Uranus**

Orson's Uranus is extremely powerful. To recap, it is in its own sign; in a stellium with the Moon, North Node and the MC; it is almost exactly square the Sun; also square Mercury, which is the chart ruler; it sextiles Mars and Venus; and is in a wide trine to the Ascendant.

The energy of Uranus was a major driving force in Orson's life, making him a law unto himself – rebellious, erratic, unpredictable – and he often seemed to bite off more than he could chew. But above all Uranus represents the gifts of the Germination soul that Orson Welles expressed par excellence – his creative genius, originality and innovation; his artistic and political vision that was years ahead of his time; and his inexhaustible creative drive pouring out through the Moon, the Sun, Mercury and the Ascendant.

### Moon in Aquarius

Cool, unemotional Aquarius is not an easy placement for the Moon and the conjunction to Uranus and square to Mercury trebles the indications of Schizoid wounding. Orson described his parents as reserved and distant and the overall impression was of a family life that was unusual and highly cultured but somewhat lacking in warmth and affection. Typifying the energy of an Aquarius Moon, his mother Beatrice was a powerful woman, an intellectual and a progressive thinker interested in women's rights. Orson once said:

*My mother was very beautiful, very generous and very tough. She was rather austere with me.*

### Uranus Square the Taurus Sun

Orson's father is represented by the Sun in Taurus; like Aquarius, a Fixed sign, powerful and stubborn! Where Beatrice was the progressive intellectual, Richard was a practical businessman and their conflicting values appear in the square between the materialistic Taurus Sun and the idealistic Aquarius Moon. Taurus brings a very different energy from that of Aquarius: warm and earthy and sensual and in his Taurus Sun we see Orson's (and his father's) enjoyment of wealth and good living. The Sun in Taurus is normally a sign of body awareness, grounding and stability, a good antidote to Schizoid fragmentation. But Orson's Sun falls in the mystical 12th house and it is so closely squared by Uranus that the hope of Taurean stability and harmony is shattered by the electric energy of Uranus.

### Gemini Ascendant

The Ascendant and the ruling planet speak of the soul's entry into the world of manifestation and a person's way of bringing themselves through into the world. We have seen that Orson's Gemini Ascendant, with ruling Mercury square Uranus, goes with the brittle energy of the *puer aeternus*. Always, the signs of wounding are also an expression of Essence struggling to come through. Gemini is all about communication and it is one of the signs most often linked with literary and dramatic talent. Gemini and Mercury are associated with speech, and with Sun-Mercury in musical Taurus and Jupiter almost exactly sextile his Mercury, Orson was celebrated for his beautiful, deep, melodious voice. With Mercury square Uranus, Orson was happiest when working spontaneously, in the moment, breaking new ground with total creative freedom. Orson was not interested in doing things by the book, and while filming he was continually making changes and rewriting the script while being open to input from the actors – there was nothing rigid about Orson's approach to his art. Backed up by the love of art and beauty that goes with the Sun in Taurus and the ground-breaking vision of Uranus, Orson was the embodiment of the literary brilliance of Gemini and he will be remembered as one of the great communicators of the twentieth century.

### Radical Change – Moon, Uranus, North Node and the MC in Aquarius

With the Moon, the North Node and the Midheaven all together in Aquarius, Orson was a progressive left-wing thinker. This is also indicated by the Venus-Mars conjunction in the 11th house, which has to do with vision for a better society. He was deeply concerned about humanitarian and political issues and for a while he wrote a newspaper column on political issues. At one point he seriously considered running for office but the political climate wasn't right for him and he eventually fell foul of the McCarthy anti-communist witch hunt.

Aquarius and Uranus are, of course, signs of rebellion as well as originality and Orson must have been aware of the likely consequences of his refusal to toe the line with the media moguls. It was widely surmised that in *Citizen Kane* the mysterious last word 'Rosebud' was a deliberate taunt directed at William Randolph Hearst for whom it had a private sexual meaning (though this kind of provocation is more typical of Masochist spite than straightforward Uranian rebellion). Orson's problem with Hollywood was that he was an artist who was ahead of his time and in both his message and his vision he was too radical for the businessmen who ran the studios and only wanted a reliable return on their investments.

# 71

# Indications of Characterology in Orson Welles's Chart

## Rooting/Oral Energy

### THE MOON

- *Moon conjunct Uranus (orb 3 ° 14')*
- *Moon square the Sun (orb 3 ° 53')*
- *Moon conjunct the North Node (orb 3 ° 37')*

### NEPTUNE

- *Neptune in the 2nd house*
- *Neptune quintile the Sun (orb 0 ° 56')*

### TWELFTH HOUSE

- *Sun in the 12th house*

### The Moon

The Moon, representing the infant years, is an indication of the kind of relationship a person forms with their body. The Aquarius Moon conjuncting Uranus is a classic indication of Schizoid wounding and to a lesser extent it also indicates Oral wounding: Uranus and Aquarius are cool, mental energies and do not support the tender bonding process of mother and child. The personal planets in this chart are all in Earth, Air and Fire, and the lack of Water echoes the idea of difficulty with tenderness and vulnerability.

Orson had lifelong issues with his weight, and eating disorders are usually associated with Schizoid and Oral wounding. Even when he was seriously short of money he wined and dined at the most expensive restaurants, and in later life he became seriously obese. The Sun in Taurus is always inclined to overindulge in the sensual pleasures of food and wine and, exacerbated by the square to his disassociated

Moon, Orson's overeating went with the fundamental Schizoid difficulty with being in a body compounded by Oral wounding.

### Boundary Issues

The Sun in the 12th house and Neptune in the 2nd echo this theme of the infant Orson's difficulty in developing a healthy sense of boundaries and containment. The 12th house represents the place where we dissolve our human boundaries and become one with All That Is; it is the house of the collective, where we experience oneness with the group. But the Sun represents our sense of a personal, individual, separate self and so the house of Universal Consciousness and the collective is a difficult placement for the Sun. Orson always had problems in maintaining a realistic sense of personal limitation and there were repeated incidents of boundary confusion in Orson's life, such as the dispute over the authorship of the screenplay for *Citizen Kane*.

If the 1st house represents our first raw consciousness of being alive, the 2nd house represents our sensual experience of being in a body. Our most primal experience of boundaries is something so automatic that we don't even think about it: living inside our biological skin, the border of the territory of our physical body. The 2nd house has everything to do with what happens inside that skin and the needs of the body, such as nourishment, physical health and sensual, sexual well-being. The 2nd house also has to do with our way of surviving in the physical world, including our relationship with money. Just as Orson's Taurus Sun has no certainty of self tucked away in the house of Spirit, so Neptune, perhaps the most 'cosmic' of all the planets, brings confusion to his 2nd house awareness of the real needs of the body and a chaotic disregard for limitations around money.

The Rooting/Oral stage is about anchoring the new life safely into physical existence and setting up a sense of personal boundaries. Neptune in Cancer in the 2nd house represents a wonderful sense of bonding and merging with the mother, and here we can feel Beatrice's love for Orson. But this placement also lays down a fundamental confusion about boundaries and limitation. Orson suffered from asthma, which can be associated with too much merging – a sense of suffocation from a mother who has, in some way, overstepped the boundaries.

Neptunian confusion about the nature of the body meant that Orson never learned to pay attention to his health and fitness, and lacked a sense of limitation regarding his diet and lifestyle. Oceanic Neptune in the 2nd house also explains the tidal fluctuations in Orson's financial fortunes. Together, the 12th house Sun and 2nd house Neptune make a double-whammy, a kind of mutual receptivity of the Oral difficulties with boundaries.

In traditional astrology, planets in the 2nd house represent values and the way of making a living. Neptune is the planet most associated with the cinema and theatre.

72

# Indications of Characterology in Orson Welles's Chart

## Budding/Masochist Energy

**THE SUN**

- ***Sun in the 12th house***
- ***Mercury in the 12th house***
- ***Sun semi-square Pluto (orb 0° 47')***

**PLUTO**

- ***Pluto conjunct Saturn in the 1st house (orb 1° 13')***
- ***Pluto conjunct the Ascendant (orb 6° 18')***
- ***Saturn conjunct the Ascendant (orb 5° 05')***

**VENUS AND CHIRON**

- ***Venus conjunct Mars (orb 3° 51')***
- ***Chiron conjunct Jupiter (orb 0° 49')***

The other dominant Characterology in Orson's chart is the Budding/Masochist type.

**Sun Conjunct Mercury in the 12th House**

We have seen that Orson has the Sun conjunct Mercury in the 12th house. Planets in the 12th house represent the gift we offer to the world. Orson's Mercurial Solar energy coming through the house of the collective represents his destiny as a creator who would change the course of history.

However, planets in the 12th house represent aspects of the self that are not easy for the individual to bring into consciousness. The Sun is the prime symbol of the radiance of self and Mercury is the symbol of self-expression. With both planets in the 12th house we see that during his childhood Orson's unique individual Essence was not really welcomed in its entirety and his authentic voice was not properly heard. His advanced intelligence and verbal brilliance were gifts that he was required to parade before his mother's friends but things about him that were less than special were not praised or valued. When the child experiences a lack of recognition for their wholeness, when they are not accepted for simply being who they are, their Solar sense of self gets repressed and slips away into the unconscious. Orson's 12th house Sun/Mercury placement is a classic sign of Masochist wounding.

So we see that, although everyone else could clearly see the shining light of his talent, Orson himself suffered from profound feelings of uncertainty about his true identity, i.e. as someone separate from the demands and expectations of others, particularly his parents. Orson's personality seemed so big (and that was what his parents demanded of him) but underneath the apparent confidence he was not at all certain who he really was. It is notable that a number of Orson's films dealt with the issue of identity.

The 12th house placement of the Sun speaks in particular of Orson's father Dick who became increasingly invisible and succumbed to alcoholism. So Orson never received support from his father to help him discover and assert his own sense of his Solar nature. Just as Marilyn Monroe somehow drew people in to try and rescue the motherless girl they felt in her, so Orson attracted a string of male mentors into his life who tried to bridge the gap in his fathering and help this talented boy to get a grip on his overpowering creativity.

### Saturn and Pluto Conjunct the Ascendant from the 1st House

The Ascendant is the key to the expression of the self and the 1st house is the house of identity. These are the major issues for the Budding/Masochist type and we have seen that Orson's 1st house conjunction of Saturn, Pluto and the Ascendant is an indication of considerable Masochist wounding. Saturn and Pluto standing at the gateway of individuality make for an extremely challenging configuration and in their negative expression these two dark energies seriously impede and distort the expression of the life force. Saturn and

Pluto are always inclined to express in a negative way, and in the 1st house they appear as an invading and controlling force bearing down on little Orson's fragile budding sense of identity. On their own, either Saturn or Pluto in the 1st house and aspecting the Ascendant is a sign of Masochist wounding, so together this difficult grouping indicates major life issues around domination and control.

This conjunction first manifested as the atmosphere in the home into which Orson was born. Dick and Beatrice each battled to assert their own set of values and Orson's future became a football kicked around in the competition between intellect and commerce. The fact that his parents demanded different things from him only deepened Orson's confusion about his sense of identity.

**Saturn**

Saturn in the 1st house is also indicative of Rigid wounding. Saturn here represents the Superego, the internalized voice of parental demands, and Orson's intellectual mother had quite an agenda for her child prodigy. For example, Orson was taught to read by the age of three and his first reading primer was Shakespeare's *A Midsummer Night's Dream*. This seems a little extreme, and Saturn in Gemini in the 1st house represents the negative impact of a parent who needs their child to be brilliant and gives them Shakespeare for their first reader. Gemini rules everything to do with words and literature but Saturn goes over the top and tries to take the ephemeral butterfly of Gemini's poetry and nail it down. Beatrice required her son to be literary, cultured and intellectual and this overrode her recognition of his right to be himself. A family friend described Beatrice as:

> *A cool, self-centred woman who had little tolerance for children in their natural state.*

However, things in astrology always express through a continuum ranging from positive to negative. And so another way of looking at this is to say that Beatrice was only trying to foster her child's amazing literary gifts. Orson grew up with a passion for Shakespeare – of the films he made, one of his favourites was *Chimes at Midnight*, which he compiled from five Shakespeare plays. However, as a child presented with such a Rigid plan of who he was supposed to be, Orson inevitably lost confidence in his own natural response to life.

The 1st house is one of the more difficult placements for Saturn as it is often goes with individuals who are crippled by the fear that they are fundamentally not good enough, and Saturn operates as the shaming, blaming Inner Critic. Orson's way of dealing with a negative Saturn was to identify with the adolescent escapism of the *puer* (Moon-Uranus in Aquarius) and reject the Saturnian principles of order and patience. In Voice Dialogue terms, any planet in the chart that is disowned distorts into a force that appears to come AT the individual in an adversarial way. Time and time again in his career, Orson came up against authority figures and his creative vision was sabotaged and defeated by movie moguls, financiers or other distorted representatives of Saturn.

**Pluto**

Whereas a negative Saturn expresses as the cold, critical voice of the Superego, the issue with Pluto is power. Even more frightening than Saturn, the negative expression of Pluto is the voice of Ereshkigal – the bitter fury of someone who will stop at nothing to gain the upper hand. This is not a voice that many of us openly express, but in many families unexpressed fury over issues of power hangs in the air like looming thunder. In mythology Pluto wore a helmet of invisibility and very rarely revealed himself in the world of mortals. So we find that the power struggles indicated by Pluto tend to be somewhat invisible – often underhand manipulation very different to the forthright anger of Mars. Pluto in the 1st house is often a sign of this kind of repressed dark struggle going on in the family and it added to the difficulties in Orson's relationship with his mother. Beatrice's need for Orson to excel in her world of culture was part of the power struggle in her battle with her husband and appeared to override all other considerations. For example, from a very early age Orson was taught to play piano and raised as a musical prodigy. There is an anecdote of a childhood drama when little Orson rebelled against taking music lessons and threatened to jump off a hotel balcony. His mother, correctly calculating that this would dissuade him from such histrionics, told his hysterical piano teacher:

*Well, if he wants to jump, let him jump!*

Beatrice and Dr Bernstein were more interested in seeing Orson as a genius than in seeing him as a child. Orson recalled that in childhood, though he was precocious and appeared supremely confident, he felt increasingly anxious that he would not come up to his parents' expectations:

*I always felt I was letting them down, that's why I worked so hard. That's the stuff that turned the motor.*

True to the Masochist template, Orson became dominated by his anxious and impossible struggle to please and comply. Throughout his life, Orson had difficulty in receiving praise as this triggered his fundamental fear that he would always end up being a disappointment.

On the deepest level, beneath Orson's wounding around this difficult placement, we see the life purpose of the Budding soul, seeking the buried treasure of his authentic self and finding a mirror to his Essence through his creativity. In its positive expression Pluto is connected to the raw power of the Lower Tan T'ien, the root of the life force. Pluto has more to do with real transformation of old wounds than any other planet. Similarly Saturn brings the energy of the central Hara line that holds the soul's life purpose. Though the Saturn/Pluto conjunction was at the heart of Orson's experiences of frustration and defeat, the placement also gave him an unstoppable drive to find himself through his creativity. On its own, the artistic energy of Gemini can sometimes be superficial but in Orson's case the Saturn-Pluto conjunction brought depth to his work and gave him the creative integrity, power, persistence and sheer grit to hold himself together in the face of adversity and continue to make his films.

## Chiron

Orson has Chiron conjunct his Jupiter and Venus conjunct his Mars; these two sets of 'couplets' in the chart are a secondary indication of Masochist restraint because the fiery planets are impeded in the expression of their energy.

Orson has Jupiter in Pisces, prominent in the 10th house, but the close conjunction with Chiron brings in the energy of wounding. The 10th house is generally associated with the mother, and so we see again that Beatrice's presence loomed large in a way that was also hurtful. We might say that Chiron represents that sense of disappointment in Orson's career following his youthful success. But Chiron is not a force for evil or destruction. Chiron here in the 10th house speaks of the deeper need of his soul to escape from the infantile grandiosity of the demand for him to be 'special' and to discover a sense of his own truth.

Mars in Aries expresses the aggression and heroic leadership of the warrior. With Venus conjuncting Mars, the angry fire of Mars is softened. This is not a difficult placement: it speaks of Orson's sexual charisma and love of women. It is worth mentioning here as it also echoes the idea of something in Orson that held back from the most direct and straightforward assertion of the self.

73

# Indications of Characterology in Orson Welles's Chart

## Flowering/Psychopathic Energy

**MARS**

- *Mars sextile the Moon (orb 3 ° 28')*
- *Mars in the 11th house*

**THE SUN**

- *Leo South Node*
- *Leo IC*

**JUPITER**

- *Jupiter square the Ascendant (orb 3 ° 34')*
- *Jupiter sextile chart ruler Mercury (orb 0 ° 10')*

Orson clearly had many of the heroic and creative gifts of the Flowering soul. However, he has the South Node in Leo (and a Leo IC) which indicates that the Flowering/Psychopathic energy was not Orson's major direction in this life. The Moon's nodal axis is not a planetary energy but speaks of the overall path of the soul through this life from the South Node towards the North (similar to the MC which represents that which we most aspire to in life). The South Node in Leo gave Orson an innate feeling for drama and performance, and the Sun and Mercury square the Nodal axis indicate that the Solar exploration of self-expression was an integral part of his life journey.

Orson has Uranus, the Moon and the Midheaven all conjunct the North Node in Aquarius. But Aquarius is not interested in stardom and this meant that Orson was required to look beyond the glory of being a movie star. Aquarius is the sign of the humanitarian – of those who seek to create a better society – and Orson's Venus-Mars conjunction in the 11th house echoes the emphasis on the Aquarian, Promethean drive to create a more just and enlightened society. Orson had Aquarian faith that the viewing public was capable of understanding theatre and films that were challenging and thought-provoking and so he was unable to knuckle down and simply make more easy-watching movies that the studios wanted him to make. Overriding his need to be a star was his Uranian urge to challenge the status quo and push back the frontiers of art.

## Jupiter

Orson has Jupiter in Pisces in the 10th house squaring his Gemini Ascendant, almost exactly sextile the chart ruler Mercury. This is a powerful indication of extrovert Flowering/Psychopathic energy. In its own sign of Pisces (associated with all the arts, but photography and cinema in particular), and highly visible in the 10th house, Jupiter represents Orson's prolific creativity, his accomplishments and achievements, and his persona as a giant of the movie industry. However, as we have seen, Jupiter is conjuncted by Chiron, a placement that speaks again of Orson's Narcissistic wounding and Jupiterian grandiosity and it describes the pain of his struggle to match up to his mother's need for him to be a genius. Jupiter sextiles the 12th house Sun and trines Neptune, so it also links to Orson's primal wounding in relationship with his alcoholic father. Orson appeared to be the embodiment of his 10th house Jupiter, an overpowering presence in person as well as professionally, large in every sense! But Chiron conjunct Jupiter gives us the image of the wounded king – the king who so often failed in his attempts to manifest his vision.

Larger-than-life Jupiter is the planet most associated with fame and acting, and the energy of Jupiter is what people remember of Orson Welles. Jupiter gave Orson charisma and tremendous stage presence and it is this visionary combination of Jupiter, Uranus and Mercury that symbolizes the creativity of Orson's Germination and Flowering gifts.

## The Sun

We have seen that Orson's Sun in the 12th house was indicative of Masochist wounding. The aspects from Uranus, Jupiter and Neptune all added to Orson's confusion about his father and his own self-doubt, and they showed up in the form of his long string of male mentors, surrogate father figures drawn like moths to the flame of his talent.

## Mars

Orson's Mars was strong in its own sign of Aries exactly sextile the powerful Uranus. Uranus electrified Orson's Flowering/Psychopathic energy and he often came across as a temperamental artist, shifting between explosive outbursts (Mars) and moments of tenderness and sweetness (Venus).

Venus was less powerful in its detriment in Aries, but it worked in two ways – it expressed Orson's passion for beauty, art and romance but it also brought in the Rigid energy operating as a restraining influence on Mars and bringing the qualities of the Masochist 'Pleaser'.

Nevertheless, Orson's Mars in Aries sextile Uranus was wilful and impulsive. The heat of Mars made it difficult for Orson to approach his work calmly. It gave him a drive and a passion that fuelled his prolific output but it also got him into fights and propelled him into making impulsive decisions that often did not serve him.

# 74

# Indications of Characterology in Orson Welles's Chart

## Harvest/Rigid Energy

### VENUS

- *Venus conjunct Mars (orb 3° 51')*
- *Venus semi-square the MC (orb 1° 59')*

### SATURN

- *Saturn conjunct the Ascendant (orb 5° 05')*
- *Saturn in the 1st house*
- *Saturn trine the MC (orb 1° 07')*
- *Saturn semi-square the Sun (orb 0° 30')*

Orson was not a typically controlled and repressed Rigid type. He was unconventional in his art and in his lifestyle, reckless and impulsive and non-conformist. But the gift of the Harvest soul is the ability to manifest vision, to achieve a result in the physical world, and this Orson clearly did, albeit via a labyrinthine Masochist route. Because he achieved greatness at such a young age it is easy to think of Orson's career as a tragedy and even a failure. Actually, he regularly produced magnificent works of art and achieved numerous awards as an actor, a writer and a director.

### Venus

The least integrated planets in Orson's chart are the feminine energies of Neptune and Venus. Venus is in its detriment in Aries and neither the conjunction to Mars nor the sextile to Uranus support the Venusian principle of relationship. Venus is in a wide sextile to the Moon and in a quintile to the Ascendant, and these aspects came through as a kind of sweetness that Orson had and his sheer love of art and beauty. But the energy of Venus that seeks union and relationship is not a dominant force in Orson's chart. This is echoed by the fact that the chart has no oppositions – the aspect associated with the issues of relationship. With all the planets gathered in the Bowl configuration mostly occupying the southern hemisphere, Orson focused his energy on his creative projects out in the world. With passionate Mars conjunct romantic Venus Orson was attracted to many women; he had countless affairs and was married to three very beautiful women.

But the archetype of the *puer aeternus* is often found polarized with the dark devouring face of the Feminine – Ereshkigal or the Gorgon. In Orson's chart the youthful energies of Uranus, Mercury and Jupiter were on the run, escaping from the power and control issues of Pluto in the 1st house. The *puer* loves falling in love but his fear of the negative Feminine means that he is unable to stay still and commit to an intimate relationship. So Orson did not know how to be faithful to his women; he could not restrain his roving eye, his marriages ended painfully and his three daughters from three different marriages all felt estranged from him. In his late forties Orson entered into relationship with a younger woman, Oja Kodar, who he lived with until he died.

**Saturn**

As well as an indication of Masochist wounding, Saturn in the 1st house is a sign of the Harvest/Rigid soul. We have seen that in youth this is a difficult placement with Saturn as the Inner Critic in the house of identity, leaving the individual with the fear that in their Essence they are just no good – the root of Masochist wounding. The Rigid type compensates for their inner doubt by seeking to match up to an external standard of success.

However, we can also recognize that Saturn is one of the most important principles in human life. Saturn is the gatekeeper of the material realm and nothing manifests in this world without Saturn. Saturn is associated with the deepest levels of the HEF where we hold our soul's purpose and the power of intention, giving us determination, stamina, self-discipline and authority. A person who is aligned with their Saturnian energy can become an unstoppable force guided by an innate knowing that they are fulfilling their destiny.

Clearly Orson suffered from the impact of the negative Saturn and he never found a way of integrating his radical Uranian vision with the grounded patience and presence that is the highest expression of Saturn. If there was a tragedy around Orson Welles it was that his Saturn and Pluto so often appeared in the negative form of struggles with external authority figures. Nevertheless, though he was always dogged by this conflict, it was the positive energy of Saturn and Pluto that gave Orson the steeliness and the raw power to drive through his massive creative projects – but it was a rocky road.

The pairing up of all the planets in the chart into a collection of couplets is another illustration of Orson's overwhelming talent and echoes the theme of the lifetime's challenge for him to learn to gain mastery of his creative drive. All the planets associated with patience, embodiment, stillness and grounding are in pairings with planets that are fiery and impulsive – Venus with Mars, the Moon with Uranus and Chiron with Jupiter.

A significant aspect of Orson's wounding is that there is a widespread sense of regret about his career. Orson sometimes spoke of his life as if he had failed instead of recognizing the great things that he had achieved. It is easy to get caught up in the idea that what he did was not enough; as though we have been deprived of what he might have been. Unfortunately this is a world-scale echo of Orson's core belief that sooner or later he would be seen as a disappointment.

The struggle for an artist to manifest their vision in the physical world is beset with challenges and Orson never achieved the sense of peace and fulfilment which is the final gift of the Harvest stage. Nevertheless, if we draw back from his unhappy conviction that he was a disappointment we see that Orson counts as one of the great artists of the twentieth century. Orson's Saturn in the 1st house operated very powerfully, giving him the drive of a man who stepped up to meet a great destiny – a sense of purpose that enabled him to manifest astonishing performances and inspiring works of art throughout his life.

# 75

# Orson Welles's Human Energy Field

The theme that dominates Orson's chart is the struggle between the planets of Air and Fire and the dark energies of Pluto, Saturn and Chiron.

## In the Human Energy Field

Often when we look at someone's HEF the first impression we get is of the energy patterns coming through the Ascendant. Orson had a Gemini Ascendant ruled by Mercury in the 12th house exactly sextile Jupiter and in a wide sextile with Neptune, bringing the flickering light of the shape-shifter, the god of many disguises – the trickster gods Loki, Coyote and Puck.

The outer level of Orson's energy field was a moving kaleidoscope of artistic and verbal brilliance – words and images gliding across his HEF. Orson had a very big energy field and these swirling rivers of poetry, philosophy, stories and pictures could easily extend to fill a stage, a film set or a theatre. This was an entrancing pageant but it also served as a mask for Orson – a way for him to protect himself by shifting into a suitable disguise.

## The Auric Level

The light in the HEF around Orson's head was expansive and brilliant. Orson's 6th chakra was large and often overcharged both from his restlessly fertile imagination and from over-vigilant Masochist watchfulness. The 7th was also very active and it was through these chakras that Uranus and Mercury brought through ideas and inspiration.

From his shoulders down Orson's HEF became much more clouded, the colours more opaque, and he lacked the Neptunian radiance that lit up the energy fields of Jimi Hendrix and Marilyn Monroe. The dominant placement of his Saturn and Pluto and the fact that these energies were often operating in a negative way made shadows and blockages in Orson's HEF. Beneath the flamboyant exterior of the Gemini Harlequin there is the sense of withheld energy accumulating around the core of the field where it lost its transparency and became dense. These shadows lodged in and around his lower chakras, particularly the 3rd chakra, hold the energy of his Masochist resistance – resistance to fully liberating the power held in the Lower Tan T'ien. And there was a reason for this – beneath his complex Mercurial exterior Orson's heart was in trouble.

The heart chakra is possibly the most important chakra in the Human Energy Field. The heart is the meeting place where the fine high energies of the non-physical realms flow down through the upper chakras and unite with the slower, denser energies of the physical world rising up through the lower chakras. The human heart is the place where the energy of the earth comes into communion with the energy of the sky. In different ways, many on a spiritual path believe that developing the human heart has a vital role in the evolution of the Universe. It is the nature of the sacred human heart – our capacity to love that makes us the bridge between Spirit and Matter.

Orson had a big heart, a generous heart overflowing with goodwill and bonhomie. But he also had a broken heart. If we picture a chakra as a little world unto itself then we see that deep in the energy field of Orson's heart there was a lost boy who felt abandoned and believed that he could not trust anyone. And in the shadows that surrounded this lonely child I sense the presence of ancestral issues and past lives. When Pluto, Saturn or Chiron (but particularly Chiron and Pluto) are a dominant influence in a chart I feel we are looking at the outcome of events from beyond this life. With Orson's Pluto closely semi-square to his Sun and Chiron closely conjunct his Jupiter there is an issue about the appropriate use of power, i.e. the possibility of past lives where there were distortions around power. The Leo South Node and 12th house Sun also suggest ancestral concerns around the kingly power of the Sun. Seen in this light, the conjunction of Saturn and Pluto and the square from Jupiter and Chiron to the Ascendant are all indications of a soul in the process of learning about the right use of power. In keeping with this, *Citizen Kane* and many of Orson's other films are about issues of power and corruption. The Aquarius North Node and stellium that surrounds it are further indications of this educative process – like the learning of Sir Percival who suffered from Solar Leo egotism before he learned to ask 'Whom does the Grail serve?'

A person with Masochist wounding has a deep fear that in their Essence they are 'bad'. The Masochist urge to withhold and resist the flow of the life force is often based on a fear that if they allowed their life force free reign they would do something terrible. Something about the placement of Pluto, Saturn and Chiron brings up the possibility of a past life in which Orson's use of power was involved in some kind of catastrophe. Orson himself never spoke about any such memory or issue but the placement of these planets could suggest the lingering vibration of something that once went very wrong.

The heart is the key to the right use of power. If those who rule are not guided by love, compassion and the will to be of service then the raw power of the life force follows the will of the Little Mind and can cause great harm. Difficulties with misuse of power go with difficulties with love.

And if we return to the lonely boy in Orson's heart, we see the impact of wounding in his relationships with his parents as well as grief at the loss of both parents in childhood and the anguish of having rejected his father just before his death. In addition to this, all Orson's marriages and relationships in the first half of his life ended in separation. So in Orson's chart and HEF we see a combination of issues around power and a wounded heart.

### The Haric Level

On the auric level we can see the energies of Saturn and Pluto as causing a major disturbance in Orson's HEF – a weight of constricted withheld energy that blocked the flow of energy through the field. However, on the deeper level of the Hara something else is happening. Here we come into the presence of Orson's core qualities, the soul of an artist with an intense passion for art, beauty, poetry and his innovative cinematic vision. Here we feel the energy of Pluto as the root power of the Lower Tan T'ien that sustained his vast creative drive while Saturn is the energy of the central Hara line, bringing the steady persistence, dedication and focus necessary to complete a creative project.

Higher up the Hara line is the Middle Tan T'ien, which seems to be filled with the light of Aquarius – Uranus, the Moon, the North Node and the Midheaven – the love of fairness and justice but, above all, the longing for freedom. And higher still in Upper Tan T'ien we feel the warm, expansive radiance of Piscean Jupiter, with unlimited imagination and accessing the Gemini Ascendant to communicate his vision to the world.

76

# THE FLOWERING OR PSYCHOPATHIC SOUL:

## Frida Kahlo

> *Frida began work on a series of masterpieces which had no precedent in the history of art – paintings which exalted the feminine quality of truth, reality, cruelty and suffering. Never before had a woman put such agonized poetry on canvas.*
> Diego Rivera

The Mexican artist Frida Kahlo was one of the outstanding artists of the twentieth century. Her work was a subjective, autobiographical, pictorial representation of her own life and her paintings are instantly recognizable, unique in both subject matter and style. More than half of her paintings were self-portraits symbolically representing her psychological state, which was often physically and emotionally painful. Frida was sometimes classed as a surrealist painter but she refuted this label, saying:

> *I have never painted dreams. What I represented was my own reality.*

Whereas the work of the surrealists was marked by the detachment of a dreamer, an observer, sometimes voyeuristic, Kahlo's work is remarkable for its direct expression of her personal emotional experience.

As a politically progressive and revolutionary thinker, Kahlo recognized the value of her Mexican heritage and she incorporated spiritual symbolism from traditional Mexican folk art into her paintings to create her unique style. Frida achieved considerable fame in her own lifetime, bringing Mexican art to the attention of the western world, and when she died she was honoured with a state funeral in Mexico. In her life she exhibited in New York and Paris, she was the first Mexican artist to have a painting bought by the Louvre in Paris, and major retrospectives of her work have been held in Europe and America in recent years. The home where she was born, lived and died – La Casa Azul, the 'Blue House' in Coyoacán, Mexico City – is now a museum devoted to her life and work.

## Characterology

At the core of Frida Kahlo's life was her relationship with her husband Diego Rivera, the Mexican mural artist. Theirs was an all-consuming, passionate and turbulent relationship. They were both highly emotional, both had extra-marital affairs and at one point they divorced and then re-married.

Frida was also very involved with politics. She was born just before the Mexican Revolution and she was a champion of radical left-wing politics and a member of the Communist Party. With her fiery temperament, her immense creativity, the intensity of her involvement in her relationship including many experiences of betrayal and her passion for freedom and justice, Frida Kahlo is a classic example of the Flowering/Psychopathic soul.

## Childhood

Frida's father, Guillermo Kahlo, was born in Germany and, as a young man he emigrated to Mexico where he became a photographer. Her mother was Matilde Calderón y González, a devout Catholic of indigenous Mexican and Spanish descent. Guillermo and Matilde did not have a happy marriage, but the couple had four daughters of which Frida was the third. Frida was a spirited and lively girl, her father's favourite. She adored her father and remained close to him throughout her life.

In a typical version of both Oral and Psychopathic wounding, Frida had a difficult relationship with her mother. Matilde fell pregnant again immediately after having Frida and gave birth to her youngest daughter, Christina, only 11 months later. She hired an Indian nurse to look after Frida and so we see early disruption to the mother-and-baby bonding during the Oral stage of Frida's infancy. During her adolescence Frida reacted against her mother's religious dogma, which did not fit at all with Frida's rebellious nature and love of freedom and change.

Frida had lifelong issues with her health. At the age of six she contracted polio which left her with a withered right leg; however, she remained an active and tomboyish little girl. She was an extremely bright child and later she was enrolled in the Escuela National Preparatoria, a prestigious school where she was one of only 35 female students. Frida planned to train to be a doctor but when she was 18 her life changed forever. The bus she was riding in crashed into a streetcar and Frida was very seriously injured. She broke her back, her collarbone and her pelvis, suffered multiple fractures to her right leg, and part of the bus pierced her abdomen and womb. Frida never fully recovered from her injuries. She lived with pain for the whole of her life, underwent numerous episodes of surgery and the injury to her uterus meant she was never able to carry a child. After the accident Frida was immobilized, encased in plaster body casts for three months, and it was during this time that she started painting. Her mother fixed up an easel over her bed and she had a mirror hung above her so that she could draw self-portraits.

Eventually Frida recovered enough to return to school. Here the famous artist Diego Rivera was painting a mural and Frida audaciously approached him and asked what he thought of her paintings. Diego encouraged her to continue to paint and became very interested in the young woman. Frida enjoyed flirting with Diego and provoking his jealous wife. Diego's marriage ended and in the summer of 1929 the 22-year-old Frida married the 42-year-old Diego. But Rivera was a notorious womanizer, and he continued to have affairs even a short time after marrying Frida, who was his third wife.

## Career

In 1930 Frida and Diego travelled to the US where Diego was commissioned to paint murals in San Francisco and had an exhibition in New York. Frida did not like America and as a communist she was offended by the trappings of capitalism. She longed for her native soil, took great pride in her Mexican heritage and caused a stir by going about dressed in her brightly coloured, traditional Mexican costumes.

In 1932 Frida became pregnant but had a miscarriage and became extremely depressed. Once again it was her art that helped her through a very dark time. She made paintings that symbolically represented her grief at her loss and graphically portrayed the physical pain of her experience. Frida wanted to return to Mexico but Diego enjoyed his celebrity status in America and the couple had fierce battles before Diego agreed to return to Mexico at the end of 1933. Here Diego had a special house built for them in Mexico, comprised of two separate homes, one small and one large, joined only by a bridge.

Diego resented having to return from the US and for a long time he was apathetic and dissatisfied before he started painting again. Then Frida was devastated to discover that he had started an affair with her younger sister Christina. Frida felt utterly betrayed by the two people in the world that she loved the most. It was an agonising time for her. Diego refused to put an end to the affair, and in one of his murals Diego included a portrait of Christina and her two children that obscured the image of Frida, pushed into the background. Frida, who was already in a poor state of health, had another miscarriage. In her grief Frida stopped painting altogether for a year. The next painting she did portrayed a murder scene and for many years in her paintings she returned to the theme of the agonising heartbreak she experienced in reaction to Diego's affair with Christina. She cut off her long hair and gave up wearing her beloved Mexican dresses. Eventually Frida moved out of the house Diego had built and went on a visit to New York. Frida began having love affairs of her own with both men and women but she discovered that nothing could replace her love for Diego and so she returned to him.

Diego was a Trotskyite, and when Leon Trotsky was expelled from Russia Diego helped to ensure that Trotsky was given asylum in Mexico. When Trotsky and his wife arrived in Mexico, Frida had a brief liaison with him. The affair did not last but Frida regained her self-confidence and now devoted herself to her painting, often returning to the theme of her childlessness.

Frida's art began to receive serious acclaim and in 1938 she participated, for the first time, in an exhibition in Mexico City. After that she staged a one-woman show in a gallery in New York. She was much admired by André Breton, the leader of the surrealist movement, who invited her to exhibit in Paris. Frida hesitated because she wanted to return to Mexico but Diego persuaded her to go to Paris. Frida's exhibition was a resounding success and she met many artists, including Kandinsky and Picasso, who greatly admired her work. One of her self-portraits was bought by the Louvre, the first work by a Mexican artist ever purchased by the renowned museum. But Frida came to despise the chic Parisian intellectuals she met in the surrealist circles and she returned to Mexico.

When Frida got back to Mexico, Diego asked her for a divorce. In his own autobiography Diego maintained that the divorce was his attempt to protect Frida from the pain of their marriage when he knew he could not be faithful to her. Diego wanted his freedom and he wanted Frida to be more independent. But Frida did not welcome this kind of independence and she became depressed and turned to drink.

Once again Frida sublimated her grief through her art, and after the divorce she painted one of her most famous works, entitled *The Two Fridas*. It is a double self-portrait showing two versions of herself, both with her heart exposed to view and bleeding to death. Later, Diego wrote of this painting:

*Frida is the only person ever to have ripped open her breast and torn out her heart to tell the truth in biological terms and say what is felt inside.*

Soon Frida was proud to be earning money from her commissions and claimed that she would never again take money from Diego.

When Trotsky was assassinated in Coyoacán, Mexico City, Diego fled to San Francisco as he was suspected of being an accomplice. Frida joined him there to undergo surgery conducted by her American friend Dr Eloesser. The doctor recognized that a large part of Frida's illness was brought on by her emotional suffering after the divorce, and he worked hard as the go-between in an aim to reunite the couple. He explained to Frida that Diego loved her very much but she could not hope that he would ever be faithful to one woman. To Diego, he explained the ill-effects of the divorce on Frida's health. Dr Eloesser was successful and on Diego's birthday in 1940 the couple remarried. When Frida and Diego returned to Mexico City, Frida went to live in the Blue House, the house where she was born, and this now became her world. Her success as a painter continued to grow and she was appointed to teach at the Academy of Painting and Sculpture.

However, by 1944 Frida had to reduce her teaching hours because of her declining health. She spent a good deal of time in bed and had to wear a steel brace to support her back. In the following years she painted several pictures depicting her suffering. *The Broken Column* is a self-portrait showing her naked body encased in the brace, her spine symbolized by a broken column of stone and her skin pierced all over with nails. Another painting shows the scars on her back after surgery and in another of her most famous paintings, *The Wounded Deer*, she portrays herself as a deer, bleeding and pierced with many arrows.

Her relationship with Diego was now one of equals: Frida was financially independent and much more assertive than when they married the first time. But now Frida knew how important Diego was to her and a number of her paintings depict her powerful love for him. In two of her self-portraits, *Diego in My Thoughts* and *Diego and I*, she paints herself with a picture of Diego's face on her forehead in the place of the third eye or the 6th chakra. Always Frida's face shows much sadness, possibly because Diego had launched into yet another love affair. She now related to Diego in a more maternal way.

*He's my child every minute, my newborn, every minute of the day, my very own.*

Frida depicted Diego in one of her paintings as a wise child held in her arms while she is held in the arms of Mother Earth who is held in the arms of the Universe. In one of his murals painted at this time, Diego also includes a portrait of himself as a child with Frida standing behind him as a protective maternal figure. However, in Frida's diary she revealed that Diego was much more than a substitute child: he was everything to her – her whole world.

> *Diego beginning*
> *Diego founder*
> *Diego my child*
> *Diego my darling*
> *Diego painter*
> *Diego my lover*
> *Diego 'my husband'*
> *Diego my friend*
> *Diego my mother*
> *Diego my father*
> *Diego my son*
> *Diego = me*
> *Diego universe*
> *Diversity in unity*
> *Why do I call him my Diego? He has never been,*
> *and never will be, mine. He belongs to himself.*

In 1950 Frida's health went into a serious decline. She spent a year in hospital, having seven operations on her spine. Diego took a room next to hers in the hospital but he was not consistently supportive. Her doctor noted:

> *The fluctuations in her health while she was in hospital depended entirely on Diego's behaviour.*

When she returned from the hospital to the Blue House, Frida's style of painting changed. She was in constant pain, drinking and surviving on pain-killers. In a series of still-life pictures of fruits and vegetables she used thick paint and heavy brushwork, and the torn fruits and vegetables appear as symbols of her broken body.

In April 1953 a friend organized Frida's first one-woman show in Mexico City. Frida made a dramatic entrance, arriving in an ambulance and carried in on a stretcher to where her four-poster bed had been set up in the gallery as an integral part of the exhibition. Diego described her sitting happily in the room, pleased that so many people had come to honour her. But he also recognized that this was Frida's farewell to life. Later it was discovered that Frida's right leg had become gangrenous. It had to be amputated and she sank into a deep depression.

On 2 July 1954, Frida made her last public appearance. She defied her doctor's orders and went with Diego on a demonstration of solidarity with the overthrown left-wing government of Guatemala. She died eleven days later. There was some speculation that she may have finally ended her life by taking an overdose of drugs. Frida's last painting depicts slices of a watermelon, with one bearing the inscription 'Viva la Vida' – Long Live Life.

77

The Flowering or Psychopathic Soul

# Interpreting the Horoscope of Frida Kahlo

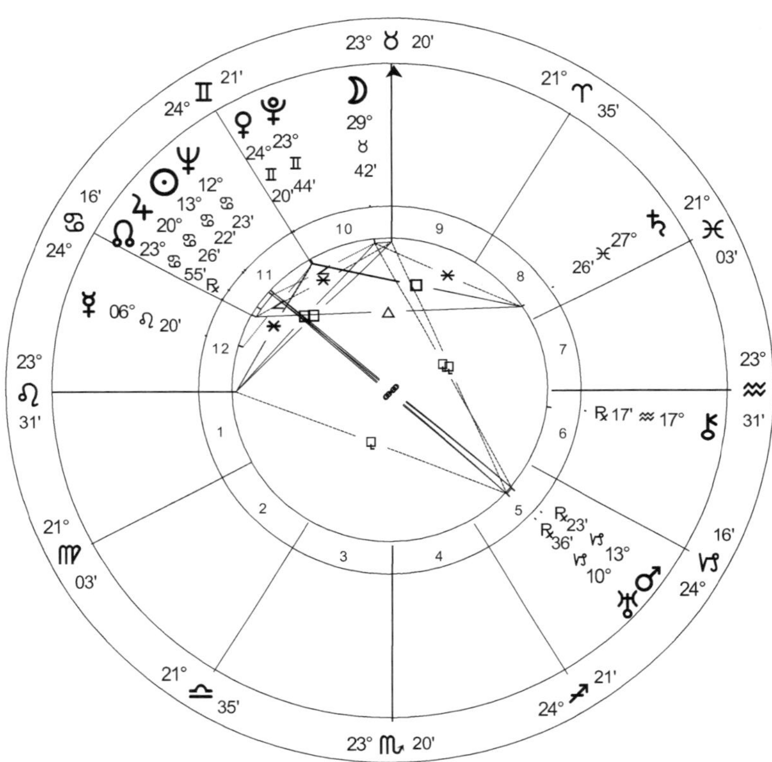


**Frida Kahlo**

8.30 am Saturday July 6 1907, Coyoacan Mexico

Placidus House System

Chart from Solar Fire version 7 Astrolabe, www.alabe.com.

## Dominant Planets and Themes

Frida's chart has two major themes: the influence of the Moon and the configuration formed by the fiery planets the Sun, Jupiter and Mars.

### The Moon

Frida's chart is overlit by the Moon, shining out from the zenith of the chart. The Moon is exalted in Taurus, square to the Ascendant, semi-square the Sun, conjunct the Midheaven and it is the ruler of the stellium in Cancer that includes the Sun and the North Node.

The Moon, Neptune and Venus represent different facets of the feminine principle: the non-rational world of feelings and the urge for relationship. In Frida's chart the prominence of the feminine principle is echoed by Neptune closely conjunct the Sun in Cancer; a huge emphasis on feelings and the longing for union and communion. Venus is in a difficult placement, besieged by a conjunction with Pluto and a square from Saturn. However, the involvement of the outer planets with Venus also emphasizes the importance of relationship and the likelihood that much transformational work will be undertaken in this area.

### Mars

There are three sets of conjunctions in this chart but the Mars-Uranus conjunction is particularly influential and in its 5th house placement it is one of the major indications of Frida's creative genius. This conjunction is at the apex of an uneasy triangle, a 'Finger of the World' formed by sesquiquadrates to the Ascendant and the Moon and MC. The closer the orb between two planets, the more powerful is their influence on each other. The opposition from Mars to the Sun is exact; it represents one of the core issues of the chart and gives a major key to Frida's passionate and heroic character.

#### Sun and Moon

With her Leo Ascendant, the ruler of Frida's chart is the Sun which is in Cancer and conjunct Neptune. From that information alone we can see that the dominant Characterologies described by the chart are the Rooting/Oral type – associated with Neptune, the Moon and the sign of Cancer – and the Flowering/Psychopath type – associated with Mars, Jupiter and the Sun. The emphasis on the Rooting/Oral and Flowering/Psychopath Characterologies also appears in the sesquiquadrate between the Moon and Mars, and the semi-square between the Sun and Moon. Symbols of the duality of the Sun and the Moon appeared in many of Frida's paintings.

# 78

## Indications of Characterology in Frida Kahlo's Chart
## Germination/Schizoid Energy

### URANUS

- *Uranus opposition the Sun (orb 2° 56')*
- *Uranus conjunct Mars (orb 2° 47')*
- *Uranus sesquiquadrate the Ascendant (2° 05')*
- *Uranus sesquiquadrate the MC (2° 44')*

### MERCURY

- *Mercury in the 12th house*

### CHIRON

- *Chiron in the 6th house*

**Uranus**

Frida's Germination/Schizoid energy is indicated by the opposition from Uranus to the Neptune-Sun-Jupiter conjunction. At first glance this resembles Jimi Hendrix's Sun-Uranus opposition and both artists were fantastically innovative and original creators. But the other planets involved are different. In Jimi's chart, the opposition has a cool energy with the Sun in the cosmic 12th house conjunct harmonious Venus and his Uranus was conjuncted by cold Saturn. In Frida's chart the configuration has heat! The Sun is in Watery Cancer and sensitized by the conjunction to Neptune but Cancer is a turbulent and emotional sign. The Sun is warmed by the conjunction with golden Jupiter and by the opposition to Mars. Frida's Sun is in the 11th house, bringing the heroic Flowering energy of the revolutionary. So, where Jimi's Uranus is restrained by the calming influences of Venus and Saturn, Frida's Uranus is fired up and expanded by the influences of Mars and Jupiter.

The Schizoid wound brings difficulty in the life of the body and Frida's physical health was a dominant factor in her life. Many of Frida's paintings communicated her physical sufferings and one of her most famous pictures, *The Broken Column*, is a powerful image of her fractured spine. We can see this and the shattering impact of the bus accident in the Uranus conjunction with Mars. Mars is the planet that rules blood and muscle and it represents the instinctual, visceral life of the body.

Aspects to Uranus are indications of a soul open to the higher vibrations of the 6th and 7th chakras and the gifts of the Germination soul – radical innovation and genius. With Uranus placed in the 5th house of creativity and Neptune closely conjunct the Sun we see Frida's expressing her creativity in an original symbolic visual language that completely transcended the limitations of the prevailing concepts of what a painting might be.

The stellium in Cancer, which includes the Sun and the North Node, falls in the 11th house, which is the house of group awareness and political ideals, and Frida expressed her Uranian spirit through her passionate involvement in revolutionary left-wing politics

### Mercury

Frida's Mercury is in the 12th house and is almost unaspected, with only a very wide sextile to the Moon and a wide semi-square to Pluto. The 12th house represents the gestation period and so we can interpret Mercury in the 12th as an indication of the presence of the Germination/Schizoid energy during Frida's time in utero – i.e. as a primal energy very close to the source of life. The 12th house represents the collective, and Mercury in the 12th house gave Frida the ability to go into the dream-world, beyond the limitations of everyday thinking, and to communicate through the language of symbols in her emotional self-portraits. As is so often the case with 12th house planets, Frida's communication through art was her gift to the world.

## Chiron

Frida's Chiron falls in Aquarius in the 6th house, the house to do with issues of health, and this is a prime indication of a life in which consciousness is entwined with the physical challenges of being in a body. So this placement is another indication of Germination/Schizoid energy emerging as Frida's lifelong problems with her health and her chronic pain following her accident. We can speculate that someone with greater emphasis on the Schizoid defence might have dealt with the physical distress caused by the accident by escaping to the mental plane and attempting to completely disassociate from the life of the body. However, Frida has the Moon in Taurus, the Sun in Cancer and Mars in Capricorn. These are signs and planets that emphasize the experience of being in a body; of a life lived in the material world – the opposite of the Schizoid defence. So we see that in Frida's life she had to deal with Uranus and Chiron bringing the Schizoid dread of the suffering of the body while her Taurus Moon and Cancer Sun could only be expressed through the life of the body. With Frida's Neptune conjunct the Sun, I am reminded of the image of Hans Andersen's Little Mermaid who felt every step she took with her human feet was as if she were walking on knives. Chiron trines Frida's Venus-Pluto conjunction in Gemini and this brings wounding to Frida's image of herself as a woman and in the unfolding of her relationships (including her relationships with women).

This placement is a classic illustration of the impact of Chiron, who brings irremediable anguish – a pain that is often nobody's fault but which cannot be reversed. In this kind of situation the individual is presented with a choice: whether to succumb to bitterness (the poison which comes from Ereshkigal's realm) or to following Chiron's numinous light into a place of acceptance and opening to Spirit. The way that Frida worked through this distressing paradox gave us the gift of her paintings that express both the agony and the beauty of the body.

# 79

## Indications of Characterology in Frida Kahlo's Chart

## Rooting/Oral Energy

### THE MOON

- *Moon square the Ascendant (orb 0 ° 11')*
- *Moon conjunct the MC (orb 6 ° 22')*
- *Moon sextile Saturn (orb 2 ° 16')*
- *Moon semi-square the Sun (orb 1 ° 20')*
- *Sun and stellium in Cancer*
- *North Node in Cancer*
- *Moon sesquiquadrate Mars (orb 1 ° 19')*

### NEPTUNE

- *Neptune conjunct the Sun, chart ruler (orb 0 ° 59')*
- *Neptune semi-square the Moon (orb 2 ° 19')*

### SATURN

- *Saturn in the 8th house*

### The Moon

The Moon is a powerful influence in Frida's chart: square to the Ascendant and conjunct the Midheaven. Here we see the emotional nature of the Moon and the Rooting/Oral soul as a dominant part of Frida's identity, influencing both her way of meeting with life (Ascendant) and her aspirations in life (MC). The Moon is exalted in Taurus where it expresses the Essence of the feminine principle – embodiment in the world of matter. Taurus brings a profound love for the fauna and flora of the earth and this was evident in Frida's paintings, which included images of plants and animals as well as symbols of the fertility of the earth such as the Mexican earth goddess Cihuacoatl. Frida's paintings expressed the feminine nature of both

Cancer and Taurus: a manifest recording of a lifetime's experience of what it is to be a woman. Diego described Frida as:

> *The first woman in the history of art to treat, with absolute and uncompromising honesty, those themes which exclusively affect women.*

Frida's Moon is semi-square to Neptune and these are the two planets associated with the Rooting/Oral stage. We know that there were difficulties for baby Frida during her nurturing phase. Frida was less than one year old when her sister Christina was born and her exhausted mother gave Frida into the care of an Indian wet-nurse. Frida explored the psychological impact of this in the painting *My Nurse and I*, depicting herself in the arms of the nurse who wears a Mexican-Indian stone mask instead of a face. This premature separation from her mother goes with Oral wounding and this shows up in Frida's chart in the sextile to the Moon from Saturn in Pisces, and the placement of Saturn in the 8th house. The 8th house has to do with intimacy in adult relationships but the foundation for the capacity for emotional communion is laid down in bonding with mother during the Oral stage. Saturn in the 8th house represents something harsh in close relationships that interferes with trust.

Apart from the sextile from Saturn, the other planet in aspect to the Moon is a sesquiquadrate from Mars and these two aspects illustrate the basic wounding in Frida's personality – swinging between the feeling of Oral abandonment represented by the Saturn aspect and the volatile Psychopathic fire represented by Mars. Oral wounding is a classic foundation for Psychopathic wounding when a girl, feeling deprived of maternal care, transfers her attachment to her father so that the natural father-daughter bond becomes unbalanced and overcharged. So begins the cycle of triangular relationships and betrayals that are the hallmark of Psychopathic wounding. A person with Oral wounding tries to meet their needs by clinging on to others, particularly in romantic partnerships. Frida Kahlo appeared to be a powerful, fiery woman but she was also sensitive, vulnerable and needy, and her Oral wounding was part of the difficulties she encountered in her relationship with Diego.

**Neptune**

Frida's Neptune is also strong in the chart: conjunct the Sun and in aspect to all the planets involved in the Cancer/Capricorn opposition. Neptune here emphasizes the Rooting/Oral soul's longing for love. However, Neptune is very closely opposed by Mars and yet again we see Frida oscillating between the feminine energy of Neptune's longing to merge and the masculine energy of the Martian urge to separate. The classic expression of the opposition between Neptune and Mars is the polarity of victim and perpetrator (also represented by the Pluto-Venus conjunction) and this dynamic played out repeatedly in the drama of Frida's relationship with Diego.

The nature of Neptune is essentially mystical, taking us into the non-physical realms of Spirit and the imagination. Frida's facility with artistic symbolism arose from her Neptune-Sun conjunction (as well as her 12th house Mercury) as she found a way to communicate feelings that could not have been expressed in a literal way. Frida lived out the entire range of expression of Neptune and the Rooting/Oral soul – going from heartbroken feelings of victimization and abandonment to the exalted capacity to create exquisite images that conveyed the longing and loving and suffering of her human heart.

# 80

## Indications of Characterology in Frida Kahlo's Chart
## Budding/Masochist Energy

**PLUTO**

- *Pluto conjunct Venus (orb 0 ° 36')*
- *Pluto exactly sextile the Ascendant (orb 0 ° 13')*

**SATURN**

- *Saturn square Venus (orb 3 ° 06')*
- *Saturn trine Jupiter (orb 7 ° 00')*

**CHIRON**

- *Chiron trine Venus (orb 7 ° 03')*

### Pluto Conjunct Venus

Frida's Leo Ascendant, the emphasis on watery Cancer and the fiery combination of the Sun, Jupiter and Mars made Frida passionately, emotionally expressive, the opposite of Masochist withholding. But the conjunction of Venus and Pluto has a different energy. Venus is more of a 'Solar' goddess in that, unlike the Moon and Neptune, she can operate in the outer world, happy in the rational light of consciousness. On its own Venus in Gemini is charming, playful, artistic, intelligent, witty and light. But with a close conjunction from Pluto, a trine from Chiron, and Saturn squaring from Pisces, Frida's Venus is besieged by difficulty.

Venus and Pluto represent the polarity of Inanna, the naive and charming sky goddess, and Ereshkigal, the vengeful 'Dark Lady from Below'. Negative Pluto goes with power struggles, envy and jealousy and this placement suggests rivalry among the women in Frida's family. Frida's mother was a strict, repressive Catholic and the Pluto-Venus conjunction in the 10th house describes mother and daughter struggling with oppression versus freedom in the expression of sensual, sexual Venus. Venus and Pluto are widely semi-square to Mercury, which represents siblings: this aspect relates to Frida's terrible hurt when her sister Christina had an affair with Diego. Frida was shattered when she discovered the affair and went into a prolonged depression. This is a painful story of Psychopathic betrayal, wounding and defeat in the arena of relationship and it is when a person feels rejected and defeated that Pluto turns into Medusa's paralysis or Ereshkigal's despair.

Pluto in aspect to Venus often brings experiences of profound wounding in relationship, but in Essence Pluto is about the deep instinctual power of the body. Frida's Venus-Pluto conjunction represents the potential to express the Goddess energy through deep intimate contact and sexual passion, and Frida certainly brought that into her relationship with Diego and with others. Frida's was never an easy Venus and Frida's heart was definitely broken; however, Frida's heart did not give way. Pluto gives a person great stamina and, ultimately, Pluto is about transformation and healing. The aspects from Chiron, Saturn and Pluto to Frida's Venus can be regarded as an indication of a lifelong process of transformation in the area of relationship. Frida never shut down her feelings, she did not stop loving, and in the course of her life she healed much of her Oral wounding and became a stronger and more independent woman. In the end she found that she could not give up on Diego and I like to think that this was a love that transcended her Oral dependency, Masochistic defeat and Psychopathic lust for conquest.

Venus in Gemini in the 10th house is, of course, yet another sign of the soul of an artist. Venus squaring Saturn often represents a career as an artist; the aspect from Pluto gave Frida's paintings their incredible psychological depth; and from the Venus Chiron trine she got her subject matter, which was so often an expression of the pain of the body. With her highly personal autobiographical images she took Venus into Pluto's realm and broke many artistic and cultural taboos, particularly those surrounding female sexuality and the female body.

# 81

## Indications of Characterology in Frida Kahlo's Chart

## Flowering/Psychopathic Energy

### MARS

- *Mars exactly opposite the Sun (orb 0° 01')*
- *Mars opposition Jupiter (orb 7° 03')*
- *Mars sesquiquadrate the Moon (orb 1° 19')*
- *Mars in the 5th house*

### THE SUN

- *Leo Ascendant*
- *Sun conjunct Jupiter (orb 7° 04')*
- *Sun semi-square the Moon (orb 1° 20')*

### JUPITER

- *Jupiter conjunct the North Node (orb 3° 29')*
- *Jupiter sextile MC (orb 2° 54')*

### ELEVENTH HOUSE

- *Stellium of Neptune, Sun, Jupiter and the North Node in the 11th house*

We have seen that Frida's infant bonding with her mother was disrupted and she transferred her affections to her father. With Jupiter and Neptune either side of the Sun, Frida adored her father and she was his favourite child. Guillermo Kahlo was born in Germany and came to Mexico as a young man, and Frida's Sun-Jupiter conjunction speaks of a father who brought into her life the idea of faraway lands and the possibility of other ways of living. Frida disliked her mother's rigid Catholicism, her parent's marriage was not a happy one and so Frida was a typical example of the Psychopathic type – with an idealized view of her father, and in a tangle of rejection and rivalry with her mother.

Frida has a Leo Ascendant and Mercury in Leo but these are the only placements in Fire, the majority of the planets are in Water and Earth and this is not typical of the Flowering/Psychopathic type. What we can see is that the energy of Fire comes through the fiery nature of the planets in aspect to the Sun; in particular the exact opposition from Mars.

### Leo Ascendant and the Sun

Frida's Leo Ascendant is a classic indication of the heroic, temperamental persona of the Flowering/Psychopathic soul. Leo needs to shine and Frida loved attention. With expansive and dramatic Jupiter conjunct the Sun in Cancer, and the Moon squaring the Ascendant, Frida's feelings were never far from the surface and her emotions would easily boil over into big emotional displays. The Neptune-Sun conjunction in Cancer is an indication of sensitivity and vulnerability but it is also an indication of unbounded emotion and, with Leo rising and Mars exactly opposing the Sun and Jupiter, Frida's expression of her feelings came with heat! Frida's Sun is closely aspected by all the planets of Fire and, typical of the valiant Flowering soul, Frida always spoke her truth; it was not in her nature to repress her emotions.

### Sun in the 11th House

Cancer is a Cardinal sign and Cardinal energy brings initiative and leadership, which are core qualities of the Flowering/Psychopathic individual. Like the Knights of the Round Table, the Flowering/Psychopathic soul is a heroic champion of justice and they are often inclined to take up the cause of the underdog.

Frida has a heavily tenanted 11th house, including the Sun and the North Node. This is a prime indication of the Flowering/Psychopath soul as a visionary leader seeking social justice and Frida's political aspirations were of paramount importance in her life. She was a communist and a crusading revolutionary and she despised the trappings of capitalism that she found in the US and the effete intellectualism of the European surrealists. Frida was strongly identified with the development of the Mexican nation and her political and philosophical idealism is a major theme that runs through her art. In a time when inequality between genders and races was still the norm, Frida's art was focused on her experience of being female and it incorporated imagery derived from her indigenous Mexican ancestry. When she was abroad she often caused a stir by wearing her traditional Mexican costume. In the last years of her life Frida's paintings became more overtly political and two of her final paintings were homages to Marx and Stalin: a statement of her utopian hopes that egalitarian politics would free the world. In her last public appearance, just eleven days before she died, Frida came in her wheelchair to a demonstration against political interference from the CIA.

**Mars**

Mars is the planet most associated with the energy of the Flowering/Psychopathic type. Although Frida's Mars falls in an Earth sign it is exalted in Capricorn. Mars is very powerful in the chart, and in the exact opposition to the Sun it appears like the head of an arrow channelling the Sun's radiance through the 5th house of creativity and love affairs. Mars represents the raw power of the Will, driving into action, making a person impetuous and often oblivious to the consequences or to the impact of their actions on others. It is likely that Frida would have experienced post-traumatic stress disorder in the wake of her accident, leaving her with a heightened sense of tension and anxiety, giving a raw edge to her natural Leonine fire and making her Mars extra volatile and impulsive. Mars represents the red-blooded energy of desire and gave Frida her passionate sexual nature and, with the conjunction to free-spirited Uranus, Frida had numerous love affairs with women as well as men. Above all, the placement of Frida's Uranus-Mars conjunction describes her creative drive, the divine fire of her genius and the inspired visual language through which she expressed her inner life.

Uranus is a mental energy and in its positive expression it brings the unemotional clarity of the Witness, the capacity to observe without involvement. When in aspect to Mars, the Airy Uranian detachment often has a cooling effect on Martian aggression. However, the extremes of hard Mars-Uranus aspects can bring icy cold detachment and an absence of empathy that represents the potential for cruelty. Dealing with cruelty, their own or when it comes at them from others, is one of the major challenges for the Psychopathic defence.

Frida's Uranus and Mars fall in close opposition to her Neptune-Sun conjunction. Neptunian individuals often become victims and Frida might often have felt herself the victim of the cruelty of life through the very nature of her accident. Frida also experienced cruelty in her relationship with Diego and it is interesting to note that the issue of Uranus aspecting Mars was one that they both shared. Diego had a Cardinal T-square with Mars in Capricorn opposition Saturn in Cancer and square to Uranus in Libra. Diego also had Neptune conjunct his Taurus Moon and we can see how their two charts were a mirror of each other and of the polarization of Neptunian tenderness and Martian cruelty that played out in their relationship.

The hallmark of the Psychopathic wound is the turmoil of triangular relationships and the issue of betrayal. Frida was still a very young woman when she set out to win Diego from his wife – from the outset their relationship was founded in a love triangle. Diego Rivera was twenty years older than Frida, so clearly the relationship had an element of the Psychopathic father-daughter bonding patterns. And, on another level, Frida and Diego were twin souls with a destiny to work out and, however complicated their story became, their relationship was a journey of consciousness, learning and growing through the challenges of the Rooting and Flowering stages.

## Jupiter

Frida has Jupiter conjunct the Sun, which is yet another classic indication of the heroic nature of the Flowering/Psychopathic soul. In her life Frida expressed all the positive qualities of Jupiter: an inspired visionary, an adventurous traveller, physically journeying to distant lands as well as making great inner journeys of the mind. However, Jupiter represents the principle of expansion and, overheated by intense contact with the Sun and Mars, expansion can easily turn to inflation. Frida's Jupiter is an indication of the grandiosity of Narcissistic wounding and the Psychopthic defence – the child oscillating between the demand to match up to some inflated ideal and her inner feelings of worthlessness. A strong Jupiter is often associated with fame or with individuals who appear larger than life, and one effect of Frida's Jupiter was to inflame her emotional life into high drama acted out in a very public way.

However, Jupiter is more impersonal than the other planets of Fire. In the HEF the energy of Jupiter is associated with the upper reaches of the Hara line – to do with purpose and meaning on the soul level. Its placement in the 11th house, conjunct the North Node, speaks of Frida's intense concerns for political and philosophical questions and the issues of justice and freedom. Frida was someone who could see beyond the accepted limitations of society to an expanded vision of a better world.

# 82

## Indications of Characterology in Frida Kahlo's Chart

## Harvest/Rigid Energy

### VENUS

- *Venus square Saturn (orb 3 ° 06')*
- *Venus sextile the Ascendant (orb 0 ° 49')*

### SATURN

- *Saturn sextile the Moon (orb 2 ° 12')*
- *Saturn sextile the MC (4 ° 16')*
- *Saturn trine Jupiter (orb 7 ° 00')*

### TENTH HOUSE

- *Taurus MC*
- *Moon in Taurus in the 10th house*

#### Venus

Frida had Venus square Saturn, a notoriously difficult placement when the goddess of love and happiness meets the lord of judgement and limitation. The negative expression of Saturn is the cold criticism of the Patriarch and, together, the two planets associated with the Rigid ideals of the Superego can easily coalesce into a Perfectionist Inner Critic.

In a woman's chart the placement of Venus describes her image of herself as a woman. Saturn square Venus becomes the voice of the Inner Critic who constantly reminds her of the ways in which she is not good enough, not beautiful enough, not fertile enough, not pleasing enough. When she discovered that Diego was having an affair with her sister, Frida suffered agonies, comparing herself unfavourably to Christina, and she sank into a depression which lasted a year – depression is frequently associated with Saturn and Pluto, particularly when in aspect to Venus.

Venus is the principle of relationship but the first requirement of Venus is that we are in good relationship with ourselves – self-esteem and the ability to love and nurture the self are prerequisites for a healthy relationship. We have seen that the undervalued and undernourished Oral type desperately seeks love and reassurance from others in the belief that on their own they are simply 'not enough'. But as long as they remain trapped in the belief of their inadequacy they can never create a relationship of equals. While Frida remained caught in the patterns of Oral dependency and Psychopathic betrayal her relationship with Diego brought her much pain – the negative expression of Venus conjunct Pluto and square Saturn.

Frida's fragile Gemini Venus was beset with difficult energies, and she had a strong connection to what Eckhart Tolle calls the 'pain-body of the Feminine'. Yet over the course of her life we can see the challenging aspects from Saturn, Pluto and Chiron emerging as agents of transformation and healing. It was through her 10th house Venus, in the form of her paintings, that Frida expressed her Essence and with the square to Saturn and semi-square to Mercury she achieved mastery and greatness as an artist. And, over time, we can see the healing light of Chiron and the alchemical transformation of Pluto occurring as Frida took more and more of her own power and found her strength. In her later years Frida grew away from her Oral dependency; she was no longer financially reliant on Diego but earned an income of her own and gained worldwide recognition and respect for her paintings. Saturn rules the passage of time and the coming of maturity, and in her later years Frida found the wisdom of acceptance, which is the gift of the Harvest soul, bowed to her fate and remarried Diego, this time negotiating the relationship on her own terms.

## Saturn

Frida's Saturn falls in the 8th house, the house to do with intimacy and deep contact in relationship. The 8th house is connected to the Oral stage for it is in our infant relationship with Mother that we first learn to trust in the possibility of communion with another human being. Saturn in the 8th house often expresses as something harsh: coldness and rejection in relationships of intimacy where we are most vulnerable and exposed in our longing for contact. So Frida's Venus square Saturn in the 8th speaks of her early Oral wounding. However, it also speaks of long-term loyalty, one of the qualities of the Harvest/Rigid type.

We have seen that with Venus in Gemini, the sign of communication, in the 10th house of ambition and achievement, Frida sublimated her suffering through her art. From the view of Saturn and Venus as symbols of the positive expression of the Harvest soul, Saturn squaring Venus gave Frida the determination to manifest her artistic vision, to continue to paint even when she was in pain and confined to her bed. And it was in this positive use of her Saturnian power of determination and clarity of intention, and in the resulting success that she achieved as an artist that Frida's Oral wounding began to heal.

## Taurus Moon and MC

Frida has the Moon in Taurus in the 10th house, conjunct the MC, square her Ascendant and sextile Saturn, and it is the ruler of the North Node and stellium in the 11th house. This emphasis on Taurus at the zenith of the chart expresses the energy of the Harvest/Rigid soul.

The concern of the Harvest soul is to manifest results in the physical world. Taurus is associated with the sensual pleasures of the body including love of the arts; Venus, the ruler of the MC, is also in the 10th house, the Moon and Venus are both in aspect to Saturn, and these are the energies of earthly creative manifestation contributing to Frida's great success as an artist.

The emphasis on the Moon and Venus, on Taurus and Cancer, represents the energy patterns of a soul expressing through the feminine principle, and Frida's experience of being female was central to her art. In a classic expression of the energy of Cancer and Taurus, 'home' was of great importance to her. In all her trials Frida was sustained by her sense of home and roots – the nourishment she got from places like the Blue House where she was born and where she died, and the deep roots that anchored her into her homeland, Mexico. However unconventional and tempestuous her life seemed, with her Taurus MC Frida's ultimate aspiration was to find peace. Having lived through half a century of political upheaval and two world wars, Frida's Taurus Moon speaks of her longing for harmony and stability, and the dove of peace appears several times in the last of her paintings

**Conclusion**

Frida's physical illnesses gave her an awareness of the fragility of the human body which she expressed in all her paintings. Nor did she flinch from communicating the truth of her emotional world. Above all it was her heroic Flowering/Psychopathic courage that sustained her through the storms of her great love for her husband and left us with the gift of her vision.

# 83

# Frida Kahlo's Human Energy Field

We have seen that the dominant theme in Frida's chart is the contrasting energy of the sensitive nature of the Moon and the extrovert energy of the planets of Fire – the Sun, Jupiter and Mars.

Much of Frida's chart expresses through Water, through the Sun and the stellium in Cancer; through the overlighting presence of the Moon (ruler of Cancer). The emphasis on Water is echoed by the influences of Neptune (ruler of Pisces) conjuncting the Sun, and Pluto (ruler of Scorpio) conjuncting Venus. The element of Water is strongly associated with the Rooting/Oral phase, and Saturn in Pisces in the 8th house is a likely indication of Oral wounding. Nevertheless, I consider Frida's dominant Characterology to have been the Flowering/Psychopathic type. This may seem strange because I have said that the Flowering/Psychopathic soul is associated with Fire and Frida has only one planet in a Fire sign – Mercury in Leo – however, her Ascendant is in Leo and this demonstrates the importance of the Ascendant in the chart. Above all, I see the powerful influence of the intertwining of the planets of Fire in the opposition between Mars and the Sun-Jupiter conjunction. This opposition appears as the central drive of the chart, with Mars directing the energy into the creativity of the 5th house and all electrified by the brilliance of Uranus.

Both the Rooting/Oral and the Flowering/Psychopath are strongly emphasized and we see how Frida used the Fire of her creative Fire to express the Water of her Lunar world.

### In the Human Energy Field

With Leo rising and with the exact aspect between the Sun and Mars, the first thing we perceive in Frida's HEF is the radiance of the Sun and her whole energy field lit up with the red glow of Mars. Beneath the surface of this red-gold light the feeling of Frida's HEF is the sensation of liquid, like water flowing, often turbulent – the oceanic, tidal, emotional energy of Cancer. Deeper in and lower down we come to the powerful light of her Taurus Moon. Frida's HEF differs from those of Marilyn Monroe and Jimi Hendrix in that the lower half of her field is not cold and deserted but filled with iridescent energy patterns arising from her connection to the fecundity of Nature and the fauna and flora of the physical world. In the core of her HEF Frida's central Hara line reaches down into the earth, illuminated with a rich stream of light arising from her Mexican heritage of indigenous peoples living from the land.

However, also in the lower part of Frida's aura are signs of the shattering impact and physical shock of her accident. In a person's HEF, the energy of the Moon appears as a translucent sphere of silvery light seated in the pelvic cradle, and this is the place where Frida is wounded. In the accident a metal rod went right through Frida's pelvis and pierced her womb. The line of tension that runs across Frida's chart in the opposition between Uranus-Mars and Neptune-Sun appears in her HEF as the energetic version of something cold and metallic driving through the lower part of her HEF, piercing her 2nd chakra and painfully fracturing the liquid light of the Moon. This configuration also has the resonance of past lives and ancestral issues of violent disturbance to the feminine energy of the Moon.

## The Auric Level

Frida's whole HEF is run through with lines of fracture emanating from the shock of the accident, and the wounding of Chiron in the 6th house appears as a black rift like a major fault line in her base chakra and extending up towards her heart. On the 1st level of Frida's field the lines of structure appear weakened, drained of energy; easily losing structure and coherence.

Frida's 2nd chakra also appears fractured, nevertheless it remains active, darkened by pain but illuminated with red-orange light and full of longing. The 2nd level of the field is a kaleidoscope of fluctuating colour changing like the Moon, sometimes pale and collapsing, at other times surging with waves of emotion and the intense dark currents of Pluto.

The 3rd chakra is more contracted than the 2nd, sometimes caving in under the pressure of self-doubt and attacks from the Inner Critic, sometimes overextended and lit up by the red light of Mars in a forcing current trying to gain mental control through the use of the Will.

The 4th chakra is also scarred with fracture lines and shadows of pain but it is full and open and the 4th level of the field is swirling and alive with currents of emotion lit up by the rose light of the heart which, again, is often overheated by the passionate red light of Mars.

Frida's 5th chakra has a different focus to that of the lower chakras. The 5th chakra is not fragmented by shock but it holds a note of grief which connects in the first place to the sadness of disconnection from her personal mother and also her alignment with the divine energy of the Goddess – a profound longing to simply live and love as a woman. The energy of Mercury comes through the throat chakra as the Essence of speech and communication, the place where we speak our truth, and Frida's 12th house Mercury connects here to the soul level and expresses through a creativity that connects to the dream world and the realm of the archetypes.

For many people in the west, the 6th chakra is focused upwards and outwards, directed towards the higher levels of the field and extending out into space. With the strength of her love of the earth, Frida's 6th chakra is more connected to the soul of the earth and to the spirit guides of her beloved Mexican heritage – more aligned with the earth-based spirituality of shamanism and less with the Christian ideal of Heaven. Frida's 6th chakra is large and full, with a beautiful warm, rich light, very different to the cosmic energy of Jimi Hendrix 6th chakra.

In her crown chakra Frida's Uranian genius connected upwards and far out to the realm of ideas where she collected the inspired and original visions of her art. However, this connection was intermittent, sometimes lost through the collapsing, sinking energy of pain and doubt, and sometimes the connection was broken by the forceful emotional heat of Mars and the will pushing the chakra system out of alignment.

## The Haric Level

Despite the shattering of the Lunar container and the lower chakras on the level of the aura, on the Haric level Frida's connection downwards into the earth appears strong, like the roots of a tree. Whereas in the aura, the 2nd chakra is badly damaged and full of pain, in the Hara the Lower Tan T'ien is a source of great power, the deep energy of Pluto. However, above the Lower Tan T'ien the Hara line is broken up by the impact of negative Saturn – the self-doubt impacting the 3rd chakra. Frida often reacted with the heat and passion and will of Mars boiling over, pushing the Hara line out of alignment, and so the connection from the Lower Tan T'ien to the Middle Tan T'ien is broken. Frida's heart holds the beautiful Goddess light of her tender longing for love and the Upper Tan T'ien appears as a fountain of Jupiter light of vision. However, the connection up to the Upper Tan T'ien is also often weakened by doubt and depression and pushed out of alignment by the emphasis on the will.

At the core of her HEF Frida radiates the beautiful qualities of her Essence – her celebration of the beauty of the earth, the mystical vision of the shaman, the idealism of the humanitarian, the fantastic skill of Mercury and Venus communicating from the great heart of the Goddess, the feminine principle seeking union and communion and love.

84

# THE HARVEST OR RIGID SOUL:
## Teilhard de Chardin

> *There is a communion with God, and a communion with the Earth, and a communion with God through the Earth.*
> Teilhard de Chardin, *The Cosmic Life*

Pierre Teilhard de Chardin was one of the great spiritual philosophers of the twentieth century. He was both a brilliant scientist and an innovative Christian theologian and he became a world authority in both callings. Teilhard was a palaeontologist and he envisioned a synthesis of Christianity and the science of evolution to suggest a spiritual interpretation of evolution which he called Christogenesis. He envisaged that the path of evolution would lead the human race into a worldwide expansion of consciousness and ultimate union with God.

Unfortunately, Teilhard's inspired vision of Christianity went far beyond the dogma of the Catholic church of his day and got him into serious trouble with the Vatican. Teilhard had doctorates in both geology and palaeontology; he was recognized as an expert in his field and in his early forties he was offered the prestigious post of Professor of Geology at the Institut Catholique in Paris. But Teilhard was a Jesuit priest and all his movements were subject to the approval of the Catholic Church. His radical spiritual teachings were extremely popular and were seen as a threat to the stability of the Church. Teilhard was denied permission to accept the position at the Institut. Instead he received orders from the Vatican to leave France. He was also told not to publish any of his theological writings.

Through many painful struggles of conscience, Teilhard remained obedient to the decrees of the Church and he spent the rest of his life in exile. He became a traveller who crossed continents, exploring and mapping uncharted regions, and returning to France only for short visits. For twenty years he was based in China where he became a leading light in a group of pioneering scientist explorers who were the first to map out the geology and prehistoric sites of the Far East. In 1929 Teilhard joined the team working on the famous excavations at Zhoukoudian. Here he played a vital role in analysing the fossilized remains of Peking Man, one of the first discoveries of the 'missing link' between apes and homo sapiens – a major breakthrough in palaeontology and confirmation of the theory of evolution.

## Cosmogenesis – The Philosophy of Teilhard de Chardin

Teilhard de Chardin developed a profound philosophy combining his knowledge of the physical processes of evolution with his belief that these were linked to a spiritual process of evolution. I have devoted some space, here, to describing his ideas, which are relevant to anyone on a spiritual path and relate well to the themes of this book.

In Teilhard's time, Darwin's theory of evolution was not yet fully verified or widely understood, so he was one of the few people of his day with a real understanding of the vast cosmic processes that led to the evolution of life on earth. Teilhard spoke of the human difficulty in comprehending the scale of things in the universe – of the 'dimensional hiatus' that separates our understanding of our everyday world from the concept of the billions of atoms and molecules that go to make up even a tiny drop of water, or the difficulty of conceiving of the aeons of time that passed before the first particles of matter emerged from the sea of galactic dust. With scientific objectivity, Teilhard saw that all forms of life had originally evolved from basic minerals. With spiritual understanding, he saw the light of God illuminating this process. For Teilhard:

> *Spirit is not the opposite pole of Matter: rather it is its very heart.*

According to Teilhard:

> *In every region of time and space, the stuff of the universe has an inner aspect of itself: co-extensive with the 'Without' there is a 'Within' to things.*

So the exterior world of form and matter is lined with an interior world which is formless. In Brennan healing terms we would say that everything in the universe has an Essence. Teilhard talks of an interdependent energy flowing between what is 'Within' and what is 'Without'; he believed that this energy is psychic in nature; it is Consciousness. This is the forerunner of contemporary ideas such as Candace Pert's concept of a 'field of information' (see p.128).

## The Law of Complexity Consciousness

Teilhard observed that a consistent feature in the history of evolution is the tendency for single units to gather together into groups of increasing complexity. Back in the depths of time the first particles were born, which came together to form the first atoms; atoms grouped together to form molecules and molecules grouped into mega-molecules, a mysterious halfway stage between minerals and the first living things. Eventually came the evolutionary leap into biological life as mega-molecules formed into living cells, the primal building blocks of life. Biological cells grouped together to form multi-cellular organisms, which eventually evolved into extremely complex life forms. Teilhard observed that with increasing complexity came increasing consciousness and he coined what he called the Law of Complexity Consciousness:

*The more complex a being is, the more aware does it become. In other words, the higher the degree of complexity in a living creature, the higher its consciousness.*

## Significant Thresholds and Evolutionary Leaps

Teilhard attributed cosmic significance to the evolution of Consciousness and saw:

*A current that runs from what is least conscious in Nature to what is most conscious.*

He also noted that this current is irreversible: a one-way street. He observed that we no longer live in a world in which it is possible to observe inorganic molecules of chemicals evolving into living organic cells – there is no evidence of this occurring anywhere on Planet Earth today. That first 'sensational event' occurred millions of years ago, never to be repeated, and we can see how the history of evolution is periodically marked by these extraordinary thresholds when sudden leaps of progress occur and life surges on to the next level of complexity.

In aeons past when Planet Earth came into being, it was made up of nothing but minerals. The first stage of the evolution of the Earth was the formation of the core of the planet known as the barysphere, followed by the formation of the Earth's crust, known as the lithosphere. The next critical stage was the appearance of water on the surface of the Earth, vital for the development of life as we know it – this was the development of the hydrosphere. When the first biological living cells were born the focus moved from the hydrosphere into the biosphere and the evolution of the myriad forms of biological life. For millions of years the biosphere continued to evolve through the development of animal species with increasingly sensitive and elaborate nervous systems. In Teilhard's view, this rising tide came to a halt with the emergence of *Homo sapiens* twenty or thirty thousand years ago and he believed that since that time no further evolutionary advances have occurred in the Biosphere. (Today Natural Scientists such as S H Buhner believe that biological change has not ended but is much more of a constantly occurring factor than Teilhard recognised. Different but sophisticated forms of consciousness and evolving networks of exchange exist among objects that would have been called inanimate in Teilhard's day. Symbiogenesis is a term used to describe the formation of more complex life forms from the union of two dissimilar simpler ones. These ideas are consistent with Teilhard's belief that the increasing complexity of a new system is the outcome of evolutionary development.)

Teilhard believed that the development of the complex brain and nervous system of *Homo sapiens* marked the final stage of evolution in the biosphere. He suggested that at this point evolution ceased to occur on the biological level but shifted directly into the realm of the psyche and the evolution of consciousness itself. Teilhard perceived the collective consciousness of the human race forming a sphere of psychic energy surrounding the Earth; he spoke of this sphere as the 'Soul of the World' and he named it the Noosphere.

*The irreversible rise of consciousness … marks the 'take-off point' between the biosphere and the Noosphere.*

## The Omega Point – Christogenesis

Teilhard saw evolution in the Noosphere leading to a point when human beings would attain a vastly expanded state of consciousness and awaken to their Divine nature. In keeping with the patterns of evolution Teilhard saw human beings as individual cells coming together to form the collective mind of the earth, the Body of Christ, (these days many prefer to see all forms of life on earth as contributors to this collective wave). He saw the tide of evolution converging on a final moment, which he called the Omega Point – when the collective consciousness of humanity would become at one with God. Teilhard named this evolutionary process 'Christogenesis'. He believed that the Omega Point exerted a pull that was the driving force behind evolution; a force that pulled humanity into ever-expanding consciousness and to the triumph of evolution in ultimate union with God.

*The sense of the Earth opening and exploding upwards into God; and the sense of God taking root and finding nourishment downwards into Earth.*

Teilhard goes further still to see the transforming power of evolution as a two-way process – the transformation of humanity is also the transformation of the Divine:

*I see in the World a mysterious product of completion and fulfilment for the Absolute Being.*

And this is where Teilhard departed from orthodox Christian thinking. Christian mysticism separates Spirit from Matter, stating that God must only be looked for in heaven. But for Teilhard, the Material world and the Spiritual world are not divided:

*Matter is the matrix of Spirit. Spirit is the higher state of Matter.*

When he writes of the Omega Point and Christogenesis, Teilhard speaks with passionate intensity, no longer the scientist but the great-hearted visionary theologian. He knew that it was only the power of love that could bring about the complete awakening and transformation of the human race:

*Matter becomes Spirit at just the same pace that love begins to spread universally.*

### Characterology

Teilhard achieved great things in his life. He lived always with the rigours and discipline of the life of a Jesuit priest and coped with the hardships of a geologist working in the field, carrying out research in remote areas of the world. He was a prolific writer, both as a scientist and as a Christian philosopher, and he was an important influence in the development of twentieth-century spirituality. With his qualities of discipline, endurance and loyalty, his many achievements and his far-sighted wisdom, I consider Teilhard de Chardin to be an example of the greatness of the Harvest/Rigid soul.

## Childhood

Born on 1 May 1881, Pierre Teilhard de Chardin was descended from distinguished noble ancestry. His father was a landed country squire and his mother was the grand-niece of Voltaire. Pierre, the fourth of eleven children, grew up on the family's estate in the rural heart of France. He had a traditional, Catholic, disciplined and educated upbringing and a secure family life.

Teilhard often spoke of an incident that occurred when, at the age of five, he was having his hair cut by his mother. The young Pierre picked up one of the curls and threw it into the fire. When he saw the hair burn away to nothing Teilhard was assailed by 'a terrible grief' as he registered the perishable nature of living things. He was deeply upset by the insecurity of life and longed to find evidence of something that would not die. For a while he consoled himself with a treasured piece of metal, believing he had found something indestructible. Later he was appalled when he discovered that his precious piece of metal was made of iron which started to rust! So from a very early age Teilhard was drawn into the question of the nature of mortality. In his search for some kind of permanent reality Pierre moved on from his little 'gods of iron' and started collecting rocks and crystals. His father was a keen student of natural history and helped to lay the foundation for his son's interest in the natural world.

Teilhard's mother played a different role in his life, nurturing his spiritual nature. He felt that she played a vital role in the development of his personal experience of Divine Love:

*Sucked in with my mother's milk, a supernatural Sense of the Divine had flowed into me side by side with the natural Sense of Plenitude.*

When he was twelve, Teilhard went to a Jesuit boarding school. Here he continued to develop his devotional relationship with Jesus Christ and at the age of eighteen he entered the Jesuit novitiate.

## Career

After he joined the Jesuits, and for the rest of his life, Teilhard was constantly on the move. He lived in England for several years and then in Egypt where his enthusiasm for natural history continued to flourish. Wherever he went he studied the local fauna and flora including gathering an extensive collection of fossils and he began corresponding with other naturalists.

At the age of thirty Teilhard was ordained a priest. He moved to Paris where he decided to pursue the study of geology and palaeontology and started taking courses and going out on field trips with eminent palaeontologists from the museums and colleges of Paris. While Teilhard was developing a promising scientific career he became very happily established in the intellectual and social milieu of Paris.

At the outbreak of the First World War Teilhard was called up for military service and became a stretcher-bearer. For nearly four years he was active in every engagement of his regiment and saw some of the most brutal battles of the war. During these years he received military honours and medals for his heroism in rescuing comrades during battle. Despite the overwhelming horror of the war, this was a period of intense spiritual growth for Teilhard. He came to see the front lines of battle as a kind of crucible of transformation.

*This tremendous war which so afflicts us, this remoulding, this universal longing for a new order, what are they but the shock, the tremor, the crisis beyond which we may glimpse a more synthetic organization of the human world?*

After the war Teilhard returned to Paris to continue his studies. In 1922 he received a doctorate with distinction, became Assistant Professor of Geology at the Institut Catholique and was elected president of the Geological Society of France. He also gave lectures which were extremely popular, speaking of his ideas about the significance of evolution in relation to Christianity.

But Teilhard's spiritual ideas did not go down well with the Catholic authorities and the Pope made an attack on evolution, on the 'new theology'. Teilhard decided to spend a short time away from France to allow the controversy which his ideas had stirred up to die down. The opportunity for field work came in an invitation from Emile Licent, a Jesuit scientist who was doing paleontological work in China. In the spring of 1923, with Jupiter in Scorpio opposing his Taurean planets, Teilhard set sail for China and soon undertook the first of his many research trips.

A year later Teilhard returned to Paris and resumed teaching at the Institut Catholique. But a copy of a theological paper that Teilhard had written made its way to Rome and Teilhard was ordered to sign a statement repudiating his ideas. He sought counsel with Father Valensin, an old trusted Jesuit friend. Valensin and Teilhard met with Teilhard's superior, who agreed to send to Rome a revised version of Teilhard's paper and his response to the statement of repudiation. While waiting to receive the reply from Rome, Teilhard continued teaching classes at the Institut and giving talks on his ideas about the spiritual nature of evolution. Teilhard's lectures were filled to capacity with students flocking to listen to this dynamic and exciting professor but the stir he was making disturbed a group of conservative French bishops. They reported him to Vatican and in 1925 Teilhard was again ordered to sign the statement repudiating his controversial theories and to leave France.

This was a major crossroads for Teilhard. His friends from the Institut advised him to leave the Jesuits and become a diocesan priest but his Jesuit friends advised him to sign the statement as a gesture of faith and loyalty to the Jesuit Order. This time it was Saturn, transiting through Scorpio, that opposed his Sun, then Neptune and Venus. After a week of retreat and reflection Teilhard signed the document.

In the spring of 1926 Teilhard set sail again for China. He still hoped to be able to find a way to express his views in a manner acceptable to the Catholic authorities and he now wrote *The Divine Milieu* – a mystical treatise expressing his love of the world and his vision of a human being as 'matter at its most incendiary stage'. When he returned to France he was eager to engage in discussion with his superiors but in June 1928 he was told that he must put an end to all his theological work, confine himself to scientific research and leave France.

This was a severe blow and, as Chiron in the heavens conjuncted his Saturn in Taurus, Teilhard returned to China with a heavy heart.

For the next eleven years Teilhard remained in exile while slow-moving Chiron made the long transit through his 12th house, conjuncting the planets one by one and finally reaching his Ascendant in 1937. In addition to the pain of exile Teilhard also suffered the loss of his parents and two siblings, who all died in his absence.

During these years Teilhard took part in numerous scientific expeditions and carried out ground-breaking research mapping out the geological history of China. His most famous achievement came in 1929 when he joined the international team of scientists who unearthed the skull of a *Sinanthropus* – a prehistoric man and the first to be found in China. Teilhard and Chinese palaeontologist Dr Young were responsible for analysing the fossilized findings and were able to determine that this was indeed the skull of *Homo erectus*, an intermediate stage in human evolution. It was a major turning point in twentieth-century palaeontology. Teilhard continued to expand his network of contacts among the international group of research scientists in China. In 1930 he joined an expedition to Central Mongolia at the invitation of the American Museum of Natural History and after that he visited the US. He became increasingly involved in projects funded by the Americans and in 1937 at a conference in Philadelphia he was awarded the Mendel Medal for his scientific accomplishments. By now Teilhard was recognized as one of the foremost geologists alive.

The period of the Second World War coincided with Teilhard's final years in China. Central government in China was disintegrating as China moved towards the civil war that preceded the Communist Revolution.

At this time Teilhard wrote *The Phenomenon of Man*, perhaps the most significant of all his achievements. This book is the most comprehensive statement of his views and presents the fourfold sequence of the evolutionary process: the evolution of the galaxy, the evolution of Planet Earth, the evolution of biological life and the evolution of consciousness.

In 1947 Teilhard received permission to return to France and he was honoured by the French Ministry of Foreign Affairs for 'Outstanding services to the intellectual and scientific influence of

France'. Back in Paris he renewed contacts in the intellectual world and he was offered the post of the prehistory chair at the Sorbonne. He reworked The Phenomenon of Man and sent a copy to Rome requesting permission for publication. But Teilhard became exhausted by the stress of his renewed attempt to communicate his views. On 1 June 1947, with transiting Uranus exactly conjunct his Gemini Ascendant, Pluto exactly squaring his Sun, Chiron exactly opposing his Saturn and Saturn exactly squaring his Jupiter, he suffered a heart attack.

After he recovered, in the spring of 1948, Teilhard travelled to the United States. He was asked to give a series of lectures at Columbia University but permission was refused by the local Jesuit Superior. However, later that year Teilhard received an invitation to come to Rome to discuss the publication of *The Phenomenon of Man.* But the reigning Pope Pius XII held very conservative views. He saw the material world as fixed and unchanging and considered 'Spirit and Matter' to represent a duality of what was 'holy and what was profane'. Teilhard began to sink into despair as he realized that he would never be allowed to publish his works. In November every hope was dashed when the final letter came informing him that he was denied permission to publish either *The Divine Milieu* or *The Phenomenon of Man.* He was not allowed to accept the position at the Sorbonne, nor to take up offers to lecture in the US, and he was blocked from any further public discussion of his theological and philosophical ideas.

Those who spoke with Teilhard when he returned to Paris could sense his pain as he struggled to cope with forces against which he was so powerless. Soon after receiving this final rejection Teilhard came down with pleurisy. During his convalescence he wrote a short essay on the sixteenth-century astronomer Galileo who had had to cope with similar repression of his ideas. For a while Teilhard continued to live in Paris, under an enforced silence, unable to defend himself from attacks from the Catholic conservatives.

Teilhard needed to get away from oppressive atmosphere in France and in the summer of 1951, at the age of seventy, he joined an American expedition to South Africa. Before he left Teilhard faced the possibility that he might never return to France. He had to make an excruciating decision about the fate of his writings: a choice between following the official line in which his work was considered the property of the Jesuits (who would have destroyed everything) or to follow what his conscience told him was his real vocation and make provision for the preservation of his work after his death. Teilhard gathered together all his papers and made out a will leaving his entire body of writing to his secretary Mlle Mortier.

After the expedition to South Africa, Teilhard went to New York where he was given the post of research associate. Teilhard's decision to live in New York was approved by his Jesuit superiors and this resolved his uncertainty with regard to a place of residence. Here Teilhard picked up with old friends and colleagues and gave lectures at Harvard and Yale. Teilhard's letters during these final years are remarkable for their lack of bitterness. In 1954 Teilhard visited France for the last time. Hoping to spend his final years in his native country, Teilhard applied once more for permission to return to France permanently. Permission was refused and Teilhard returned to America. Back in New York, he famously mentioned at a dinner party, 'I would like to die on the day of the Resurrection.' Pierre Teilhard de Chardin died of a heart attack on Easter Sunday, 10 April 1955, at the age of 73.

> *I managed to climb up to the point where the Universe became apparent to me as a great rising surge … now at the end of my life, I can stand on the peak I have scaled and there, with ever more assurance, see the ascent of God.*

85

# The Harvest or Rigid Soul

## Interpreting the Horoscope of Pierre Teilhard de Chardin

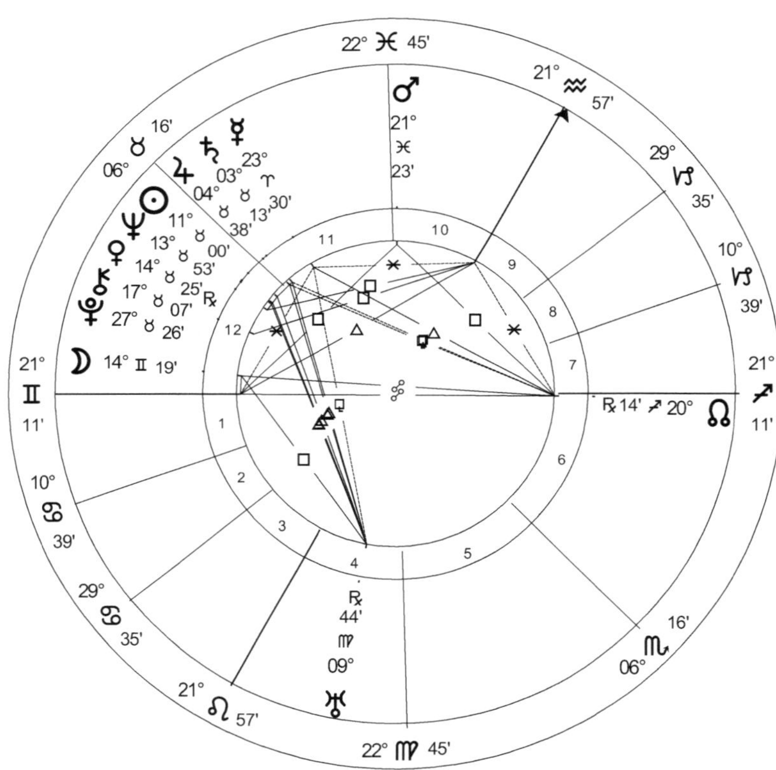


**Pierre Teilhard de Chardin**

Sunday 1 May 1881, Clermont-Ferrand France

Placidus House System

Chart from Solar Fire version 7 Astrolabe, www.alabe.com.

# Dominant Planets and Themes

We have seen that Teilhard's life was centred around his work, both as a geoscientist and as a Christian philosopher. From early childhood on he devoted his life to the exploration of the relationship between Spirit and Matter and this theme dominates his chart.

## Sun, Moon and Taurus Stellium in the 12th House

*Even at the peak of my spiritual trajectory I was never to feel at home unless immersed in an ocean of matter.*

Teilhard has seven planets in Taurus, which is Fixed Earth and the sign most associated with human life on earth. However, most of the Taurus stellium falls in the 12th house, including the Sun, the Gemini Moon and the South Node of the Moon. The 12th house represents our relationship to Spirit so we immediately see how Teilhard's Taurean love of the earth would be expressed through his spirituality. For anyone with a grasp of astrology, Teilhard's chart is astonishing in the clarity with which it represents the core issue of his life.

Venus, the ruler of Earthy Taurus, repeats the theme as it is retrograde in the 12th house and almost exactly conjunct Neptune (orb 0° 32'): a triple emphasis on exquisite sensitivity and spirituality, and Neptune is associated with Christianity. The conjunction of Saturn and Jupiter in Taurus also represents the duality of Matter and Spirit, with Saturn the precise and disciplined scientist and Jupiter the inspiring spiritual seeker.

The Gemini Ascendant and Moon trining the Aquarius MC emphasize the element of Air and it was through the verbal gifts of his Gemini Ascendant that Teilhard expressed his genius.

# 82

# Indications of Characterology in Teilhard de Chardin's Chart

## Germination/Schizoid Energy

### URANUS

- *Uranus square the Moon (orb 4° 35')*
- *Uranus trine the Sun (orb 0° 16')*
- *Uranus trine Venus, ruler of Taurus stellium (orb 4° 41')*
- *Uranus trine four other planets in Taurus: Saturn (orb 6° 31'), Jupiter (orb 5° 06'), Neptune (orb 4° 09') and Chiron (orb 7° 23)*
- *Uranus in the 4th house*
- *Aquarius MC*

### MERCURY

- *Gemini Ascendant*
- *Gemini Moon*
- *Mercury sextile Ascendant (orb 2° 19') and MC (orb 1° 33')*

### CHIRON

- *Chiron conjunct Venus (orb 2° 42')*

Teilhard's Gemini Ascendant, and his Gemini Moon square Uranus, are immediate signs of Germination/Schizoid energy. The fragmentation inherent in a Gemini Moon goes with Teilhard's lifelong uncertainty about the question of home, always split between his life in China or America and his longing to be in Paris. The Gemini Ascendant repeats the theme of restlessness and continual change. Gemini has a fragile, youthful quality and, in a classic Gemini way,

Teilhard suffered from periodic episodes of mental crisis and depression as a result of his struggles with the Church authorities. The Germination/Schizoid soul is at home in the world of ideas and much less comfortable with the body and the emotions. Teilhard's letters are Mercurial – full of his knowledge and expertise – and Neptunian – full of his love of Christ – but they avoid expression of any raw personal emotion.

The Ascendant is the lens through which we relate to the world and planets in the 12th house represent gifts that we offer to the collective, so we see Teilhard's multiple talents focused through the mental brilliance of his Gemini Ascendant. His Gemini nature kept him continually curious, eager to pass on his understanding, and he was an inspiring lecturer and a prolific writer. His contributions as a scientist, theologian, philosopher, speaker and writer are the fruits of the highest expression of Gemini.

**Uranus**

Teilhard has Uranus in the 4th house square his Gemini Moon re-emphasizing the energy of the Germination/Schizoid soul and the possibility of fragmentation – finding home in the realms of Spirit rather than on earth.

Uranus, psychologically the most detached of all the planets, is the only one that falls below the horizon and so we see that for Teilhard the emphasis was never going to be on his personal life or the world of close relationships. Teilhard's Uranus in the 4th can be seen as an indication of wounding: firstly representing his childhood in an upper class family where relationships were formal and rather remote and, later, as an indication of a man who never found the comfort of a stable, earthly home. Not unlike planets in the 12th, planets in the 4th house are not so obvious on the surface of things, but they can represent a more hidden but very powerful force in the personality. Teilhard might not have wished to be identified as a revolutionary but nevertheless we can see Teilhard's Uranus, down at the root of the chart, as an indication of the fundamental Essence of his nature as a genius who brought through ground-breaking ideas in science and theology.

### Mercury

Mercury is the chart ruler and sextiles the Ascendant, thereby doubling the emphasis on the abstractions of the mind. Teilhard's Mercury is in Aries, trining the North Node in Sagittarius, and these are the only placements in the element of Fire. Aries brings the quality of the pioneer, and the fire of Teilhard's Mercury gave him the capacity to break new ground and courage to speak of the vision coming to him from the cosmic realms of the 12th house, despite the challenges that he met.

Much of Teilhard's work as a geoscientist involved the precise classification of rocks and bones and other archaeological artefacts, and this level of discernment is one of the main functions of Mercury. The mental function of specifically differentiating one thing from another is echoed by the placement of the North Node in the 6th house. Yet again we see the theme of the relationship of Spirit and Matter as the North Node in Sagittarius brings cosmic vision, which is successfully grounded by the 6th house's focus on the systemic order of things and the way that they function.

The 11th house represents groups and networks on a planetary scale – the interdependence of all of humanity and the ideal of the 'global village'. Mercury in the 11th gives voice to Teilhard's vision of the ultimate unification of the human race. Gemini, Uranus and the 11th house are all associated with computer technology and the vast leap in the human capacity for communication represented by the birth of the World Wide Web. Even back in 1950, Teilhard saw the new technology as part of the process of Noogenesis, creating structures for the exchange of information within the collective consciousness:

*The network of radio and television communication, which already link us in a sort of 'etherised' universal consciousness.'*

The 11th is the house of friendship and Teilhard was always happiest amongst his friends in the intellectual circles of Paris. and he generated loyal friendships wherever he went.

### Chiron

The placement of Chiron conjunct Venus echoes the theme of the Germination/Schizoid tendency to disassociate from the life of the body. Venus is dignified in Taurus, where she is normally happy representing the sensual pleasures of the body and romantic relationships, but the conjunction of Chiron represents wounding to the Venusian principle. Teilhard was a monk and his Venus was not to be expressed through intimate sexual relationships. Teilhard never expressed any personal regret around this issue but this Venus represents heartbreak of a different kind. Teilhard was charming and made friends easily. However, like many great minds he was often lonely for people who truly understood and shared his views. He was quite often surrounded by Jesuits who opposed his ideas, and when he did find kindred souls he spent much of his life separated from them by his life of exile. So Teilhard's wounded Venus neither lived out the sensuality of Taurus nor found an easy path of human companionship.

# 86

## Indications of Characterology in Teilhard de Chardin's Chart

## Rooting/Oral Energy

**THE MOON**

- ***Moon in the 12th house***
- ***Moon conjunct the Ascendant (orb 6 ° 52')***

**NEPTUNE**

- ***Neptune conjunct the Sun (orb 2 ° 53')***
- ***Neptune conjunct chart ruler Venus (orb 0 ° 32')***

### The Moon

The sense of coolness and distance in relationships in the family home is echoed in Teilhard's 12th house Moon, which is often an indication of a family in which the child's needs are overlooked. So in psychological terms we can see the likelihood of some Oral wounding in the form of insufficient personal contact in Teilhard's early years when there were a lot of other siblings around as well as servants to take over many of the tasks of child-rearing. However, Teilhard spoke with gratitude of his pious and mystical mother as the inspiration for his passionate relationship with God.

*A spark had to fall upon me, to make the fire blaze out. And, without a doubt, it was through my mother that it came to me.*

The 12th house Moon repeats the theme of a chart that is intrinsically transpersonal. Teilhard was a great soul with a mission to fulfil and the importance of his spiritual message transcended everything else.

Always in his writings Teilhard returned to the importance of love and, through his 12th house Moon, Venus and Neptune, Teilhard was radiant with the gift of the Rooting soul, the Essence of love.

> *Love – in the pure state displays its astonishing power to transform everything.*

## Neptune

Teilhard's Neptune is in the 12th house, conjuncting the Sun, Venus and all of the Taurean planets except Pluto. This powerful Neptune is the source of Teilhard's heartfelt faith in divine love and his celestial vision of the ultimate relationship between humanity and Christ. Neptune in the 12th house feels at one with all of life and often comes with the loss of a healthy sense of boundaries. But with the Gemini Moon squared by Mars (the principle of individuation), and with detached Uranus trining the Sun and squaring the Moon, there is not so much risk of Neptunian enmeshment in this chart. A strong Neptune often indicates a person who becomes some kind of a victim and we can see Teilhard's life of exile and the suppression of his work as a form of Neptunian martyrdom to the Catholic establishment. However, above all, Neptune represents Teilhard's devotion to God, his love of Jesus Christ and his great-hearted compassion for humanity.

# 87

# Indications of Characterology in Teilhard de Chardin's Chart

## Budding/Masochist Energy

**THE SUN**

- ***Sun in the 12th house***

**PLUTO**

- ***Pluto in the 12th house***
- ***Pluto sextile Mars (orb 6 ° 03')***

### The Sun

The Sun in the 12th house is a further indication of a childhood in which Teilhard was not fully 'seen' in his Essence, and this is reinforced by the conjunction from Neptune. Yet we know that Teilhard's mother supported his devotional nature, his father supported his exploration into natural history, and Teilhard never spoke as if he had an unhappy childhood. However, I think we can interpret the 12th house Sun as representing a traditional Rigid style of upbringing – habits of piety, conformity and discipline laid down in childhood. Something about the transpersonal emphasis of the 12th house points to Teilhard's doubts about his right to express the revolutionary teachings that were the calling of his Solar Essence. In his deeply ingrained Christian faith Teilhard had to contend with painful confusion when the representatives of his religion forbade him to pursue the calling of his heart. Teilhard spent his adult life struggling with the rulings from the Church, and the placement of Pluto in the 12th house represents the disempowering impact of the decisions that came from the Vatican. To illustrate this we can see that in 1948, when the final ruling came from Rome, prohibiting him publishing *The*

*Phenomenon of Man*, transiting Chiron was in Scorpio opposing his natal Pluto, and Pluto was in Leo squaring his natal Chiron.

**Pluto**

Teilhard has Mars in Pisces almost exactly squaring his Ascendant, and here we see his pioneering adventurous spirit and his ability to take the lead. However, just as the light of Teilhard's Sun becomes lost in the 12th house and diffused by the conjunction from Neptune, so the raw courage of Mars is watered down by the soft energy of Pisces and held back by the sextile to Pluto. Although Pluto and Mars have much in common, even harmonious aspects between the two planets tend to cause problems for the assertion of the individual will, which is symbolized by Mars. In Teilhard's case this is reinforced by Pluto's placement in the 12th house which speaks of issues of control, difficulty with the instinctual urges of the body and restrained expression of the life force.

Planets in the 12th house represent something that is struggling to come into consciousness – both for the individual and in the human collective – and we can regard Teilhard's Pluto as a classic representation of the Budding/Masochist challenge to undertake a deep exploration of the true nature of personal power.

At the end of his life, realizing that he might be close to death, Teilhard finally made the difficult decision to defy the rulings of his Jesuit order, which stated that all his writings were the property of the Jesuits who would certainly have destroyed his work after his death. Teilhard realized that his life's work was too important to be lost and he made a will bequeathing all his work to his secretary. So we see Teilhard's lifetime of struggle with the Masochist issues of bondage and freedom. Always alongside this were his prolific writings, expressions of his knowledge and wisdom, the upwelling of his Solar light – the outpouring Essence of the Budding Soul. And in the end it was the light of the Sun that triumphed when he made the final decision to allow his work to live on.

# 88

## Indications of Characterology in Teilhard de Chardin's Chart

## Flowering/Psychopathic Energy

**THE SUN**

- *The Sun conjunct Jupiter (orb 6° 22')*

**MARS**

- *Mars square the Ascendant (orb 0° 22')*
- *Mars square the Moon (orb 7° 04')*
- *Mars square the Nodal Axis (orb 1° 09')*
- *Chart ruler Mercury in Aries*

**JUPITER**

- *Jupiter conjunct the Sun (orb 6° 22')*
- *Ruler of the North Node*
- *Jupiter sesquiquadrate the North Node (orb 0° 36')*
- *Jupiter quintile MC (orb 0° 41')*

Teilhard has Jupiter conjunct the Sun, Mars closely square his Ascendant and widely square the Moon, and Mercury, the chart ruler, is in Aries, sextile the Ascendant and trine the Sagittarius North Node. Although the heat of the Sun is dissipated in the vast cosmic spaces of the 12th house, his life was warmed by the influence of the other planets of Fire – his Jupiterian vision and love of travel and adventure, and the pioneering courage of Mars.

In Teilhard's history it is not relevant to pursue the idea of Psychopathic wounding expressed through triangular romantic relationships. Teilhard lived a celibate life; he had many deep friendships with women, some of whom were in love with him, but his destiny did not lie in the arena of romantic relationships. However, we can look on his relationship with the Catholic Church as a version of Psychopathic wounding and betrayal. Teilhard loved Christianity with a passion and he felt that if he left the Jesuits it would cause a damaging rift for himself and for many Christian followers. So he submitted to the decrees from the Vatican that caused him great personal pain, continually sacrificing his own well-being in order to protect the Church – very much in line with the honourable, heroic actions of the Flowering/Psychopathic soul.

Although the chart is heavily weighted to Earth and Air it is interesting to look at Teilhard's North Node in Sagittarius – the sign associated with images of the traveller, the explorer, the spiritual seeker, the High Priest and the teacher of higher knowledge. The South Node represents the foundation of Teilhard's life in the hidden world of the 12th house. As the years pass we see the pull towards the North Node, which develops momentum, expanding towards the full expression of the inspiring energy of Sagittarius. Over the course of a lifetime, we see the gradual emergence of the fire of his vision, like a light of the sun dispersing the mists of dawn. With this Nodal axis we can see Teilhard's life as a bridge between the formless 12th house world of Spirit and the embodied, specific, communicable 6th house world of Matter.

# 89

# Indications of Characterology in Teilhard de Chardin's Chart

## Harvest/Rigid Energy

**VENUS**

- ***Venus conjunct the Sun (orb 4° 25')***
- ***Venus square the MC (orb 7° 32')***

**SATURN**

- ***Saturn conjunct the Sun (orb 7° 47')***
- ***Saturn conjunct Jupiter (orb 1° 25')***
- ***Saturn quintile the MC (orb 0° 44')***

**EMPHASIS ON EARTH**

- ***Eight planets in Earth signs; seven planets, including the Sun, in Taurus***

The Sun sits at the heart of the Taurus stellium, conjuncting all the Taurus planets except Pluto. The planets associated with Harvest/Rigid energy are Venus and Saturn and both are conjunct the Sun: Venus retrograding towards the Sun with an orb of 4° 25', and Saturn conjunct the Sun with an orb of 7° 47'. Although we shall look at the influence of Venus and Saturn, it is the overall emphasis on the sign of Taurus that is the first indication of the Harvest/Rigid energy.

**Taurus**

One of the key images associated with the sign of Taurus is the Garden of Eden – the beauty and wonder of the earth. The deep purpose of the Taurean soul is to honour the earth and to live as a responsible guardian of the manifest world of Matter.

In this respect Taurus can express the best of the Harvest/Rigid soul like a gardener working in harmony with the limitations of the material world to bring forth the fruits of life on earth. With his Gemini Ascendant Teilhard was not a gardener but he was a geologist who fell in love with the rocks and crystals of his homeland at a very young age. The love of the land and of all life on earth was his driving passion. Despite the extraordinary emphasis in his chart on the 12th house, his spirituality was always anchored in the Taurean experience of being human and living on the earth.

### Saturn

Teilhard's love of the material world cost him dearly, putting him at loggerheads with the Catholic establishment. Teilhard's Saturn is conjunct Jupiter and this combination represents a double emphasis on the archetypes of Judgement and the Law. Teilhard was often deeply frustrated and depressed by the rulings from the Vatican. In later life he became ill from the stress of struggling to make his views understood, and this is the Rigid wounding of the negative expression of Saturn – bondage to law which feels oppressive. With his revolutionary Uranus and heroic Mars, Teilhard must have often wanted to throw off the rulings handed down to him by theologians who were not scientists and did not even understand his message. Indeed, a man with more of an emphasis on Flowering/Psychopathic energy might well have left the Church. But always Teilhard came back to his Saturn, steadfastly upholding the decree of the Church in the name of unity. And this is where we see the patience, endurance and far-sighted wisdom of the Harvest/Rigid soul. Teilhard had a love of Christ that transcended everything else and he believed that Christianity was essential to the progress of evolution – the only religion that would lead to the Omega Point, to the Christogenesis of the human race. Rather than cause a scandal that would have created deep divisions in the Catholic Church, Teilhard submitted to the papal rulings and kept the peace. We could see Teilhard only as the disempowered victim of the rigidity of the Church but I think that is to underestimate his compassionate understanding of all the ramifications of his dilemma.

Teilhard knew that the road to the Omega Point would not be easy:

*Evil – injustice, inequality, suffering, death – ceases to be outrageous when the immense travail of the world displays itself as the inevitable reverse side of an immense triumph.*

So Teilhard put his faith in the Omega Point and the coming of Christ, and it was the positive energy of Saturn that gave Teilhard wisdom, stoical strength and unyielding loyalty to the ideals of Christogenesis and his love of humanity.

**Venus**

Venus is in the 12th house and we have noted earlier the effects of the conjunction from both Neptune and Chiron. Venus is also trined by Uranus and it is the most spiritualized of all Teilhard's personal planets: not to be expressed through earthly romance but representing the quality which was at the core of everything that mattered most in Teilhard's life – love. Teilhard had a precise, scientific mind but he never lost sight of the overriding importance of love. In his observations on evolution he said:

*With love omitted there is nothing ahead of us except the forbidding prospect of standardization and enslavement – the doom of ants and termites.*

Teilhard had a profound sense of personal love for God and heartfelt awareness of the love of Christ permeating all things, and this was his guiding star. His writing overflows with his feelings of Divine Love and when he looked into the future to the advent of the Omega Point Teilhard saw:

*A current of love is released to spread over the whole breadth and depth of the world … a fundamental essence which will metamorphose all things.*

**Teilhard de Chardin: Harvest/Rigid Energy**

Teilhard radiated a magical Venusian quality of joy in life. To those who knew him he was a gentle, lovable man, inspiring deep, loyal friendships wherever he went.

*Old Mr Tayer was truly diaphanous to every moment and being with him was like being in attendance at God's own party, a continuous celebration of life and its mysteries. But mostly Mr Tayer was so full of vital sap and juice that he seemed to flow with everything. Always he saw the interconnections between things – the way that everything in the universe, from fox terriers to tree bark to somebody's red hat to the mind of God, was related to everything else and was very, very good.*

Jean Houston *writing of her childhood memory of meetings with Teilhard de Chardin*

# 90

# Teilhard de Chardin's Human Energy Field

The initial impression of Teilhard's energy field is of a clear, translucent sphere of silver white light. This crystalline light comes from the powerful influence of Neptune and Uranus, the two most spiritual planets, energizing the pearly light of the 6th chakra (Celestial Love) and the brilliant white light of the 7th chakra (the Mind of God). These two transpersonal planets trine each other and have a powerful influence on the chart: Neptune, embedded in the heart of the 12th house stellium, is conjunct all the Taurus planets except Pluto; Uranus, a singleton at the root of the chart, trines all the Taurus planets except Pluto and squares the Moon. These two planets are the signature of Teilhard's connection out into the cosmos and the unseen world of Spirit.

**The Auric Level**

Despite the emphasis on the Earth energy of Taurus in Teilhard's lower chakras there is a feeling of uncertainty and holding back from a total surrender to the energy of the earth. In the 3rd chakra there is the shadow of a rift connected to the conflicted energies of Saturn and Pluto.

Negative Saturn brings the archetype of Judgement and the 3rd chakra fracture holds a version of the Christian split from the body: the rejection of the world of emotion, passion and the instincts – Pluto's world. The split in Teilhard's 3rd chakra also holds the energy of Chiron – a wound that blocks access to the instinctual realm, disassociation from the life of the body and detachment from the energy of the lower chakras. And so the 3rd chakra is overcharged, big and bright yellow, with the brilliance of the mental energy of Gemini overcompensating in order to avoid the fracturing in the lower chakras.

Teilhard's 4th chakra is radiant and full of light. Teilhard's heart remains open; he continually returns to this fountain of love but there is also an imbalance. The 4th chakra also holds a shadow in its lower part. Here the flow is constricted by tendrils of the dark energy of Chiron extending out from the split in the 3rd chakra. This is the impact of the conjunction of Venus and Chiron, the emotional stresses of Teilhard's life causing tearing in the 4th chakra, which has a damaging effect on his physical heart.

The lower part of Teilhard's 5th chakra also shows signs of disturbance. However, the impact of the shadow energy is much reduced. Overall the 5th chakra appears clear and open, vibrant with the fluid, quicksilver light of Mercury forming into distinct streams of connection to the upper chakras and particularly to the pure white light of the 7th chakra.

The 6th and 7th chakras are both very big, clear, open channels to the cosmic realms. The 6th chakra radiates the soft Neptunian light of the unconditional love of the Divine and extends far out beyond the boundaries of the world of matter. The 7th chakra is immensely powerful, like a river of light flowing down and illuminating the whole of the HEF with the visionary light of Jupiter and the crystal clarity of Uranus.

### The Haric Level

On the deeper level of the Hara, at the core of Teilhard's energy field, the central Hara line appears as a powerful column of light rooted into the earth and extending up to the stars. Often the light of the Hara can be perceived as being gold but in Teilhard's case the Hara line has a core of dazzling white light. This light comes from his connection to the Mind of God and it illuminates the entire HEF.

In the upper part of the Hara line the connection up to the beyond is effortlessly clear, serenely flowing to and from the heavens. Here, in the stillness of the non-physical realms, the vision and wisdom of Jupiter flow down through the upper Tan T'ien, radiating celestial light throughout the field.

Lower down the Hara line there is some distortion. Through the area of the torso there are swirls of particles of light like agitated electrons splitting away, particularly over the area of the Middle Tan

T'ien. The Middle Tan T'ien has the radiance of Venus and Neptune: deep longing for union and communion but here also is the pain of the Venus-Chiron conjunction which creates a shadowy disturbance in the Middle Tan T'ien and the beginnings of a rift in the Hara line. The connection from the Middle Tan T'ien to the Lower Tan T'ien and down into the earth does not have the effortless power and clarity of the upper Hara. From the Middle Tan T'ien down, the Hara line begins to show fracture lines and the power of the Hara is diminished and out of alignment with a full connection to the earth. Despite this disturbance the lower Hara remains strong, like the trunk of a tree. There is an unbreakable quality, the enduring stoicism of Saturn, over-Rigid but holding unwavering to Jupiter's visionary light coming down from the Upper Tan T'ien; this is the awesome strength of the Saturn-Jupiter conjunction in Taurus.

91

# CONCLUSION

When we make the connection between astrology and the Human Energy Field and observe the appearance of the horoscope in the HEF it is apparent that the planets divide into those that move the energy outwards and those that draw it inwards. The Sun, Venus, Jupiter, Uranus and Neptune have an expansive effect that focuses the energy upwards and outwards towards the higher levels of the field and the higher vibrations of the non-physical realms. The Moon, Saturn, Pluto and Chiron have the effect of contraction, focusing the energy inwards into the body and the deeper levels of the field and downwards to anchor into the earth.

Mercury and Mars do not fit clearly into either group. Although Mars is extrovert and expressive and the planet most associated with the Flowering/Psychopathic type, Mars is also deeply connected to the biological body – blood, muscle and instinct. For example, we see with Frida Kahlo that although Mars is a dominant influence in her chart, giving her a fiery temperament, nevertheless she remained in contact with her physical body and feelings, unlike Orson Welles whose Uranian Aquarian energy split away from the connection to the body. Mercury often focuses energy upwards towards the head and into analytical mental activity. However, Mercury can also focus within, opening to the symbolic imagery of the dream world and the imagination as well as communication and guidance from the body through the nervous system.

At this point in human evolution we tend to value the expansive energy of the Sun, Venus and Jupiter and we tend to have difficulty with Saturn, Pluto and Chiron. From the healer's point of view, Saturn and Pluto are related to the deep inner core of the HEF – the level of the Hara. Access to the level of the Hara comes only through stillness, through the silencing of the little mind and sinking down into Presence. The ideas of inner stillness, silence and presence are new and rather difficult for many people. This was once something only available to monks and nuns and other spiritual devotees but nowadays many 'Lightworkers' are arriving on Planet Earth and more and more people are following the paths of meditation and healing. One of the symbols of Saturn is the cornucopia – the abundance of the fruits of the earth. As we learn to access the stillness, power, integrity and wisdom of Saturn and Pluto, then we learn to live from the level of the Hara where we can truly become the bridge between Heaven and Earth.

If we look back at the five stages of child development and the five Characterologies it is clear that everyone has all been through all five stages and everyone has at least some of the wounds and some of the gifts of all five types. From the spiritual view we can see them as five stages of descent – of the flowing from the non-physical realms down into the realm of Matter. At the earliest stage of the descent the Germination/Schizoid soul and the Rooting/Oral soul are both comfortable on the higher chakras and the outer levels of the HEF but the whole business of being in a body and coping with the material world is difficult for them. Further into the realm of Matter the Budding/Masochist and Flowering/Psychopathic souls are more embodied but struggling with issues of personal identity and relationship, and their path through life will often look like the labyrinth of the Masochist or the battlefield of the Psychopath. In the final stage the Harvest/Rigid souls are focused right down into physical incarnation and the risk is that they forget their spiritual Essence and lose sight of that which lies beyond the physical world. The true purpose of the Harvest soul is exactly what Teilhard de Chardin described, the spiritualization of Matter – the path of embodying Divine consciousness while living in a physical body.

# EPILOGUE

*One ship sails East,*
*And another West,*
*By the self-same winds that blow,*
*'Tis the set of the sails*
*And not the gales,*
*That tells the way we go.*

*Like the winds of the sea*
*Are the waves of time,*
*As we journey along through life,*
*'Tis the set of the soul*
*That determines the goal,*
*And not the calm or the strife.*
Ella Wheeler Wilcox, *One Ship Sails East*

One of the fondest memories of my life is of taking a boat out on Derwentwater, in the Lake District, accompanied by four children – my elder son Mat, my younger son Michael, my nephew Tom and my niece Mary. On a rather windy day we clambered into a long green canoe, each of us armed with a lifejacket and a paddle, pushed away from the shore and raced optimistically out into the middle of the lake. I am already laughing so much at this memory that I can hardly type.

I was sitting at the back of the boat in a position to shout out instructions to the children and compensate for their mistakes with my own paddle. The wind was making the water extremely choppy and soon my young and inexperienced crew got us broadside on to the waves so that the canoe was pitching wildly from side to side and threatening, at any moment, to tip us into the water. Little Michael, crouched in the bow of the boat, started to give the occasional sob but, unfortunately, at this stage we discovered that I was completely useless as cox because I was laughing so much I couldn't speak. A memory I shall always treasure is of my parents, who had hired a sensible rowing boat, gliding serenely past us and smiling benignly on the troubled canoeful of their descendants. Because that's what my parents always did – they never saw the potential threat, they had tremendous faith in life and they always knew we would be OK!

Mat, aged fourteen, did not share their faith nor perceive the humour of the situation. He soon realized that he would have to swap seats with me so that he could take charge of directing the canoe. He did a much better job than me, sitting at the back shouting out very clear instructions. Things improved for a bit but then we saw the Lake steamer approaching and a large wave from the wake of the steamer swept towards us. 'Paddle on the left, paddle on the left!' yelled Mat. Mary, the next oldest child, who was sitting at the front of the canoe, dug her paddle vigorously into the water on the right-hand side of the boat and the other children followed suit.

'What are you doing?' roared Mat, bellowing to be heard over the engine of the launch and the rising wind. 'I said paddle on the LEFT!' Pulling ever harder and with great efficiency on the right, Mary yelled back, 'I AM paddling on the left! I AM paddling on the left!'

This story is not without a point, though I mainly have told it because I like it so much and it has the faces of some of my favourite people in the world set against a backdrop of one of my favourite places in the world.

Early on in my education about the world of 'Spirit' I did a workshop with a crystal healer from Hawaii and she told us a bit about the belief system of the Hawaiian Kahunas. One of the things she said was that the Hawaiians believe that the human psyche/soul is divided into three separate but intertwined beings. There is a little being called the Unihipili who has a childlike consciousness – very primitive, a 'doer' not a thinker. The Unihipili likes to be told what to do and then it takes its powerful little self off and does whatever it's been told to do. The Unihipili doesn't ask questions, it simply brings you exactly what you have ask for, including such things as cars which break down as soon as you have parted with the cash or romantic relationships that really don't go well.

The next self is the one that does the asking. This is the self that most of us identify with most of the time and it is called the Uhane. The Uhane has the ability to think for itself and it is more or less in charge of decisions but it gets confused and distracted by worldly activity and sometimes asks for things that turn out pretty badly.

The third self is what many of us refer to as the Higher Self or guardian angel or soul, and in Hawaii it is called the Amakua. The Amakua is wise. Its job to look after the Uhane and it is also in contact with the non-physical world of Spirit so it has all the answers (though, in the place where the Amakua lives there aren't really any questions!)

The little Unihipili likes the Amakua, who can see the way for things to turn out well. Unfortunately, the Uhane often gets into quite a mess and forgets about the Amakua. Once out of contact with the Amakua, the Uhane becomes more and more confused and afraid and can get into a downward spiral of bad choosing.

Now I'm going to tell another story about people in boats. I was once down by the river watching a bunch of novice canoeists learning how to get over a couple of small weirs. When they'd received instructions from their teachers, one by one they headed for the first weir, tense but determined, and shot over the little waterfall with greater or lesser success. The last one to come was an older man and you could see from the fast and frantic way that he was paddling that he was afraid. I felt very sympathetic as I knew that I would have been terrified. However, I could also see that his fear was causing him to make a mess of things. Sure enough, he went over the weir in the wrong place and he immediately capsized. Once he got himself back into the canoe the little group paddled off to the next waterfall but by now I could see that the older man was seriously shaken up. He shot over the second waterfall, even more frantic than before, crashed onto the rocks, bumped into a little tree and fell into the water again.

Well, this is what we are all doing a lot of the time. Something doesn't go right the first time - then we become a little afraid, and when we come to try it again our fear makes it even more likely that things will go wrong. So the Uhane limps along through life, crashing into the rocks and capsizing, and every time it gets more afraid and confused. The Unihipili can't help because it only knows how to say 'Yes', often to things that get the Uhane into big trouble.

What do we need? We need the Amakua. And unfortunately it takes years to learn how to stop listening to the screams of all the terrified Uhanes and find a bit of the river that is quiet and still enough for us to hear the voice of our Amakua.

Well, I said at the beginning of this book that I seem to have dedicated my life to this journey and I am now pretty good at listening out for my Amakua, though you'd be amazed how often my Uhane suddenly gets wilful and goes crashing off into the rapids. Still, now I really do know that I have an Amakua and that when I listen to it all my troubles drop away. The Amakua lives in the place where 'Nothing bad can possibly ever happen'.

To get back to 'Paddle on the LEFT!', for most of my life this has been the state of my canoe – a bunch of kids furiously paddling as fast as they can but they can't tell their right from their left and there's a big wave coming. More recently I've learned that always standing behind me in the canoe is my Amakua. She never goes away, she has a great sense of humour but she is unfailingly kind and wise and she has all the answers. She loves me. I guess 'Me' is my Uhane who has made some really dreadful blunders when she tries to do it on her own. And I still identify with my bumbling, ignorant Uhane and I am a little in awe of my Amakua. When I give a healing my main job is to get my Uhane to stand still and allow my Amakua to come in and take over.

So my final recommendation, at the end of the years of writing this book, is to get into your canoe, take the paddle, hand it to your Amakua and sit back quietly in the boat, play with the Unihipili and enjoy the river.

> *My day is done, and I am like a boat drawn on the beach,*
> *listening to the dance-music of the tide in the evening.*
> Rabindranath Tagore *Stray Birds*

# BIBLIOGRAPHY AND REFERENCES


Alcantara, Isabel, and Egnolff, Sandra, *Frida Kahlo and Diego Rivera,* 2011. New York: Prestel.

*American Beauty,* 1990. Film. Directed by Sam Mendes. US: DreamWorks Pictures.

Arroyo, Stephen, *Astrology, Karma and Transformation*, 1992. Sebastopol: CRCS.

Herrera, Hayden *A Biography of Frida Kahlo,* 1983. New York: HarperCollins.

Brennan, Barbara, *Hands of Light*, 1988. New York: Bantam Books.

Brennan, Barbara, *Light Emerging*, 1993. New York: Bantam Books.

Campbell Joseph, *Pathways to Bliss*, 2004. Novato: New World Library.

Castaneda, Carlos, *Journey to Ixtlan*, 1991. New York: Washington Square.

Chardin, Teilhard de, *Writings in Time of War The Cosmic Life*, 1968. New York: Harper & Row.

Chardin, Teilhard de, *The Future of Man*, 2004. New York: Image.

Chardin, Teilhard de, *The Heart of Matter*, 1979. New York: Houghton Mifflin Harcourt.

Chardin, Teilhard de, *The Phenomenon of Man*, 2008. London: Harper Perennial.

Ferrucci, Piero, *What We May Be*, 1995. London: Thorsons.

Foster, Jeff, *Be Gentle With Anger* www.lifewithoutacentre.com 2015

Fritz, Robert, *The Path of Least Resistance*, 1989. New York: Fawcett.

Greene, Liz, *Relating*, 1977. Conventure.

Greene, Liz, *The Astrological Neptune and the Quest for Redemption*, 2000. Newburyport: Red Wheel/Weiser.

Greene, Liz, *The Astrology of Fate,* 1984. London: George Allen & Unwin.

Greene, Liz, and Sharman-Burke, Juliet, *The Mythic Tarot*, 1996. London: Rider.

Greene, Liz, and Sasportas, Howard, *The Dynamics of the Unconscious*, 1988. York Beach: Weiser.

Greene, Liz, and Sasportas, Howard, *The Luminaries*, 1992. York Beach: Weiser.

Houston, Jean, *Godseed*, 1992. Wheaton: Quest.

Jackson, Eve, *Jupiter: An Astrologer's Guide*, 1986. Wellingborough: Aquarian.
Johnson, Stephen M, *Characterological Transformation*, 1985. New York: Norton.
Johnson, Stephen M, *Character Styles*, 1994. New York: Norton.
Jung, CJ, *Letters of CJ Jung Vol 2, 1951-1961*, 1976. London: Routledge.
Kettenmann, Andrea, *Frida Kahlo*, 1993. Koln: Benedikt Taschen.
Leaming, Barbara, *Orson Welles*, 1993. London: Phoenix.
Lee, Stan, *Spider-Man*. New York: Marvel Comics.
Liedloff, Jean, *The Continuum Concept*, 2004. London: Penguin.
Meera, Mother, *Answers*, 1997. London: Rider.
Miller, Arthur, *Timebends: A Life*, 1987. London: Methuen.
Milton, John, *Paradise Lost*, 2003. London: Penguin.
Pert, Candace, *Molecules of Emotion*, 1997. London: Simon & Schuster.
Pierrakos, John, *Core Energetics*, 1990. Mendocino: Life Rhythm.
Pierrakos, John, *Eros, Love and Sexuality*, 1997. Mendocino: Life Rhythm.
Rawson, Philip, and Legeza, László, *Tao*, 1973. London: Thames & Hudson.
Rudhyar, Dane, *The Astrological Houses*, 2015. Sebastopol: CRCS.
Shakenstir, Jimi Hendrix Life, Times & Fire, 2015. Available from: www.shakenstir.co.uk/index.php/reviews/jimi-hendrix-life-times-fire/reviews/18780/7/ [Accessed 24 November 2015].
Spoto, Donald, *Marilyn Monroe: The Biography*, 1994. London: Arrow.
Stone, Sidra, *The Shadow King*, 2000. Lincoln: iUniverse.
Tagore, Rabindranath, *Stray Birds*, 1916. New York: Macmillan.
Tolle, Eckhart, *The Power of Now*, 2011. London: Hodder.
Tolle, Eckhart, *A New Earth*, 2009. London: Penguin.
*The I Ching* Richard Wilhelm Translation, 1989. London: Penguin Arkana.
Tzu, Lao, *The Tao Te Ching*, 2009. Nashville: Sam Torode Book Arts.
Wahlberg, Bill, *Star Warrior*, 1993. Santa Fe: Bear.
Weekes, James, Across the King's River. Available from: https://www.facebook.com/acrossthekingsriver/photos/a.10150961804138414.401470.88064493413/10152537050108414/?type=1&theater [Accessed 24 November 2015].
Welles, Orson, and Bogdanovich, Peter, *This is Orson Welles*, 1998. Boston: Da Capo.

Wilcox, Emma Wheeler, ''Tis The Set of the Sail – or – One Ship Sails West', 1916. Available from: www.womenshistoryabout.com/library/etext/bl_wilcox_set_of_the_sail.htm [Accessed 24 November 2015].

Whyte, David, *Consolations*, 2015. Langley: Many Rivers Press.

Yongey Mingyur Rinpoche, Lion's Roar – Buddhist Wisdom for Our Time. Available from: http://www.lionsroar.com [Accessed 24 November 2015].

YouTube, A Rare Jimi Hendrix Interview – Dec 1967 – Part 1 of 3, 2015. Available from: www.youtube.com/watch?v=chMrS1Qa7xs [Accessed 24 November 2015].

YouTube, Jimi Hendrix Story Episode 1 of 3 1942-1961, 2015. Available from: wwwyoutube.com/watch?v=6V4cCr_g8gg [Accessed 24 November 2015].

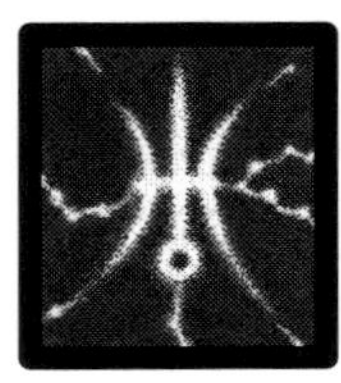

Made in the USA
Columbia, SC
23 November 2017